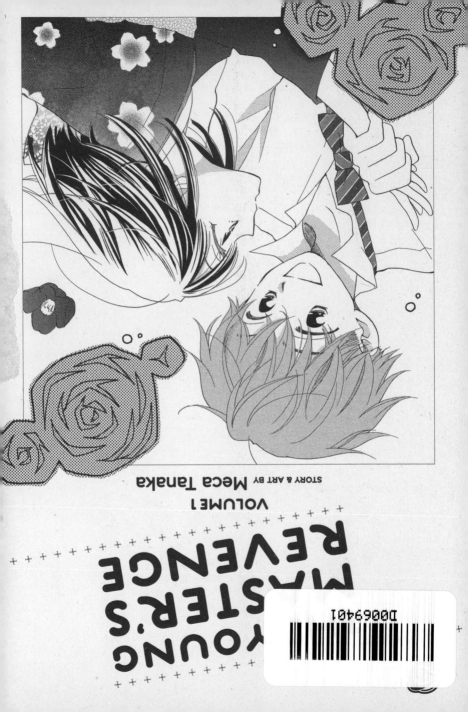

YOUNG MASTER'S REVENGE

VOLUME 1

STORY & ART BY Meca Tanaka

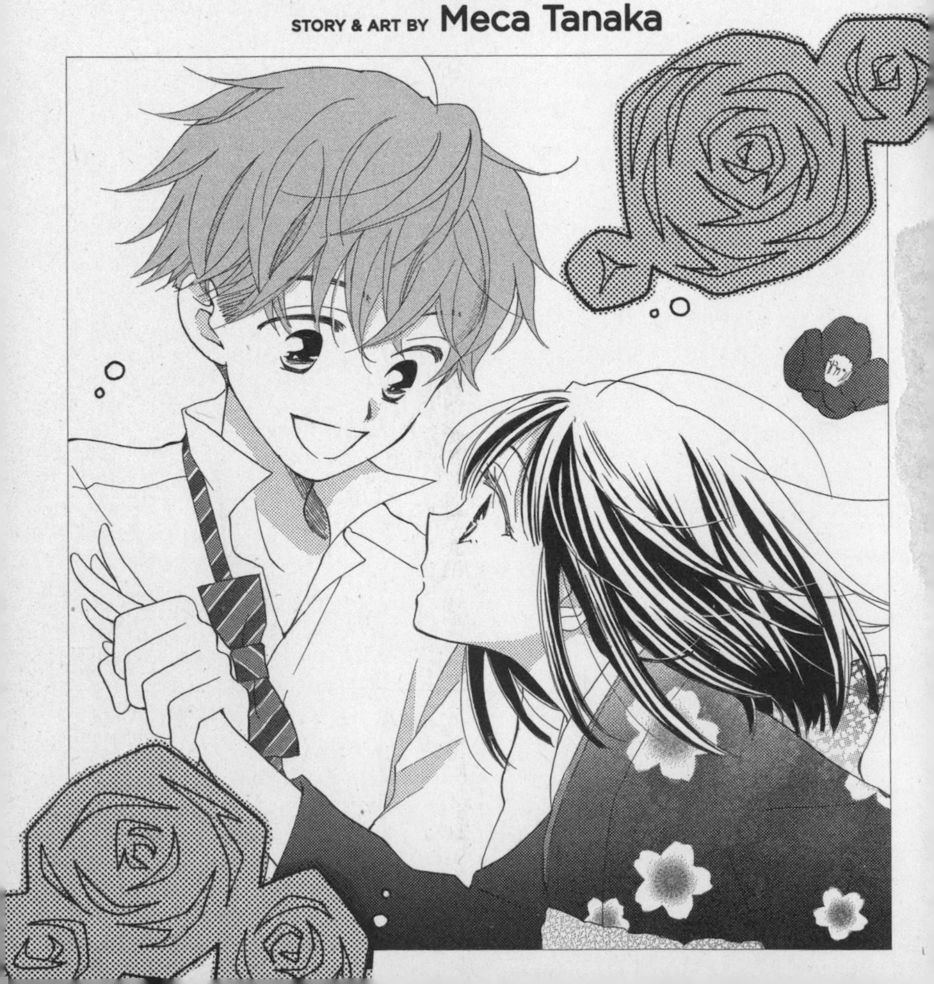

THE YOUNG MASTER'S REVENGE

1

★ CONTENTS

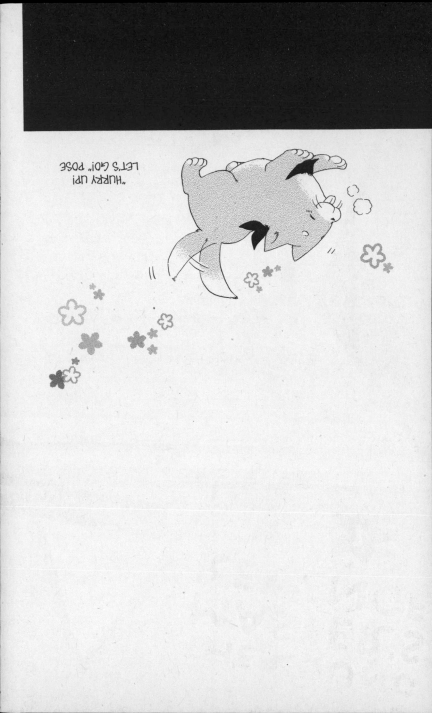

"HURRY UP!
LET'S GO!" POSE

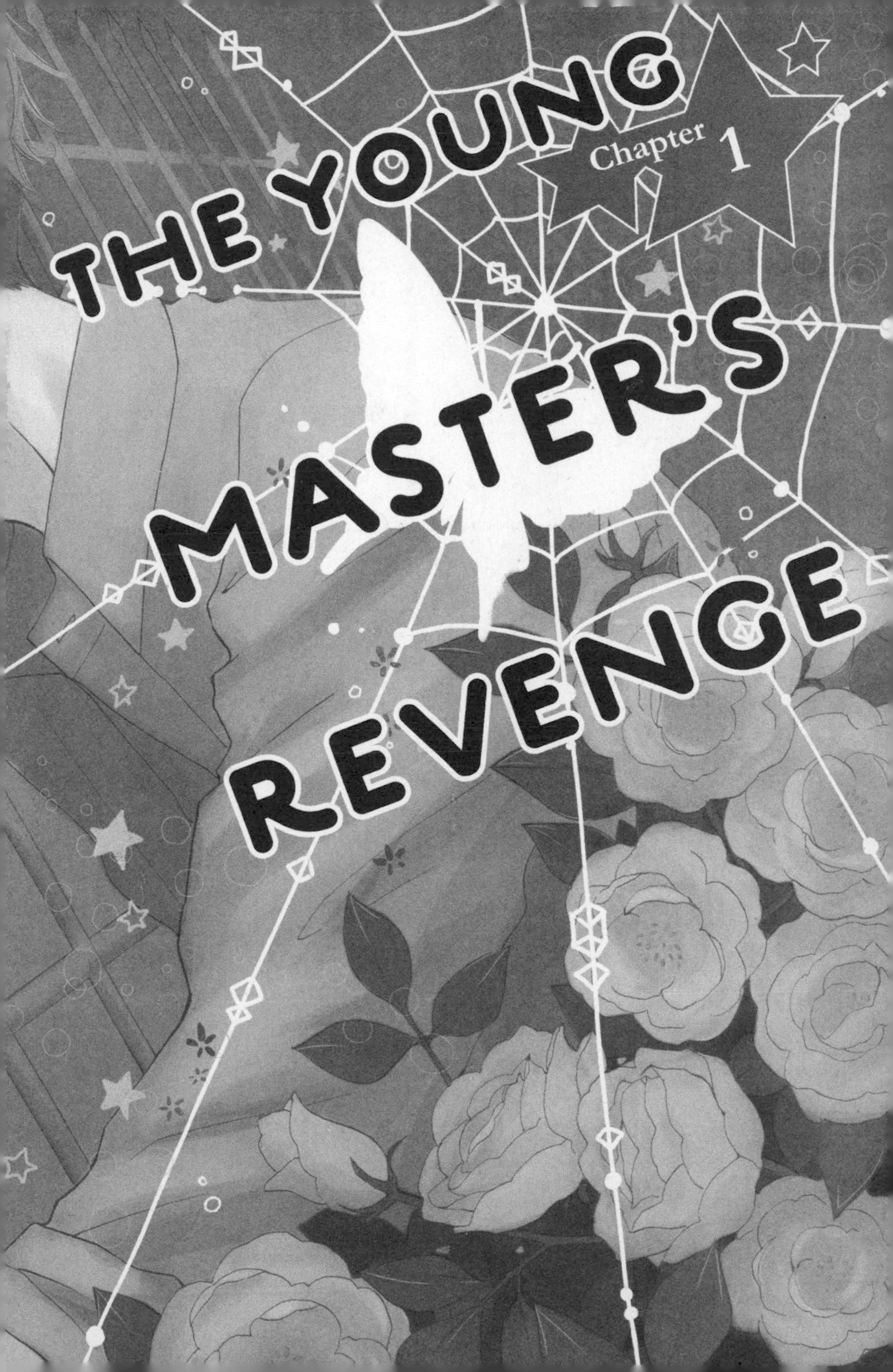
THE YOUNG MASTER'S REVENGE
Chapter 1

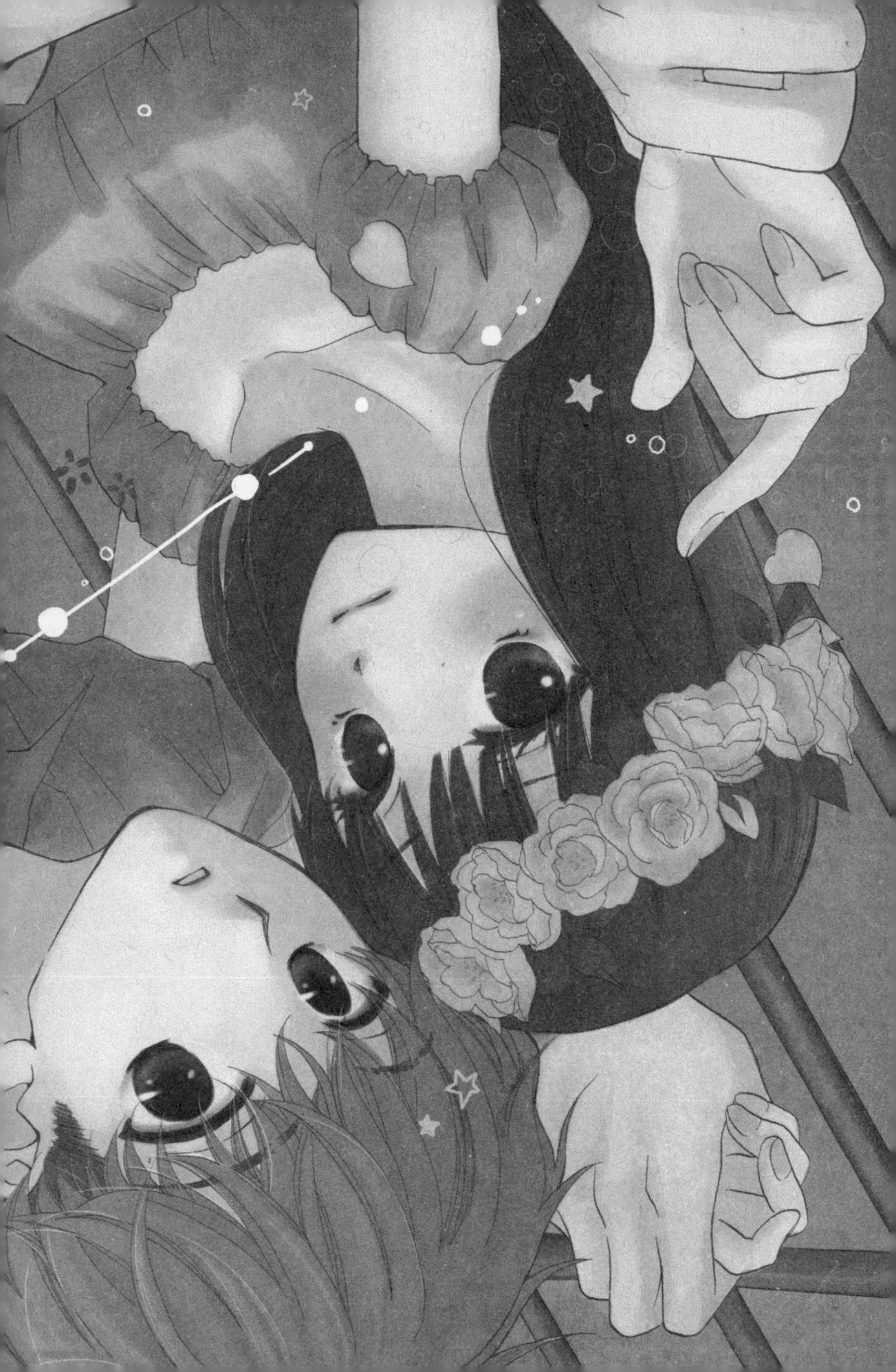

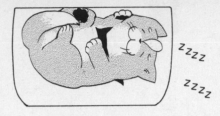

ALL HE DOES ON THE PLANE IS SLEEP.

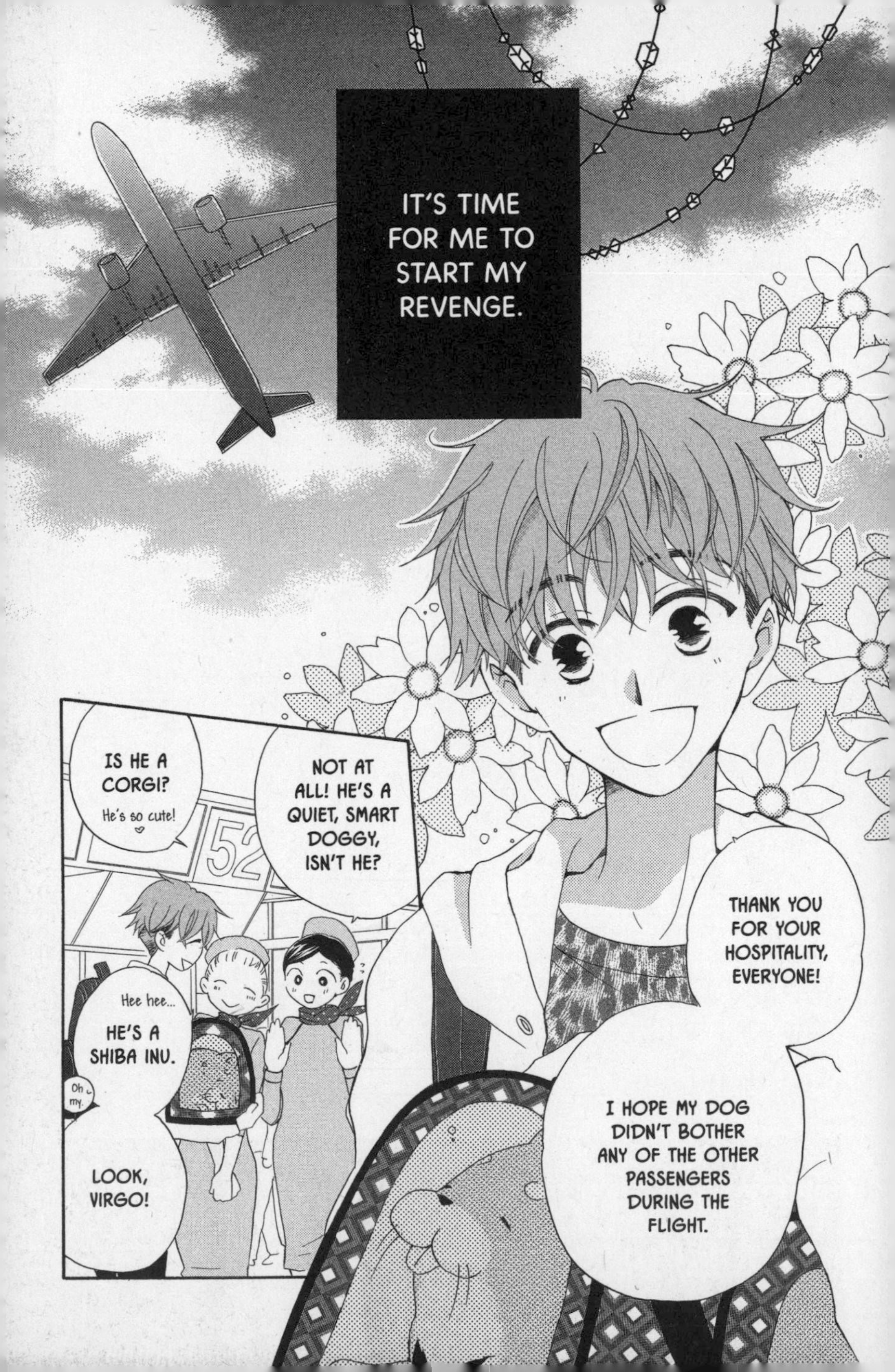
IT'S TIME FOR ME TO START MY REVENGE.
THANK YOU FOR YOUR HOSPITALITY, EVERYONE!
I HOPE MY DOG DIDN'T BOTHER ANY OF THE OTHER PASSENGERS DURING THE FLIGHT.
NOT AT ALL! HE'S A QUIET, SMART DOGGY, ISN'T HE?
IS HE A CORGI?
He's so cute!
Hee hee...
HE'S A SHIBA INU.
Oh my.
LOOK, VIRGO!

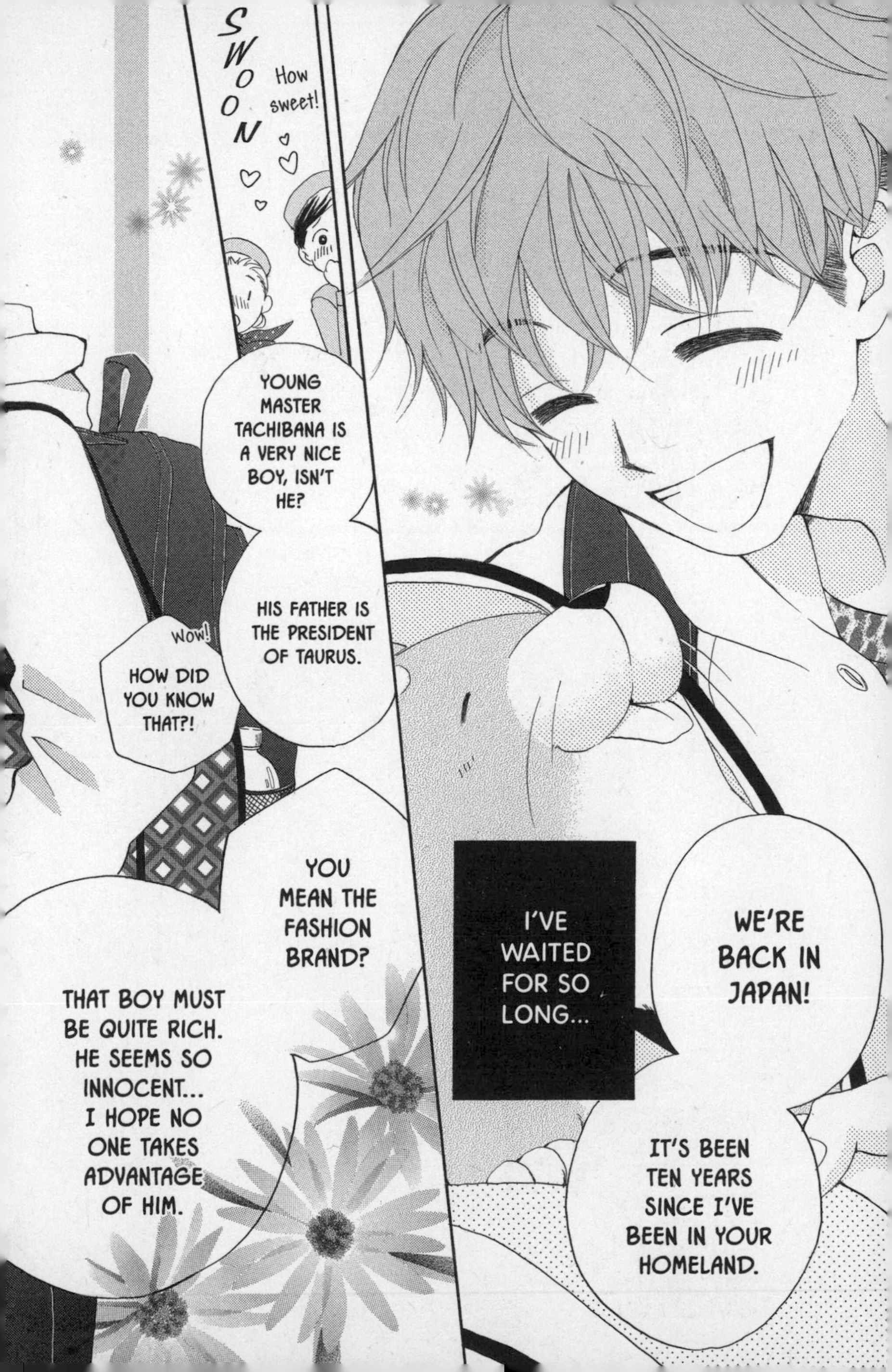
WE'RE BACK IN JAPAN!
I'VE WAITED FOR SO LONG...
IT'S BEEN TEN YEARS SINCE I'VE BEEN IN YOUR HOMELAND.
SWOON
How sweet!
YOUNG MASTER TACHIBANA IS A VERY NICE BOY, ISN'T HE?
HIS FATHER IS THE PRESIDENT OF TAURUS.
Wow!
HOW DID YOU KNOW THAT?!
YOU MEAN THE FASHION BRAND?
THAT BOY MUST BE QUITE RICH. HE SEEMS SO INNOCENT... I HOPE NO ONE TAKES ADVANTAGE OF HIM.

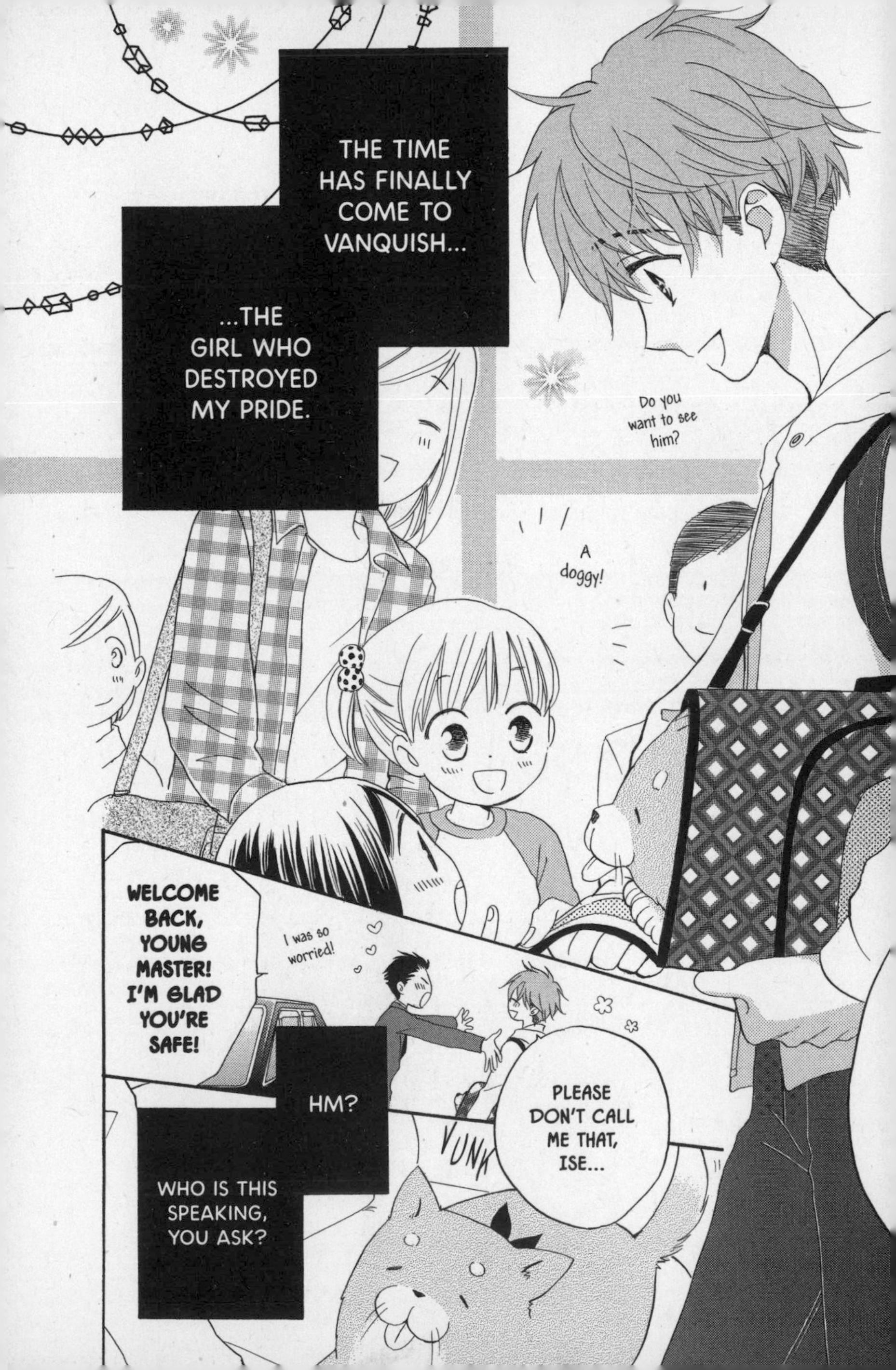
Do you want to see him?
A doggy!
THE TIME HAS FINALLY COME TO VANQUISH...
...THE GIRL WHO DESTROYED MY PRIDE.
PLEASE DON'T CALL ME THAT, ISE...
WELCOME BACK, YOUNG MASTER! I'M GLAD YOU'RE SAFE!
I was so worried!
VUNK
HM?
WHO IS THIS SPEAKING, YOU ASK?

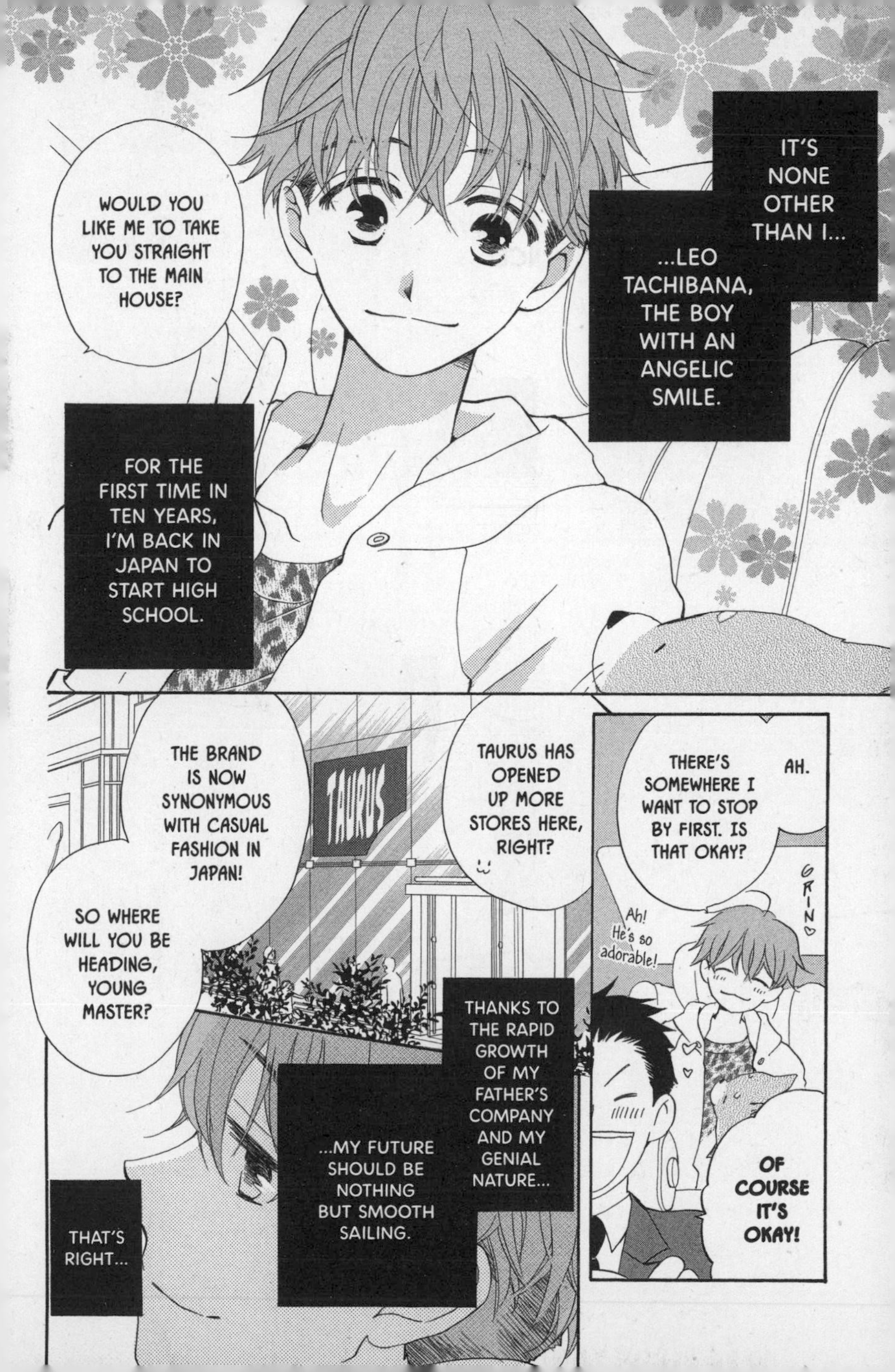
IT'S NONE OTHER THAN I...
...LEO TACHIBANA, THE BOY WITH AN ANGELIC SMILE.
WOULD YOU LIKE ME TO TAKE YOU STRAIGHT TO THE MAIN HOUSE?
FOR THE FIRST TIME IN TEN YEARS, I'M BACK IN JAPAN TO START HIGH SCHOOL.
AH.
THERE'S SOMEWHERE I WANT TO STOP BY FIRST. IS THAT OKAY?
GRIN
Ah! He's so adorable!
OF COURSE IT'S OKAY!
TAURUS HAS OPENED UP MORE STORES HERE, RIGHT?
TAURUS
THE BRAND IS NOW SYNONYMOUS WITH CASUAL FASHION IN JAPAN!
SO WHERE WILL YOU BE HEADING, YOUNG MASTER?
THANKS TO THE RAPID GROWTH OF MY FATHER'S COMPANY AND MY GENIAL NATURE...
...MY FUTURE SHOULD BE NOTHING BUT SMOOTH SAILING.
THAT'S RIGHT...

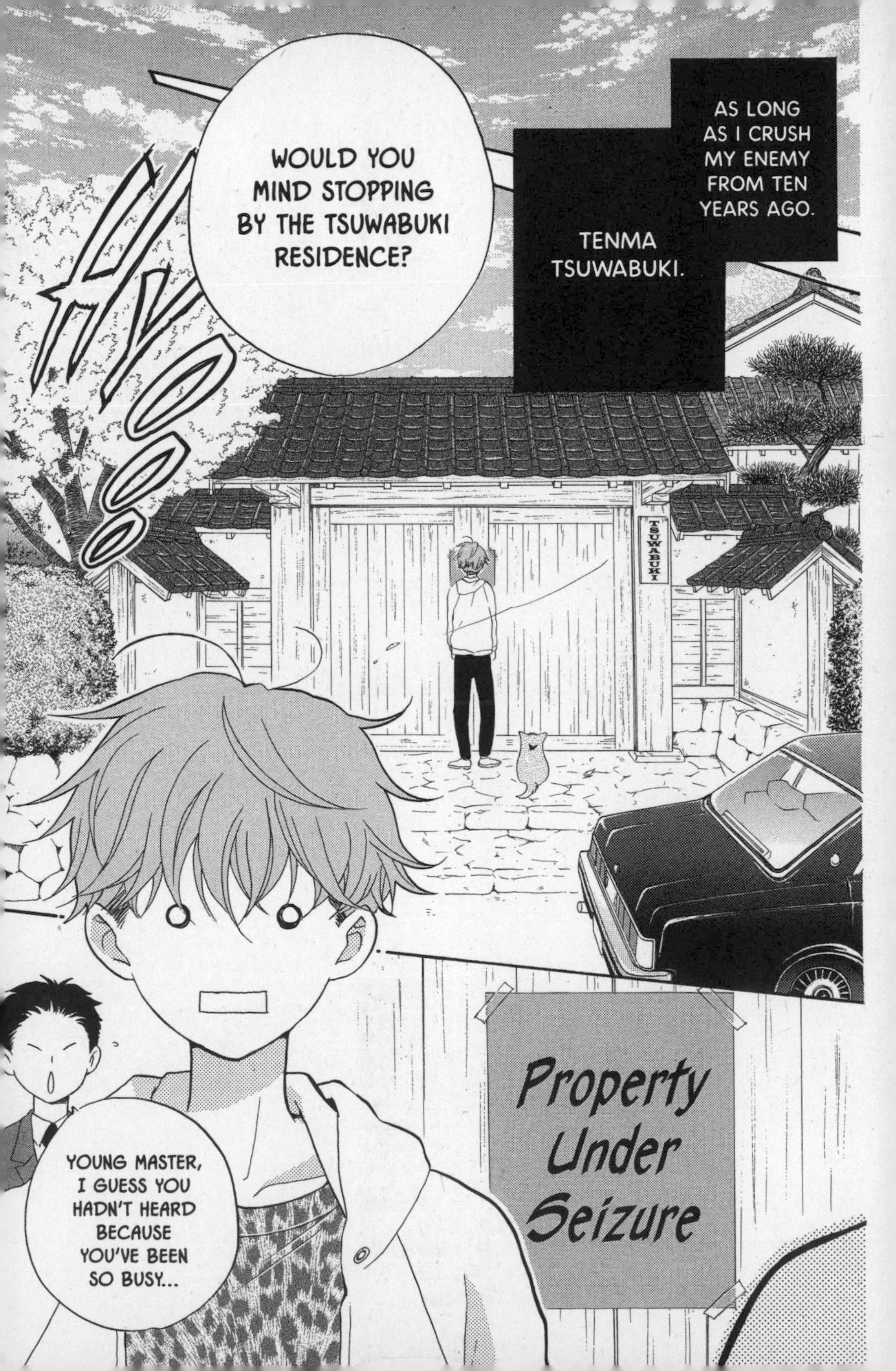
AS LONG AS I CRUSH MY ENEMY FROM TEN YEARS AGO.
TENMA TSUWABUKI.
WOULD YOU MIND STOPPING BY THE TSUWABUKI RESIDENCE?
HYOOOO
TSUWABUKI
Property Under Seizure
YOUNG MASTER, I GUESS YOU HADN'T HEARD BECAUSE YOU'VE BEEN SO BUSY...

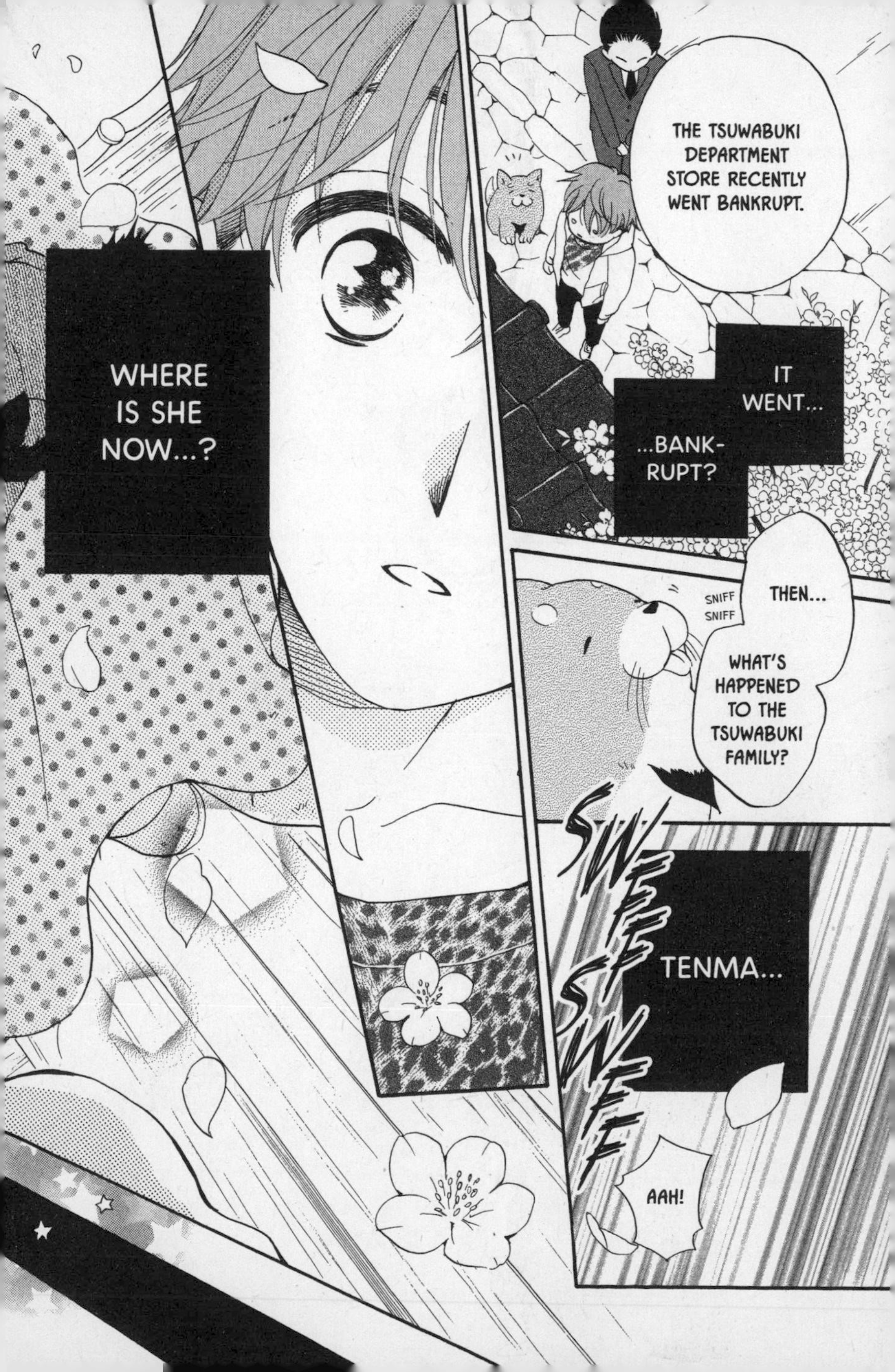
THE TSUWABUKI DEPARTMENT STORE RECENTLY WENT BANKRUPT.
IT WENT...
...BANK-RUPT?
THEN...
SNIFF SNIFF
WHAT'S HAPPENED TO THE TSUWABUKI FAMILY?
SWEFF SWEFF
TENMA...
AAH!
WHERE IS SHE NOW...?

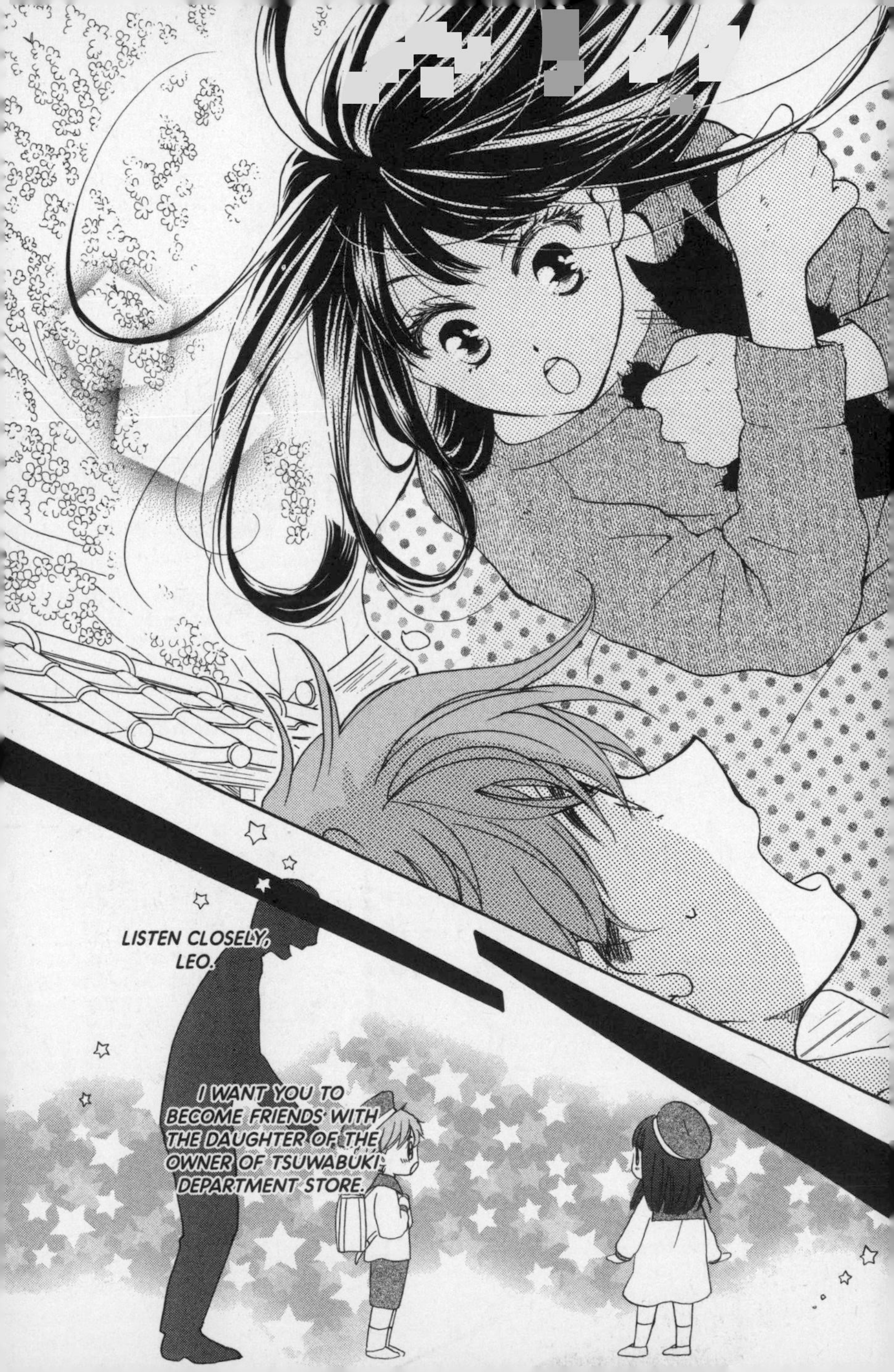
LISTEN CLOSELY, LEO.
I WANT YOU TO BECOME FRIENDS WITH THE DAUGHTER OF THE OWNER OF TSUWABUKI DEPARTMENT STORE.

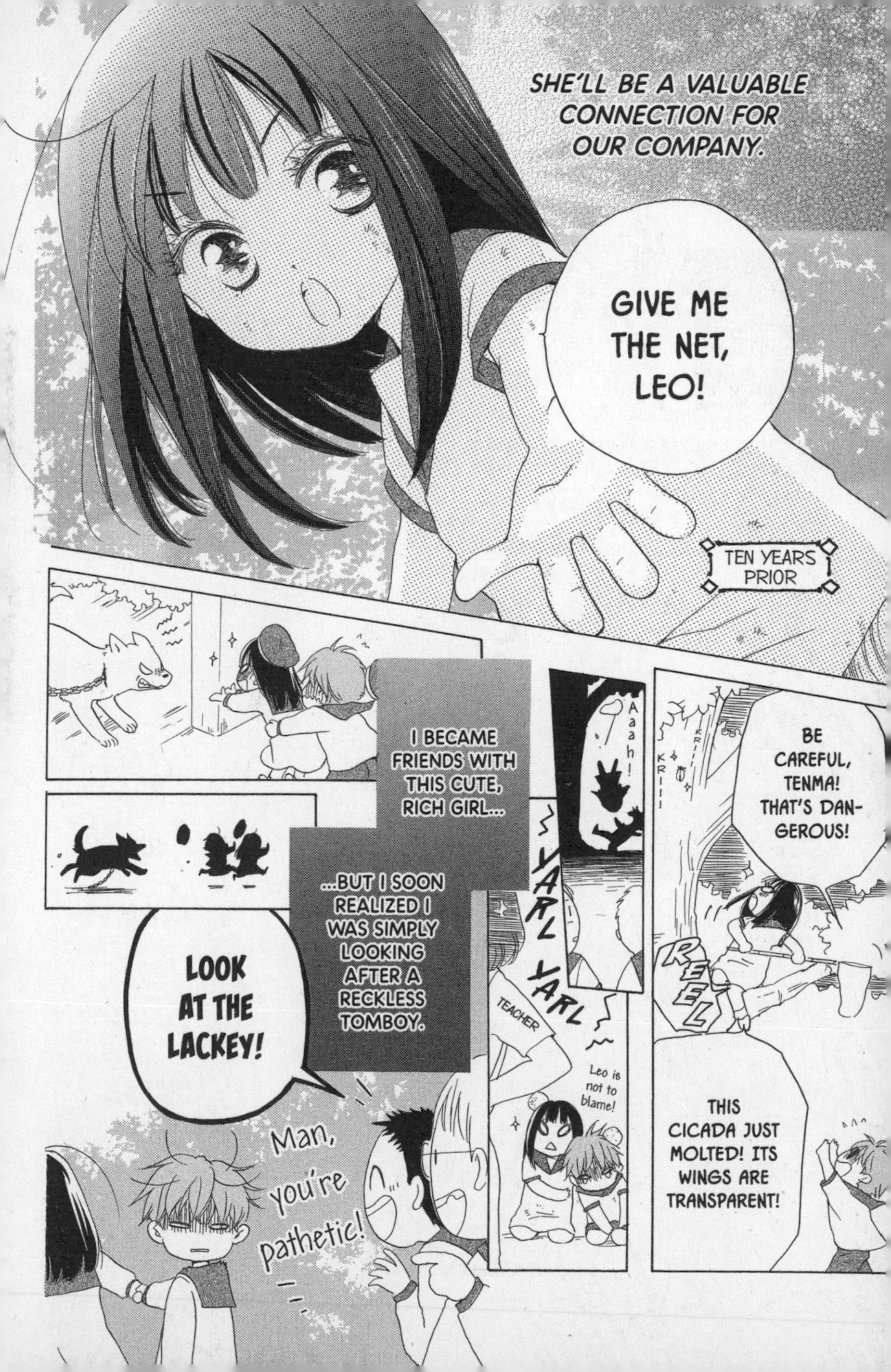
SHE'LL BE A VALUABLE CONNECTION FOR OUR COMPANY.
GIVE ME THE NET, LEO!
TEN YEARS PRIOR
BE CAREFUL, TENMA! THAT'S DANGEROUS!
KRI KRI
REEL
THIS CICADA JUST MOLTED! ITS WINGS ARE TRANSPARENT!
Aaah!
YARL YARL
TEACHER
Leo is not to blame!
I BECAME FRIENDS WITH THIS CUTE, RICH GIRL...
...BUT I SOON REALIZED I WAS SIMPLY LOOKING AFTER A RECKLESS TOMBOY.
LOOK AT THE LACKEY!
Man, you're pathetic!

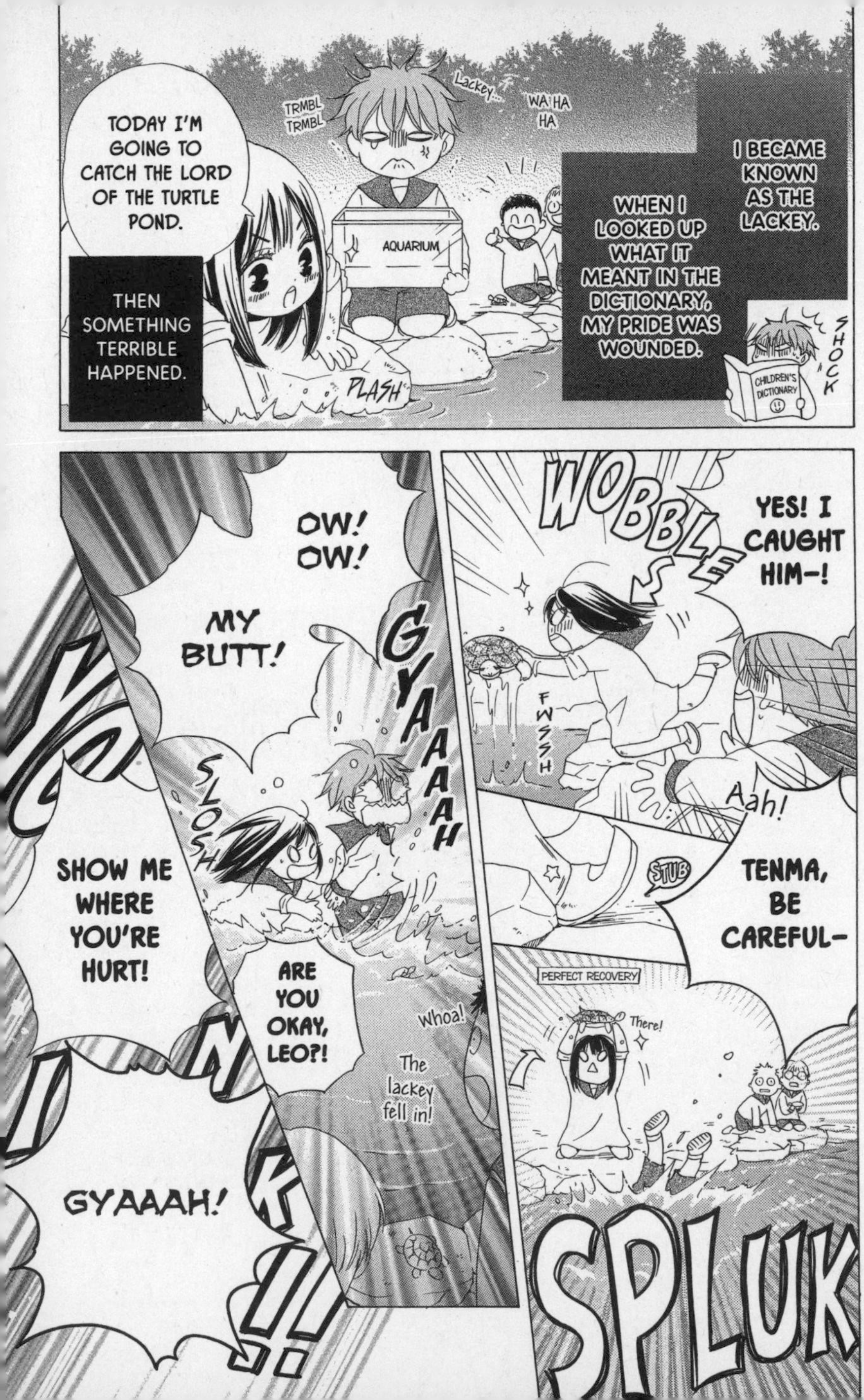
I BECAME KNOWN AS THE LACKEY.
WHEN I LOOKED UP WHAT IT MEANT IN THE DICTIONARY, MY PRIDE WAS WOUNDED.
SHOCK
CHILDREN'S DICTIONARY
Lackey...
WA HA HA
TRMBL TRMBL
AQUARIUM
TODAY I'M GOING TO CATCH THE LORD OF THE TURTLE POND.
THEN SOMETHING TERRIBLE HAPPENED.
PLASH
WOBBLE
YES! I CAUGHT HIM-!
FWSSH
Aah!
TENMA, BE CAREFUL-
STUB
PERFECT RECOVERY
There!
SPLUK
OW! OW!
MY BUTT!
GYAAAAH
SLOSH
ARE YOU OKAY, LEO?!
Whoa!
The lackey fell in!
SHOW ME WHERE YOU'RE HURT!
GYAAAH!

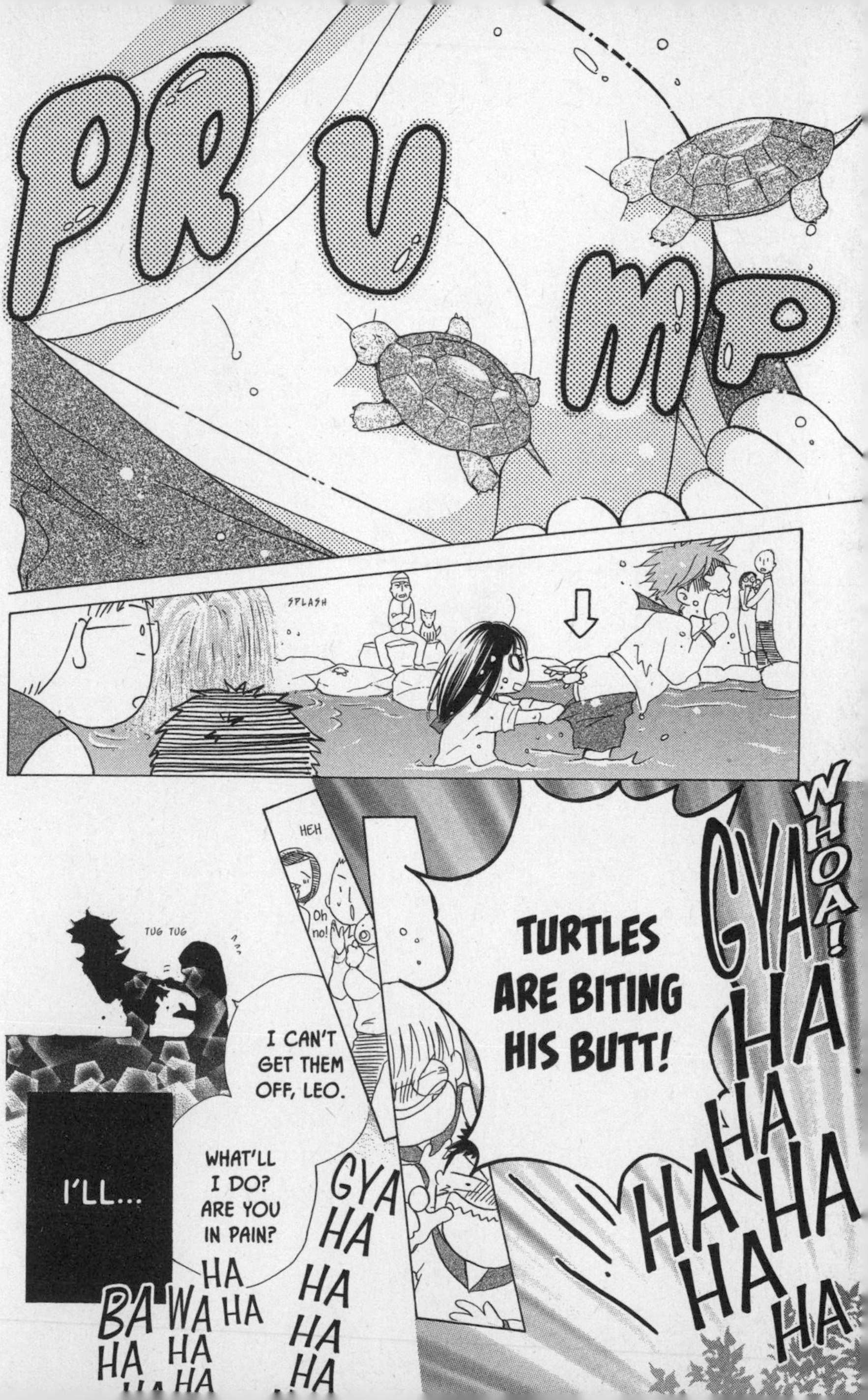
PRUMP
SPLASH
WHOA!
GYAHA HA HA HA HA HA HA HA
TURTLES ARE BITING HIS BUTT!
HEH
Oh no!
GYA HA HA HA HA HA
I CAN'T GET THEM OFF, LEO.
WHAT'LL I DO? ARE YOU IN PAIN?
BAWAHA HA HA HA HA
TUG TUG
I'LL...

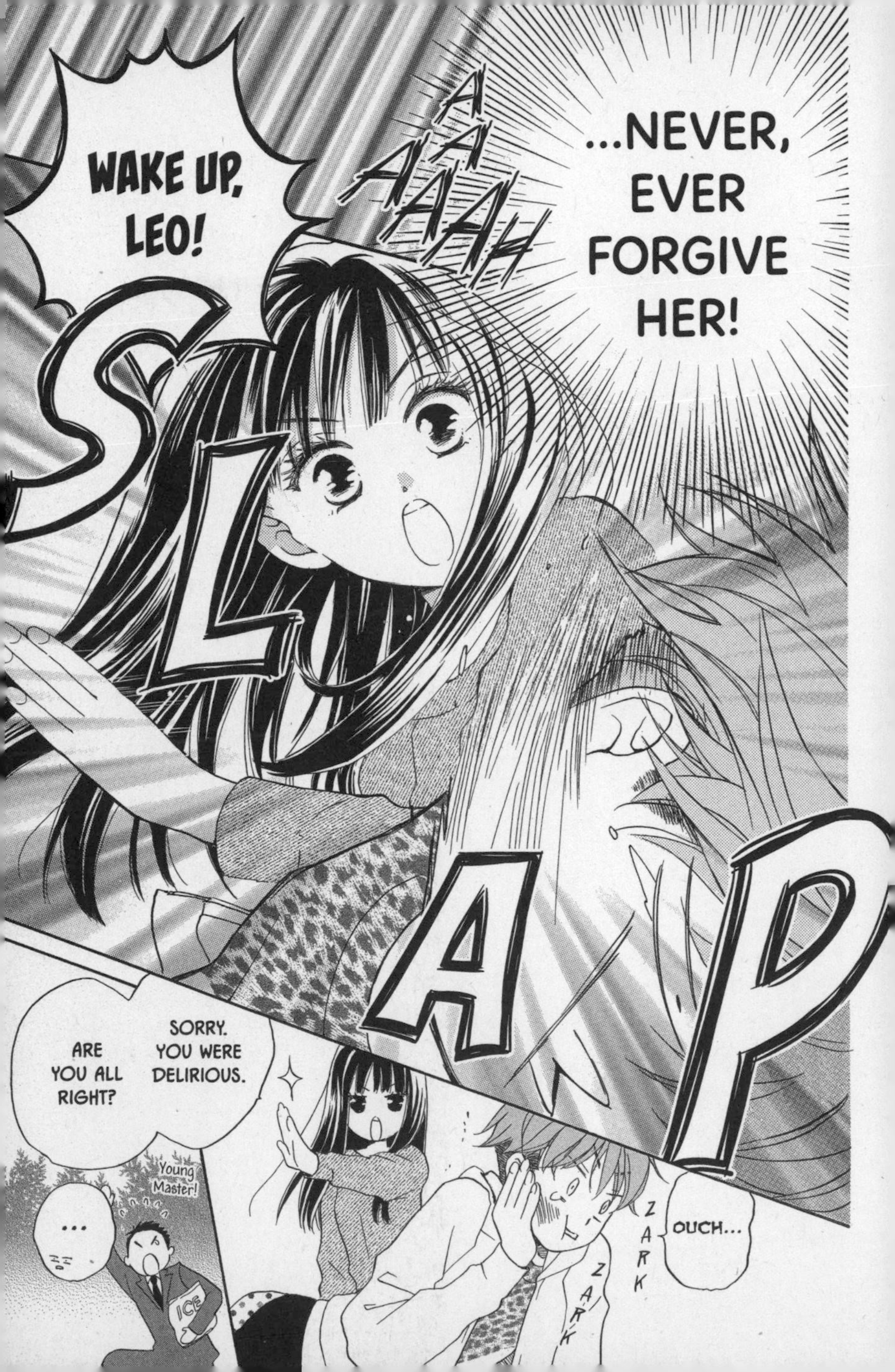
...NEVER, EVER FORGIVE HER!
AAAAAH
WAKE UP, LEO!
SLAP
ZARK ZARK
OUCH...
SORRY. YOU WERE DELIRIOUS.
ARE YOU ALL RIGHT?
Young Master!
...

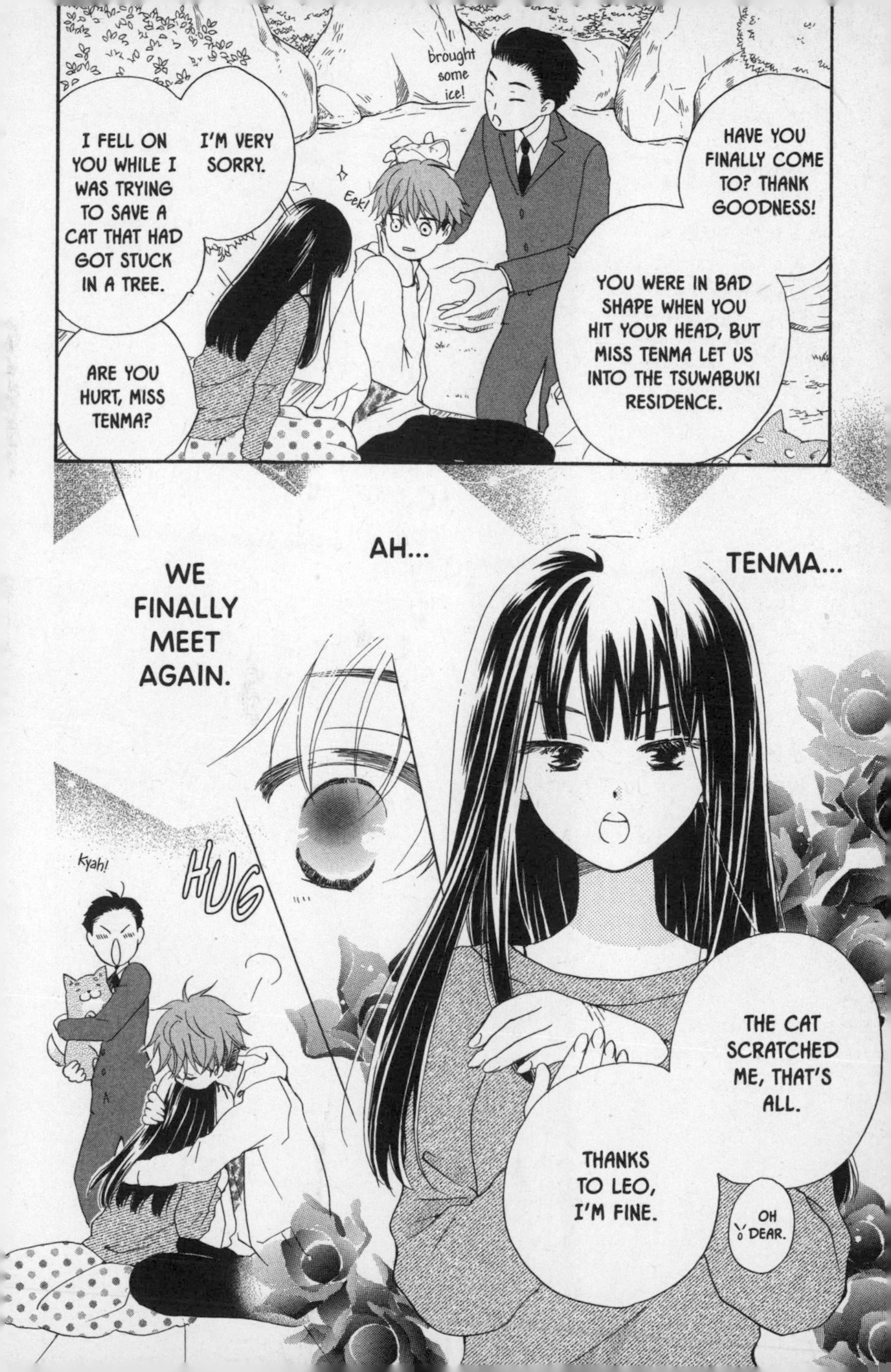
HAVE YOU FINALLY COME TO? THANK GOODNESS!
YOU WERE IN BAD SHAPE WHEN YOU HIT YOUR HEAD, BUT MISS TENMA LET US INTO THE TSUWABUKI RESIDENCE.
brought some ice!
Eek!
I'M VERY SORRY.
I FELL ON YOU WHILE I WAS TRYING TO SAVE A CAT THAT HAD GOT STUCK IN A TREE.
ARE YOU HURT, MISS TENMA?
TENMA...
AH...
WE FINALLY MEET AGAIN.
THE CAT SCRATCHED ME, THAT'S ALL.
THANKS TO LEO, I'M FINE.
OH DEAR.
HUG
Kyah!

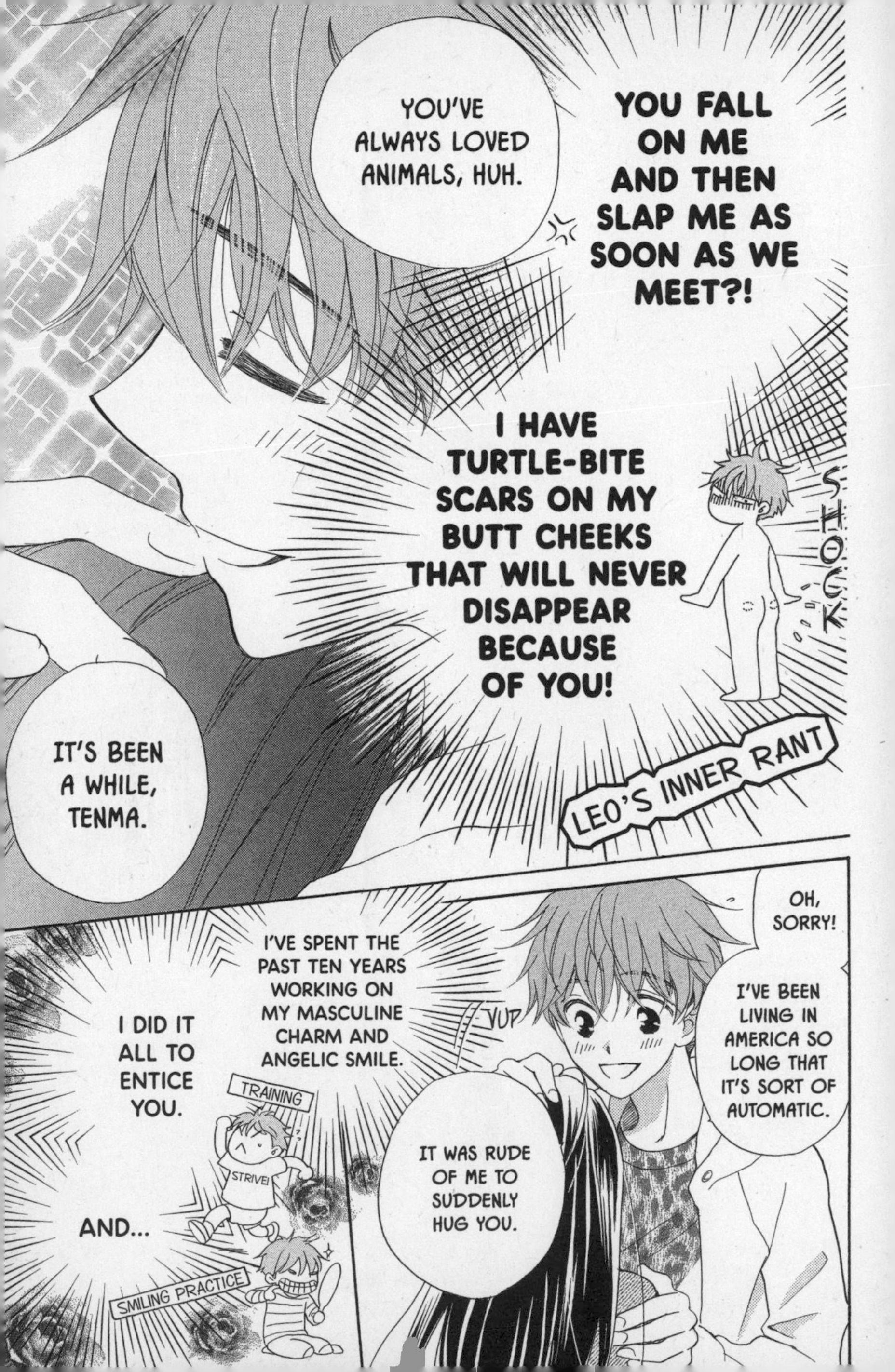
YOU'VE ALWAYS LOVED ANIMALS, HUH.
YOU FALL ON ME AND THEN SLAP ME AS SOON AS WE MEET?!
I HAVE TURTLE-BITE SCARS ON MY BUTT CHEEKS THAT WILL NEVER DISAPPEAR BECAUSE OF YOU!
SHOCK
LEO'S INNER RANT
IT'S BEEN A WHILE, TENMA.
OH, SORRY!
I'VE BEEN LIVING IN AMERICA SO LONG THAT IT'S SORT OF AUTOMATIC.
VUP
IT WAS RUDE OF ME TO SUDDENLY HUG YOU.
I'VE SPENT THE PAST TEN YEARS WORKING ON MY MASCULINE CHARM AND ANGELIC SMILE.
TRAINING
STRIVE!
SMILING PRACTICE
I DID IT ALL TO ENTICE YOU.
AND...

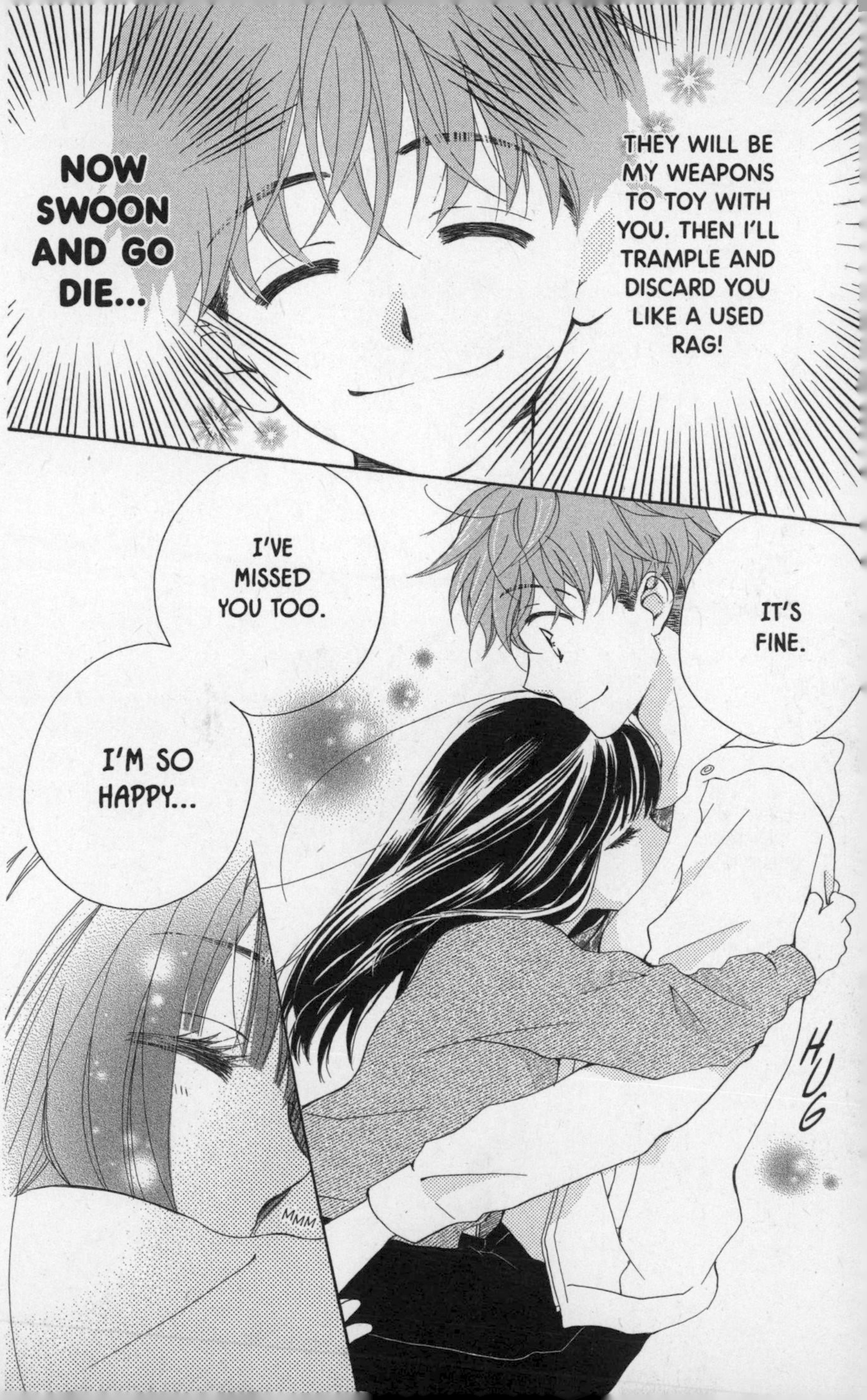
THEY WILL BE MY WEAPONS TO TOY WITH YOU. THEN I'LL TRAMPLE AND DISCARD YOU LIKE A USED RAG!
NOW SWOON AND GO DIE...
IT'S FINE.
I'VE MISSED YOU TOO.
I'M SO HAPPY...
HUG
MMM

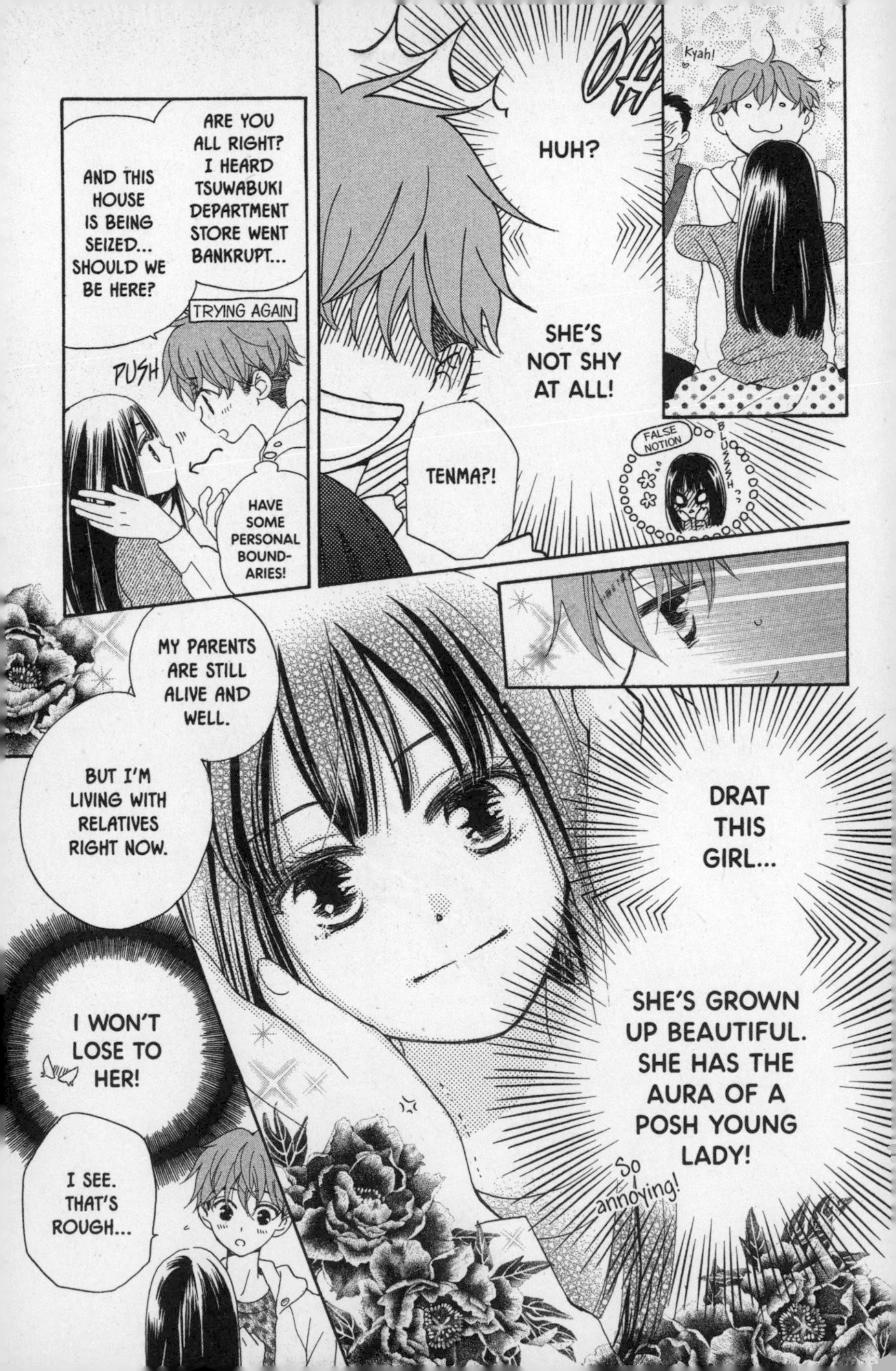
Kyah!
OH
HUH?
SHE'S NOT SHY AT ALL!
FALSE NOTION
BLUSSSH
TENMA?!
ARE YOU ALL RIGHT? I HEARD TSUWABUKI DEPARTMENT STORE WENT BANKRUPT...
AND THIS HOUSE IS BEING SEIZED... SHOULD WE BE HERE?
TRYING AGAIN
PUSH
HAVE SOME PERSONAL BOUND-ARIES!
MY PARENTS ARE STILL ALIVE AND WELL.
BUT I'M LIVING WITH RELATIVES RIGHT NOW.
DRAT THIS GIRL...
SHE'S GROWN UP BEAUTIFUL. SHE HAS THE AURA OF A POSH YOUNG LADY!
So annoying!
I WON'T LOSE TO HER!
I SEE. THAT'S ROUGH...

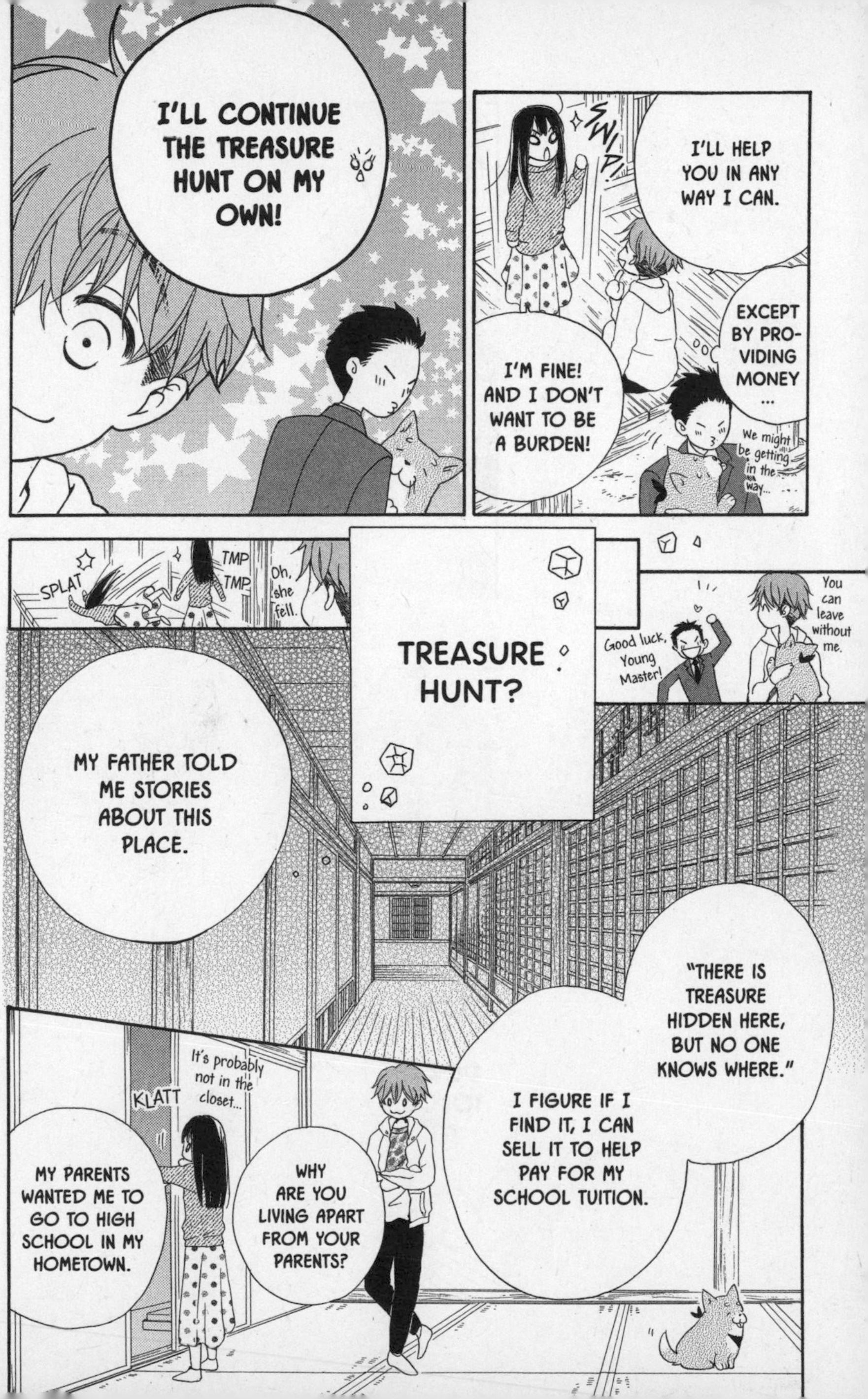
I'LL HELP YOU IN ANY WAY I CAN.
SWIP
EXCEPT BY PRO-VIDING MONEY ...
I'M FINE! AND I DON'T WANT TO BE A BURDEN!
We might be getting in the way...
I'LL CONTINUE THE TREASURE HUNT ON MY OWN!
You can leave without me.
Good luck, Young Master!
TREASURE HUNT?
TMP TMP
Oh, she fell.
SPLAT
MY FATHER TOLD ME STORIES ABOUT THIS PLACE.
"THERE IS TREASURE HIDDEN HERE, BUT NO ONE KNOWS WHERE."
I FIGURE IF I FIND IT, I CAN SELL IT TO HELP PAY FOR MY SCHOOL TUITION.
WHY ARE YOU LIVING APART FROM YOUR PARENTS?
MY PARENTS WANTED ME TO GO TO HIGH SCHOOL IN MY HOMETOWN.
KLATT
It's probably not in the closet...

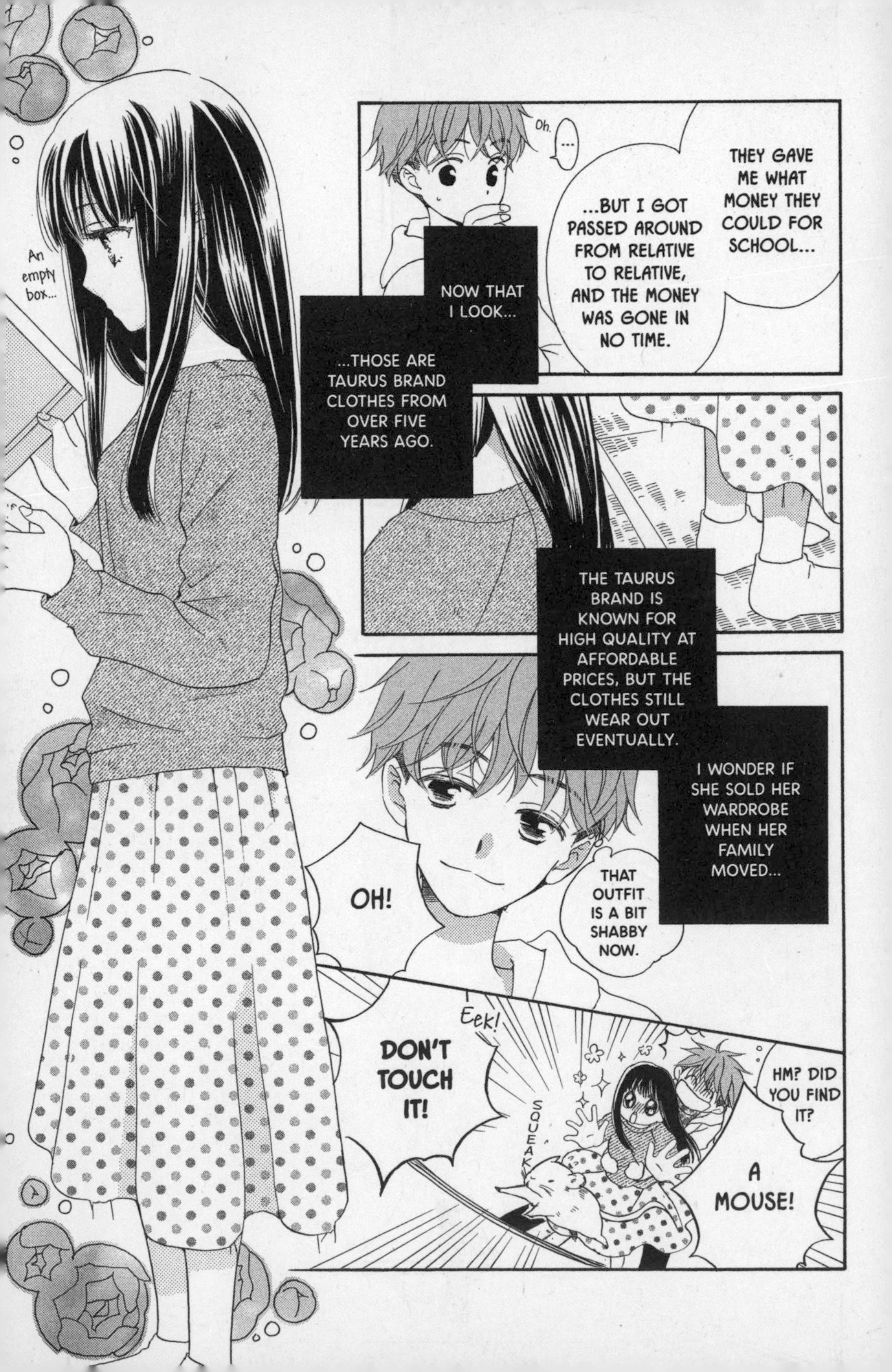
THEY GAVE ME WHAT MONEY THEY COULD FOR SCHOOL...
...BUT I GOT PASSED AROUND FROM RELATIVE TO RELATIVE, AND THE MONEY WAS GONE IN NO TIME.
Oh.
...
NOW THAT I LOOK...
...THOSE ARE TAURUS BRAND CLOTHES FROM OVER FIVE YEARS AGO.
THE TAURUS BRAND IS KNOWN FOR HIGH QUALITY AT AFFORDABLE PRICES, BUT THE CLOTHES STILL WEAR OUT EVENTUALLY.
I WONDER IF SHE SOLD HER WARDROBE WHEN HER FAMILY MOVED...
THAT OUTFIT IS A BIT SHABBY NOW.
OH!
HM? DID YOU FIND IT?
A MOUSE!
SQUEAK
Eek!
DON'T TOUCH IT!
An empty box...

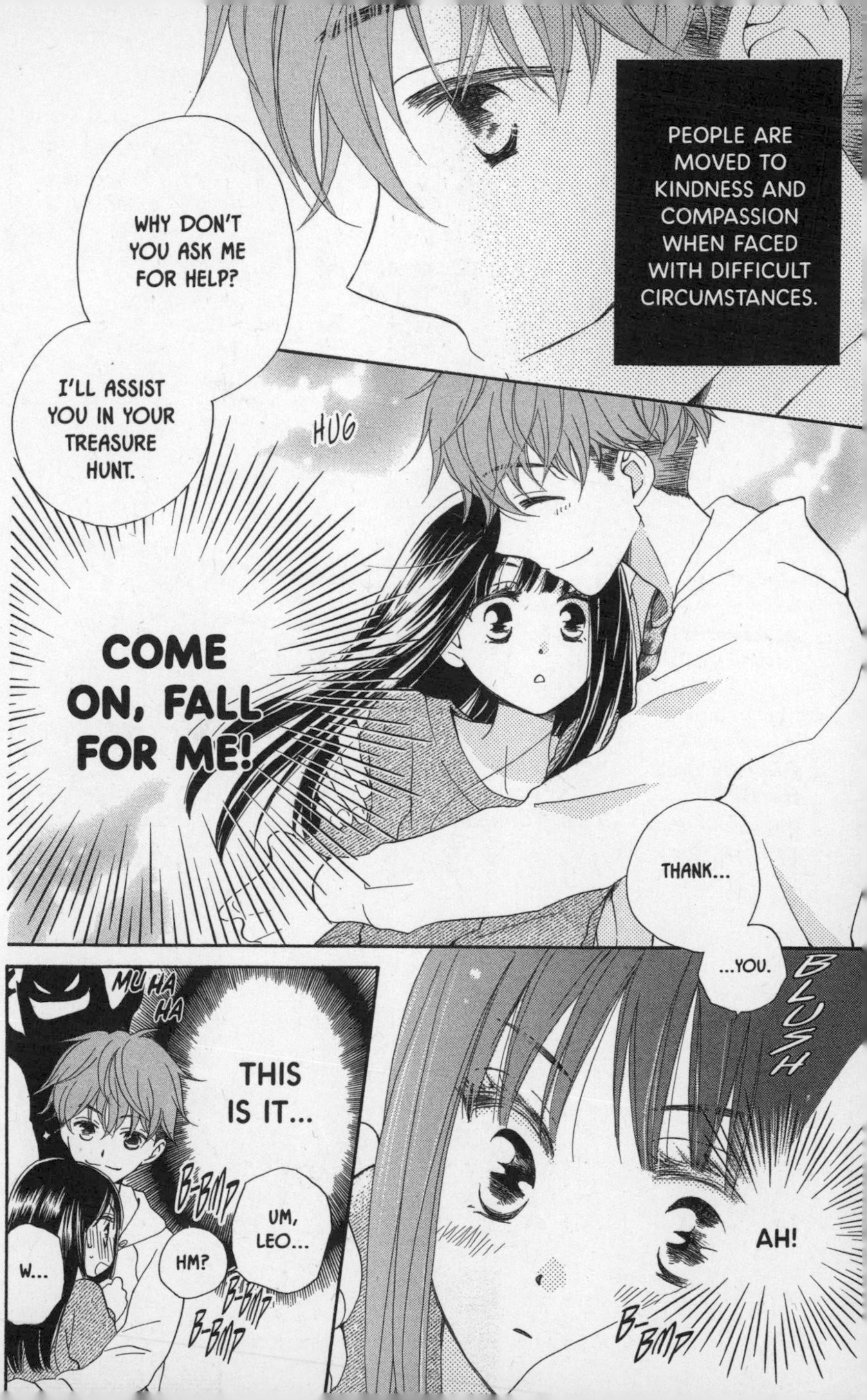
PEOPLE ARE MOVED TO KINDNESS AND COMPASSION WHEN FACED WITH DIFFICULT CIRCUMSTANCES.
WHY DON'T YOU ASK ME FOR HELP?
I'LL ASSIST YOU IN YOUR TREASURE HUNT.
HUG
COME ON, FALL FOR ME!
THANK...
...YOU.
BLUSH
AH!
B-BMP
THIS IS IT...
MU HA HA
B-BMP
UM, LEO...
HM?
B-BMP
B-BMP
W...

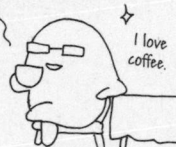

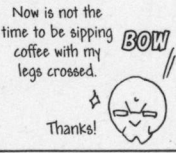

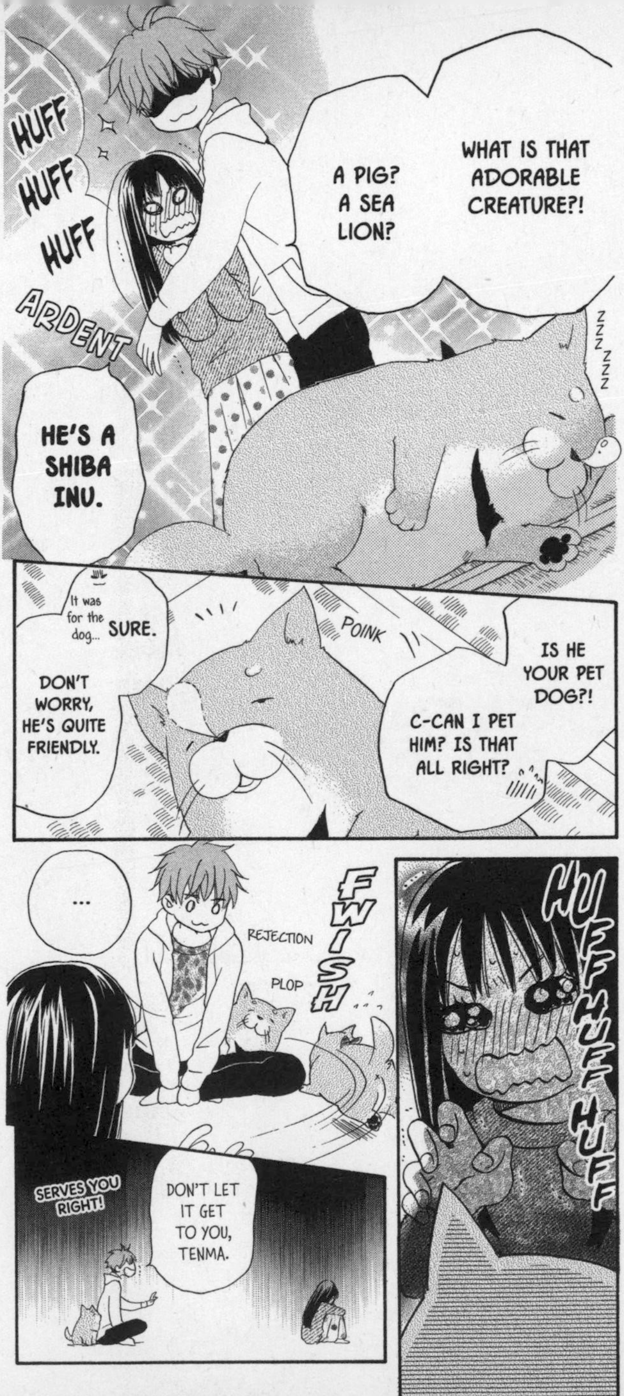
WHAT IS THAT ADORABLE CREATURE?!
A PIG? A SEA LION?
HUFF
HUFF
HUFF
ARDENT
ZZZ
ZZZ
HE'S A SHIBA INU.
IS HE YOUR PET DOG?!
C-CAN I PET HIM? IS THAT ALL RIGHT?
POINK
SURE.
It was for the dog...
DON'T WORRY, HE'S QUITE FRIENDLY.
HUFF HUFF HUFF HUFF
FWISH
REJECTION
PLOP
...
SERVES YOU RIGHT!
DON'T LET IT GET TO YOU, TENMA.

This is my 30th volume.

Hello, everyone. This is Tanaka.

I love coffee.

I've had a total of 30 volumes published by Hakusensha since my debut! What an accomplishment! I'm sure you're just as surprised as I am. I double-checked, and it is indeed 30 volumes. Isn't that amazing?! Even a heap of dust makes a mountain in time. This is all thanks to your help. Thank you very much! ♡

Whether you are new or a longtime reader, I hope you will enjoy my new series!

Now is not the time to be sipping coffee with my legs crossed.

BOW

Thanks!

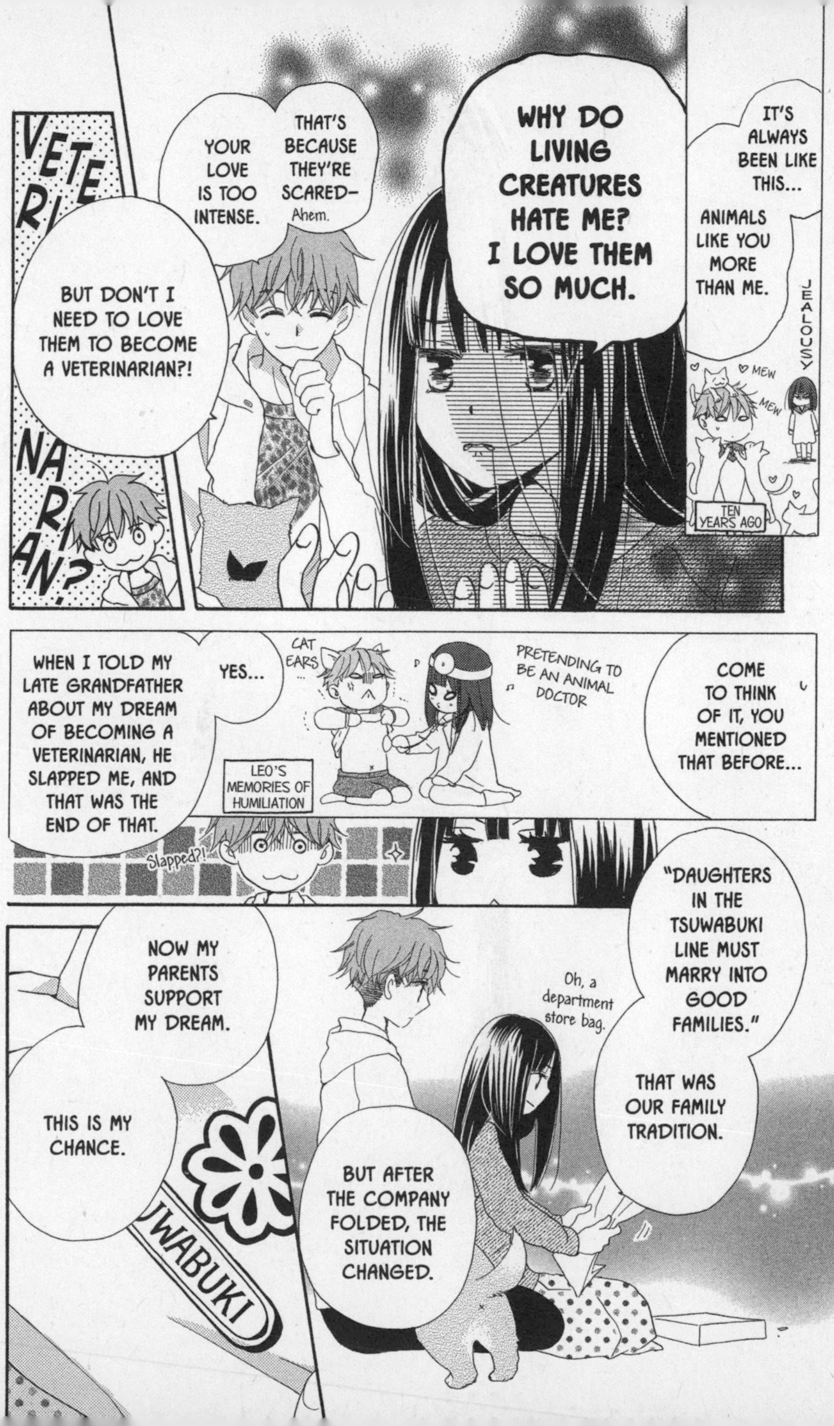
IT'S ALWAYS BEEN LIKE THIS...
ANIMALS LIKE YOU MORE THAN ME.
JEALOUSY
MEW
MEW
TEN YEARS AGO
WHY DO LIVING CREATURES HATE ME? I LOVE THEM SO MUCH.
THAT'S BECAUSE THEY'RE SCARED—
Ahem.
YOUR LOVE IS TOO INTENSE.
BUT DON'T I NEED TO LOVE THEM TO BECOME A VETERINARIAN?!
VETERINARIAN?
COME TO THINK OF IT, YOU MENTIONED THAT BEFORE...
PRETENDING TO BE AN ANIMAL DOCTOR
CAT EARS ...
LEO'S MEMORIES OF HUMILIATION
YES...
WHEN I TOLD MY LATE GRANDFATHER ABOUT MY DREAM OF BECOMING A VETERINARIAN, HE SLAPPED ME, AND THAT WAS THE END OF THAT.
Slapped?!
"DAUGHTERS IN THE TSUWABUKI LINE MUST MARRY INTO GOOD FAMILIES."
THAT WAS OUR FAMILY TRADITION.
Oh, a department store bag.
BUT AFTER THE COMPANY FOLDED, THE SITUATION CHANGED.
NOW MY PARENTS SUPPORT MY DREAM.
THIS IS MY CHANCE.
UWABUKI

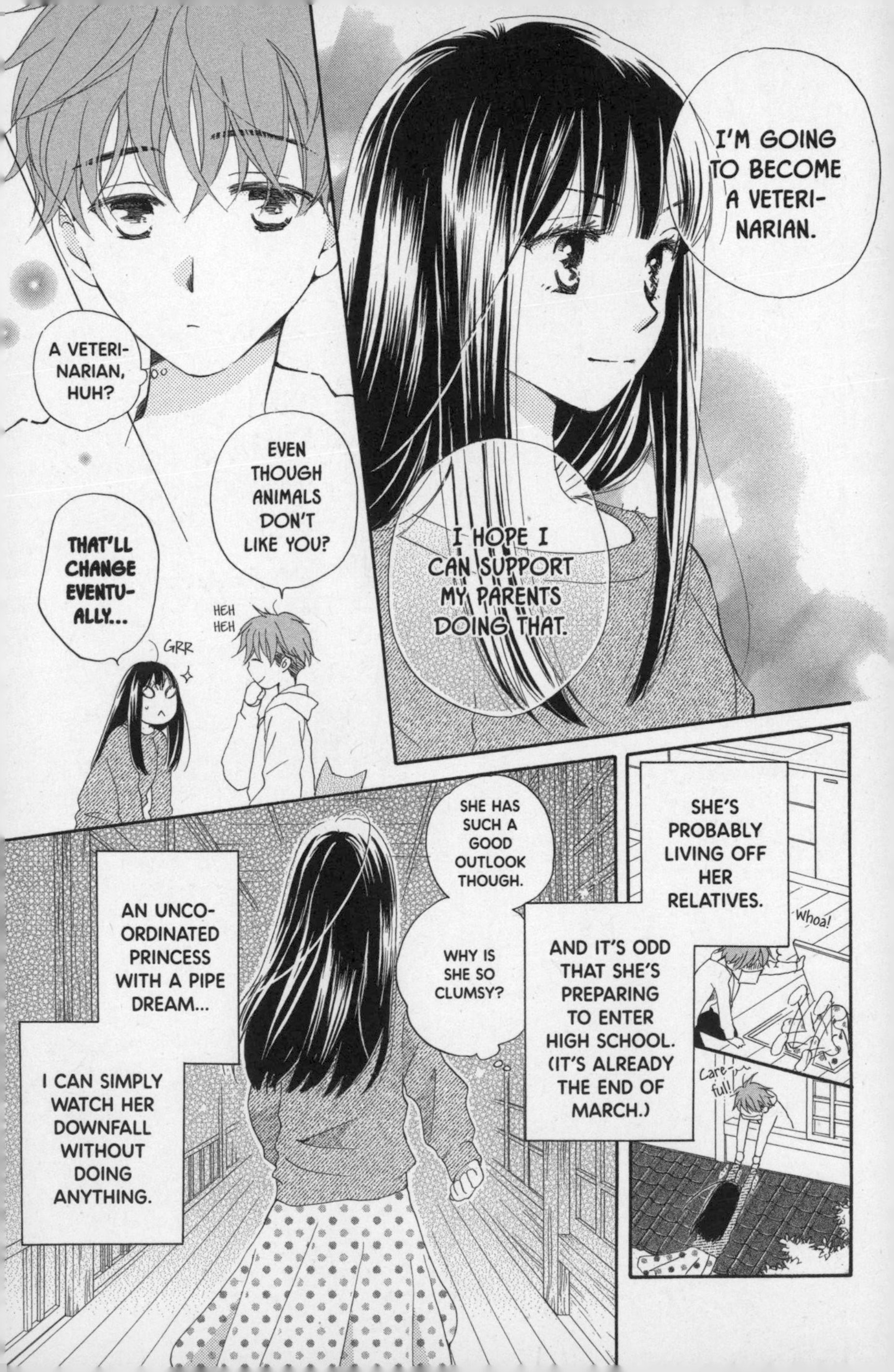
I'M GOING TO BECOME A VETERINARIAN.
I HOPE I CAN SUPPORT MY PARENTS DOING THAT.
A VETERINARIAN, HUH?
EVEN THOUGH ANIMALS DON'T LIKE YOU?
HEH HEH
THAT'LL CHANGE EVENTUALLY...
GRR
SHE'S PROBABLY LIVING OFF HER RELATIVES.
Whoa!
AND IT'S ODD THAT SHE'S PREPARING TO ENTER HIGH SCHOOL. (IT'S ALREADY THE END OF MARCH.)
Careful!
SHE HAS SUCH A GOOD OUTLOOK THOUGH.
WHY IS SHE SO CLUMSY?
AN UNCOORDINATED PRINCESS WITH A PIPE DREAM...
I CAN SIMPLY WATCH HER DOWNFALL WITHOUT DOING ANYTHING.

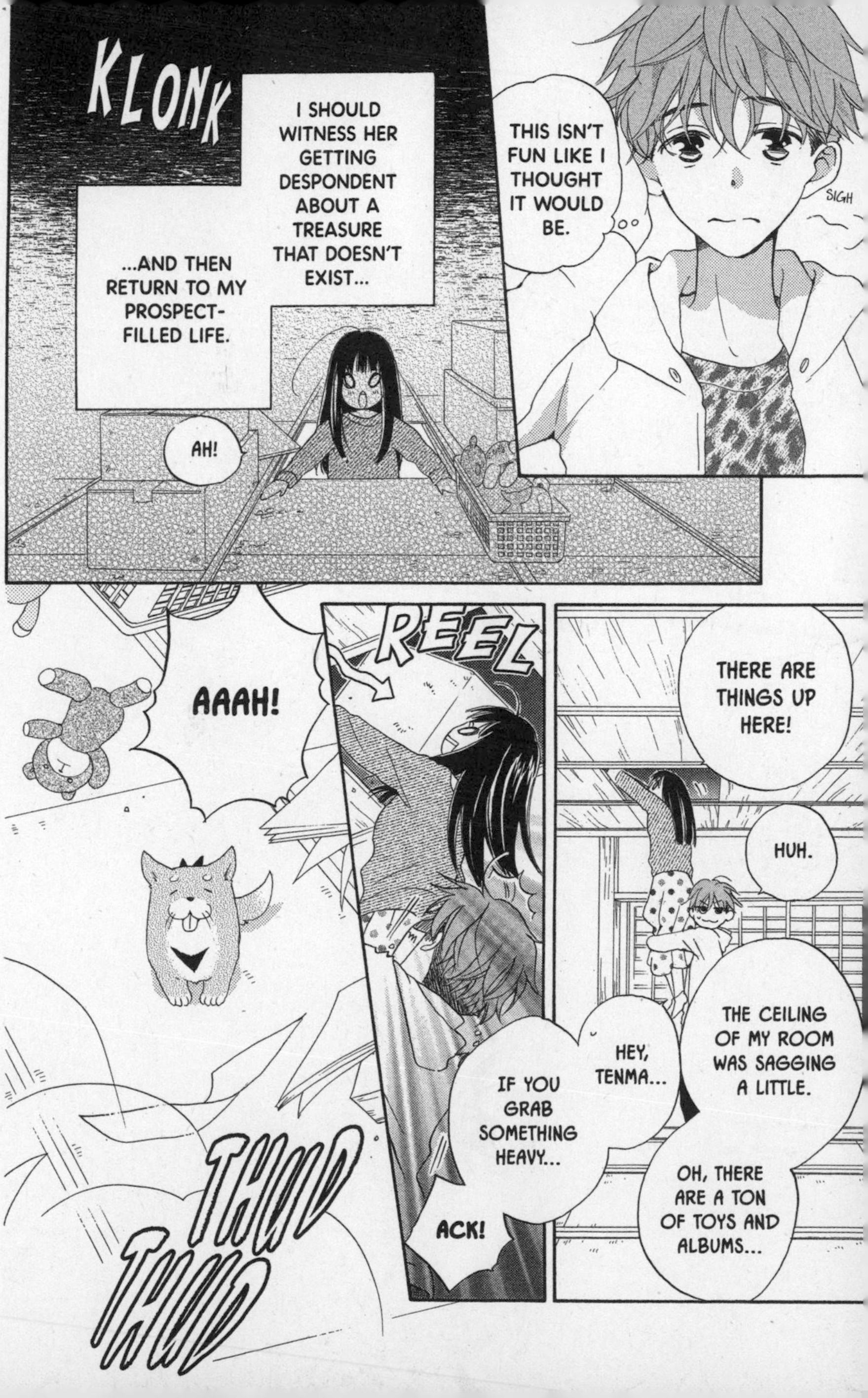
THIS ISN'T FUN LIKE I THOUGHT IT WOULD BE.
SIGH
I SHOULD WITNESS HER GETTING DESPONDENT ABOUT A TREASURE THAT DOESN'T EXIST...
...AND THEN RETURN TO MY PROSPECT-FILLED LIFE.
KLONK
AH!
THERE ARE THINGS UP HERE!
HUH.
THE CEILING OF MY ROOM WAS SAGGING A LITTLE.
OH, THERE ARE A TON OF TOYS AND ALBUMS...
HEY, TENMA...
IF YOU GRAB SOMETHING HEAVY...
ACK!
REEL
AAAH!
THUD
THUD

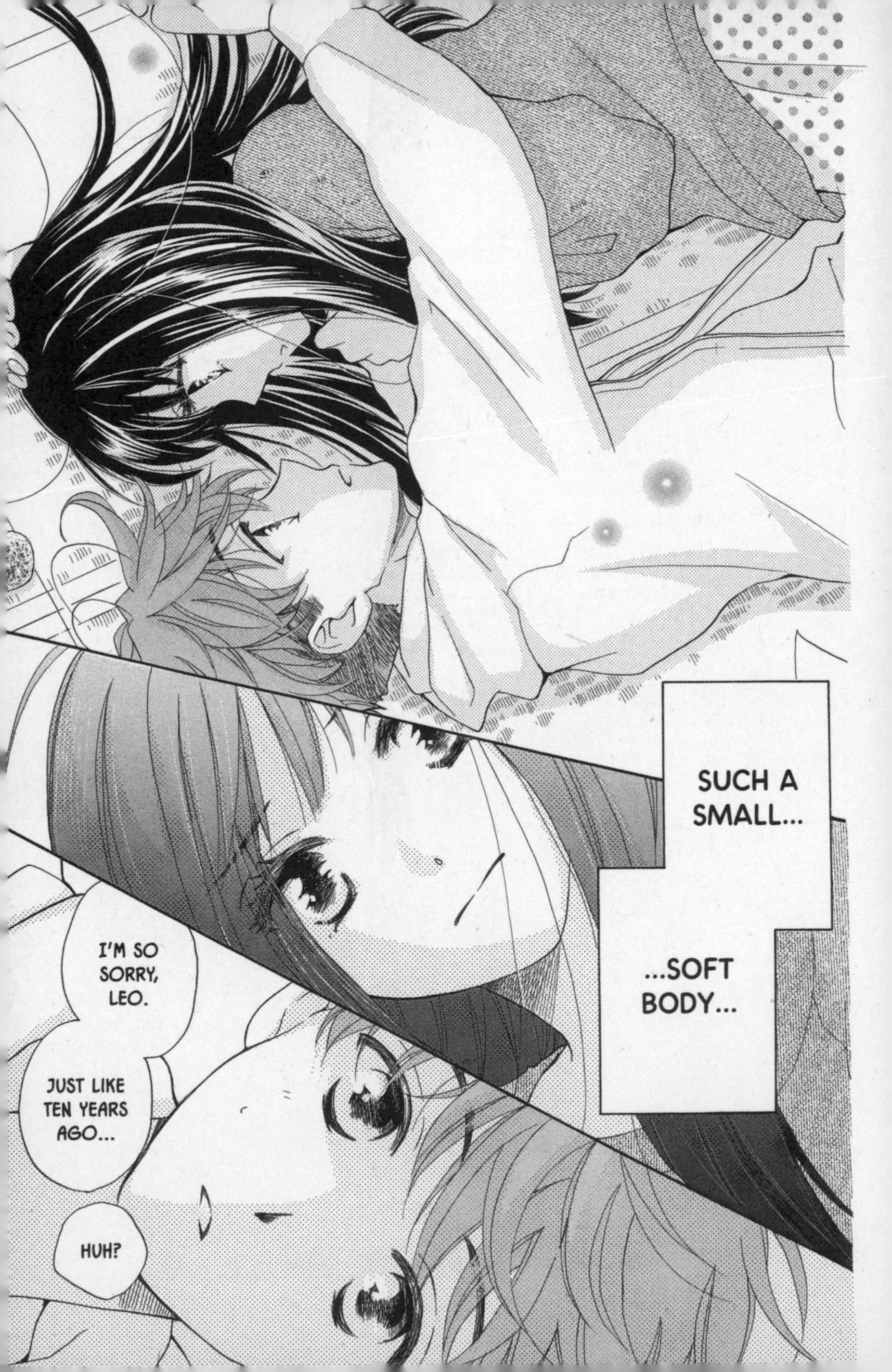
SUCH A SMALL...
...SOFT BODY...
I'M SO SORRY, LEO.
JUST LIKE TEN YEARS AGO...
HUH?

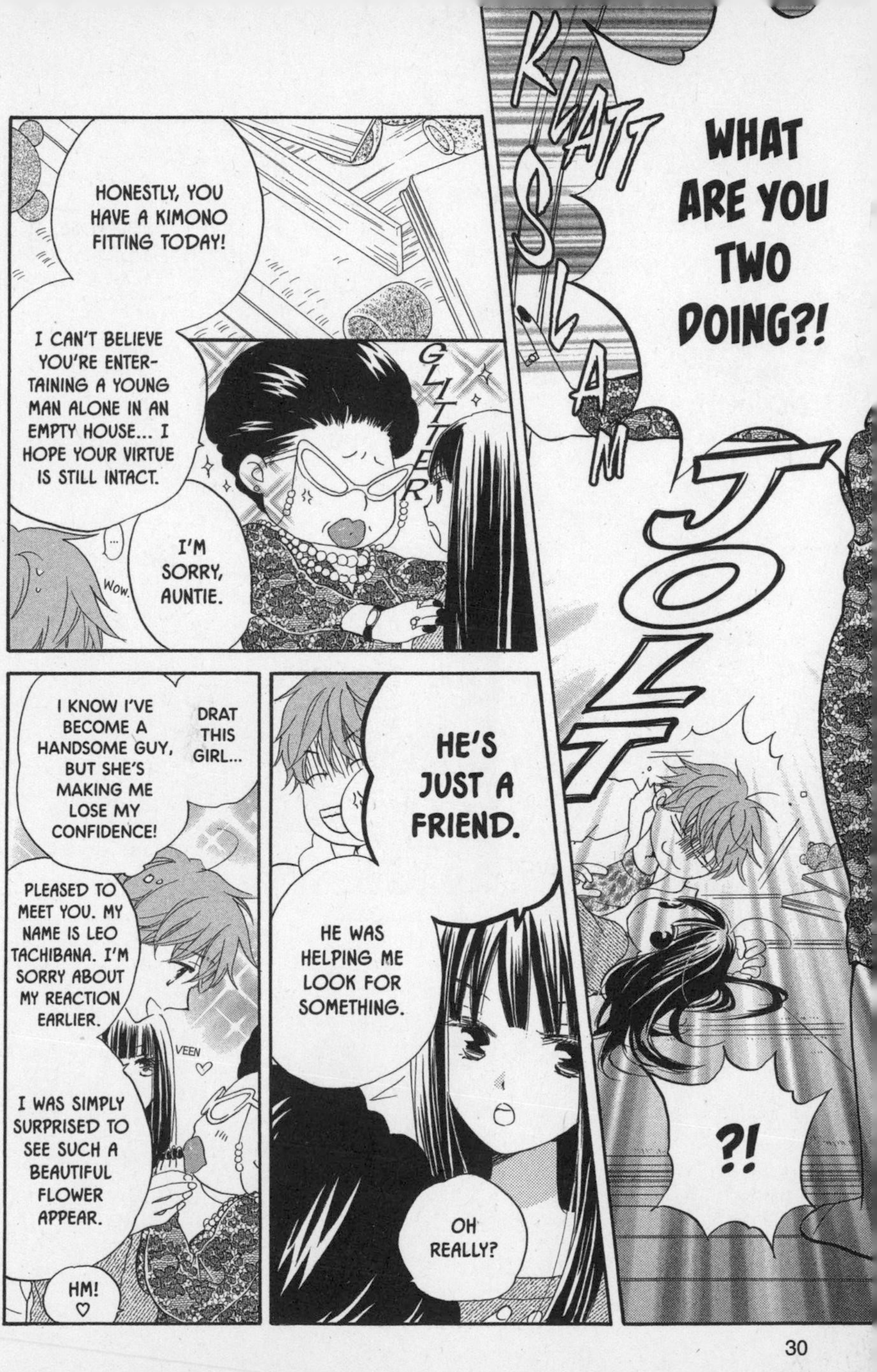
KLATT
SLAM
WHAT ARE YOU TWO DOING?!
JOLT
?!
HONESTLY, YOU HAVE A KIMONO FITTING TODAY!
I CAN'T BELIEVE YOU'RE ENTER-TAINING A YOUNG MAN ALONE IN AN EMPTY HOUSE... I HOPE YOUR VIRTUE IS STILL INTACT.
GLITTER
...
WOW.
I'M SORRY, AUNTIE.
HE'S JUST A FRIEND.
HE WAS HELPING ME LOOK FOR SOMETHING.
OH REALLY?
I KNOW I'VE BECOME A HANDSOME GUY, BUT SHE'S MAKING ME LOSE MY CONFIDENCE!
DRAT THIS GIRL...
PLEASED TO MEET YOU. MY NAME IS LEO TACHIBANA. I'M SORRY ABOUT MY REACTION EARLIER.
VEEN ♡
I WAS SIMPLY SURPRISED TO SEE SUCH A BEAUTIFUL FLOWER APPEAR.
HM! ♡

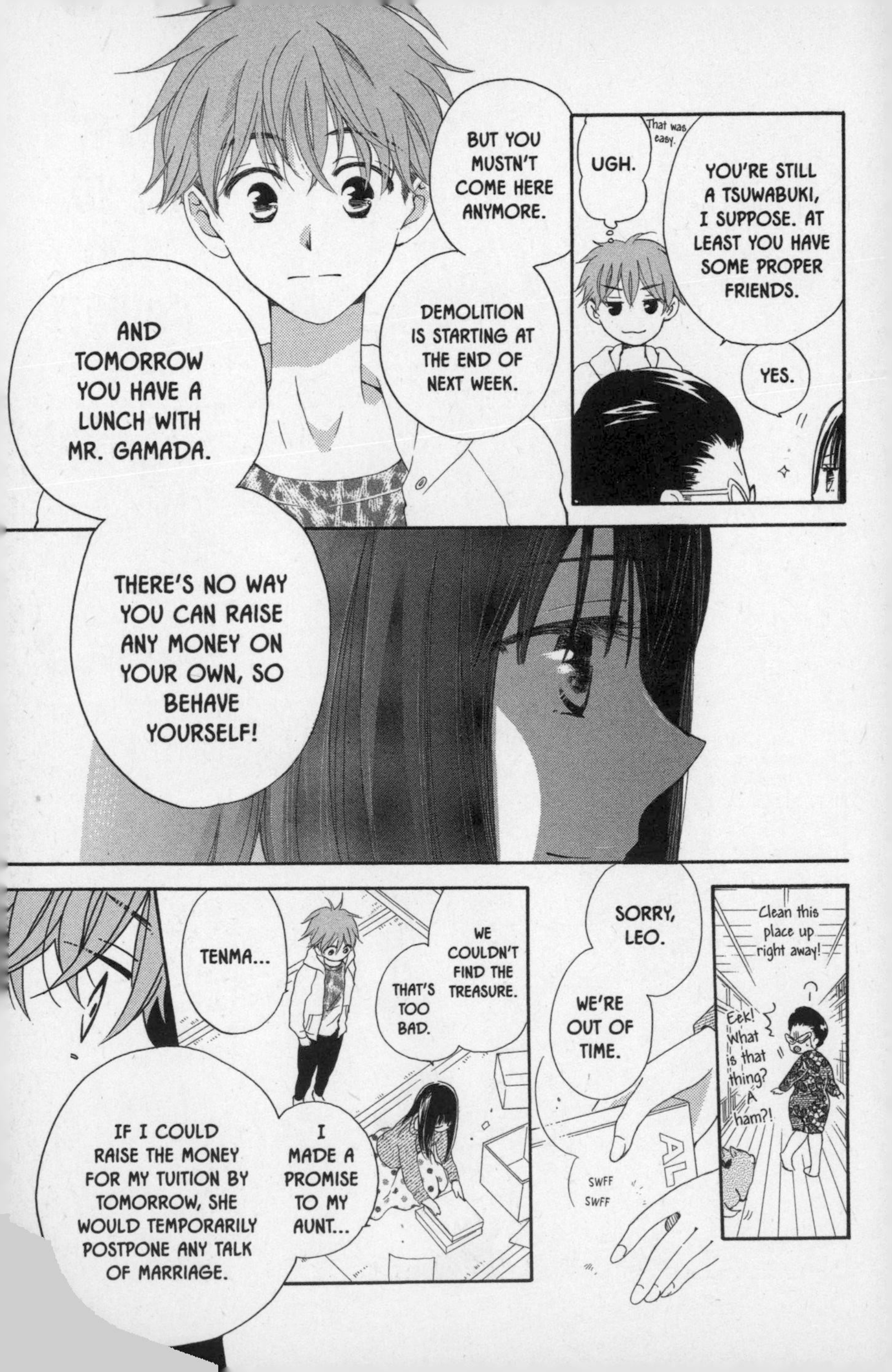
YOU'RE STILL A TSUWABUKI, I SUPPOSE. AT LEAST YOU HAVE SOME PROPER FRIENDS.
That was easy.
UGH.
YES.
BUT YOU MUSTN'T COME HERE ANYMORE.
DEMOLITION IS STARTING AT THE END OF NEXT WEEK.
AND TOMORROW YOU HAVE A LUNCH WITH MR. GAMADA.
THERE'S NO WAY YOU CAN RAISE ANY MONEY ON YOUR OWN, SO BEHAVE YOURSELF!
Clean this place up right away!
Eek! What is that thing? A ham?!
SORRY, LEO.
WE'RE OUT OF TIME.
SWFF
SWFF
WE COULDN'T FIND THE TREASURE.
THAT'S TOO BAD.
TENMA...
I MADE A PROMISE TO MY AUNT...
IF I COULD RAISE THE MONEY FOR MY TUITION BY TOMORROW, SHE WOULD TEMPORARILY POSTPONE ANY TALK OF MARRIAGE.

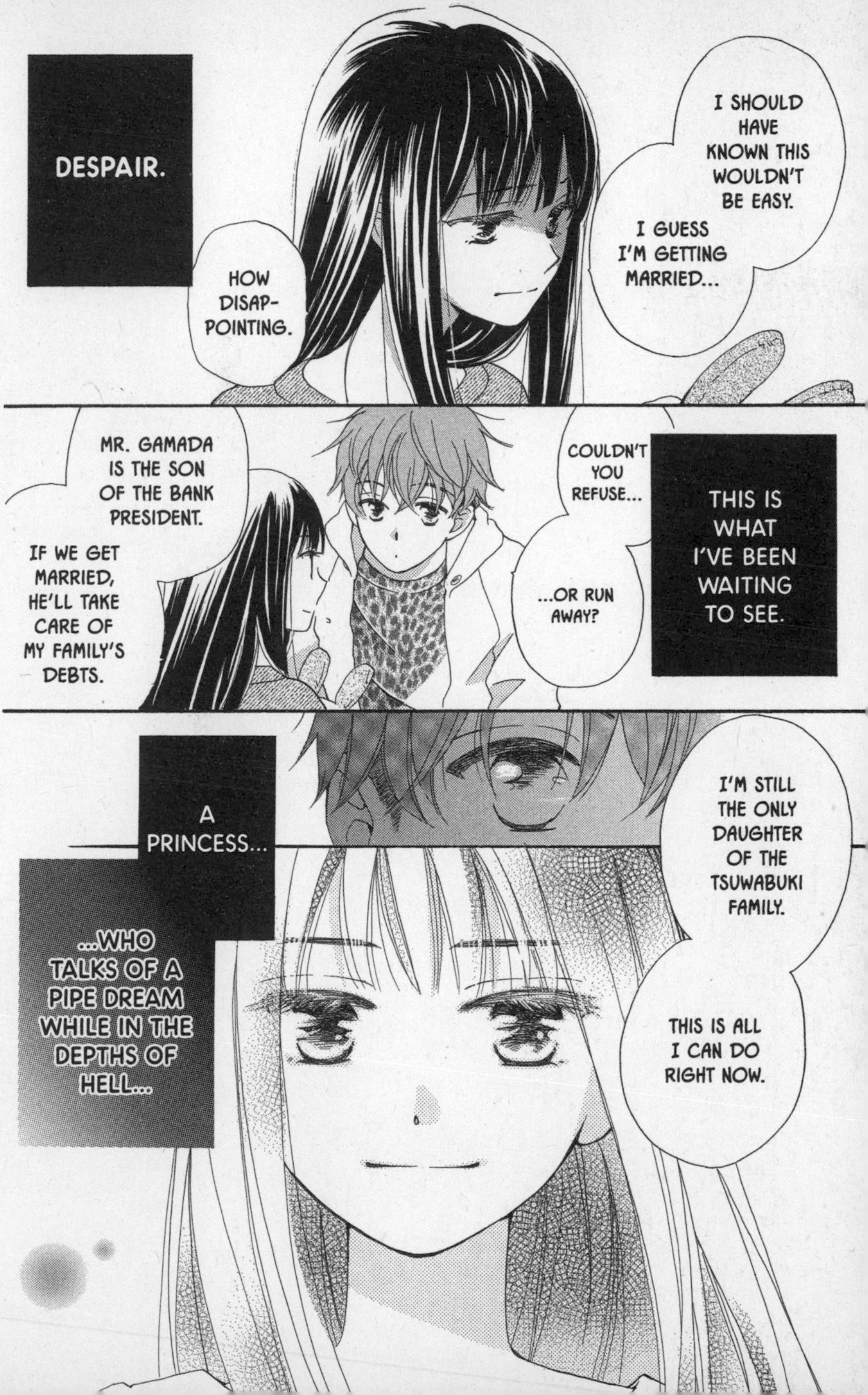
I SHOULD HAVE KNOWN THIS WOULDN'T BE EASY.
I GUESS I'M GETTING MARRIED...
HOW DISAP-POINTING.
DESPAIR.
THIS IS WHAT I'VE BEEN WAITING TO SEE.
COULDN'T YOU REFUSE...
...OR RUN AWAY?
MR. GAMADA IS THE SON OF THE BANK PRESIDENT.
IF WE GET MARRIED, HE'LL TAKE CARE OF MY FAMILY'S DEBTS.
I'M STILL THE ONLY DAUGHTER OF THE TSUWABUKI FAMILY.
A PRINCESS...
...WHO TALKS OF A PIPE DREAM WHILE IN THE DEPTHS OF HELL...
THIS IS ALL I CAN DO RIGHT NOW.

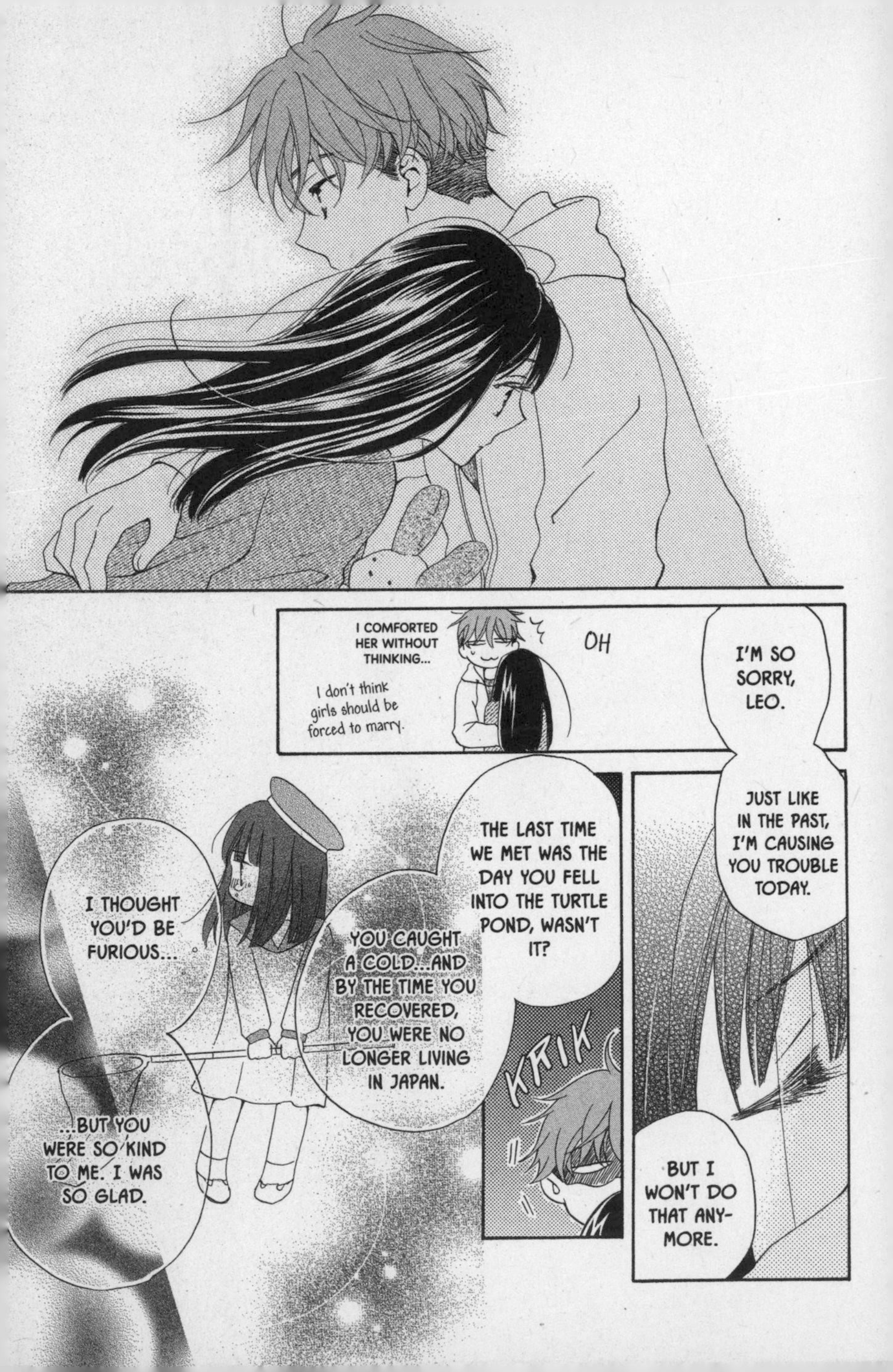
I'M SO SORRY, LEO.
OH
I COMFORTED HER WITHOUT THINKING...
I don't think girls should be forced to marry.
JUST LIKE IN THE PAST, I'M CAUSING YOU TROUBLE TODAY.
BUT I WON'T DO THAT ANY-MORE.
KRIK
THE LAST TIME WE MET WAS THE DAY YOU FELL INTO THE TURTLE POND, WASN'T IT?
YOU CAUGHT A COLD...AND BY THE TIME YOU RECOVERED, YOU WERE NO LONGER LIVING IN JAPAN.
I THOUGHT YOU'D BE FURIOUS...
...BUT YOU WERE SO KIND TO ME. I WAS SO GLAD.

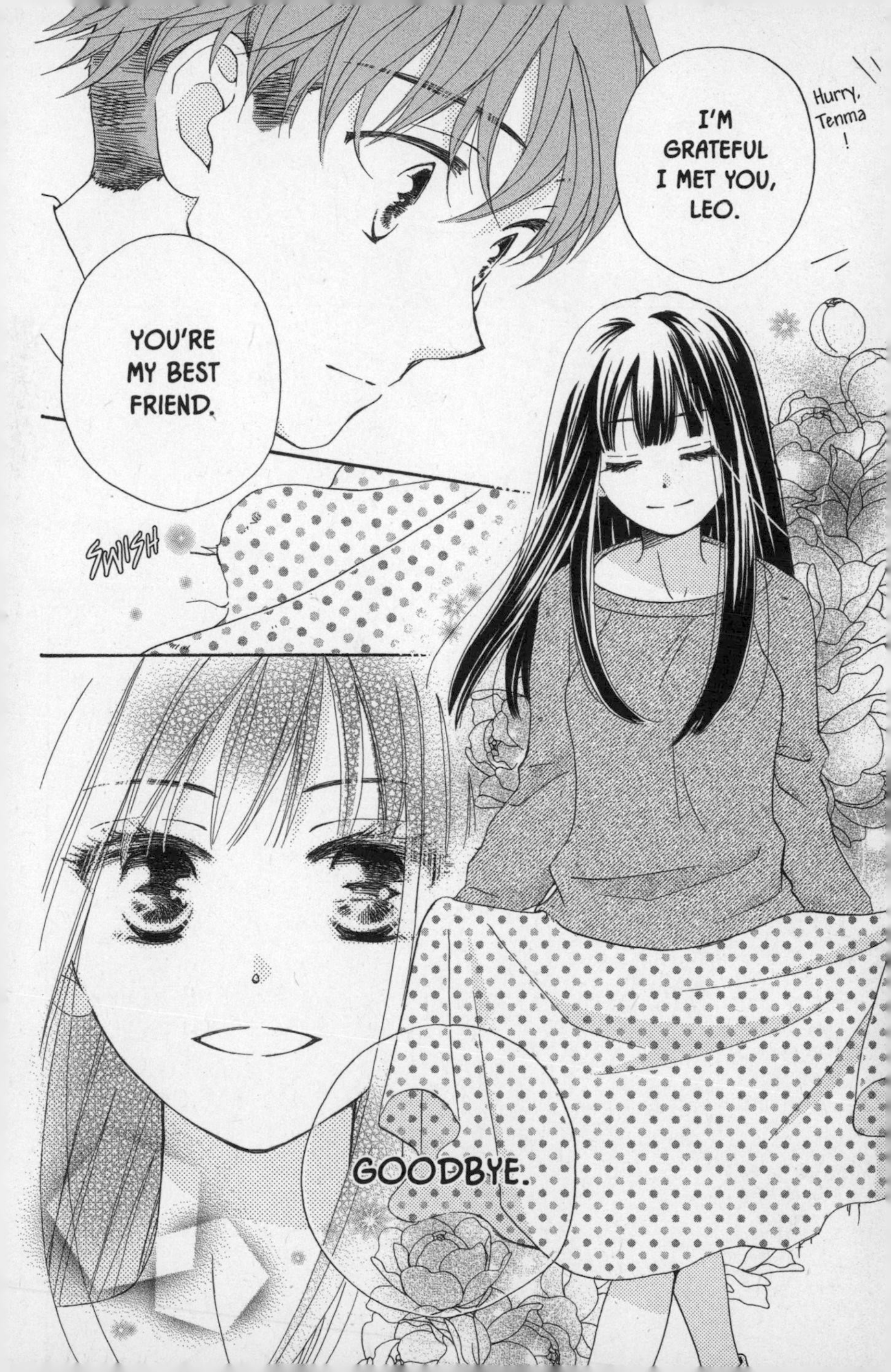
Hurry, Tenma!
I'M GRATEFUL I MET YOU, LEO.
YOU'RE MY BEST FRIEND.
SWISH
GOODBYE.

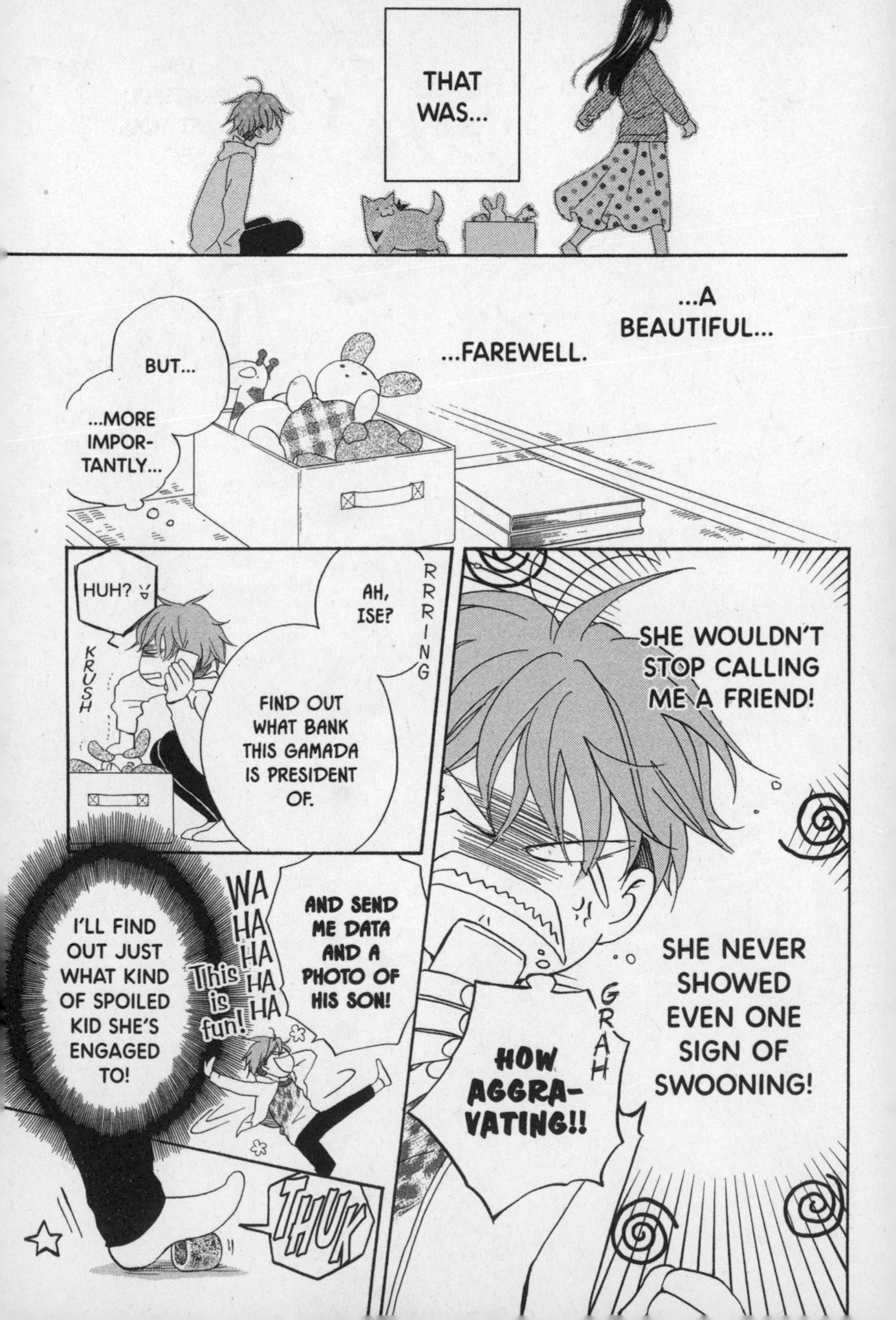
THAT WAS...
...A BEAUTIFUL...
...FAREWELL.
BUT...
...MORE IMPORTANTLY...
SHE WOULDN'T STOP CALLING ME A FRIEND!
SHE NEVER SHOWED EVEN ONE SIGN OF SWOONING!
GRAH
HOW AGGRAVATING!!
RRRING
AH, ISE?
HUH?
KRUSH
FIND OUT WHAT BANK THIS GAMADA IS PRESIDENT OF.
AND SEND ME DATA AND A PHOTO OF HIS SON!
WA HA HA HA HA HA
This is fun!
I'LL FIND OUT JUST WHAT KIND OF SPOILED KID SHE'S ENGAGED TO!
THUK

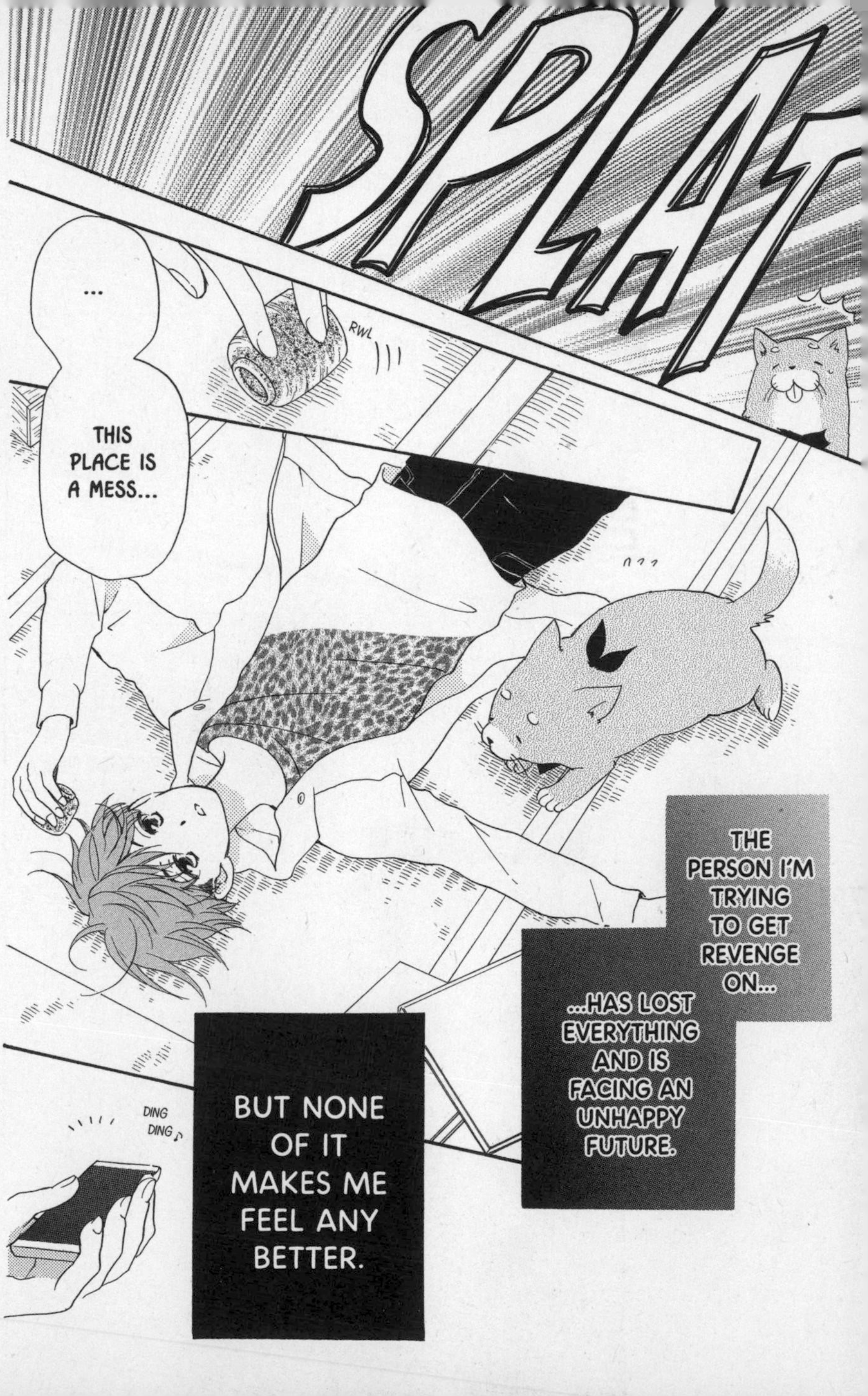
SPLAT
RWL
...
THIS PLACE IS A MESS...
THE PERSON I'M TRYING TO GET REVENGE ON...
...HAS LOST EVERYTHING AND IS FACING AN UNHAPPY FUTURE.
BUT NONE OF IT MAKES ME FEEL ANY BETTER.
DING DING

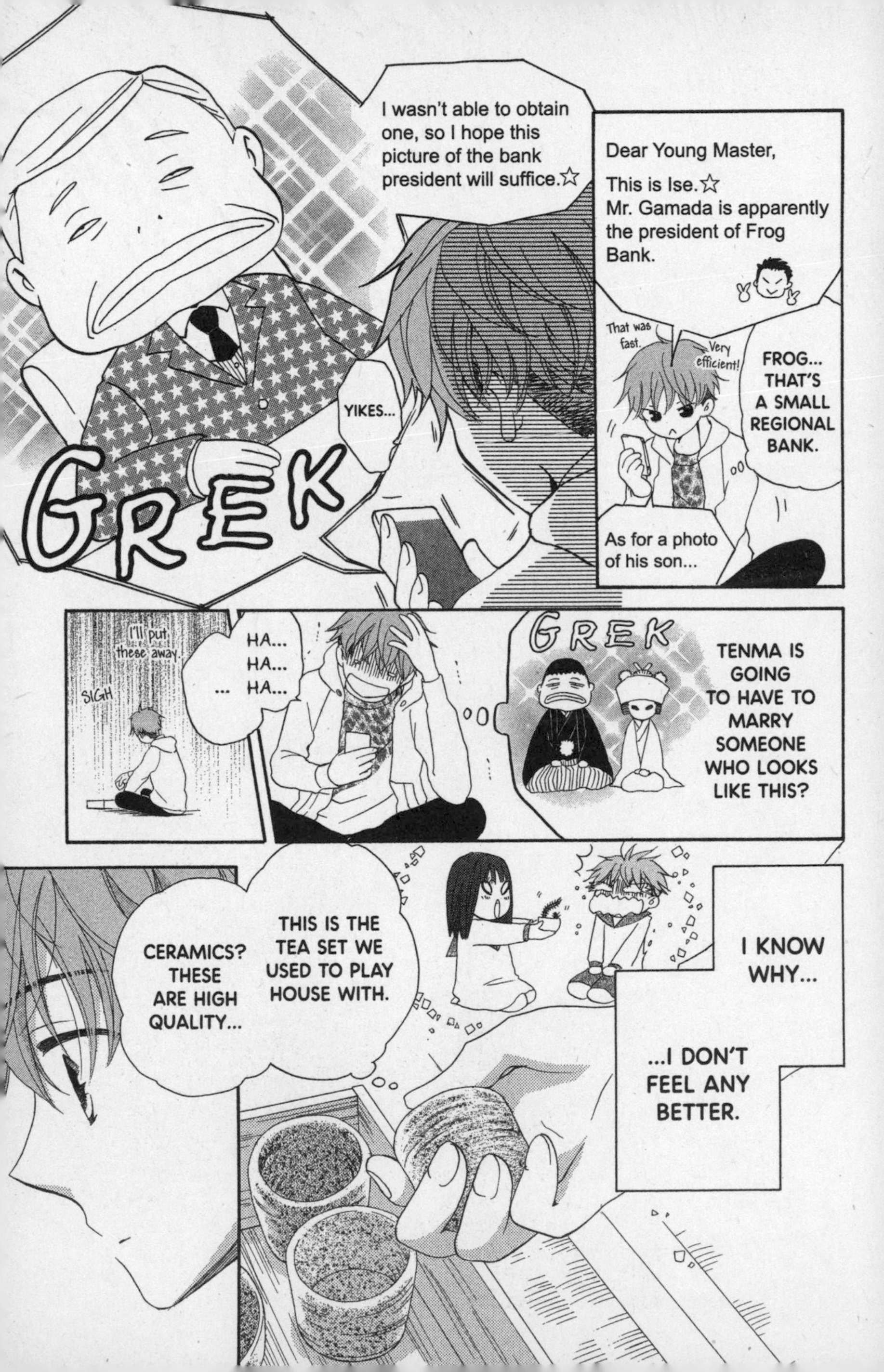
Dear Young Master,
This is Ise.☆
Mr. Gamada is apparently the president of Frog Bank.
That was fast.
Very efficient!
FROG... THAT'S A SMALL REGIONAL BANK.
As for a photo of his son...
I wasn't able to obtain one, so I hope this picture of the bank president will suffice.☆
YIKES...
GREK
TENMA IS GOING TO HAVE TO MARRY SOMEONE WHO LOOKS LIKE THIS?
GREK
HA... HA... ... HA...
I'll put these away.
SIGH
I KNOW WHY...
THIS IS THE TEA SET WE USED TO PLAY HOUSE WITH.
CERAMICS? THESE ARE HIGH QUALITY...
...I DON'T FEEL ANY BETTER.

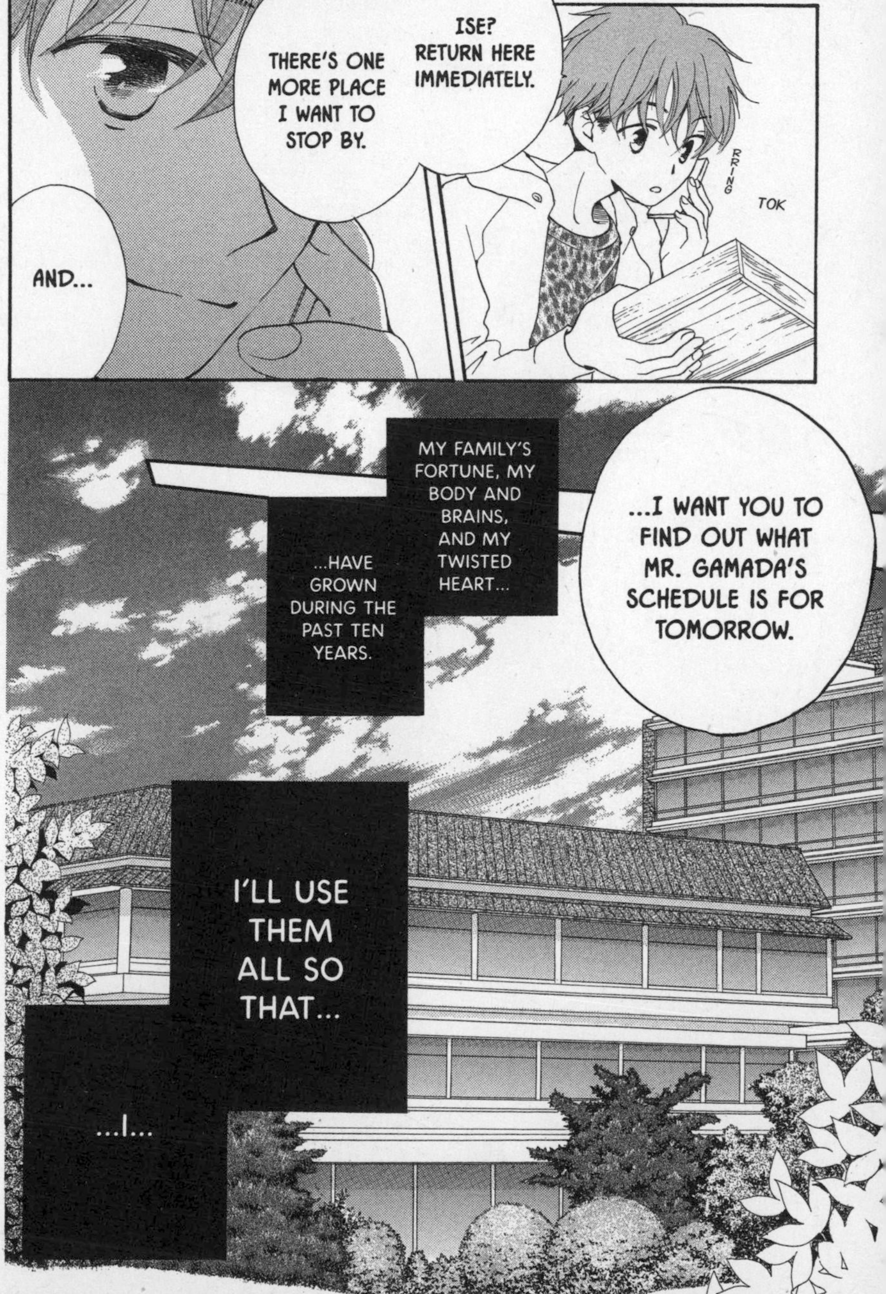
RRING
TOK
ISE? RETURN HERE IMMEDIATELY.
THERE'S ONE MORE PLACE I WANT TO STOP BY.
AND...
...I WANT YOU TO FIND OUT WHAT MR. GAMADA'S SCHEDULE IS FOR TOMORROW.
MY FAMILY'S FORTUNE, MY BODY AND BRAINS, AND MY TWISTED HEART...
...HAVE GROWN DURING THE PAST TEN YEARS.
I'LL USE THEM ALL SO THAT...
...I...

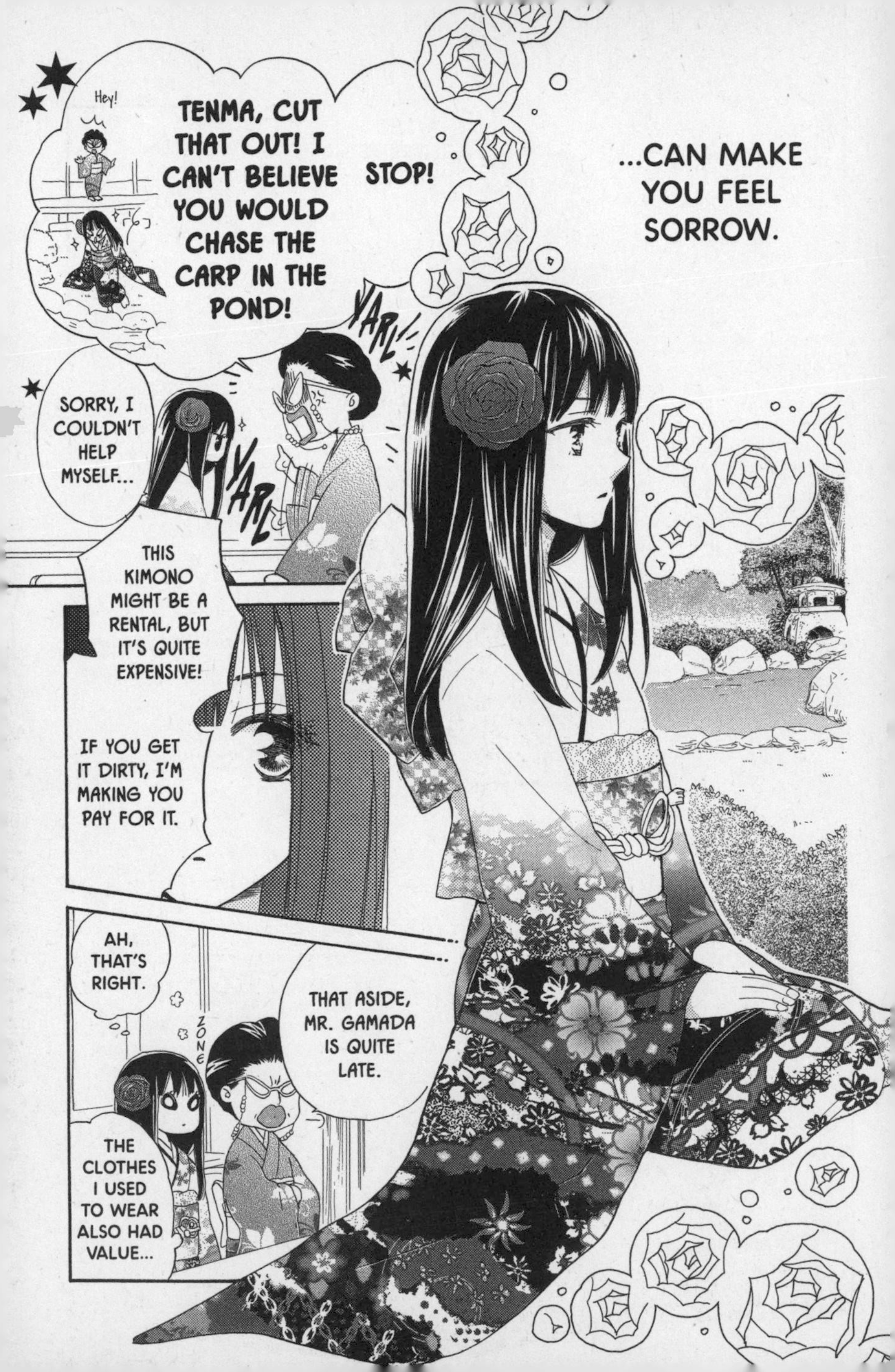
...CAN MAKE YOU FEEL SORROW.
STOP!
TENMA, CUT THAT OUT! I CAN'T BELIEVE YOU WOULD CHASE THE CARP IN THE POND!
Hey!
YARL
YARL
SORRY, I COULDN'T HELP MYSELF...
THIS KIMONO MIGHT BE A RENTAL, BUT IT'S QUITE EXPENSIVE!
IF YOU GET IT DIRTY, I'M MAKING YOU PAY FOR IT.
THAT ASIDE, MR. GAMADA IS QUITE LATE.
AH, THAT'S RIGHT.
ZONE
THE CLOTHES I USED TO WEAR ALSO HAD VALUE...

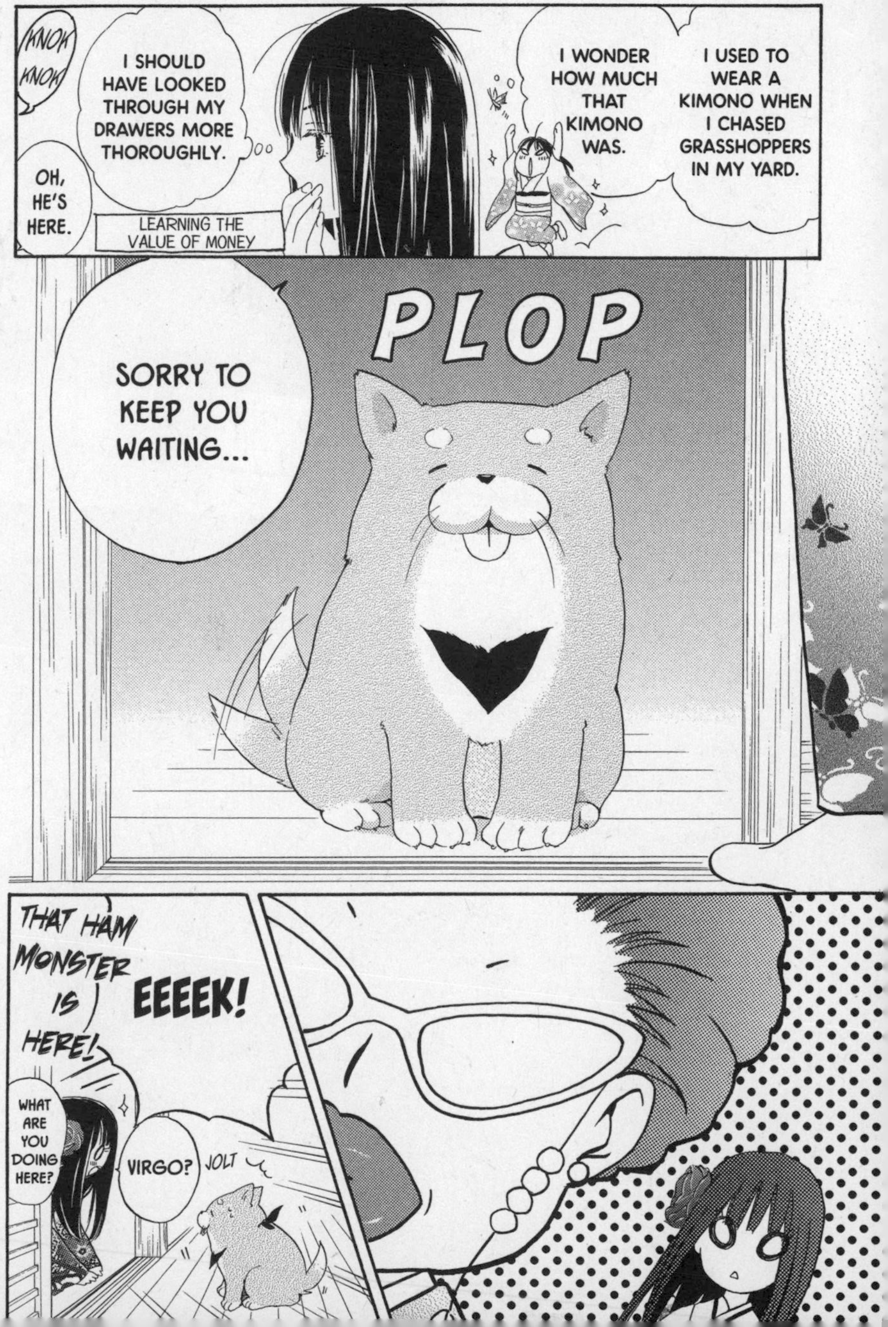
I USED TO WEAR A KIMONO WHEN I CHASED GRASSHOPPERS IN MY YARD.
I WONDER HOW MUCH THAT KIMONO WAS.
I SHOULD HAVE LOOKED THROUGH MY DRAWERS MORE THOROUGHLY.
LEARNING THE VALUE OF MONEY
KNOK KNOK
OH, HE'S HERE.
PLOP
SORRY TO KEEP YOU WAITING...
EEEEK!
THAT HAM MONSTER IS HERE!
JOLT
VIRGO?
WHAT ARE YOU DOING HERE?

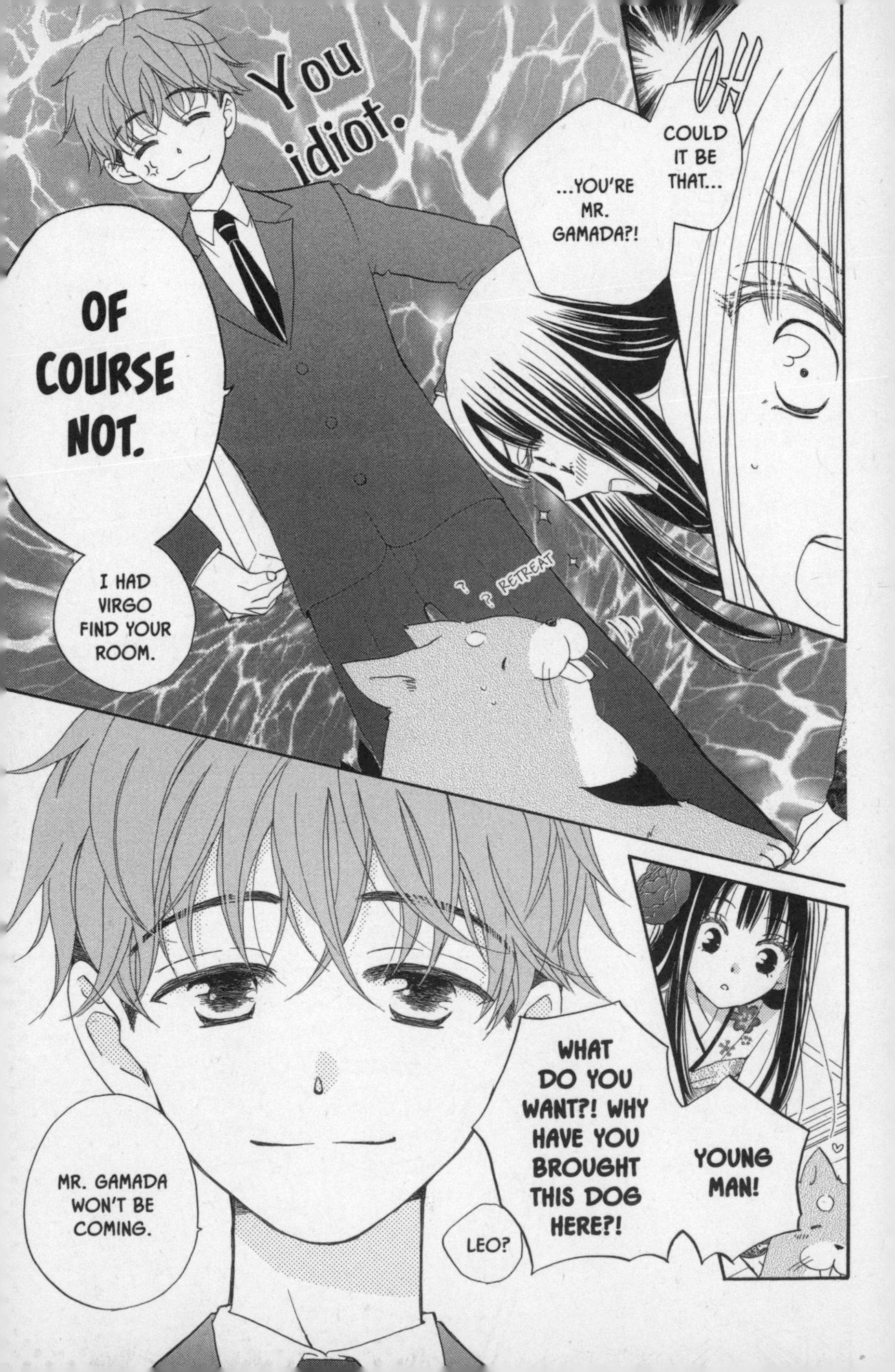
OH
COULD IT BE THAT...
...YOU'RE MR. GAMADA?!
You idiot.
OF COURSE NOT.
I HAD VIRGO FIND YOUR ROOM.
? ? RETREAT
WHAT DO YOU WANT?! WHY HAVE YOU BROUGHT THIS DOG HERE?!
YOUNG MAN!
LEO?
MR. GAMADA WON'T BE COMING.

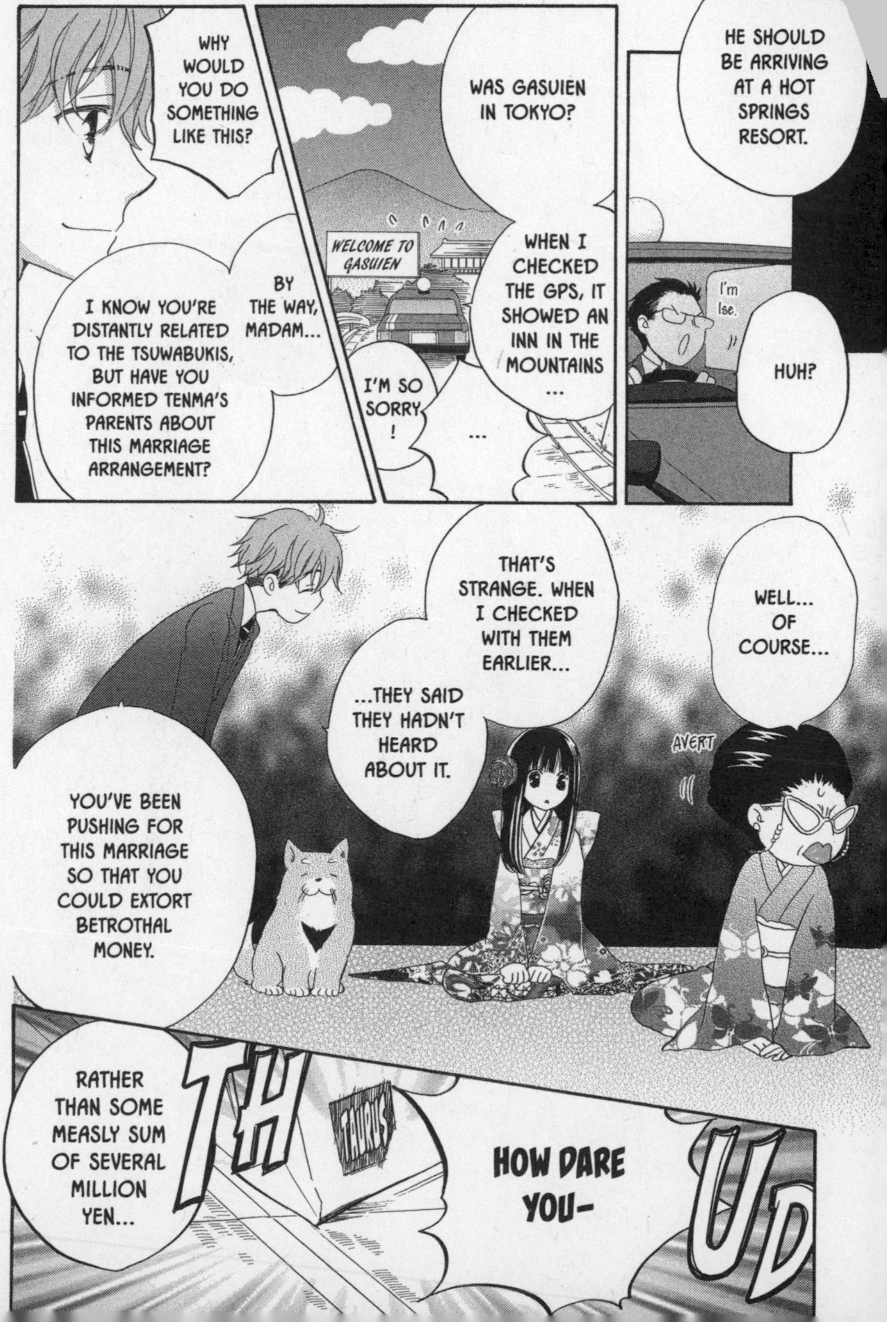
HE SHOULD BE ARRIVING AT A HOT SPRINGS RESORT.
I'm Ise.
HUH?
WAS GASUIEN IN TOKYO?
WHEN I CHECKED THE GPS, IT SHOWED AN INN IN THE MOUNTAINS ...
WELCOME TO GASUIEN
I'M SO SORRY !
...
WHY WOULD YOU DO SOMETHING LIKE THIS?
BY THE WAY, MADAM...
I KNOW YOU'RE DISTANTLY RELATED TO THE TSUWABUKIS, BUT HAVE YOU INFORMED TENMA'S PARENTS ABOUT THIS MARRIAGE ARRANGEMENT?
WELL... OF COURSE...
AVERT
THAT'S STRANGE. WHEN I CHECKED WITH THEM EARLIER...
...THEY SAID THEY HADN'T HEARD ABOUT IT.
YOU'VE BEEN PUSHING FOR THIS MARRIAGE SO THAT YOU COULD EXTORT BETROTHAL MONEY.
HOW DARE YOU-
UD
TAURUS
TH
RATHER THAN SOME MEASLY SUM OF SEVERAL MILLION YEN...

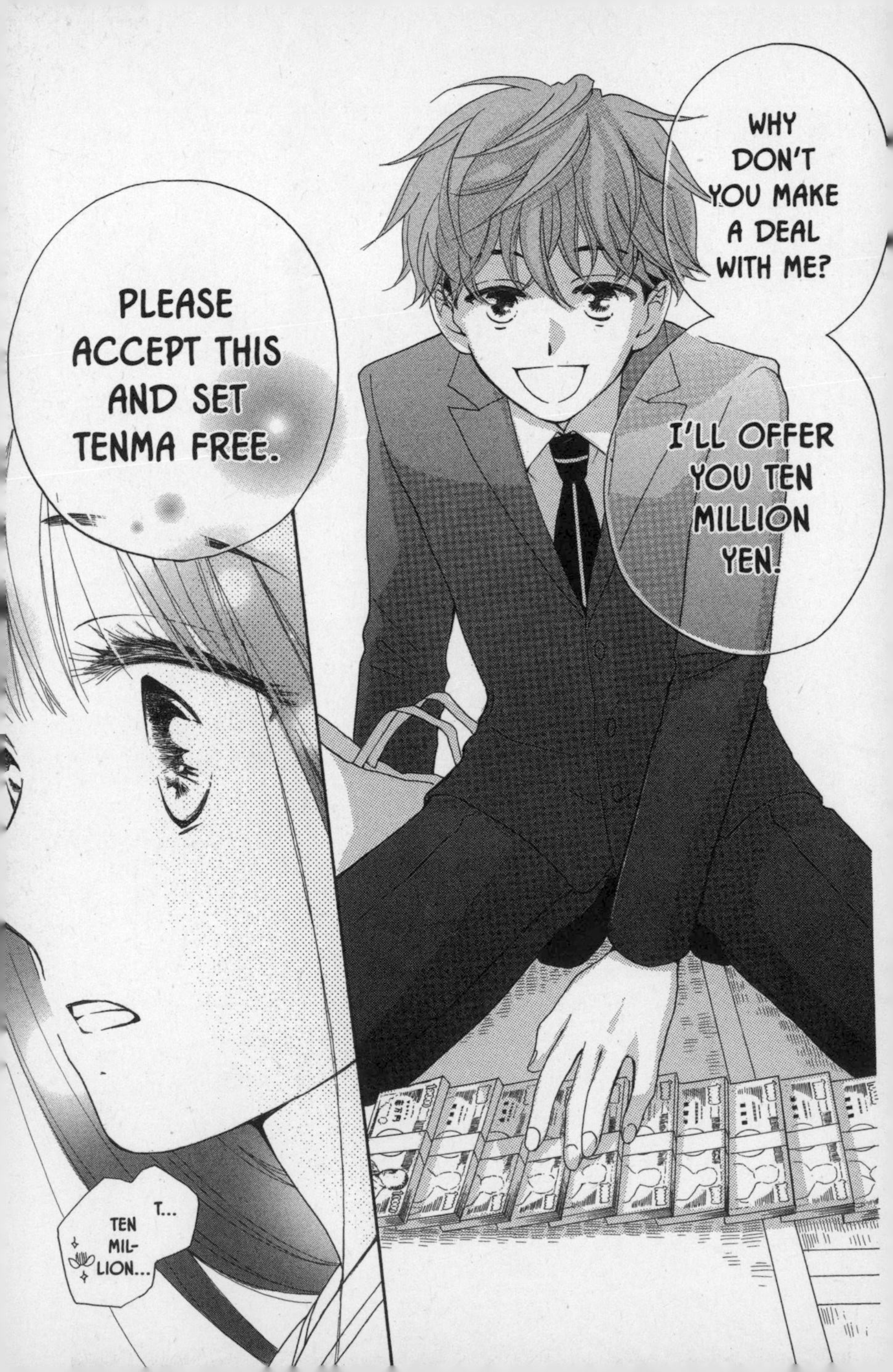
WHY DON'T YOU MAKE A DEAL WITH ME?
I'LL OFFER YOU TEN MILLION YEN.
PLEASE ACCEPT THIS AND SET TENMA FREE.
T... TEN MIL-LION...

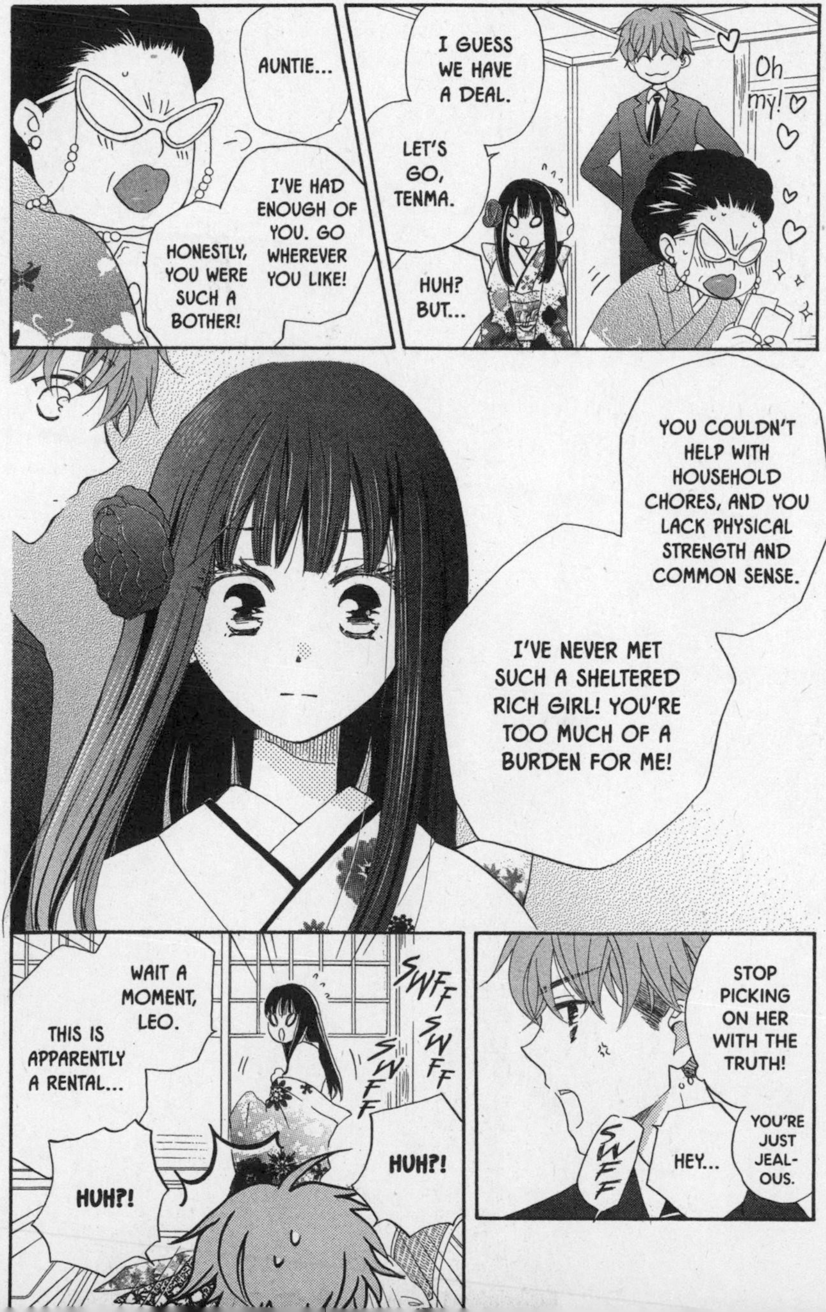
Oh my!
I GUESS WE HAVE A DEAL.
LET'S GO, TENMA.
HUH? BUT...
AUNTIE...
I'VE HAD ENOUGH OF YOU. GO WHEREVER YOU LIKE!
HONESTLY, YOU WERE SUCH A BOTHER!
YOU COULDN'T HELP WITH HOUSEHOLD CHORES, AND YOU LACK PHYSICAL STRENGTH AND COMMON SENSE.
I'VE NEVER MET SUCH A SHELTERED RICH GIRL! YOU'RE TOO MUCH OF A BURDEN FOR ME!
STOP PICKING ON HER WITH THE TRUTH!
YOU'RE JUST JEAL-OUS.
SWFF
HEY...
SWFF
SWFF
SWFF
WAIT A MOMENT, LEO.
THIS IS APPARENTLY A RENTAL...
HUH?!
HUH?!

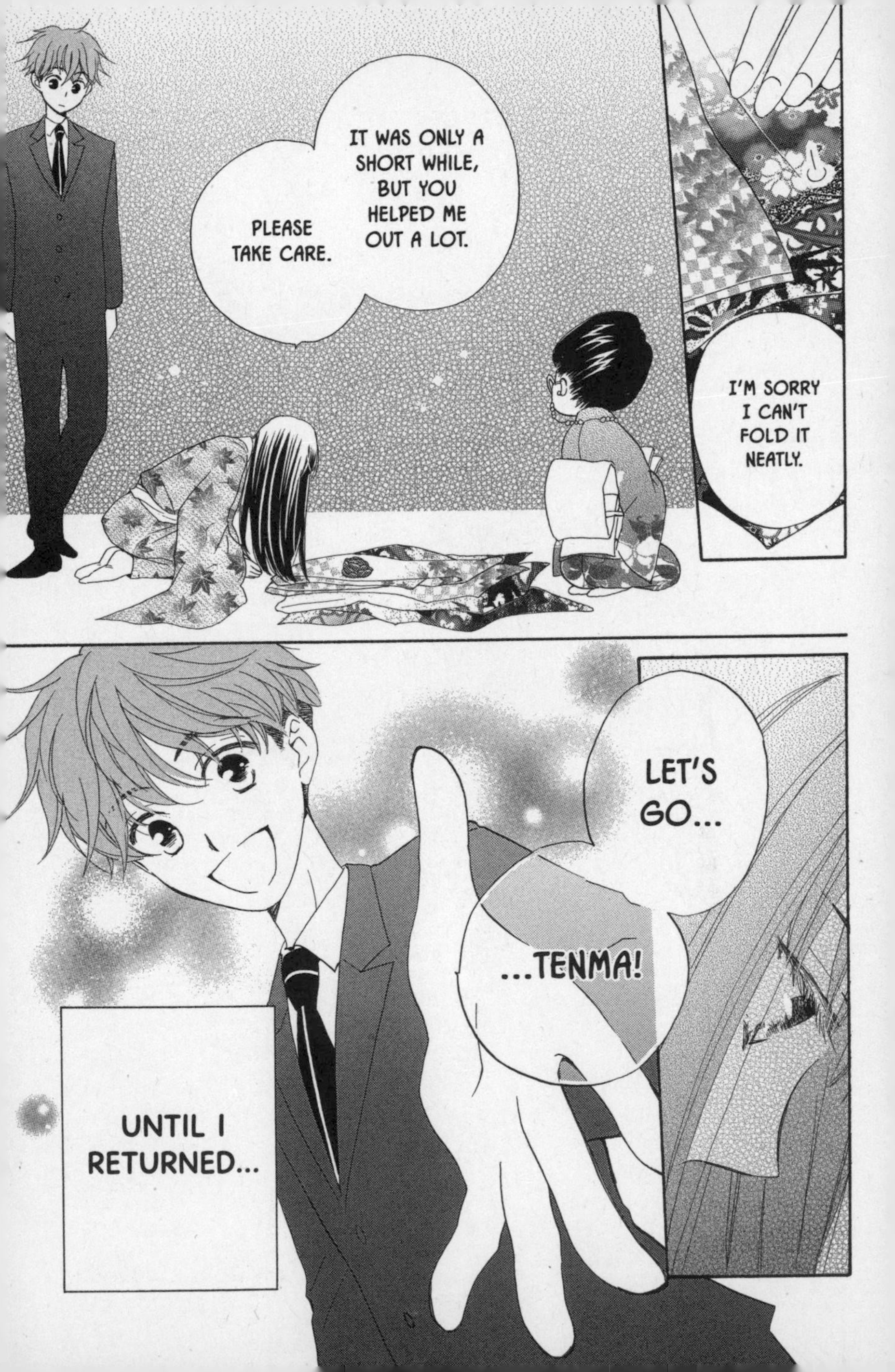
I'M SORRY I CAN'T FOLD IT NEATLY.
IT WAS ONLY A SHORT WHILE, BUT YOU HELPED ME OUT A LOT.
PLEASE TAKE CARE.
LET'S GO...
...TENMA!
UNTIL I RETURNED...

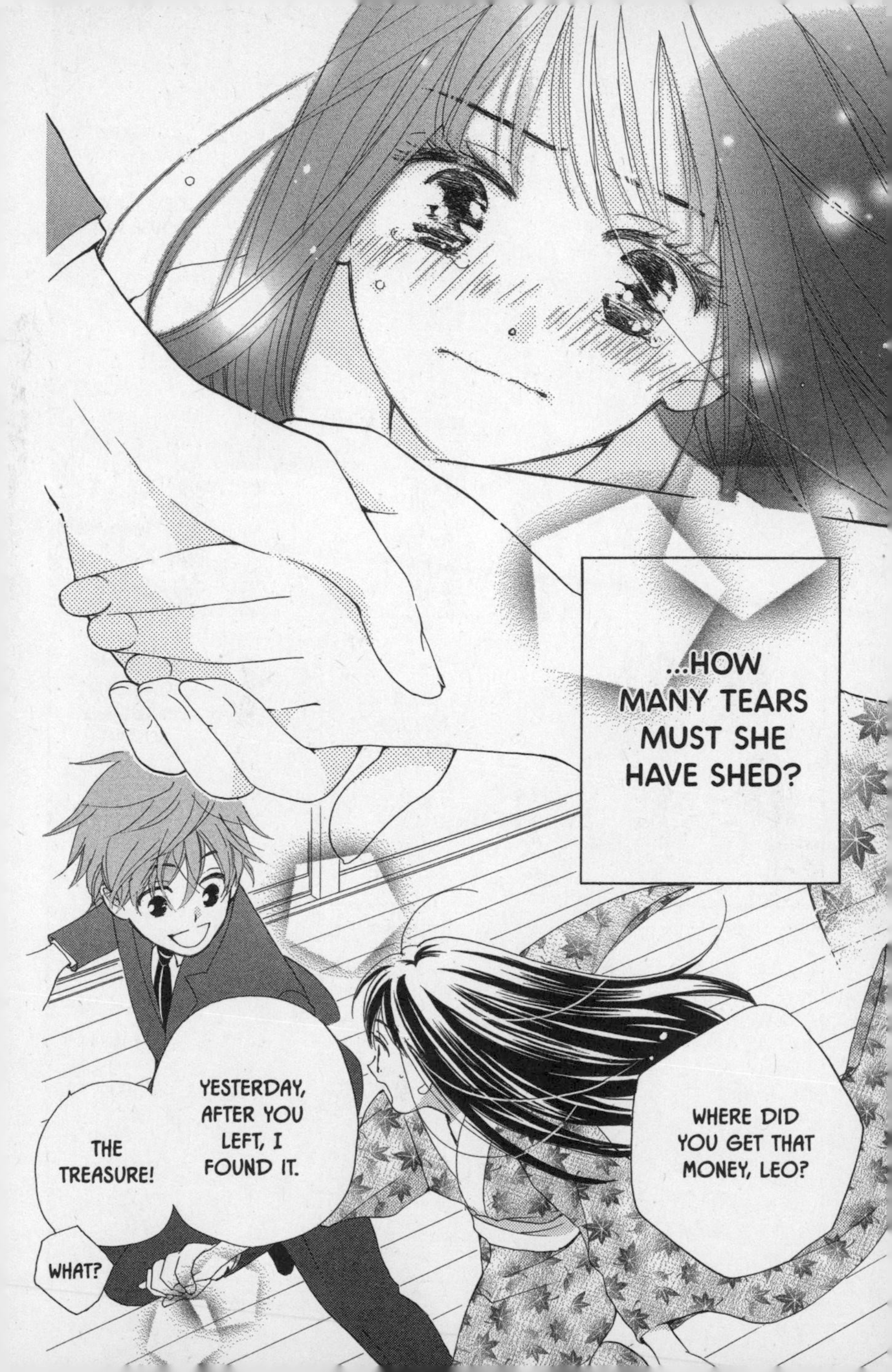
...HOW MANY TEARS MUST SHE HAVE SHED?
WHERE DID YOU GET THAT MONEY, LEO?
YESTERDAY, AFTER YOU LEFT, I FOUND IT.
THE TREASURE!
WHAT?

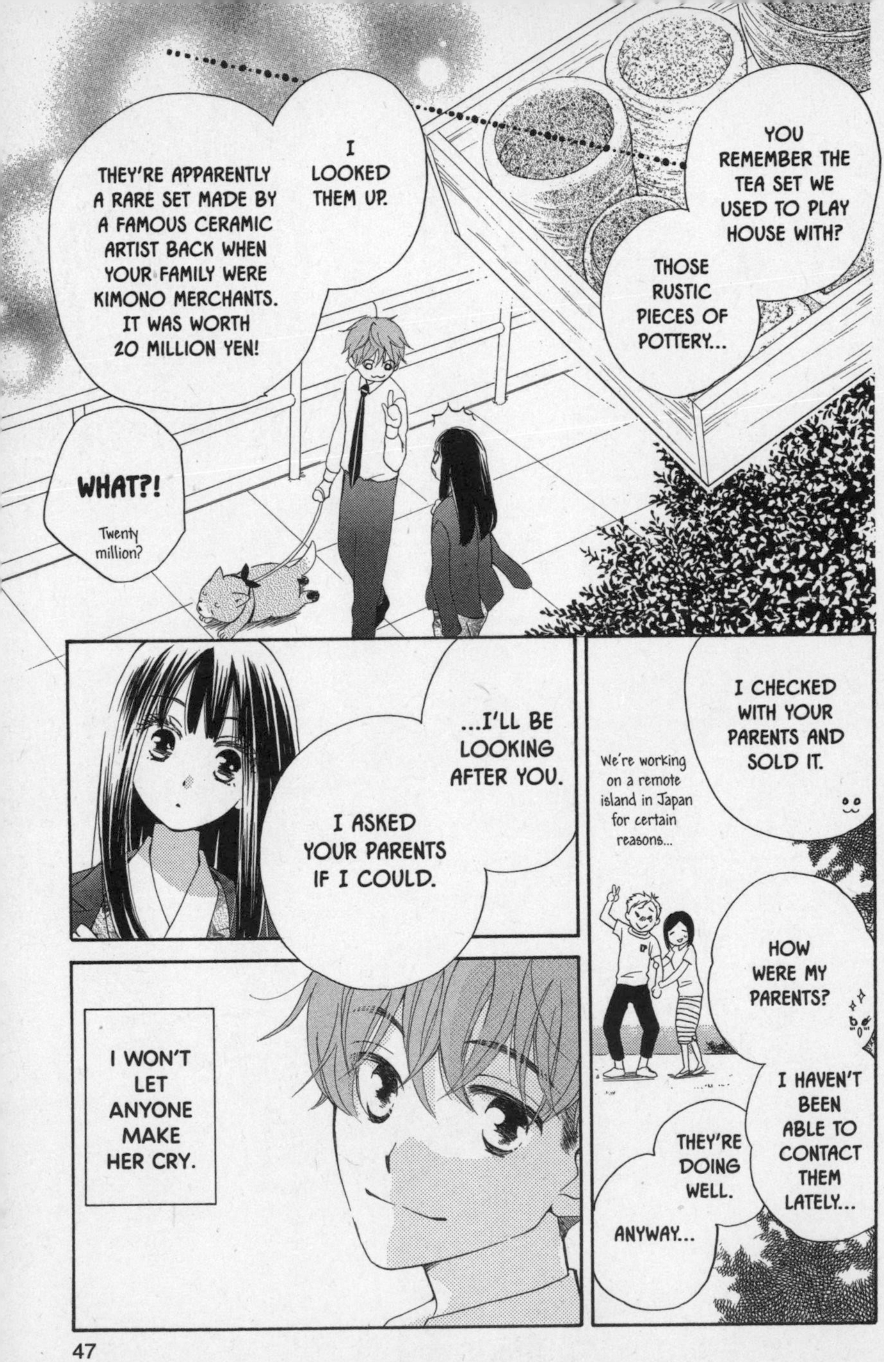
YOU REMEMBER THE TEA SET WE USED TO PLAY HOUSE WITH?
THOSE RUSTIC PIECES OF POTTERY...
I LOOKED THEM UP.
THEY'RE APPARENTLY A RARE SET MADE BY A FAMOUS CERAMIC ARTIST BACK WHEN YOUR FAMILY WERE KIMONO MERCHANTS. IT WAS WORTH 20 MILLION YEN!
WHAT?!
Twenty million?
I CHECKED WITH YOUR PARENTS AND SOLD IT.
We're working on a remote island in Japan for certain reasons...
HOW WERE MY PARENTS?
I HAVEN'T BEEN ABLE TO CONTACT THEM LATELY...
THEY'RE DOING WELL.
ANYWAY...
...I'LL BE LOOKING AFTER YOU.
I ASKED YOUR PARENTS IF I COULD.
I WON'T LET ANYONE MAKE HER CRY.

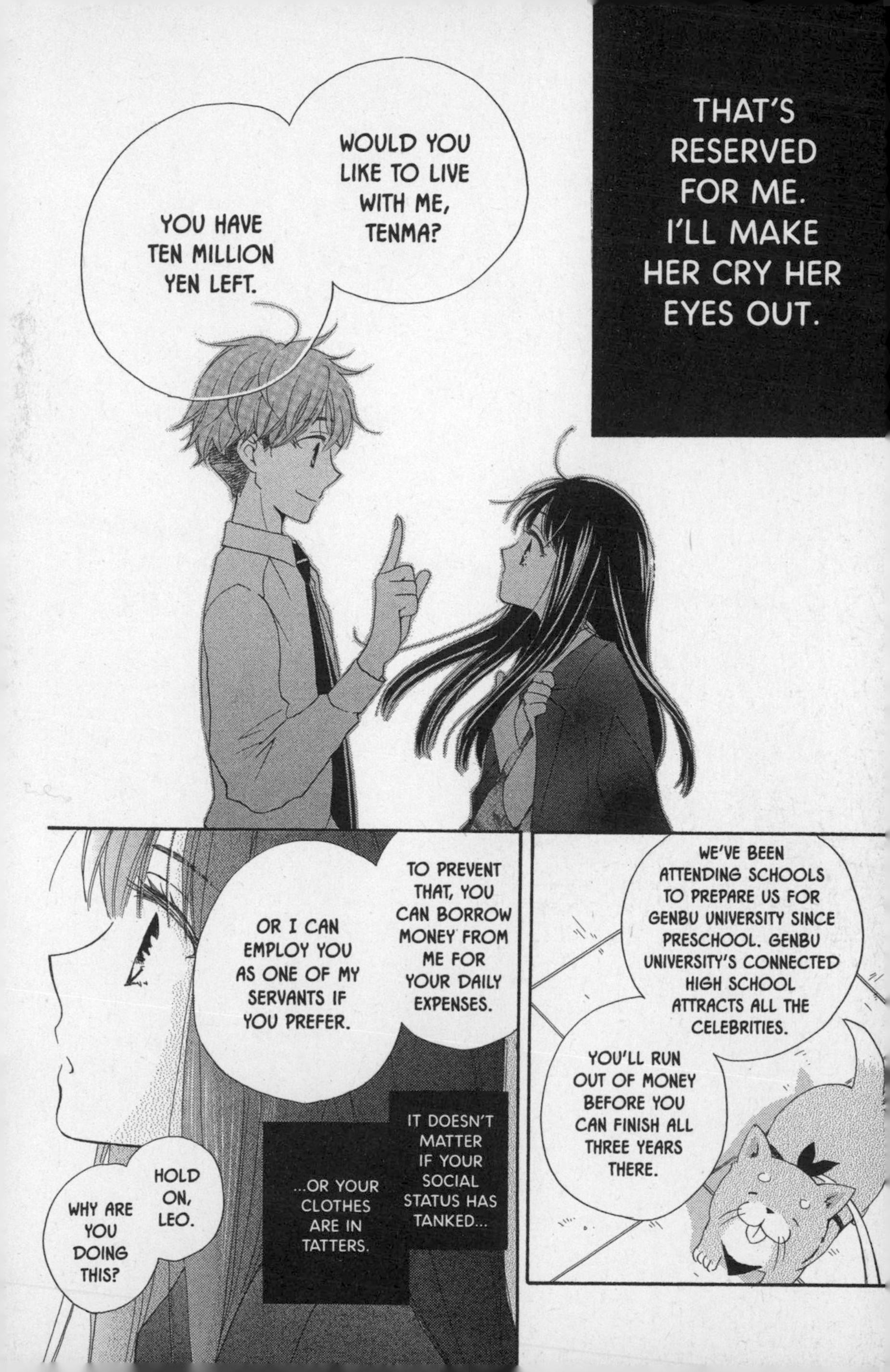
THAT'S RESERVED FOR ME. I'LL MAKE HER CRY HER EYES OUT.
WOULD YOU LIKE TO LIVE WITH ME, TENMA?
YOU HAVE TEN MILLION YEN LEFT.
WE'VE BEEN ATTENDING SCHOOLS TO PREPARE US FOR GENBU UNIVERSITY SINCE PRESCHOOL. GENBU UNIVERSITY'S CONNECTED HIGH SCHOOL ATTRACTS ALL THE CELEBRITIES.
YOU'LL RUN OUT OF MONEY BEFORE YOU CAN FINISH ALL THREE YEARS THERE.
TO PREVENT THAT, YOU CAN BORROW MONEY FROM ME FOR YOUR DAILY EXPENSES.
OR I CAN EMPLOY YOU AS ONE OF MY SERVANTS IF YOU PREFER.
IT DOESN'T MATTER IF YOUR SOCIAL STATUS HAS TANKED...
...OR YOUR CLOTHES ARE IN TATTERS.
HOLD ON, LEO.
WHY ARE YOU DOING THIS?

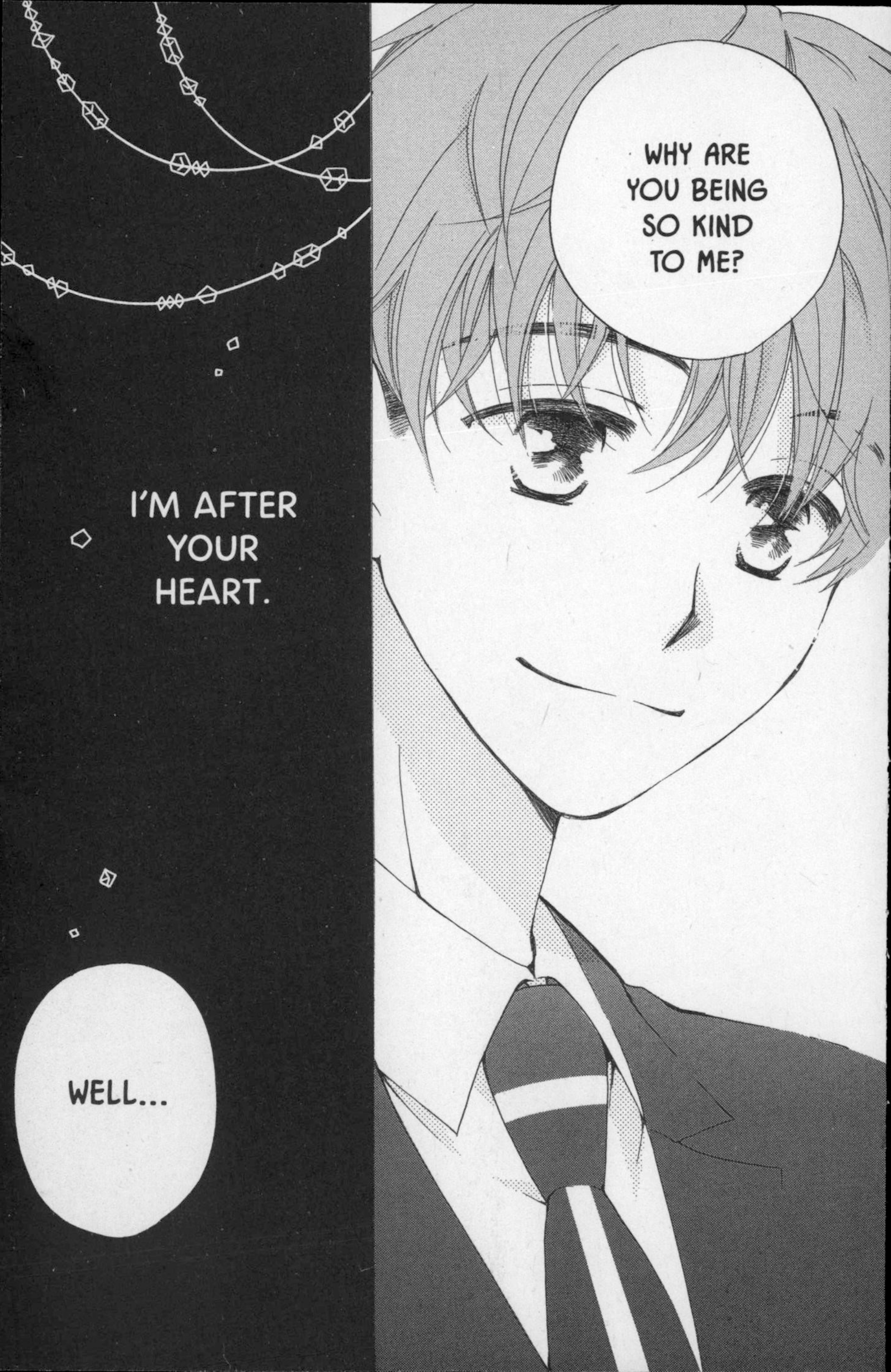
WHY ARE YOU BEING SO KIND TO ME?
I'M AFTER YOUR HEART.
WELL...

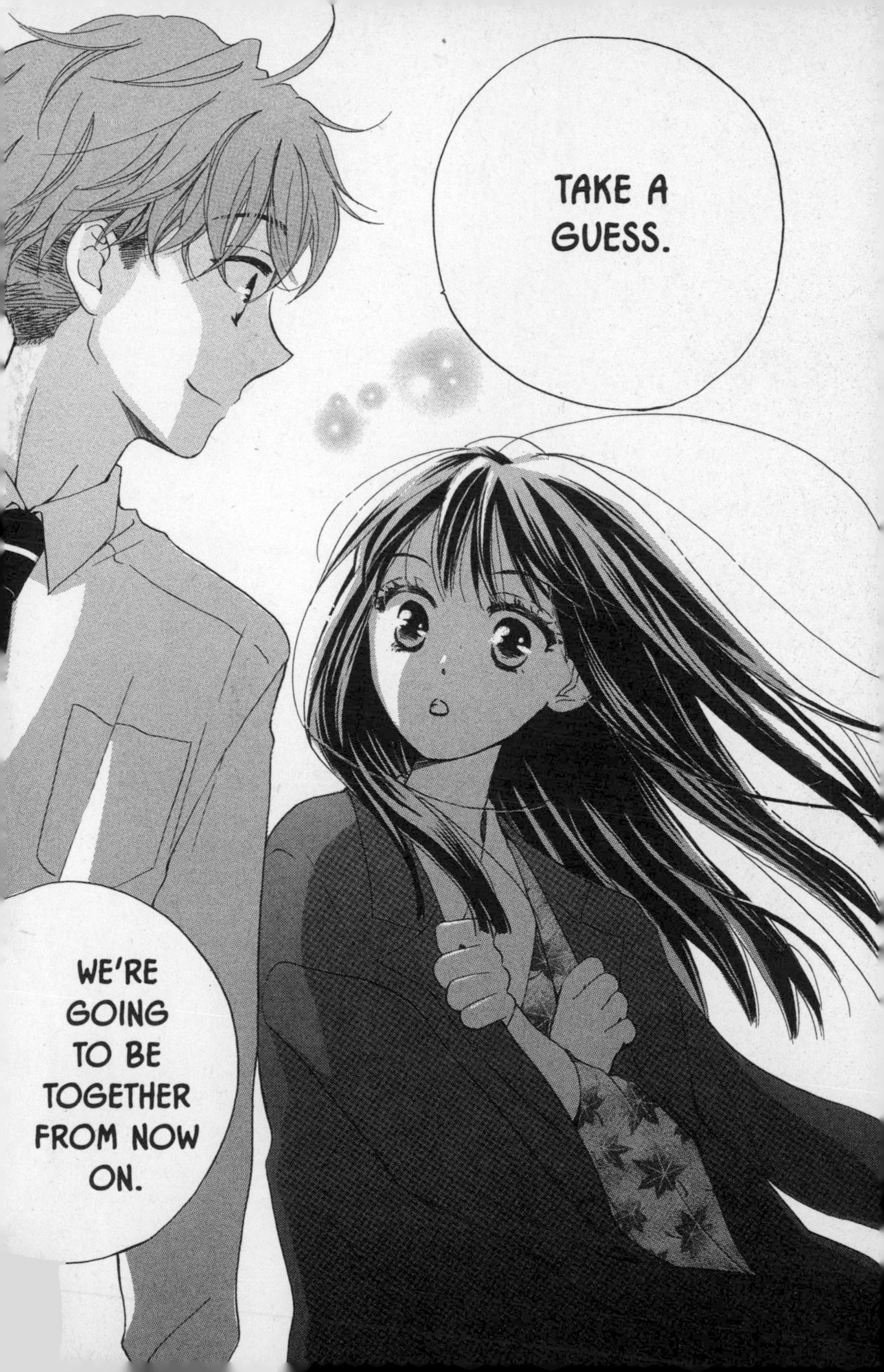
TAKE A GUESS.
WE'RE GOING TO BE TOGETHER FROM NOW ON.

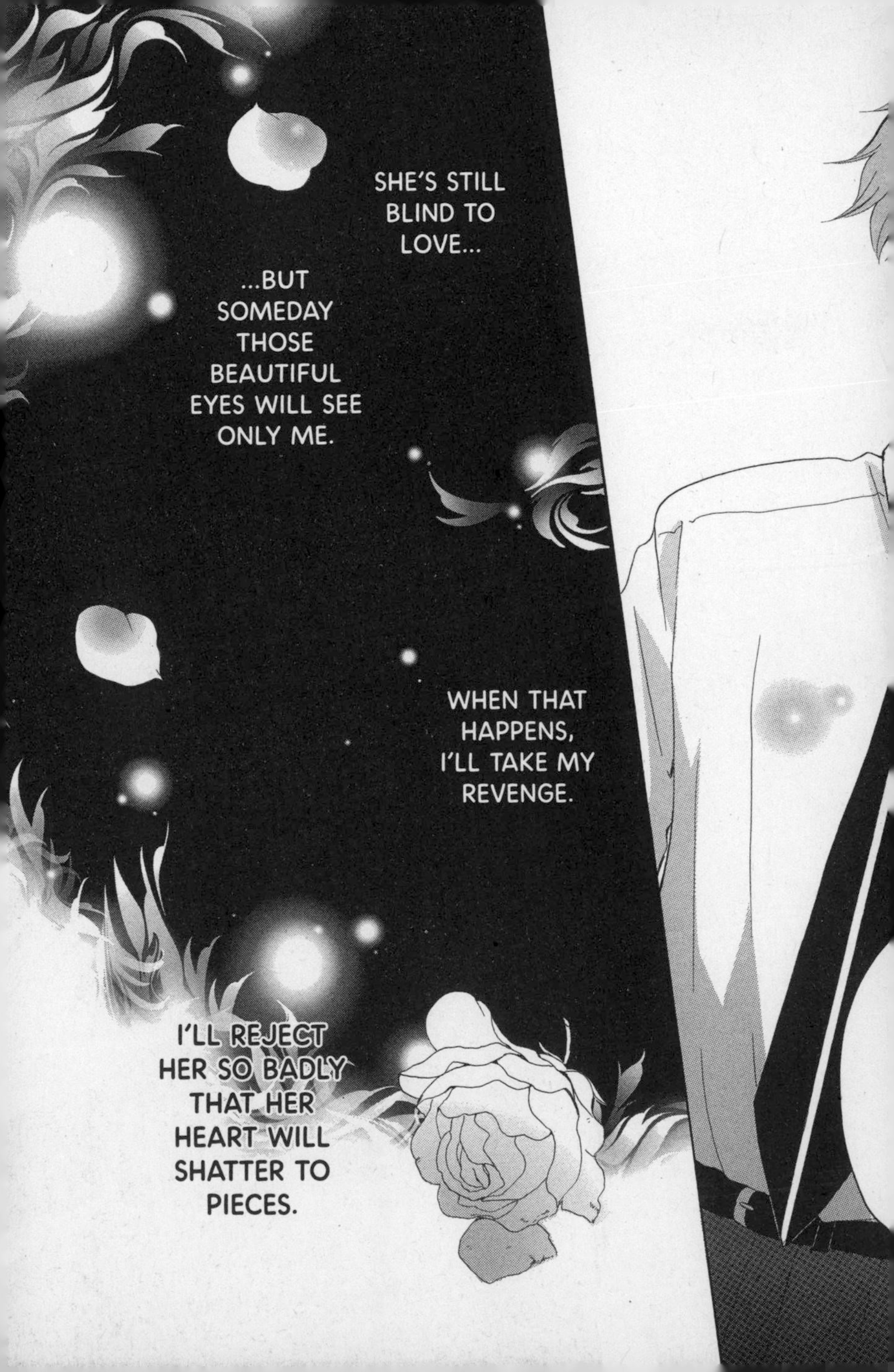
SHE'S STILL BLIND TO LOVE...
...BUT SOMEDAY THOSE BEAUTIFUL EYES WILL SEE ONLY ME.
WHEN THAT HAPPENS, I'LL TAKE MY REVENGE.
I'LL REJECT HER SO BADLY THAT HER HEART WILL SHATTER TO PIECES.

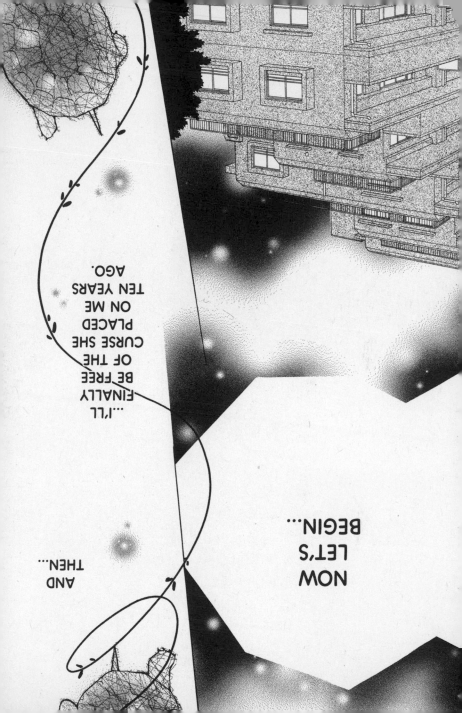

...I'LL
FINALLY
BE FREE
OF THE
CURSE SHE
PLACED
ON ME
TEN YEARS
AGO.

NOW
LET'S
BEGIN...

AND THEN...

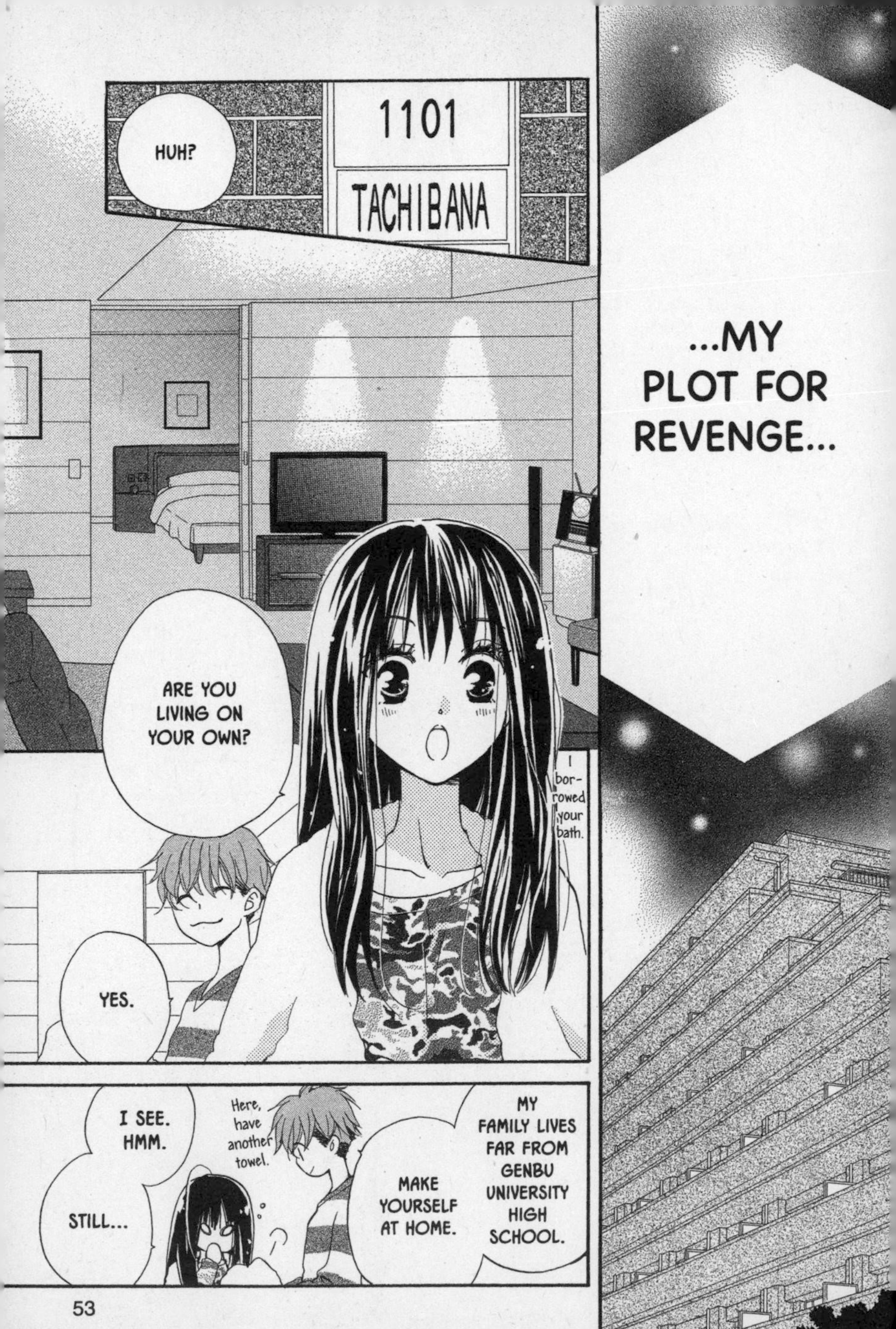
...MY PLOT FOR REVENGE...
1101
TACHIBANA
HUH?
ARE YOU LIVING ON YOUR OWN?
I borrowed your bath.
YES.
MY FAMILY LIVES FAR FROM GENBU UNIVERSITY HIGH SCHOOL.
MAKE YOURSELF AT HOME.
Here, have another towel.
I SEE. HMM.
STILL...

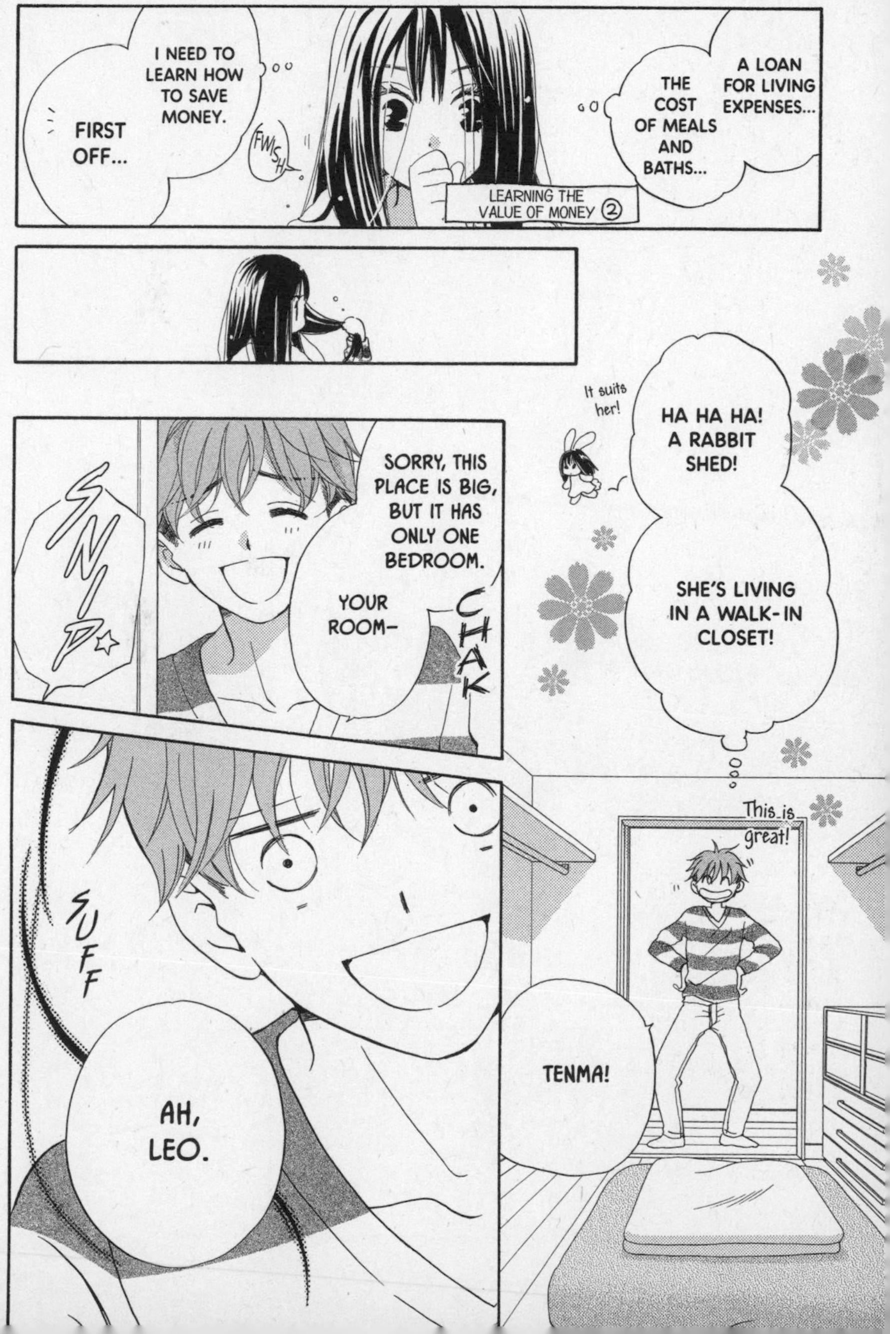
A LOAN FOR LIVING EXPENSES...
THE COST OF MEALS AND BATHS...
LEARNING THE VALUE OF MONEY ②
FWISH
I NEED TO LEARN HOW TO SAVE MONEY.
FIRST OFF...
HA HA HA! A RABBIT SHED!
SHE'S LIVING IN A WALK-IN CLOSET!
It suits her!
This is great!
TENMA!
SORRY, THIS PLACE IS BIG, BUT IT HAS ONLY ONE BEDROOM.
YOUR ROOM—
CHAK
SNIP
SUFF
AH, LEO.

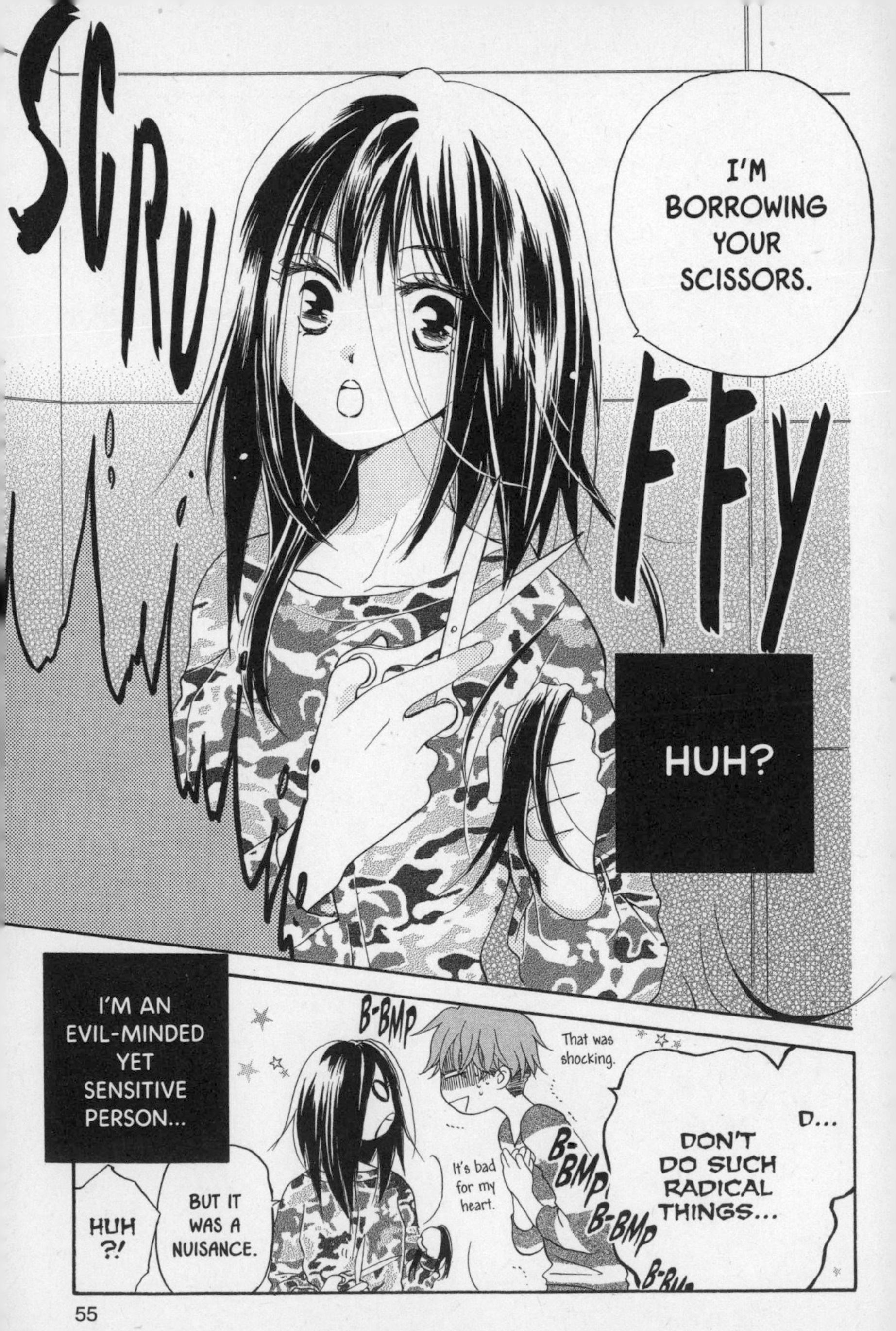
I'M BORROWING YOUR SCISSORS.
SCRUFFY
HUH?
D...
DON'T DO SUCH RADICAL THINGS...
B-BMP
B-BMP
B-BMP
That was shocking.
It's bad for my heart.
I'M AN EVIL-MINDED YET SENSITIVE PERSON...
BUT IT WAS A NUISANCE.
HUH ?!

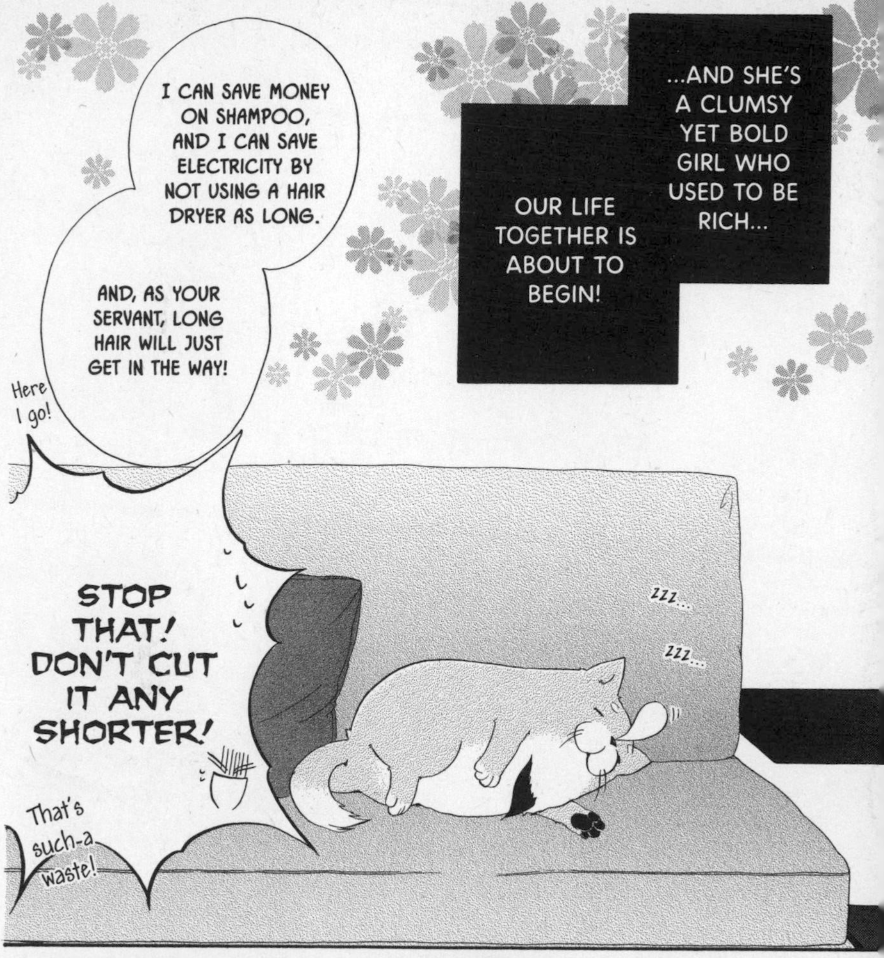
...AND SHE'S A CLUMSY YET BOLD GIRL WHO USED TO BE RICH...
OUR LIFE TOGETHER IS ABOUT TO BEGIN!
I CAN SAVE MONEY ON SHAMPOO, AND I CAN SAVE ELECTRICITY BY NOT USING A HAIR DRYER AS LONG.
AND, AS YOUR SERVANT, LONG HAIR WILL JUST GET IN THE WAY!
Here I go!
ZZZ...
ZZZ...
STOP THAT! DON'T CUT IT ANY SHORTER!
That's such-a waste!
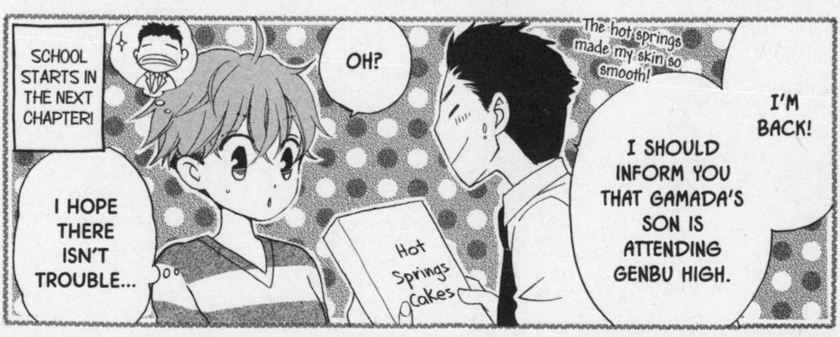
I'M BACK!
The hot springs made my skin so smooth!
I SHOULD INFORM YOU THAT GAMADA'S SON IS ATTENDING GENBU HIGH.
Hot Springs Cakes
OH?
SCHOOL STARTS IN THE NEXT CHAPTER!
I HOPE THERE ISN'T TROUBLE...

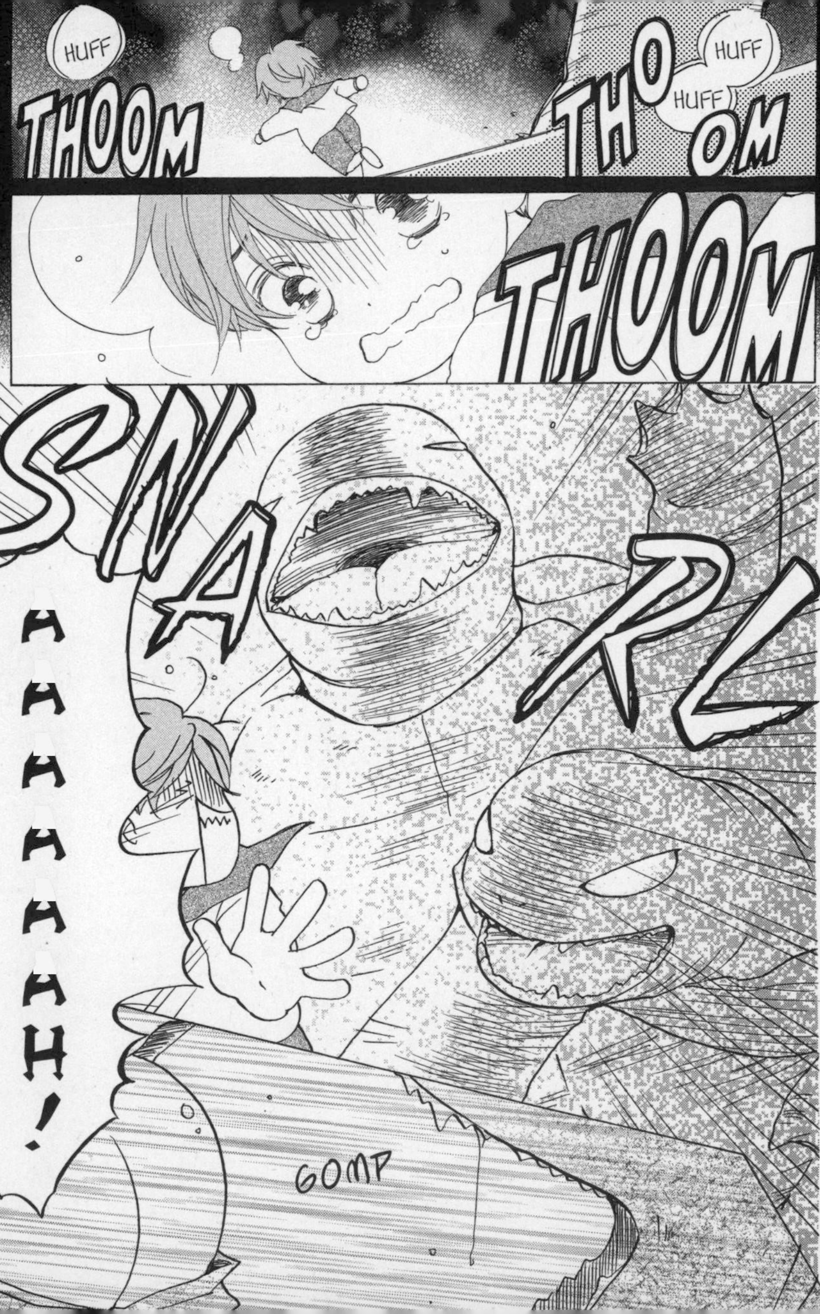
THO OM
HUFF
HUFF
THOOM
HUFF
THOOM
SNARL
AAAAAAH!
GOMP

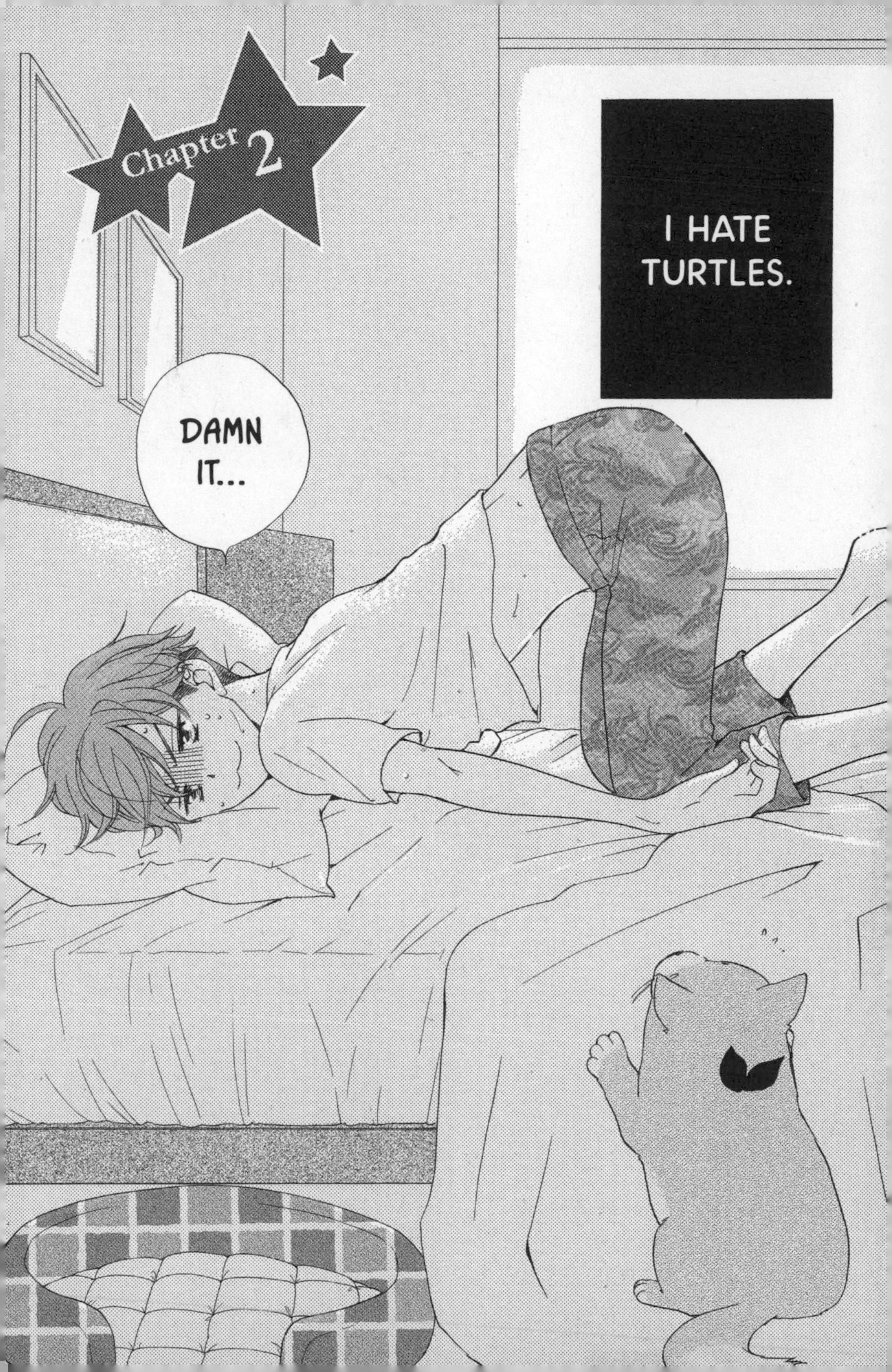
I HATE TURTLES.
Chapter 2
DAMN IT...

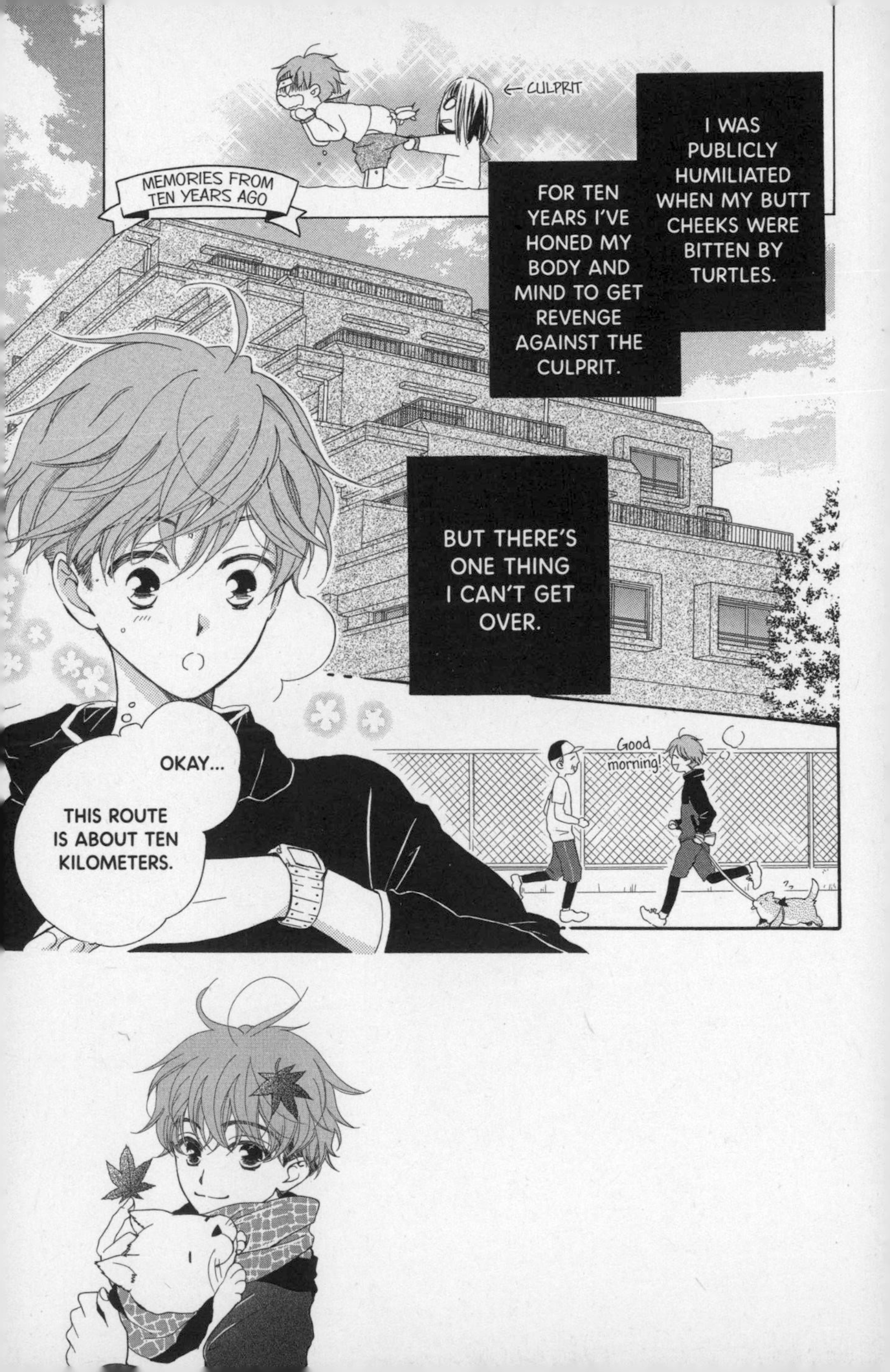
← CULPRIT
MEMORIES FROM TEN YEARS AGO
I WAS PUBLICLY HUMILIATED WHEN MY BUTT CHEEKS WERE BITTEN BY TURTLES.
FOR TEN YEARS I'VE HONED MY BODY AND MIND TO GET REVENGE AGAINST THE CULPRIT.
BUT THERE'S ONE THING I CAN'T GET OVER.
Good morning!
OKAY...
THIS ROUTE IS ABOUT TEN KILOMETERS.

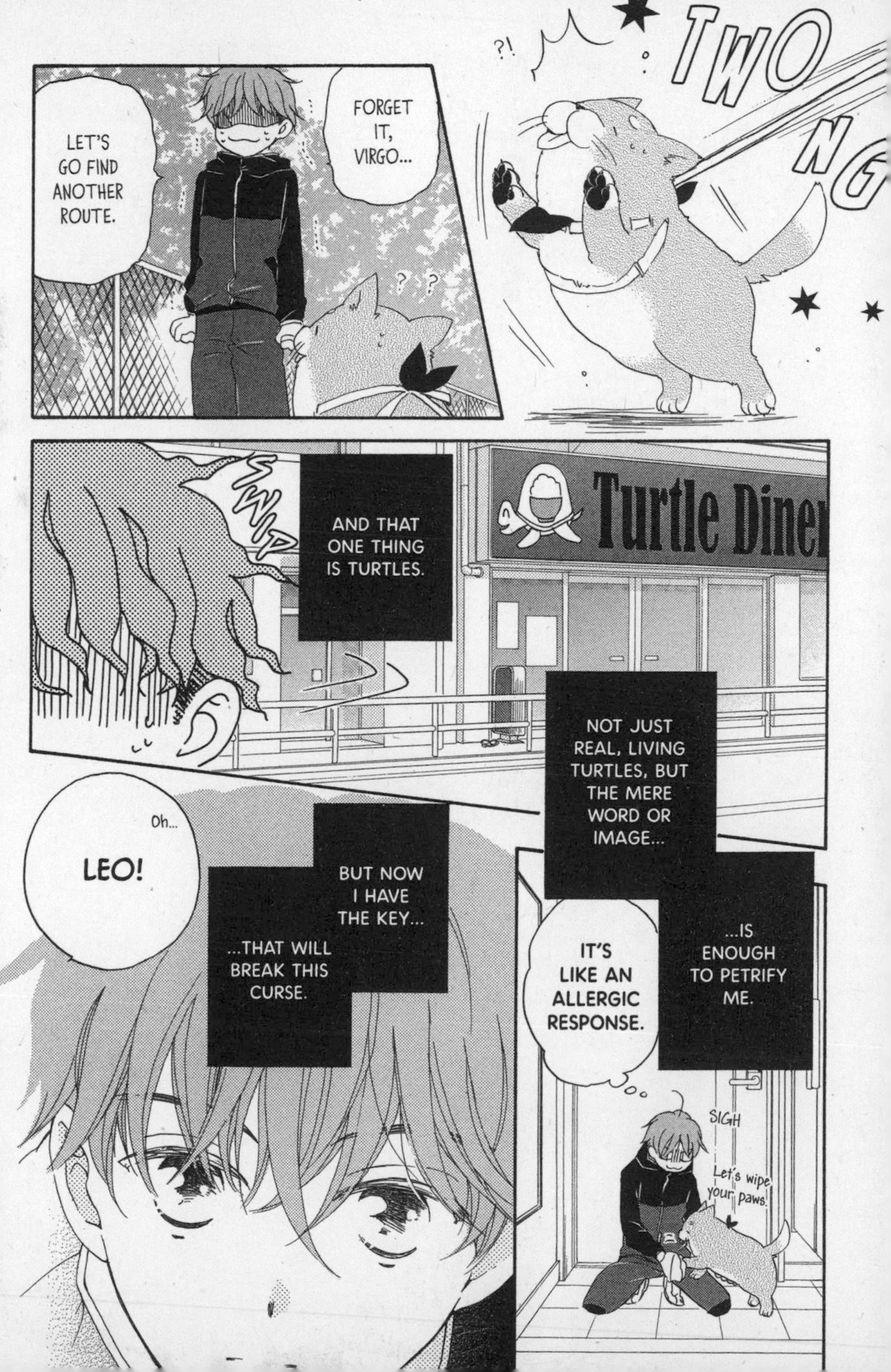
TWONG
?!
FORGET IT, VIRGO...
LET'S GO FIND ANOTHER ROUTE.
? ?
Turtle Diner
SWIP
AND THAT ONE THING IS TURTLES.
NOT JUST REAL, LIVING TURTLES, BUT THE MERE WORD OR IMAGE...
...IS ENOUGH TO PETRIFY ME.
IT'S LIKE AN ALLERGIC RESPONSE.
SIGH
Let's wipe your paws.
BUT NOW I HAVE THE KEY...
...THAT WILL BREAK THIS CURSE.
Oh...
LEO!

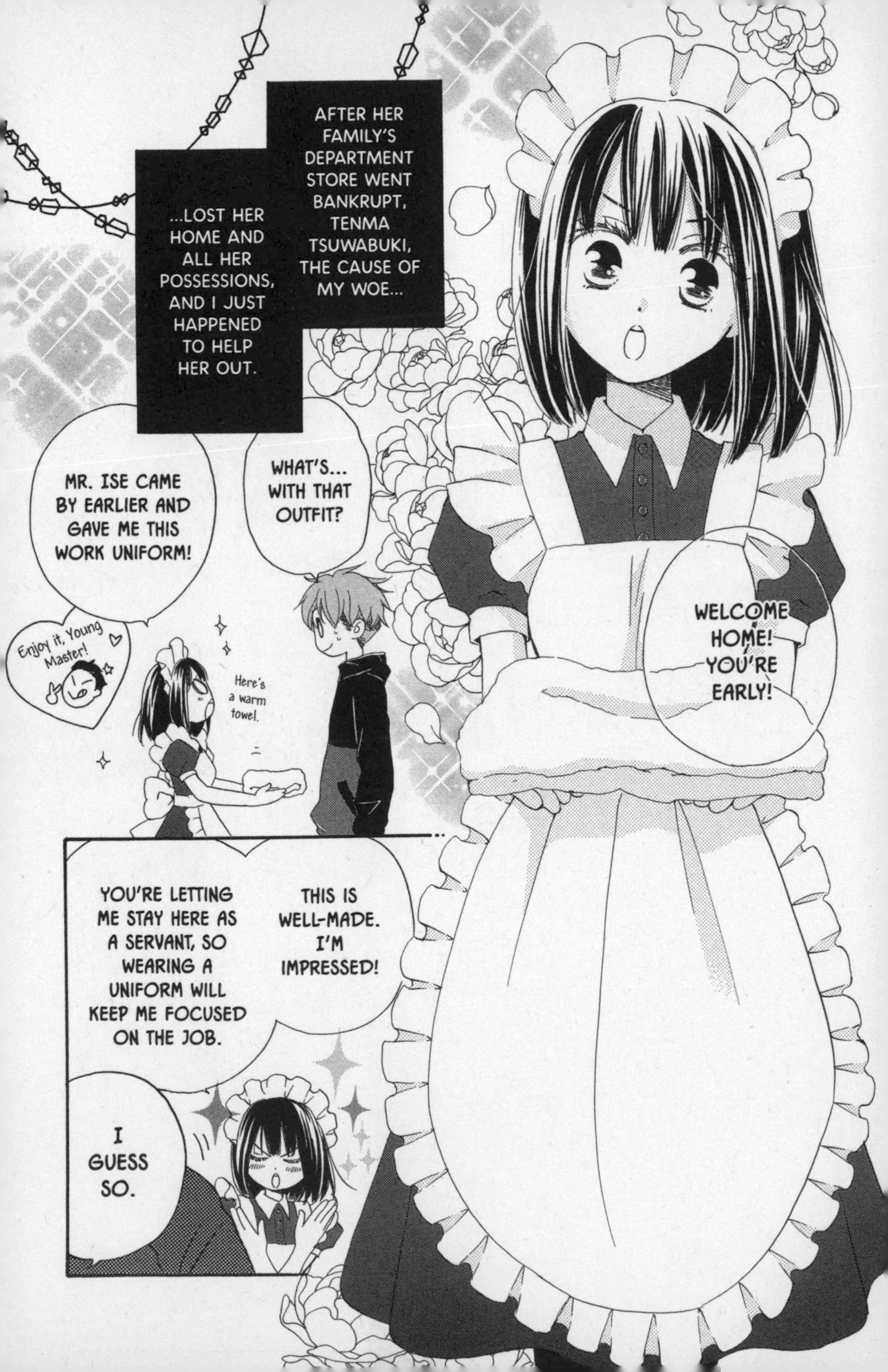

AFTER HER FAMILY'S DEPARTMENT STORE WENT BANKRUPT, TENMA TSUWABUKI, THE CAUSE OF MY WOE...
...LOST HER HOME AND ALL HER POSSESSIONS, AND I JUST HAPPENED TO HELP HER OUT.
WELCOME HOME! YOU'RE EARLY!
WHAT'S... WITH THAT OUTFIT?
MR. ISE CAME BY EARLIER AND GAVE ME THIS WORK UNIFORM!
Enjoy it, Young Master!
Here's a warm towel.
THIS IS WELL-MADE. I'M IMPRESSED!
YOU'RE LETTING ME STAY HERE AS A SERVANT, SO WEARING A UNIFORM WILL KEEP ME FOCUSED ON THE JOB.
I GUESS SO.

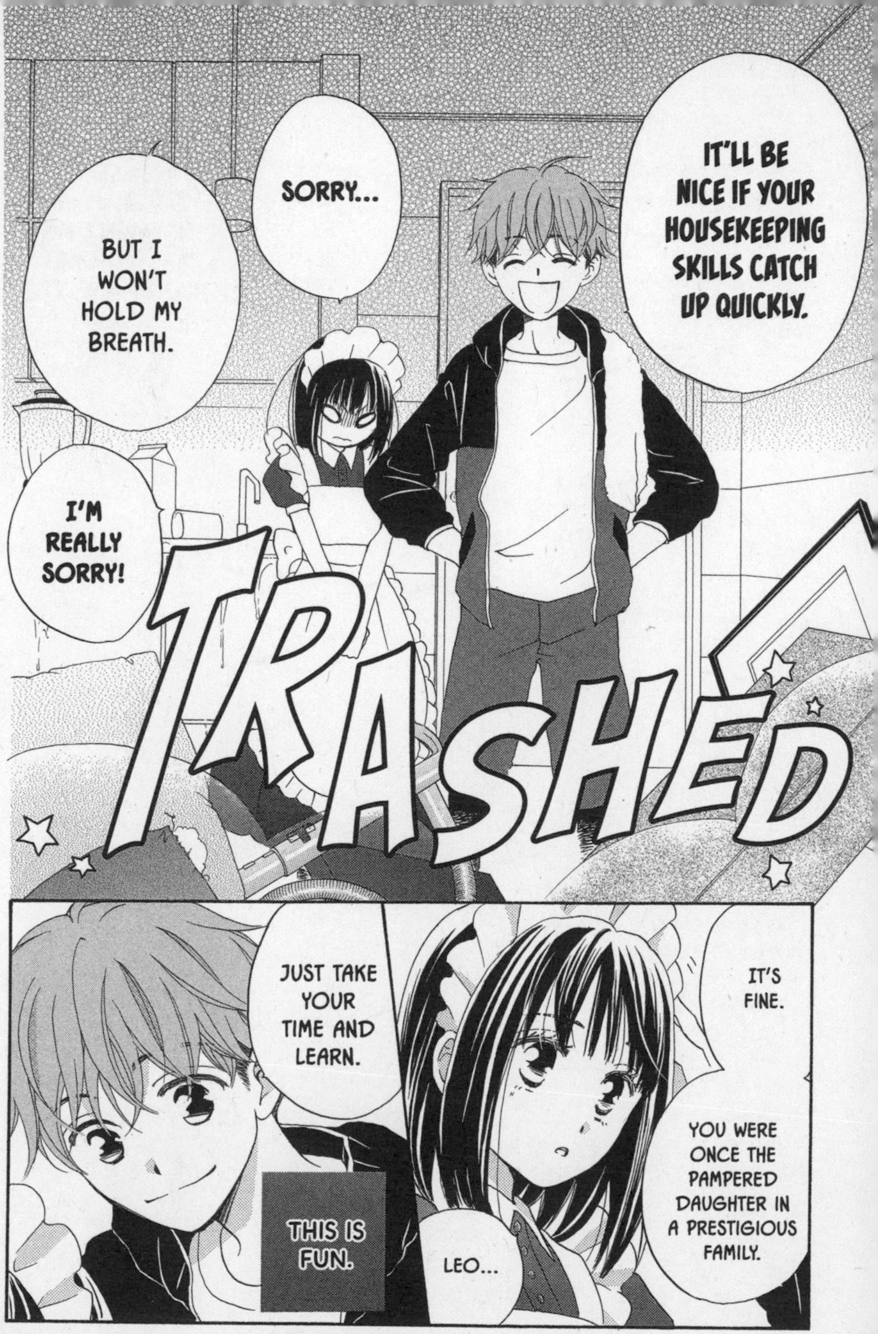
IT'LL BE NICE IF YOUR HOUSEKEEPING SKILLS CATCH UP QUICKLY.
SORRY...
BUT I WON'T HOLD MY BREATH.
I'M REALLY SORRY!
TRASHED
IT'S FINE.
YOU WERE ONCE THE PAMPERED DAUGHTER IN A PRESTIGIOUS FAMILY.
LEO...
JUST TAKE YOUR TIME AND LEARN.
THIS IS FUN.

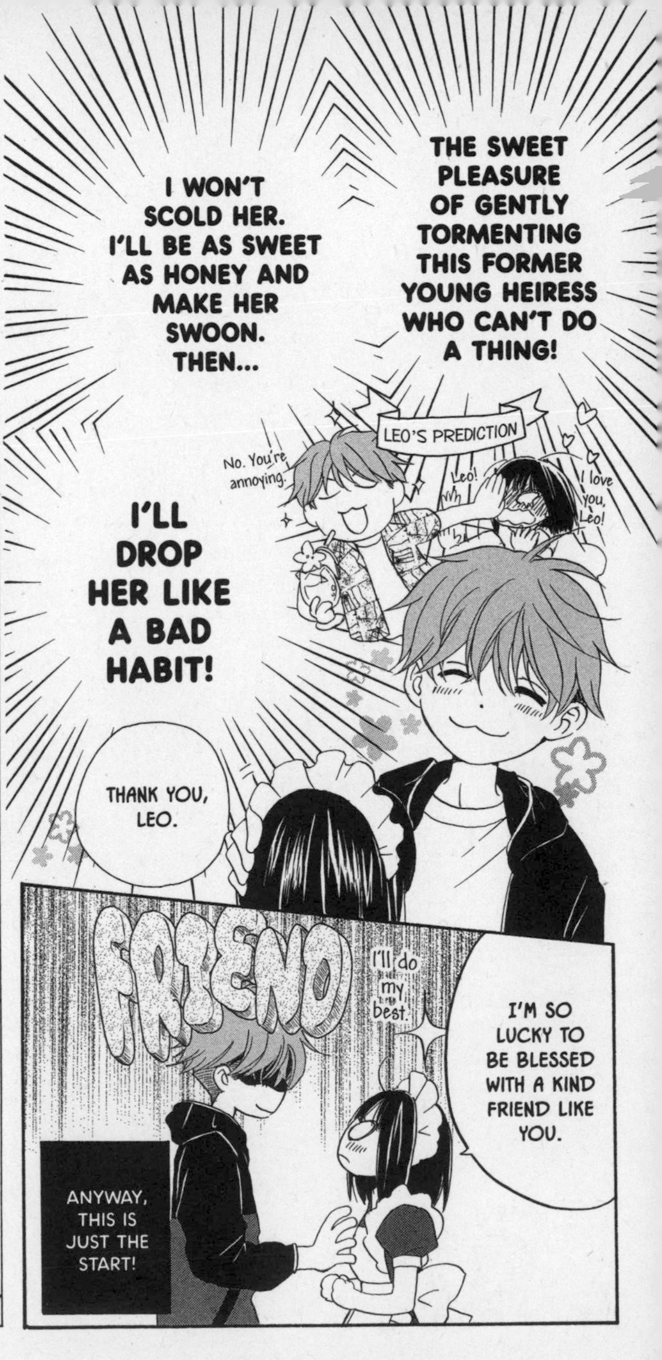
THE SWEET PLEASURE OF GENTLY TORMENTING THIS FORMER YOUNG HEIRESS WHO CAN'T DO A THING!
I WON'T SCOLD HER. I'LL BE AS SWEET AS HONEY AND MAKE HER SWOON. THEN...
LEO'S PREDICTION
I love you, Leo!
Leo!
No. You're annoying.
I'LL DROP HER LIKE A BAD HABIT!
THANK YOU, LEO.
I'M SO LUCKY TO BE BLESSED WITH A KIND FRIEND LIKE YOU.
I'll do my best.
FRIEND
ANYWAY, THIS IS JUST THE START!

About *The Young Master's Revenge*

It's a new "lyrical-revenge romance."

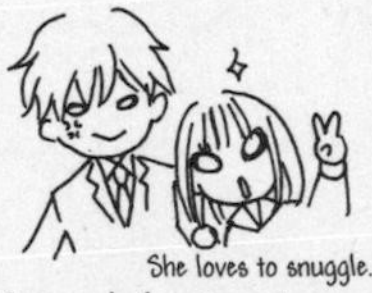
She loves to snuggle.

Around the time I was finishing up my last work, I was toying with an idea about one person getting so close to the other that love turns topsy-turvy. These two characters are the outcome of that. At first I was thinking along the lines of a really intense soap opera-like revenge. But I put my ideas on paper, and it made me think rationally. I realized something like that just wasn't me, and I came up with Leo's sad past. Actually, in the beginning, the turtles didn't chomp on Leo's butt cheeks. It happened to his little peter, but...

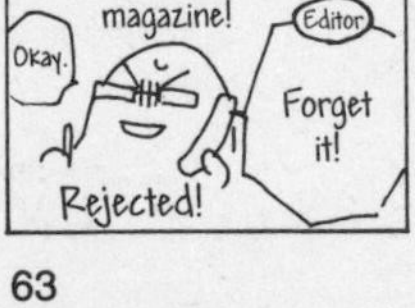
It's a shojo magazine!
Editor
Okay.
Forget it!
Rejected!

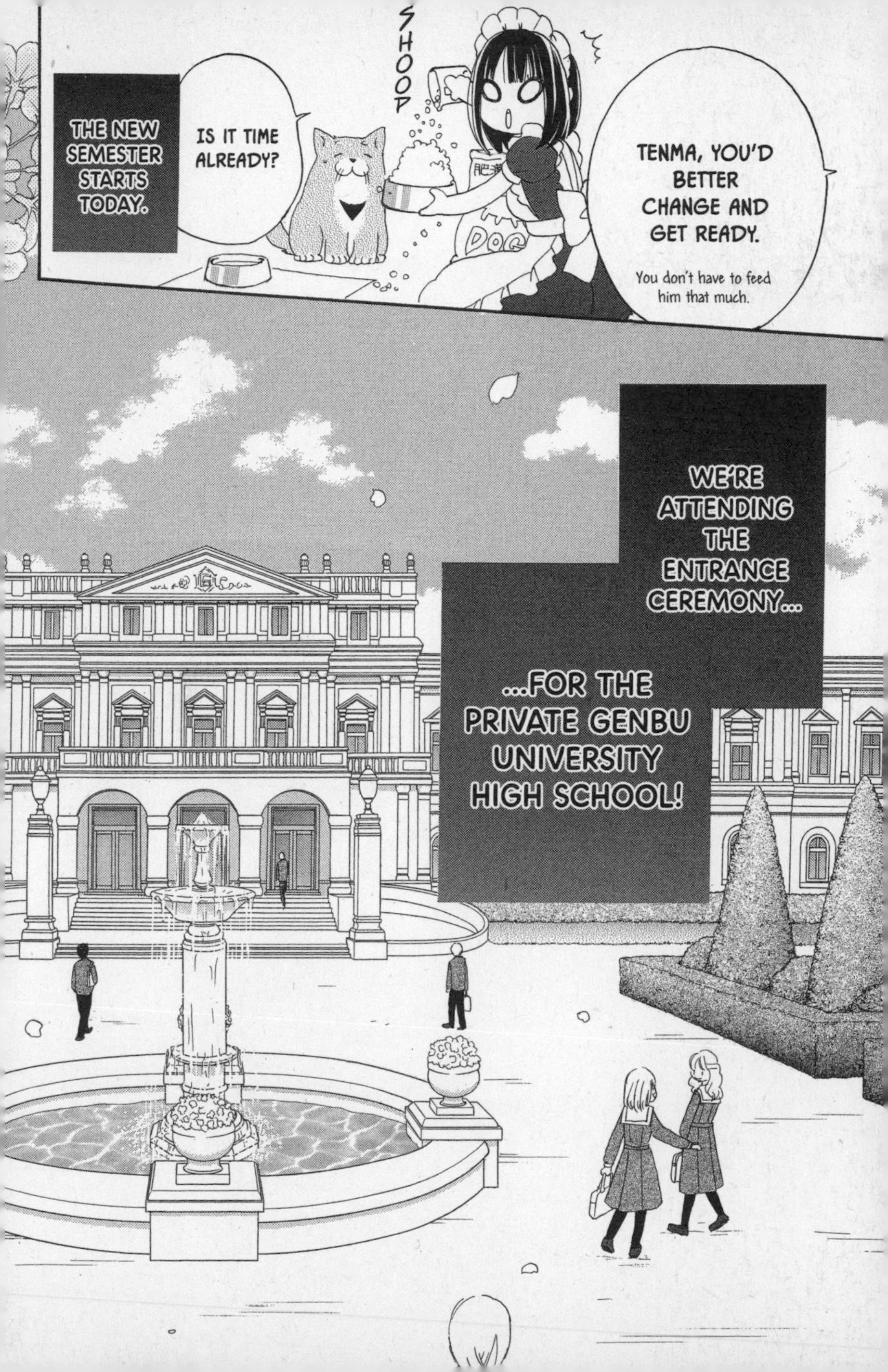
THE NEW SEMESTER STARTS TODAY.
IS IT TIME ALREADY?
SHOOP
TENMA, YOU'D BETTER CHANGE AND GET READY.
You don't have to feed him that much.
WE'RE ATTENDING THE ENTRANCE CEREMONY...
...FOR THE PRIVATE GENBU UNIVERSITY HIGH SCHOOL!

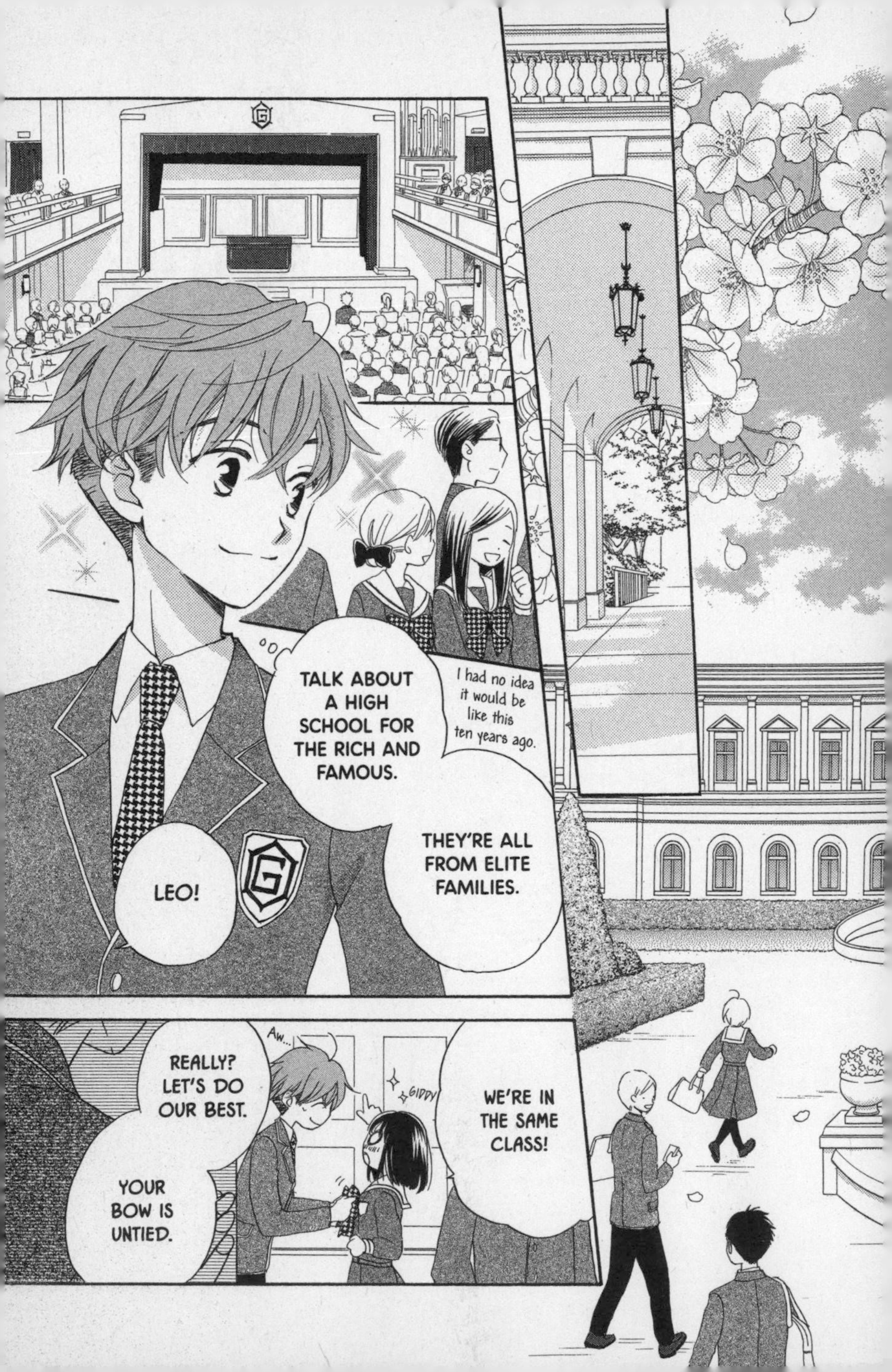
THEY'RE ALL FROM ELITE FAMILIES.
TALK ABOUT A HIGH SCHOOL FOR THE RICH AND FAMOUS.
I had no idea it would be like this ten years ago.
LEO!
WE'RE IN THE SAME CLASS!
GIDDY
AW...
REALLY? LET'S DO OUR BEST.
YOUR BOW IS UNTIED.

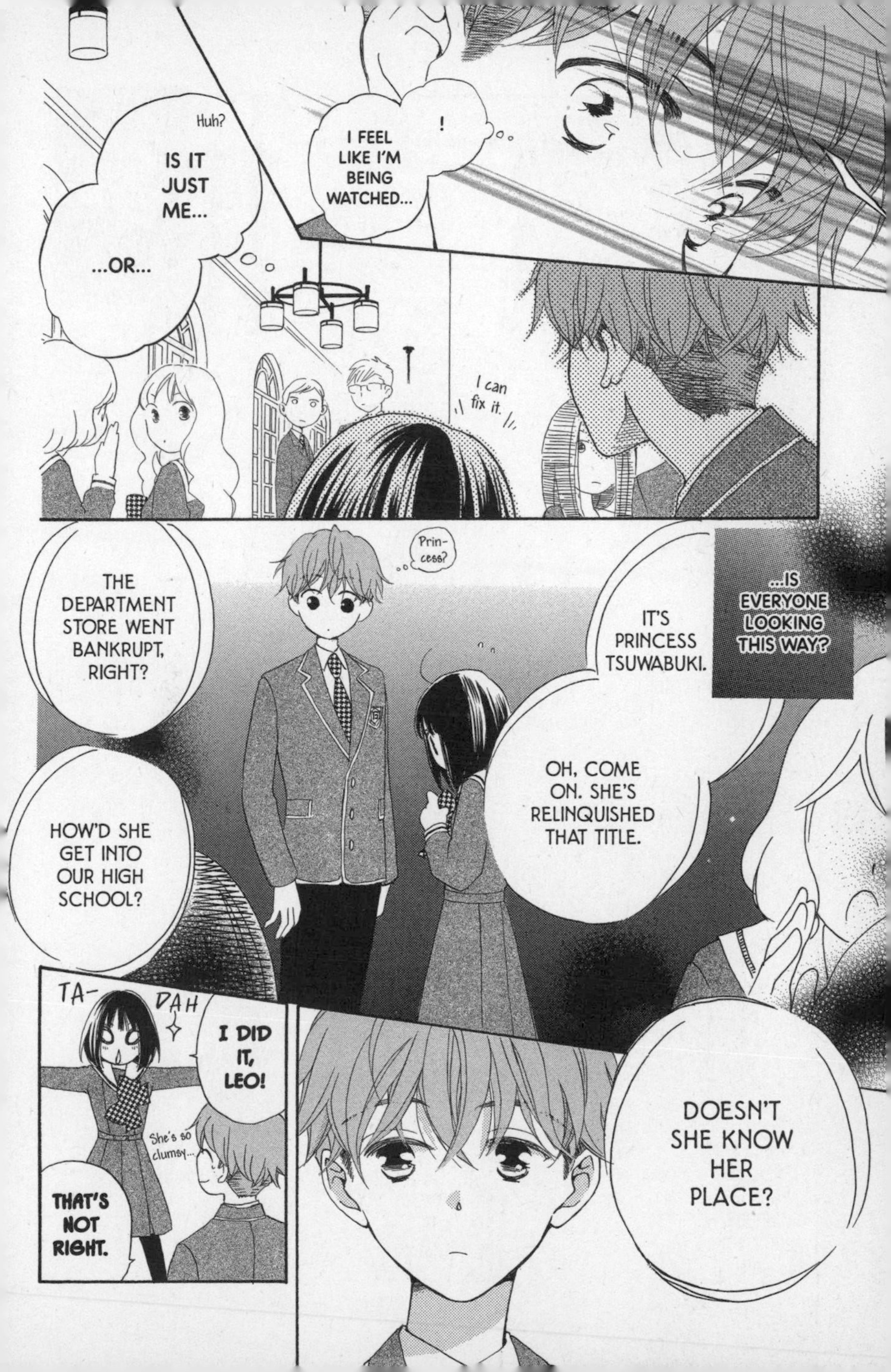
!
I FEEL LIKE I'M BEING WATCHED...
Huh?
IS IT JUST ME...
...OR...
I can fix it.
...IS EVERYONE LOOKING THIS WAY?
IT'S PRINCESS TSUWABUKI.
Prin-cess?
THE DEPARTMENT STORE WENT BANKRUPT, RIGHT?
OH, COME ON. SHE'S RELINQUISHED THAT TITLE.
HOW'D SHE GET INTO OUR HIGH SCHOOL?
DOESN'T SHE KNOW HER PLACE?
TA-DAH
I DID IT, LEO!
She's so clumsy...
THAT'S NOT RIGHT.

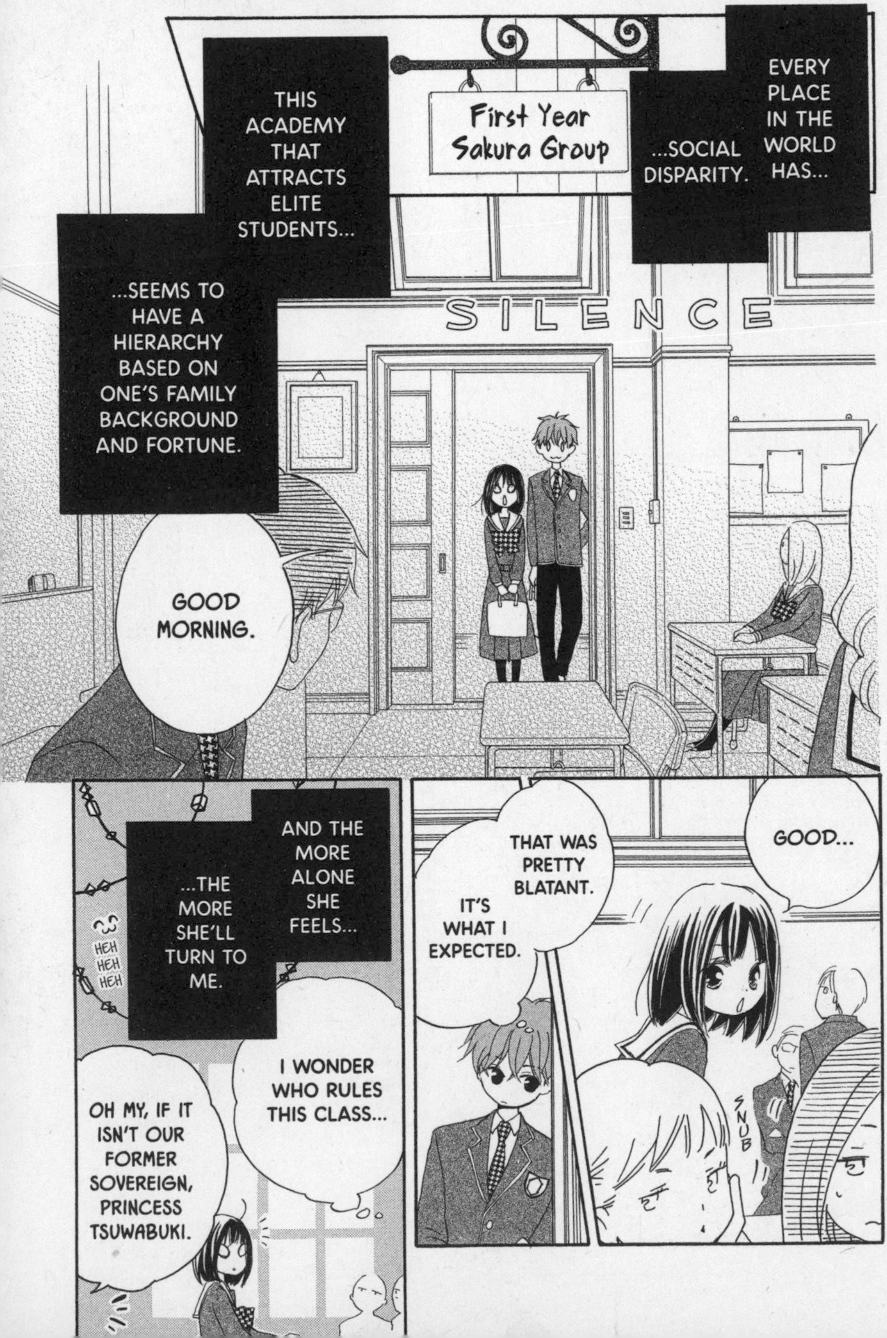
EVERY PLACE IN THE WORLD HAS...
...SOCIAL DISPARITY.
First Year Sakura Group
THIS ACADEMY THAT ATTRACTS ELITE STUDENTS...
SILENCE
...SEEMS TO HAVE A HIERARCHY BASED ON ONE'S FAMILY BACKGROUND AND FORTUNE.
GOOD MORNING.
GOOD...
THAT WAS PRETTY BLATANT.
IT'S WHAT I EXPECTED.
SNUB
AND THE MORE ALONE SHE FEELS...
...THE MORE SHE'LL TURN TO ME.
HEH HEH HEH
I WONDER WHO RULES THIS CLASS...
OH MY, IF IT ISN'T OUR FORMER SOVEREIGN, PRINCESS TSUWABUKI.

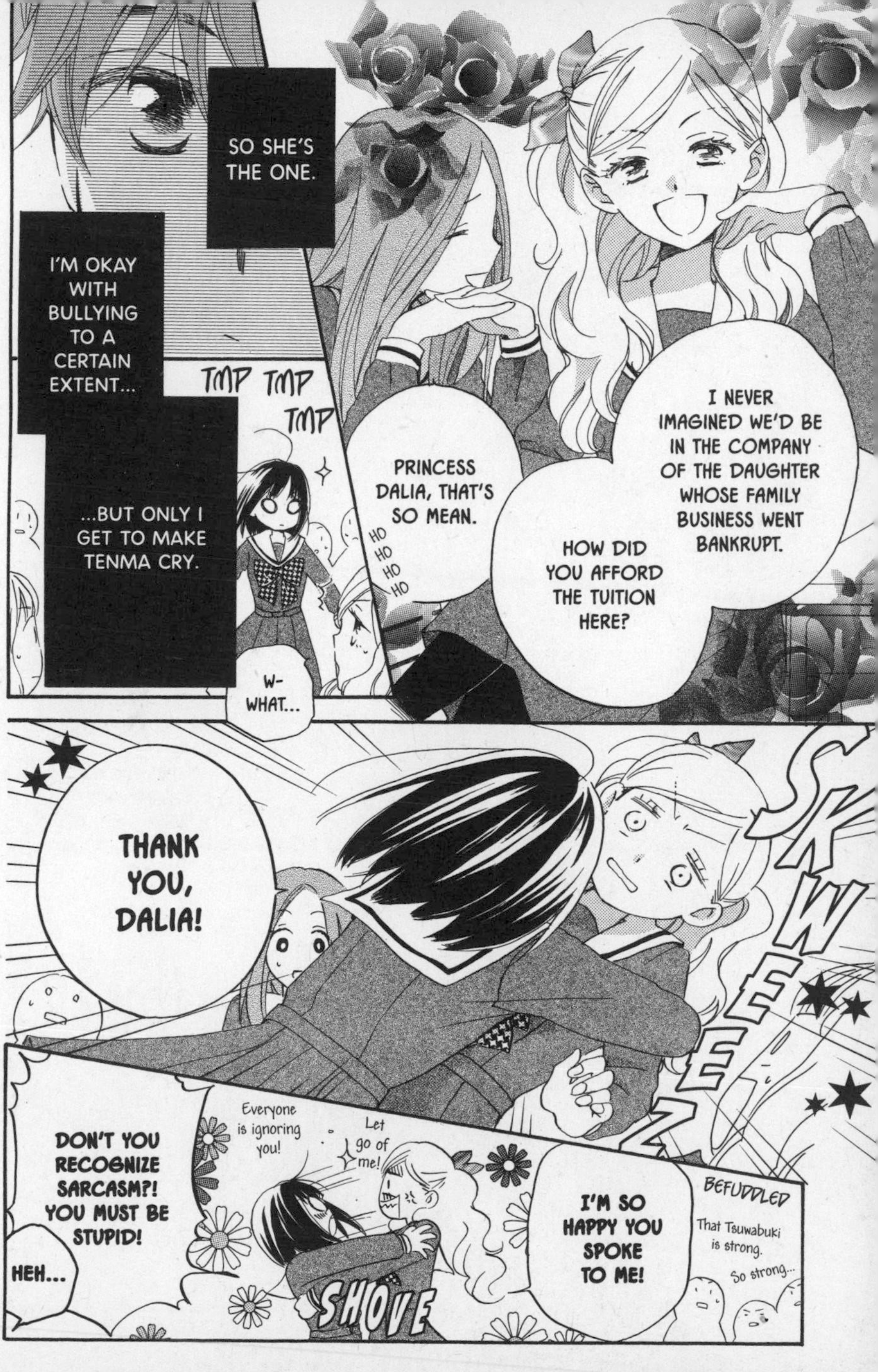
I NEVER IMAGINED WE'D BE IN THE COMPANY OF THE DAUGHTER WHOSE FAMILY BUSINESS WENT BANKRUPT.
HOW DID YOU AFFORD THE TUITION HERE?
PRINCESS DALIA, THAT'S SO MEAN.
HO HO HO HO
SO SHE'S THE ONE.
I'M OKAY WITH BULLYING TO A CERTAIN EXTENT...
TMP TMP TMP
...BUT ONLY I GET TO MAKE TENMA CRY.
W- WHAT...
SKWEEZ
THANK YOU, DALIA!
BEFUDDLED
That Tsuwabuki is strong.
So strong...
I'M SO HAPPY YOU SPOKE TO ME!
SHOVE
Let go of me!
Everyone is ignoring you!
DON'T YOU RECOGNIZE SARCASM?! YOU MUST BE STUPID!
HEH...

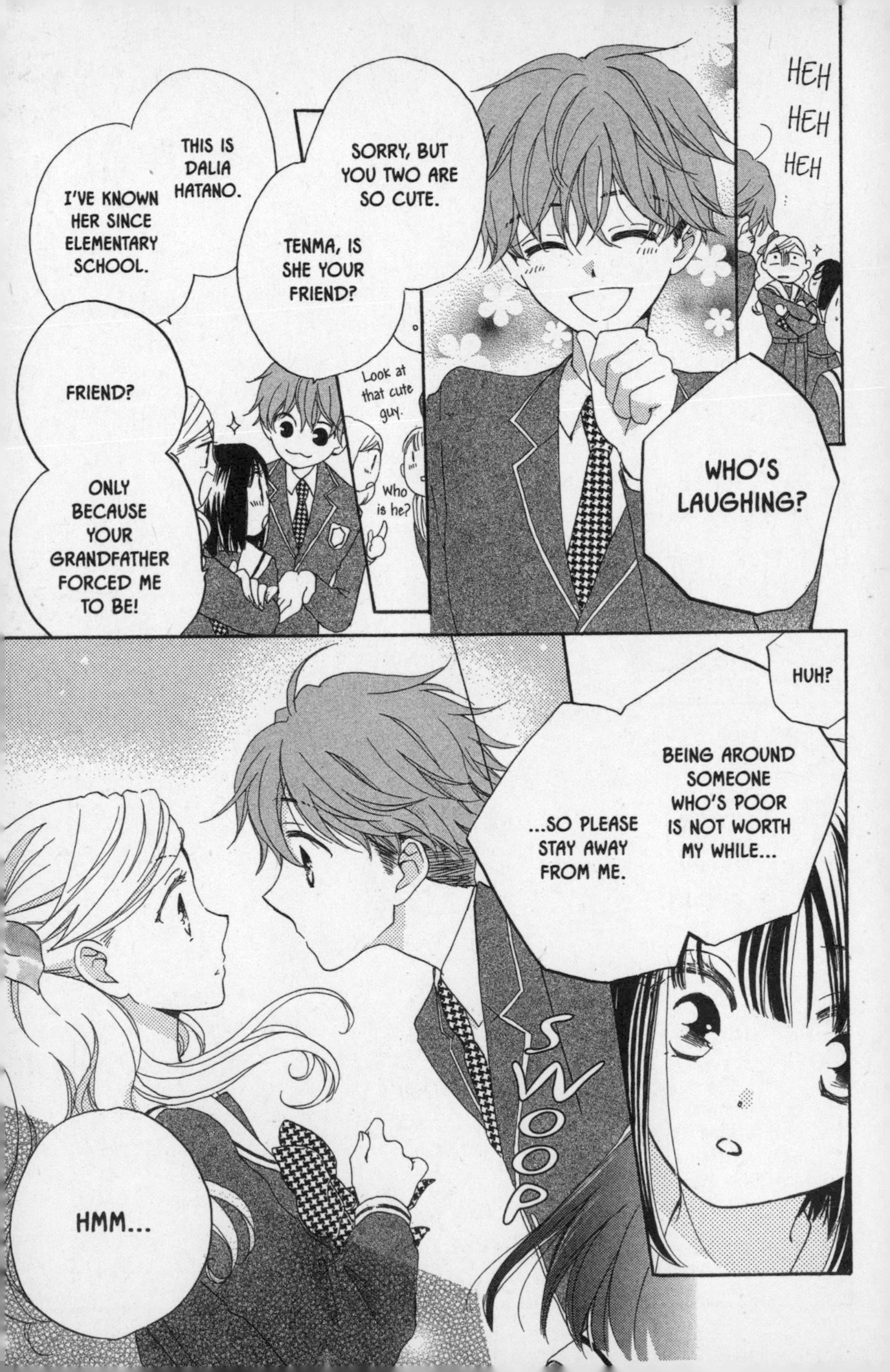
HEH HEH HEH
WHO'S LAUGHING?
SORRY, BUT YOU TWO ARE SO CUTE.
TENMA, IS SHE YOUR FRIEND?
Look at that cute guy.
Who is he?
THIS IS DALIA HATANO.
I'VE KNOWN HER SINCE ELEMENTARY SCHOOL.
FRIEND?
ONLY BECAUSE YOUR GRANDFATHER FORCED ME TO BE!
HUH?
BEING AROUND SOMEONE WHO'S POOR IS NOT WORTH MY WHILE...
...SO PLEASE STAY AWAY FROM ME.
SWOOP
HMM...

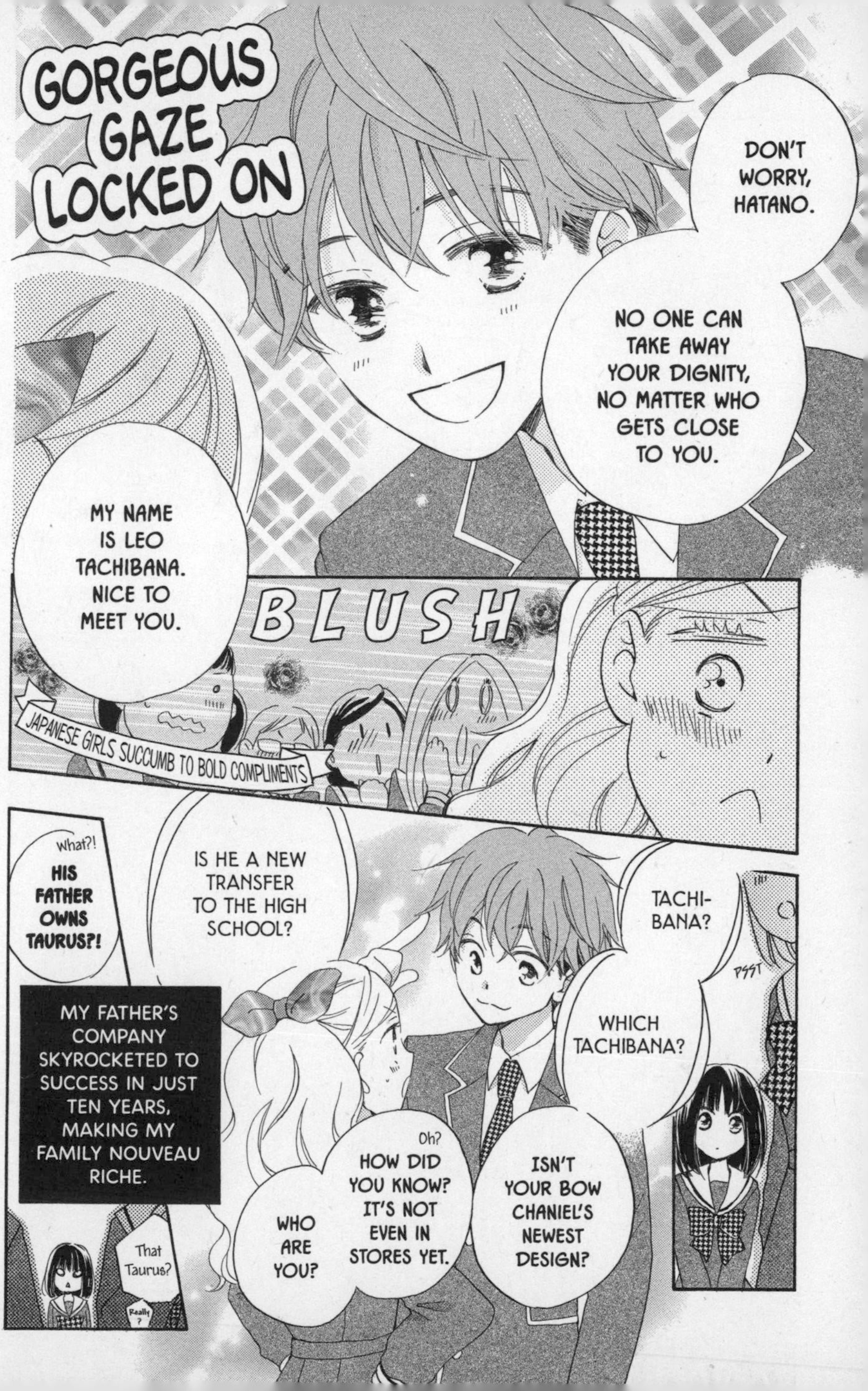
DON'T WORRY, HATANO.
NO ONE CAN TAKE AWAY YOUR DIGNITY, NO MATTER WHO GETS CLOSE TO YOU.
GORGEOUS GAZE LOCKED ON
MY NAME IS LEO TACHIBANA. NICE TO MEET YOU.
BLUSH
JAPANESE GIRLS SUCCUMB TO BOLD COMPLIMENTS
TACHI-BANA?
PSST
WHICH TACHIBANA?
IS HE A NEW TRANSFER TO THE HIGH SCHOOL?
What?!
HIS FATHER OWNS TAURUS?!
MY FATHER'S COMPANY SKYROCKETED TO SUCCESS IN JUST TEN YEARS, MAKING MY FAMILY NOUVEAU RICHE.
ISN'T YOUR BOW CHANIEL'S NEWEST DESIGN?
Oh?
HOW DID YOU KNOW? IT'S NOT EVEN IN STORES YET.
WHO ARE YOU?
That Taurus?
Really?

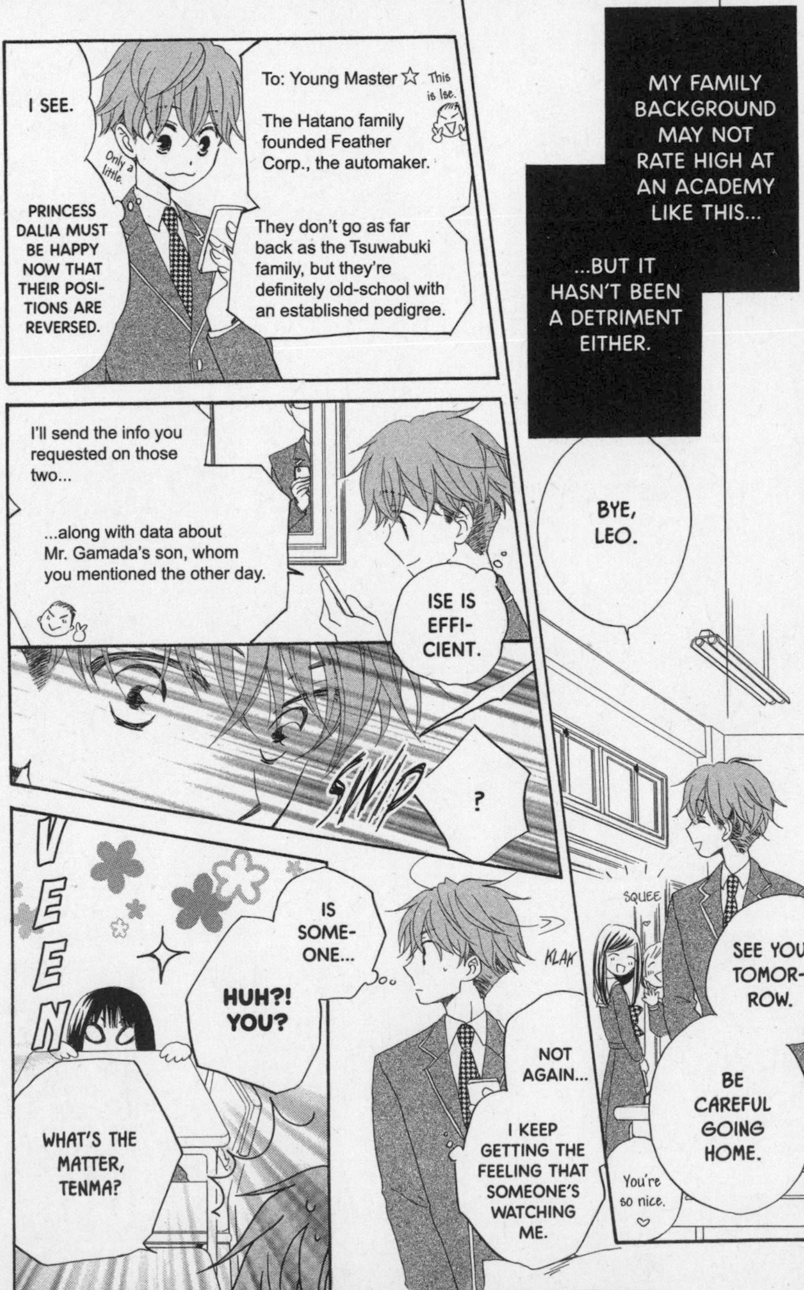
MY FAMILY BACKGROUND MAY NOT RATE HIGH AT AN ACADEMY LIKE THIS...
...BUT IT HASN'T BEEN A DETRIMENT EITHER.
BYE, LEO.
SEE YOU TOMOR-ROW.
SQUEE
BE CAREFUL GOING HOME.
You're so nice. ♡
KLAK
NOT AGAIN...
I KEEP GETTING THE FEELING THAT SOMEONE'S WATCHING ME.
I SEE.
Only a little.
PRINCESS DALIA MUST BE HAPPY NOW THAT THEIR POSI-TIONS ARE REVERSED.
To: Young Master ☆ This is Ise.
The Hatano family founded Feather Corp., the automaker.
They don't go as far back as the Tsuwabuki family, but they're definitely old-school with an established pedigree.
I'll send the info you requested on those two...
...along with data about Mr. Gamada's son, whom you mentioned the other day.
ISE IS EFFI-CIENT.
SWIP
?
IS SOME-ONE...
HUH?! YOU?
VEEN
WHAT'S THE MATTER, TENMA?

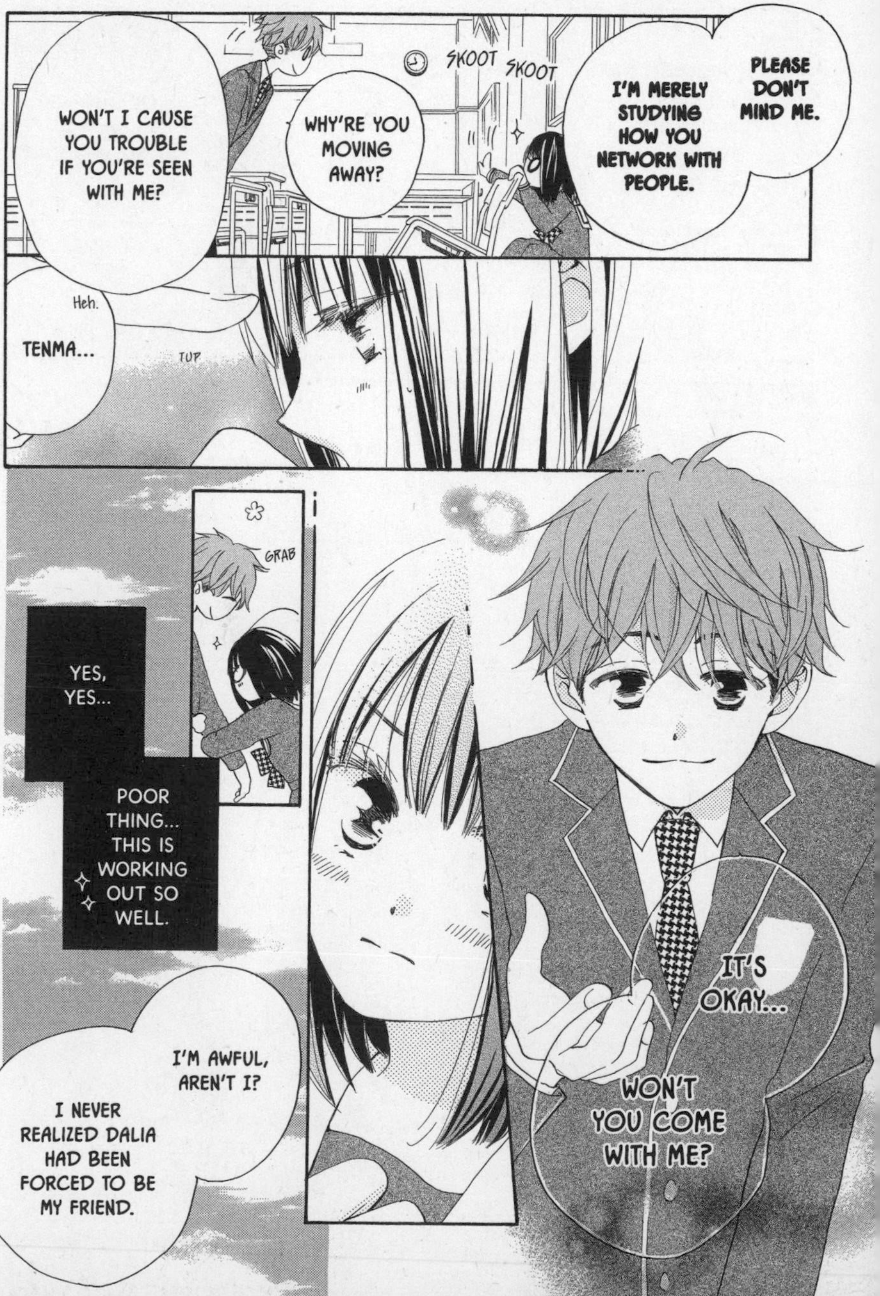
PLEASE DON'T MIND ME.
I'M MERELY STUDYING HOW YOU NETWORK WITH PEOPLE.
SKOOT SKOOT
WHY'RE YOU MOVING AWAY?
WON'T I CAUSE YOU TROUBLE IF YOU'RE SEEN WITH ME?
TUP
Heh.
TENMA...
IT'S OKAY...
WON'T YOU COME WITH ME?
GRAB
YES, YES...
POOR THING... THIS IS WORKING OUT SO WELL.
I'M AWFUL, AREN'T I?
I NEVER REALIZED DALIA HAD BEEN FORCED TO BE MY FRIEND.

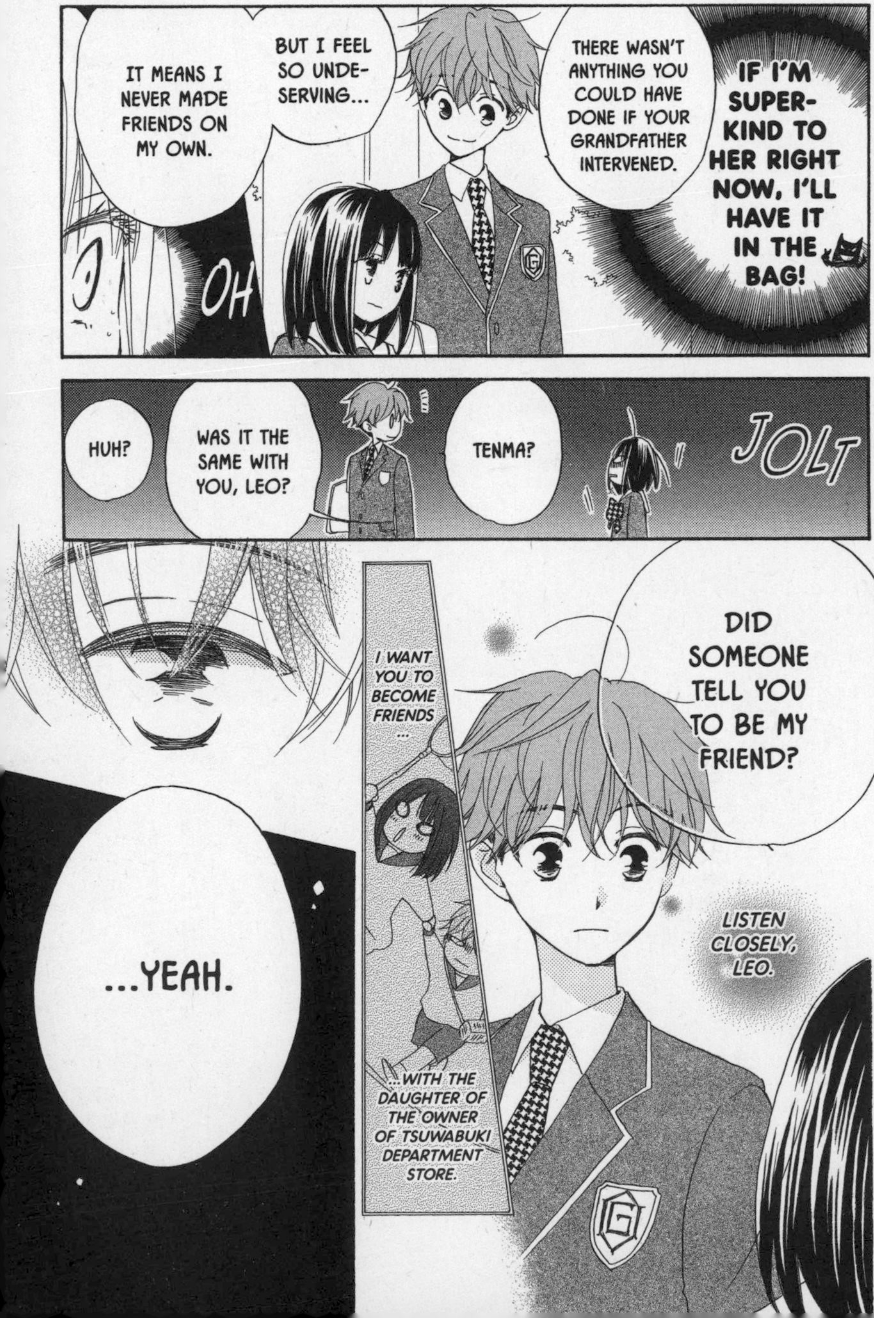
IF I'M SUPER-KIND TO HER RIGHT NOW, I'LL HAVE IT IN THE BAG!
THERE WASN'T ANYTHING YOU COULD HAVE DONE IF YOUR GRANDFATHER INTERVENED.
BUT I FEEL SO UNDESERVING...
IT MEANS I NEVER MADE FRIENDS ON MY OWN.
OH
JOLT
TENMA?
WAS IT THE SAME WITH YOU, LEO?
HUH?
DID SOMEONE TELL YOU TO BE MY FRIEND?
LISTEN CLOSELY, LEO.
I WANT YOU TO BECOME FRIENDS...
...WITH THE DAUGHTER OF THE OWNER OF TSUWABUKI DEPARTMENT STORE.
...YEAH.

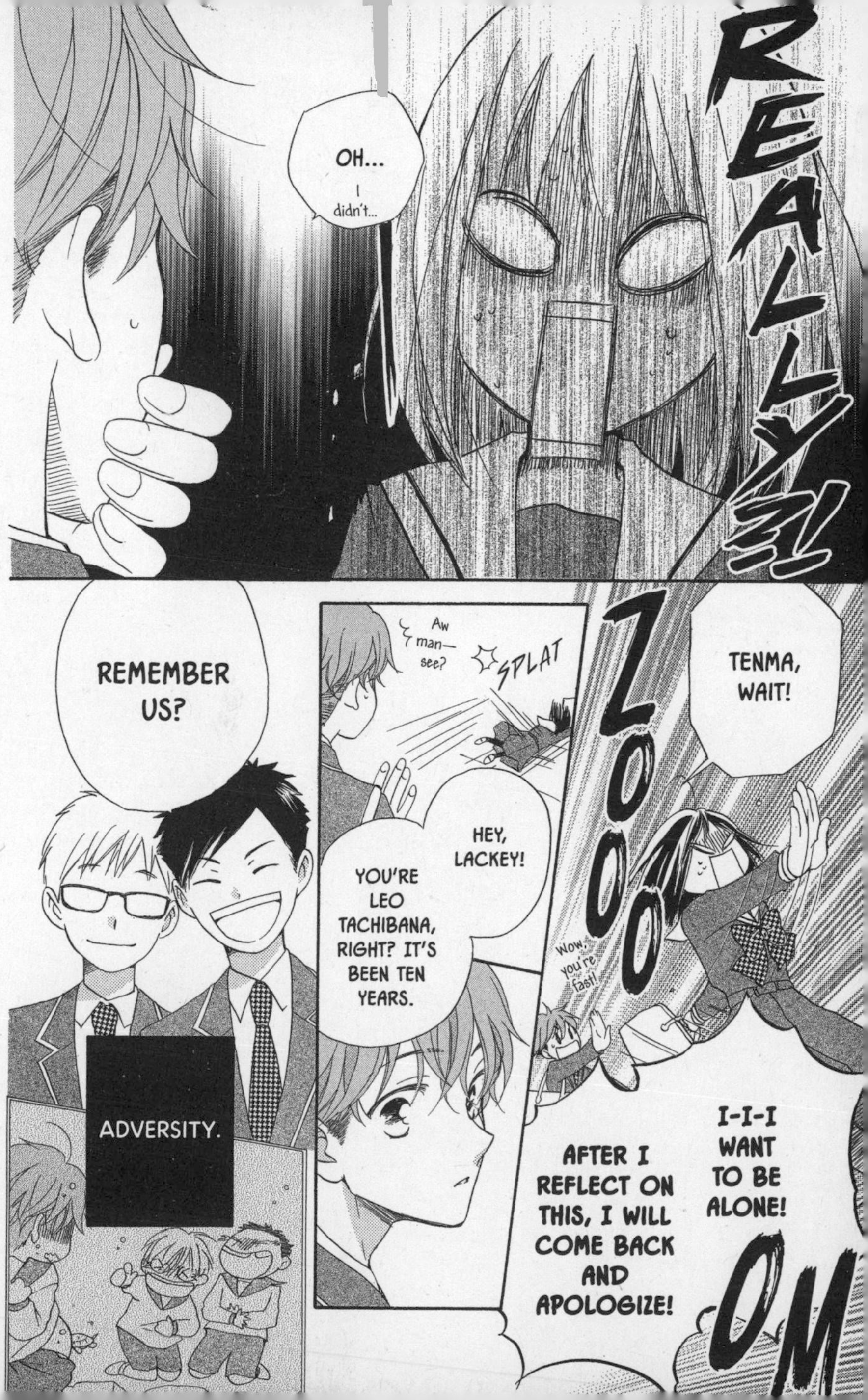
REALLY?!
OH... I didn't...
TENMA, WAIT!
ZOOOOOM
I-I-I WANT TO BE ALONE!
AFTER I REFLECT ON THIS, I WILL COME BACK AND APOLOGIZE!
Wow, you're fast!
Aw man— see?
SPLAT
HEY, LACKEY!
YOU'RE LEO TACHIBANA, RIGHT? IT'S BEEN TEN YEARS.
REMEMBER US?
ADVERSITY.

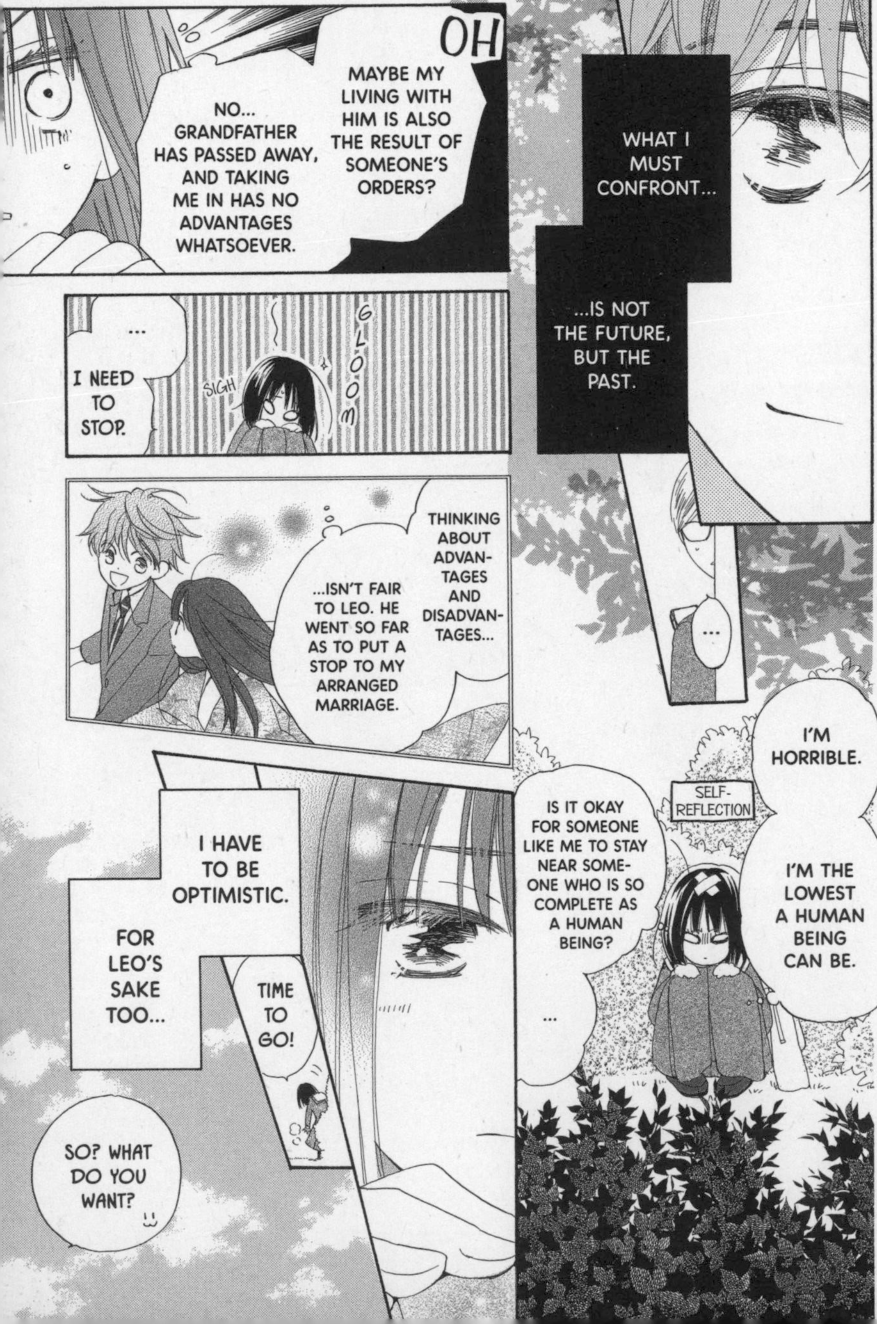
WHAT I MUST CONFRONT...
...IS NOT THE FUTURE, BUT THE PAST.
...
I'M HORRIBLE.
SELF-REFLECTION
I'M THE LOWEST A HUMAN BEING CAN BE.
IS IT OKAY FOR SOMEONE LIKE ME TO STAY NEAR SOME-ONE WHO IS SO COMPLETE AS A HUMAN BEING?
...
OH
MAYBE MY LIVING WITH HIM IS ALSO THE RESULT OF SOMEONE'S ORDERS?
NO... GRANDFATHER HAS PASSED AWAY, AND TAKING ME IN HAS NO ADVANTAGES WHATSOEVER.
GLOOM
SIGH
...
I NEED TO STOP.
THINKING ABOUT ADVAN-TAGES AND DISADVAN-TAGES...
...ISN'T FAIR TO LEO. HE WENT SO FAR AS TO PUT A STOP TO MY ARRANGED MARRIAGE.
I HAVE TO BE OPTIMISTIC.
FOR LEO'S SAKE TOO...
TIME TO GO!
SO? WHAT DO YOU WANT?

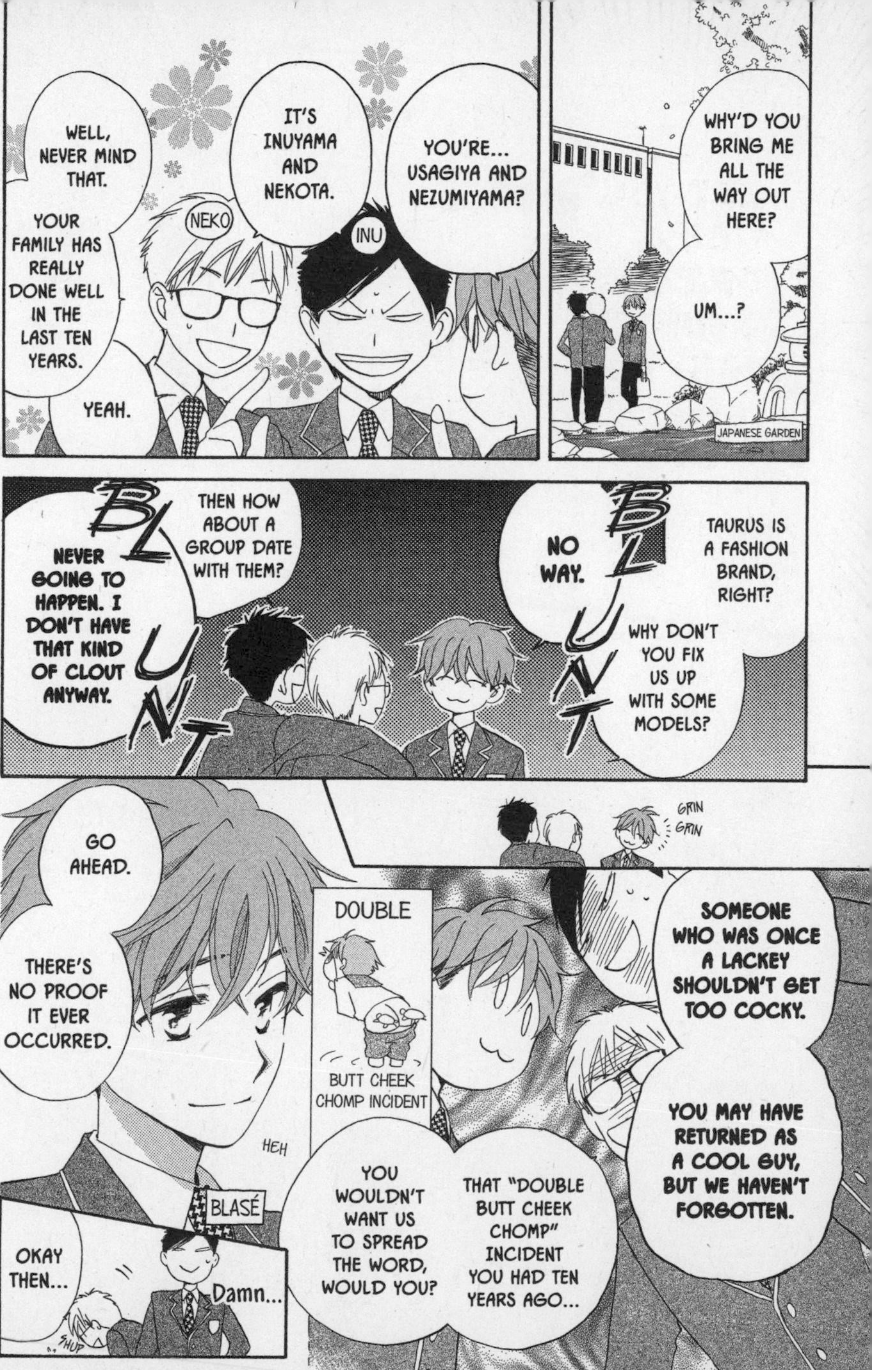
WHY'D YOU BRING ME ALL THE WAY OUT HERE?
UM...?
JAPANESE GARDEN
YOU'RE... USAGIYA AND NEZUMIYAMA?
IT'S INUYAMA AND NEKOTA.
INU
NEKO
WELL, NEVER MIND THAT.
YOUR FAMILY HAS REALLY DONE WELL IN THE LAST TEN YEARS.
YEAH.
TAURUS IS A FASHION BRAND, RIGHT?
WHY DON'T YOU FIX US UP WITH SOME MODELS?
NO WAY.
BLUNT
THEN HOW ABOUT A GROUP DATE WITH THEM?
NEVER GOING TO HAPPEN. I DON'T HAVE THAT KIND OF CLOUT ANYWAY.
BLUNT
GRIN GRIN
SOMEONE WHO WAS ONCE A LACKEY SHOULDN'T GET TOO COCKY.
YOU MAY HAVE RETURNED AS A COOL GUY, BUT WE HAVEN'T FORGOTTEN.
DOUBLE
BUTT CHEEK CHOMP INCIDENT
THAT "DOUBLE BUTT CHEEK CHOMP" INCIDENT YOU HAD TEN YEARS AGO...
YOU WOULDN'T WANT US TO SPREAD THE WORD, WOULD YOU?
HEH
GO AHEAD.
THERE'S NO PROOF IT EVER OCCURRED.
BLASÉ
Damn...
OKAY THEN...
SHUP

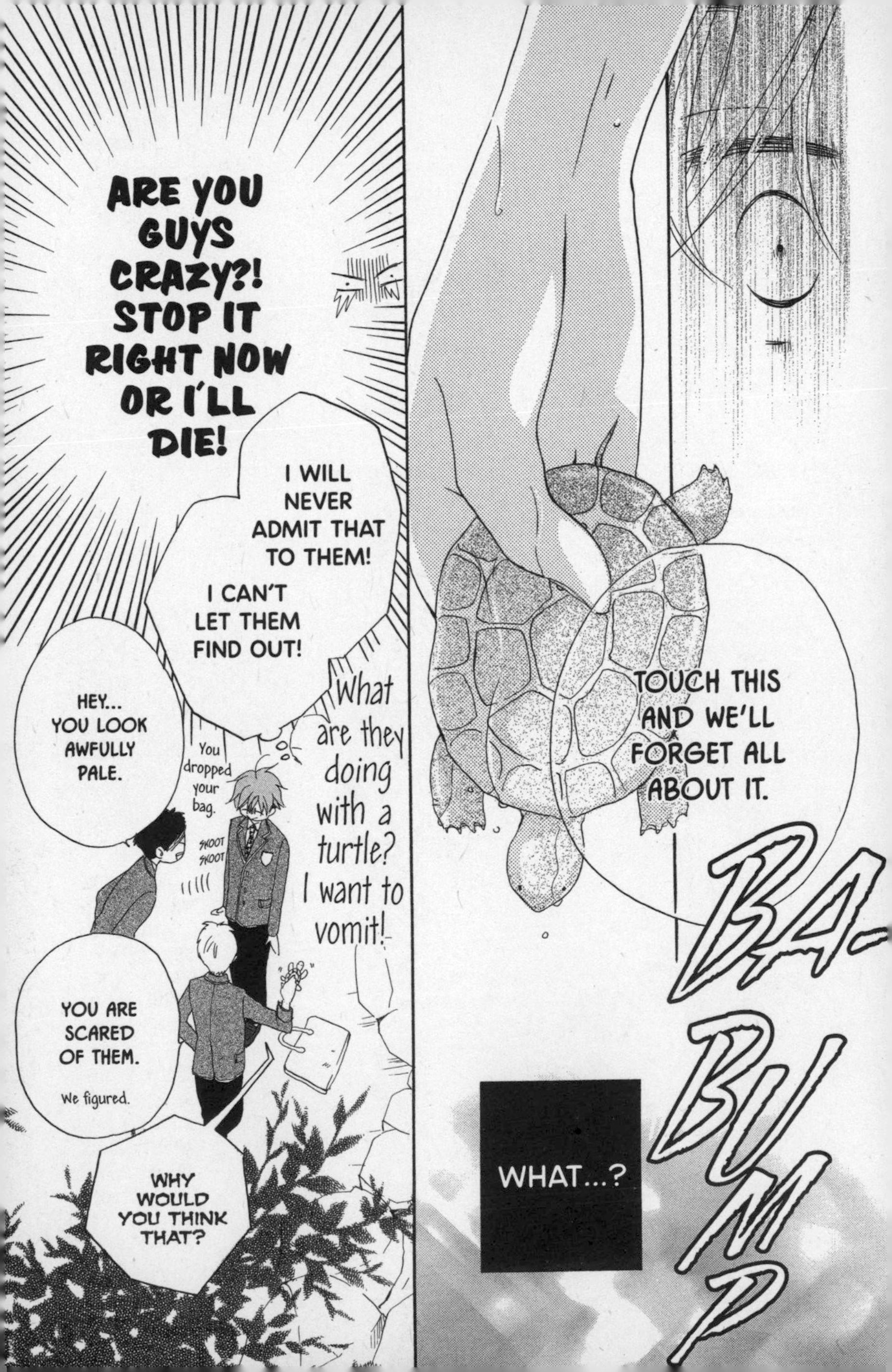
TOUCH THIS AND WE'LL FORGET ALL ABOUT IT.
BA-BUMP
WHAT...?
ARE YOU GUYS CRAZY?! STOP IT RIGHT NOW OR I'LL DIE!
I WILL NEVER ADMIT THAT TO THEM!
I CAN'T LET THEM FIND OUT!
What are they doing with a turtle? I want to vomit!
You dropped your bag.
SHOOT SHOOT
HEY... YOU LOOK AWFULLY PALE.
YOU ARE SCARED OF THEM.
We figured.
WHY WOULD YOU THINK THAT?

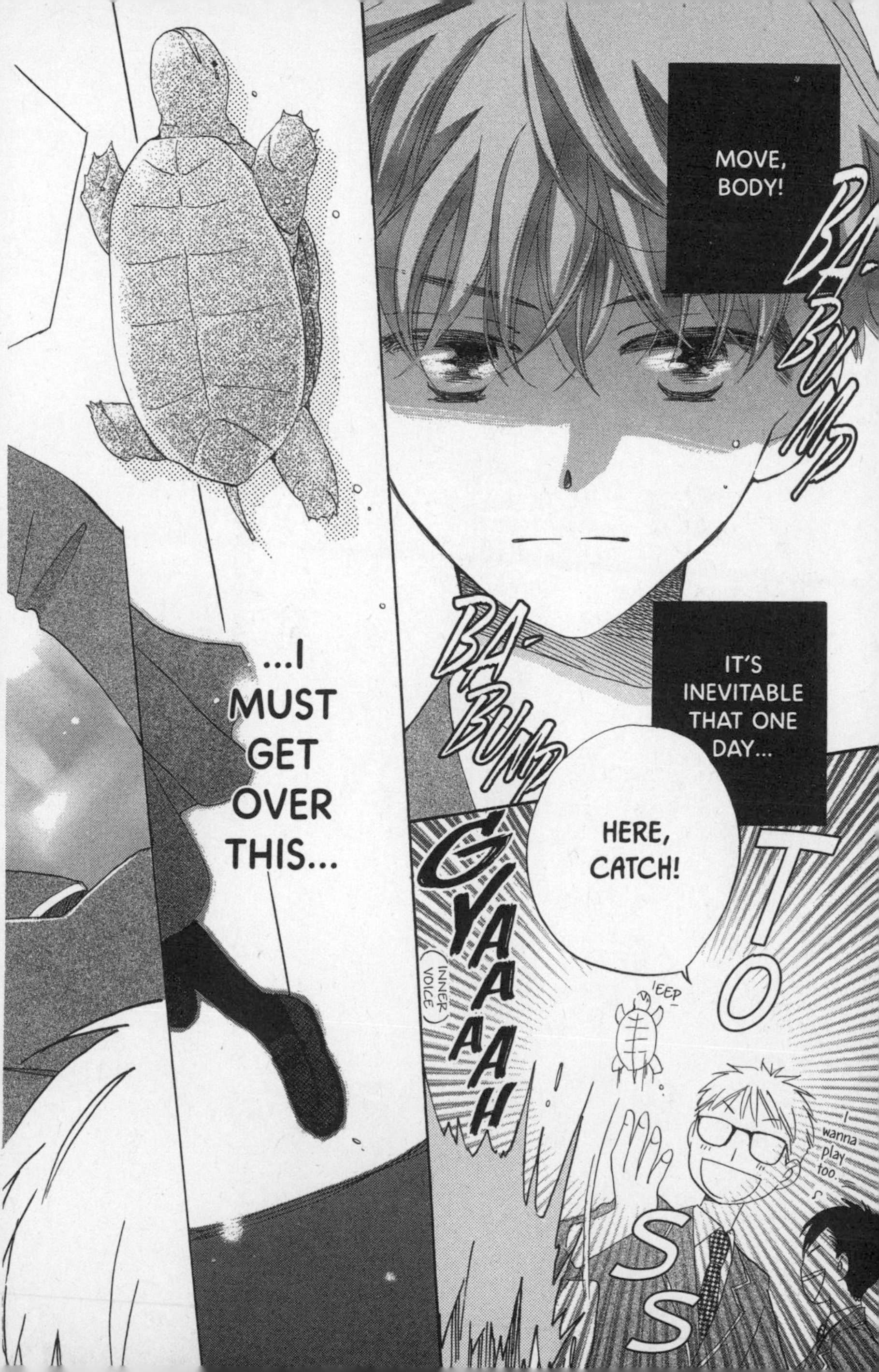
MOVE, BODY!
BA-BUMP
BA-BUMP
IT'S INEVITABLE THAT ONE DAY...
HERE, CATCH!
TOSS
GYAAAAH (INNER VOICE)
EEP
I wanna play too.
...I MUST GET OVER THIS...

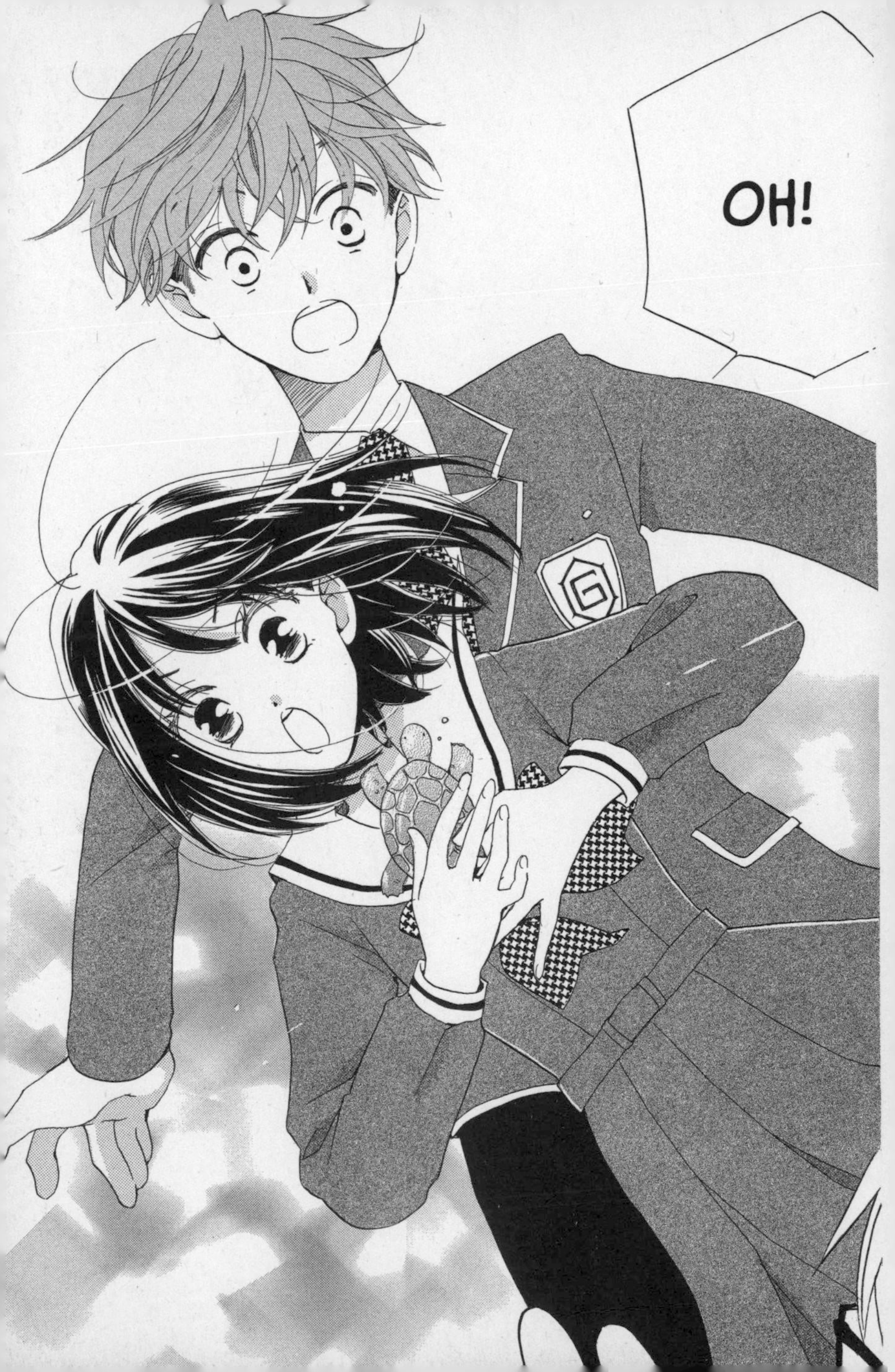
OH!

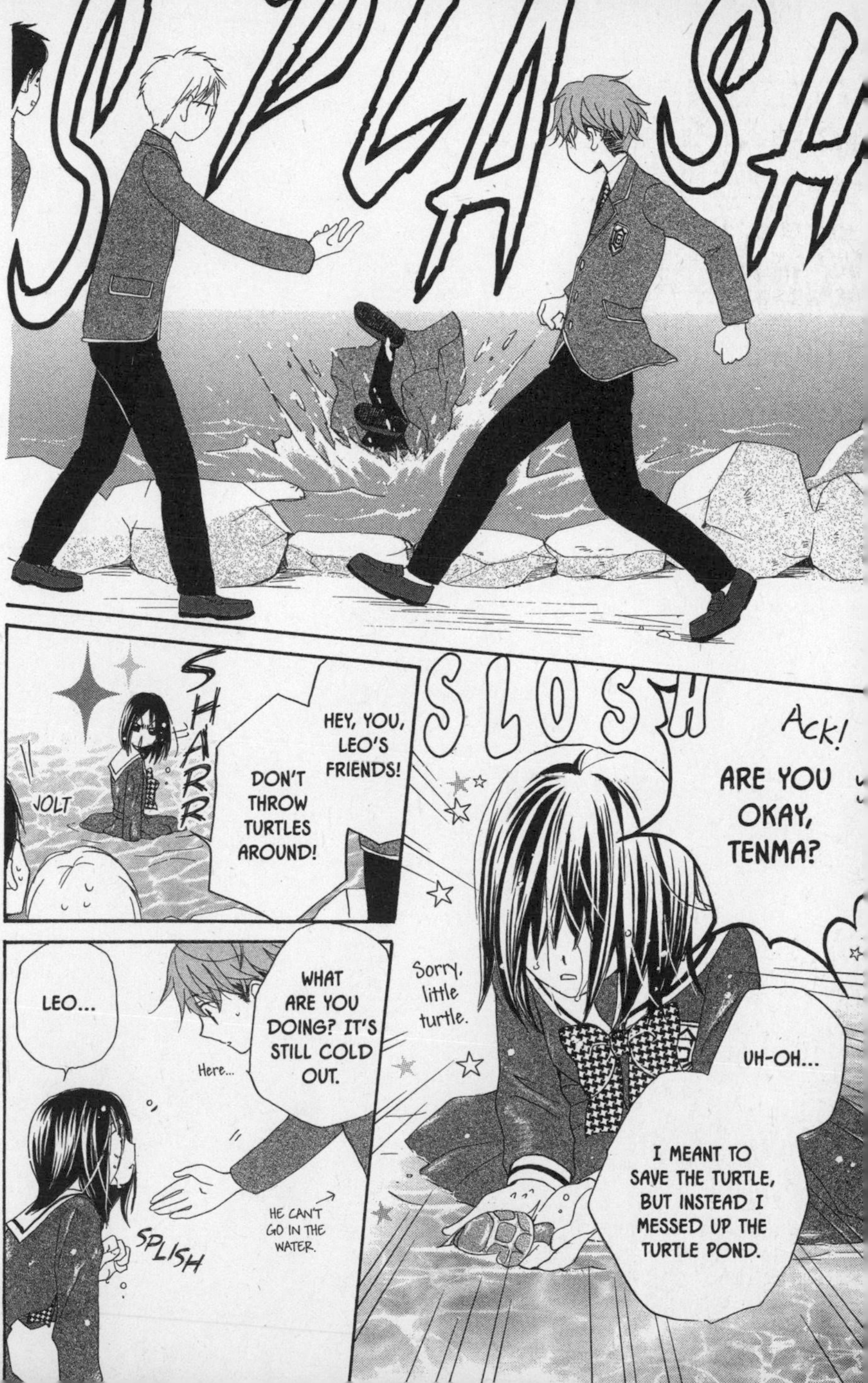
SPLASH
SLOSH
Ack!
ARE YOU OKAY, TENMA?
UH-OH...
Sorry, little turtle.
I MEANT TO SAVE THE TURTLE, BUT INSTEAD I MESSED UP THE TURTLE POND.
SHARR
HEY, YOU, LEO'S FRIENDS!
DON'T THROW TURTLES AROUND!
JOLT
WHAT ARE YOU DOING? IT'S STILL COLD OUT.
Here...
LEO...
HE CAN'T GO IN THE WATER.
SPLISH

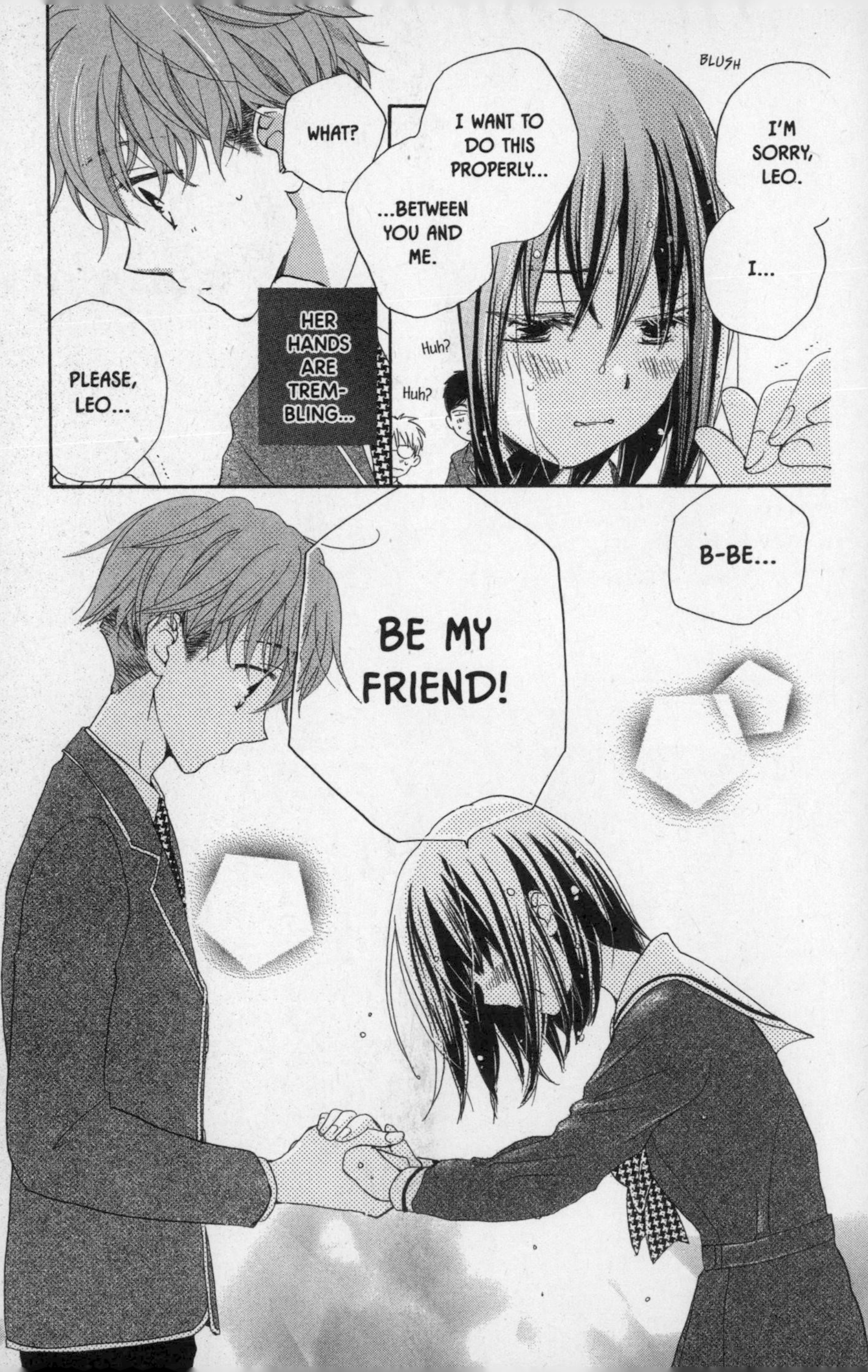
BLUSH
I'M SORRY, LEO.
I...
I WANT TO DO THIS PROPERLY...
...BETWEEN YOU AND ME.
WHAT?
Huh?
Huh?
HER HANDS ARE TREM-BLING...
PLEASE, LEO...
B-BE...
BE MY FRIEND!

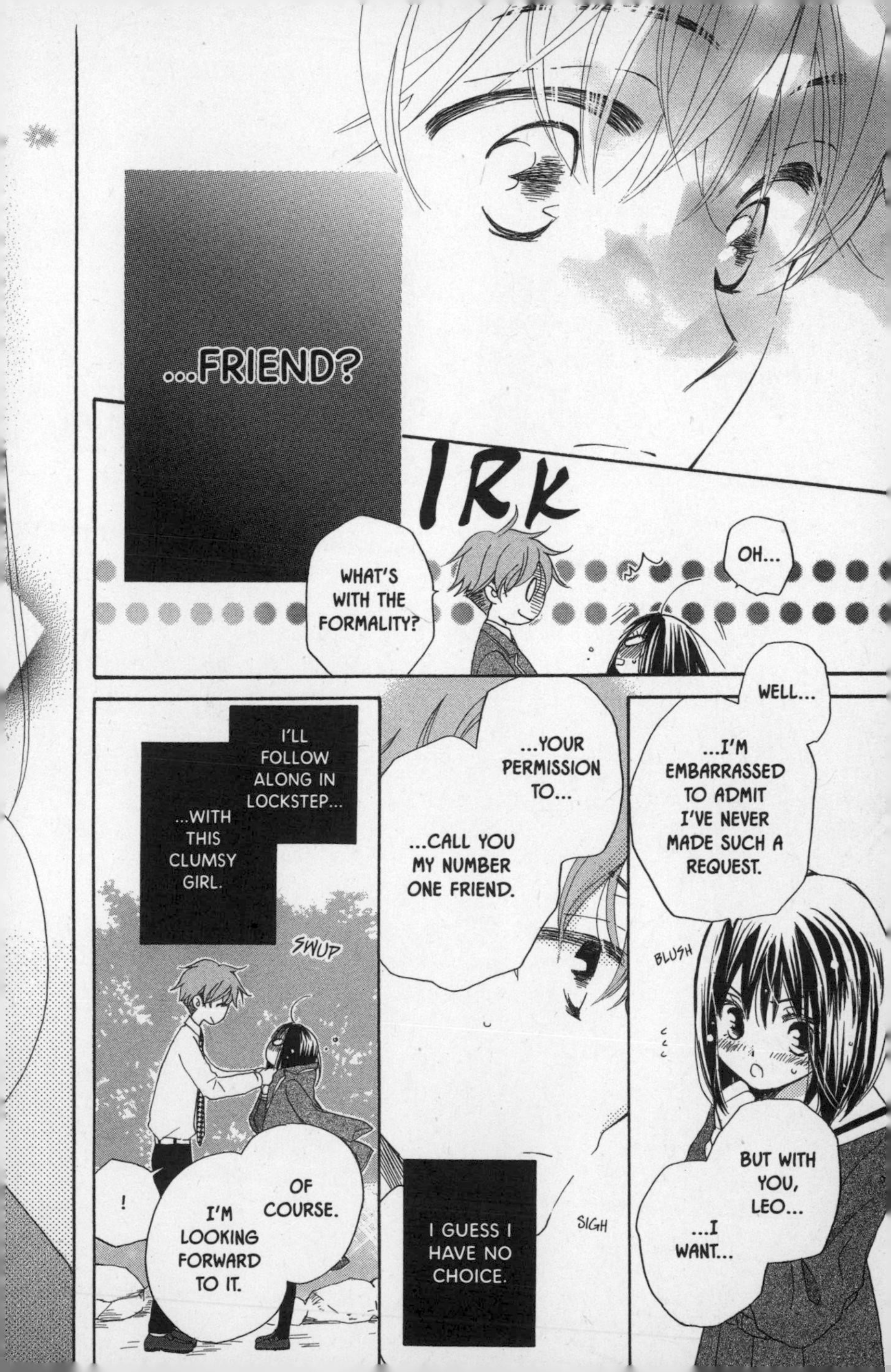
...FRIEND?
OH...
IRK
WHAT'S WITH THE FORMALITY?
WELL...
...I'M EMBARRASSED TO ADMIT I'VE NEVER MADE SUCH A REQUEST.
BLUSH
BUT WITH YOU, LEO...
...I WANT...
...YOUR PERMISSION TO...
...CALL YOU MY NUMBER ONE FRIEND.
SIGH
I GUESS I HAVE NO CHOICE.
I'LL FOLLOW ALONG IN LOCKSTEP...
...WITH THIS CLUMSY GIRL.
SWUP
OF COURSE.
I'M LOOKING FORWARD TO IT.
!

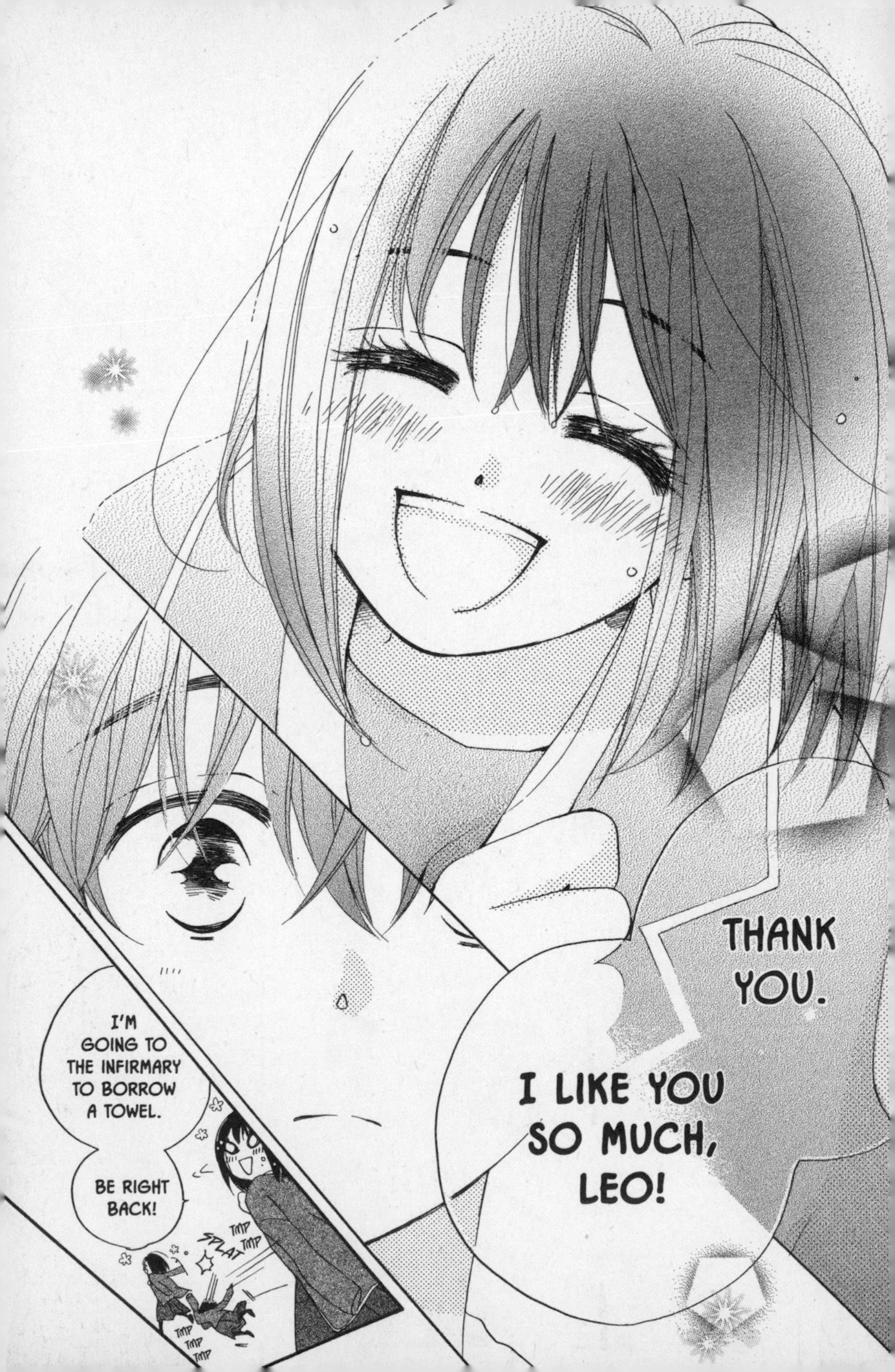
THANK YOU.
I LIKE YOU SO MUCH, LEO!
I'M GOING TO THE INFIRMARY TO BORROW A TOWEL.
BE RIGHT BACK!
TMP TMP
SPLAT
TMP TMP TMP

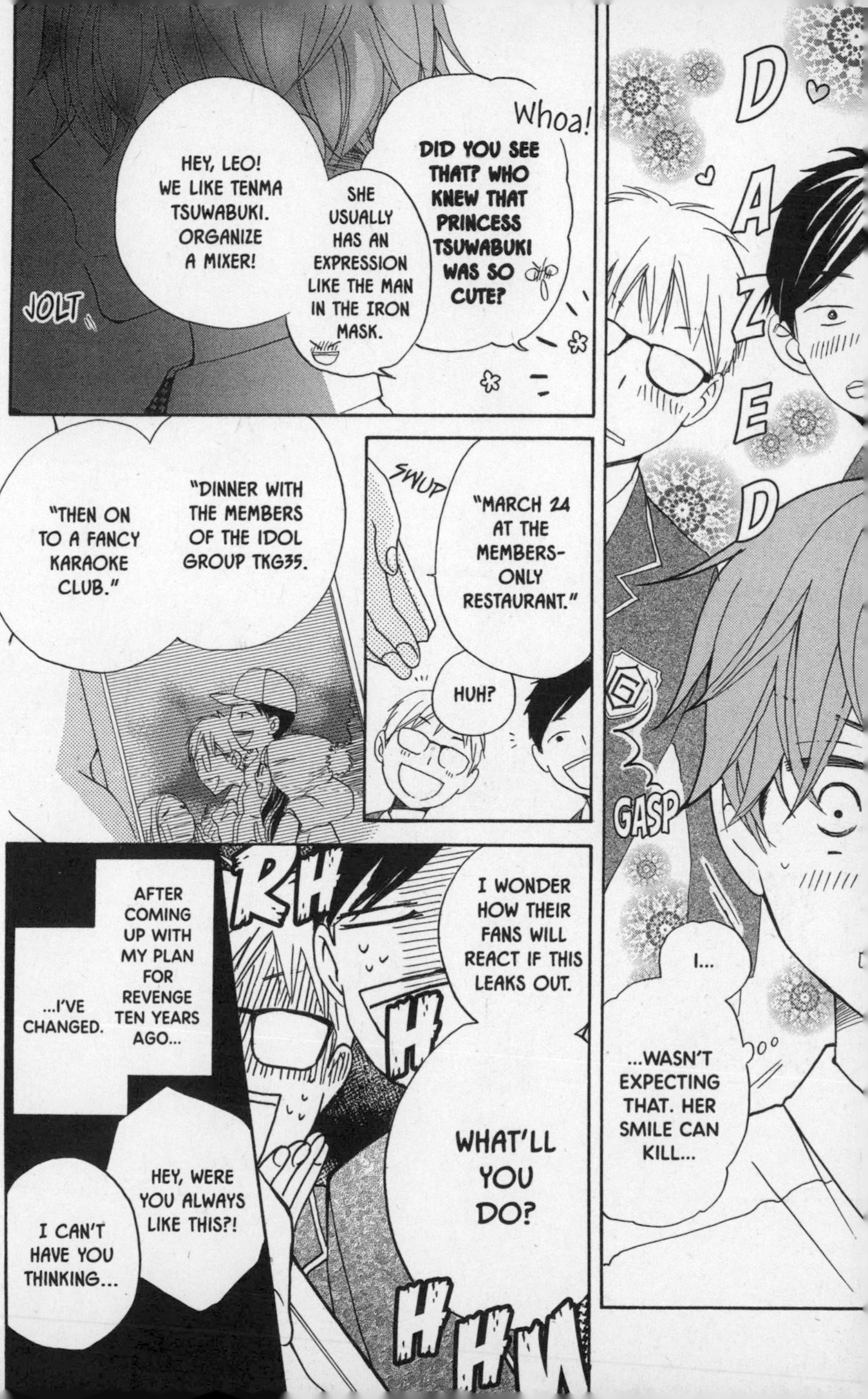
D
A
Z
E
D
GASP
I...
...WASN'T EXPECTING THAT. HER SMILE CAN KILL...
Whoa!
DID YOU SEE THAT? WHO KNEW THAT PRINCESS TSUWABUKI WAS SO CUTE?
SHE USUALLY HAS AN EXPRESSION LIKE THE MAN IN THE IRON MASK.
HEY, LEO! WE LIKE TENMA TSUWABUKI. ORGANIZE A MIXER!
JOLT
SWUP
"MARCH 24 AT THE MEMBERS-ONLY RESTAURANT."
HUH?
"DINNER WITH THE MEMBERS OF THE IDOL GROUP TKG35.
"THEN ON TO A FANCY KARAOKE CLUB."
I WONDER HOW THEIR FANS WILL REACT IF THIS LEAKS OUT.
WHAT'LL YOU DO?
RH
H
HHW
AFTER COMING UP WITH MY PLAN FOR REVENGE TEN YEARS AGO...
...I'VE CHANGED.
HEY, WERE YOU ALWAYS LIKE THIS?!
I CAN'T HAVE YOU THINKING...

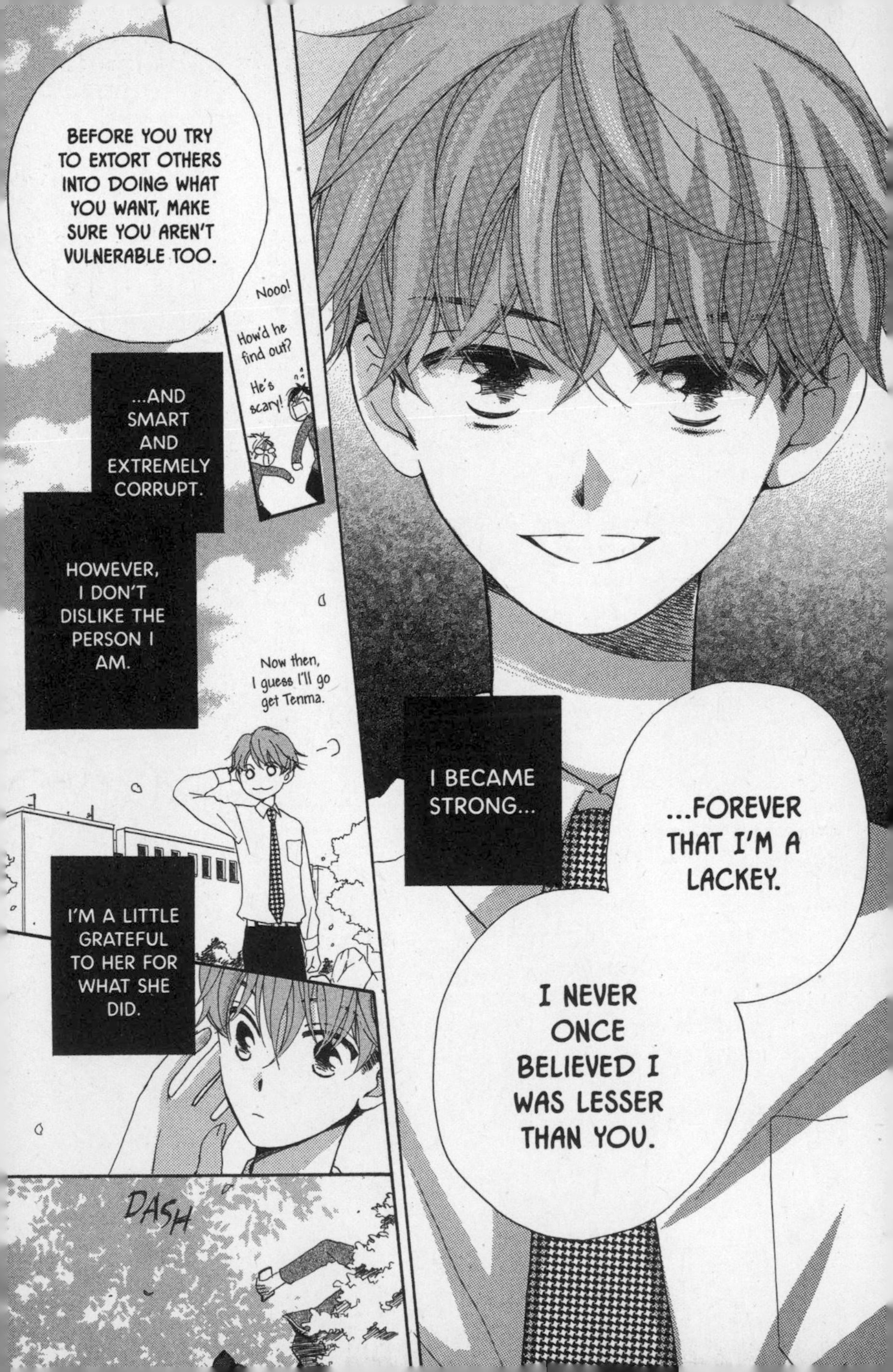
...FOREVER THAT I'M A LACKEY.
I BECAME STRONG...
I NEVER ONCE BELIEVED I WAS LESSER THAN YOU.
BEFORE YOU TRY TO EXTORT OTHERS INTO DOING WHAT YOU WANT, MAKE SURE YOU AREN'T VULNERABLE TOO.
Nooo!
How'd he find out?
He's scary!
...AND SMART AND EXTREMELY CORRUPT.
HOWEVER, I DON'T DISLIKE THE PERSON I AM.
Now then, I guess I'll go get Tenma.
I'M A LITTLE GRATEFUL TO HER FOR WHAT SHE DID.
DASH

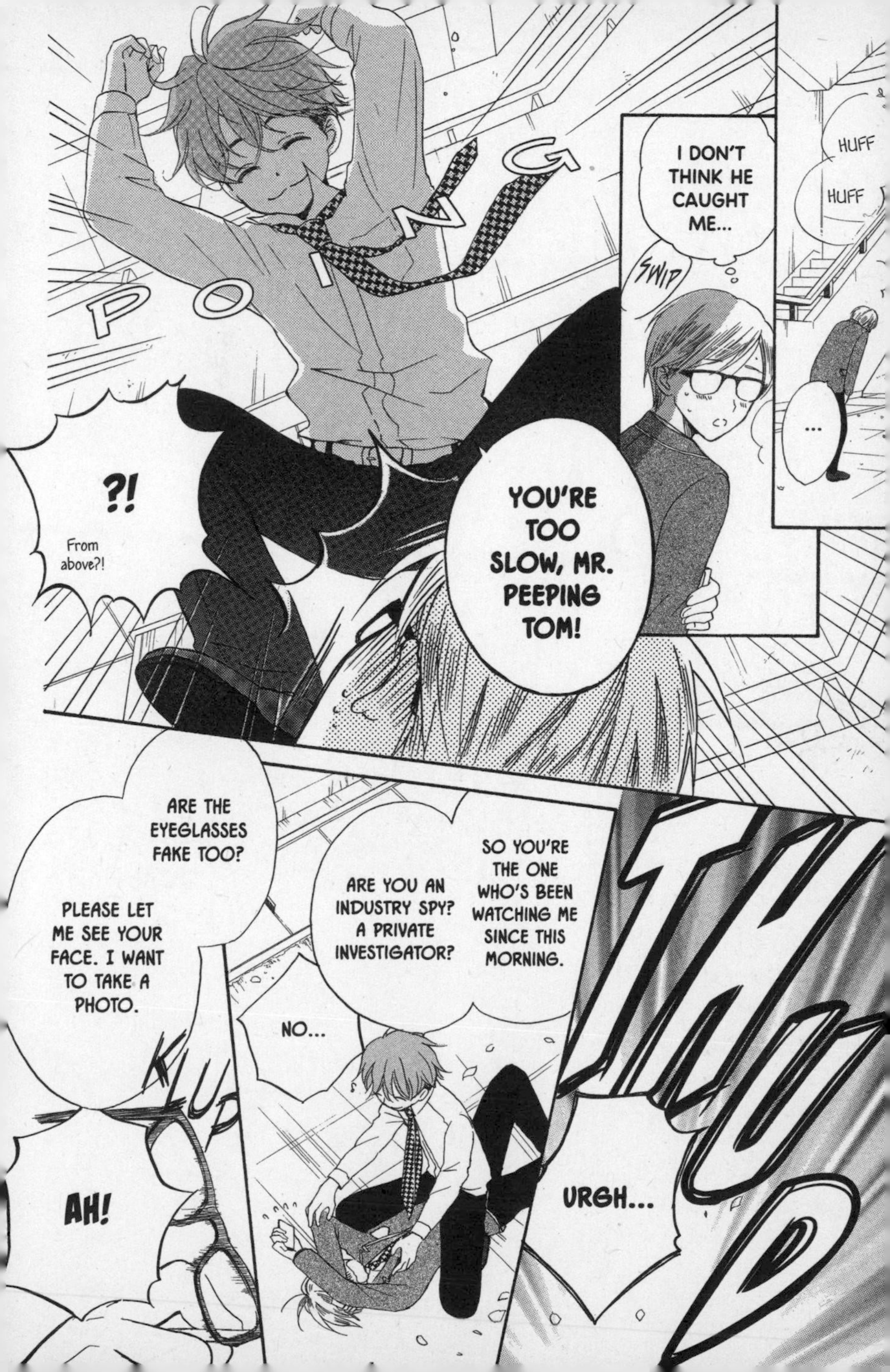
HUFF
HUFF
...
I DON'T THINK HE CAUGHT ME...
SWIP
POING
YOU'RE TOO SLOW, MR. PEEPING TOM!
?!
From above?!
URGH...
SO YOU'RE THE ONE WHO'S BEEN WATCHING ME SINCE THIS MORNING.
ARE YOU AN INDUSTRY SPY? A PRIVATE INVESTIGATOR?
NO...
ARE THE EYEGLASSES FAKE TOO?
PLEASE LET ME SEE YOUR FACE. I WANT TO TAKE A PHOTO.
KLUD
AH!

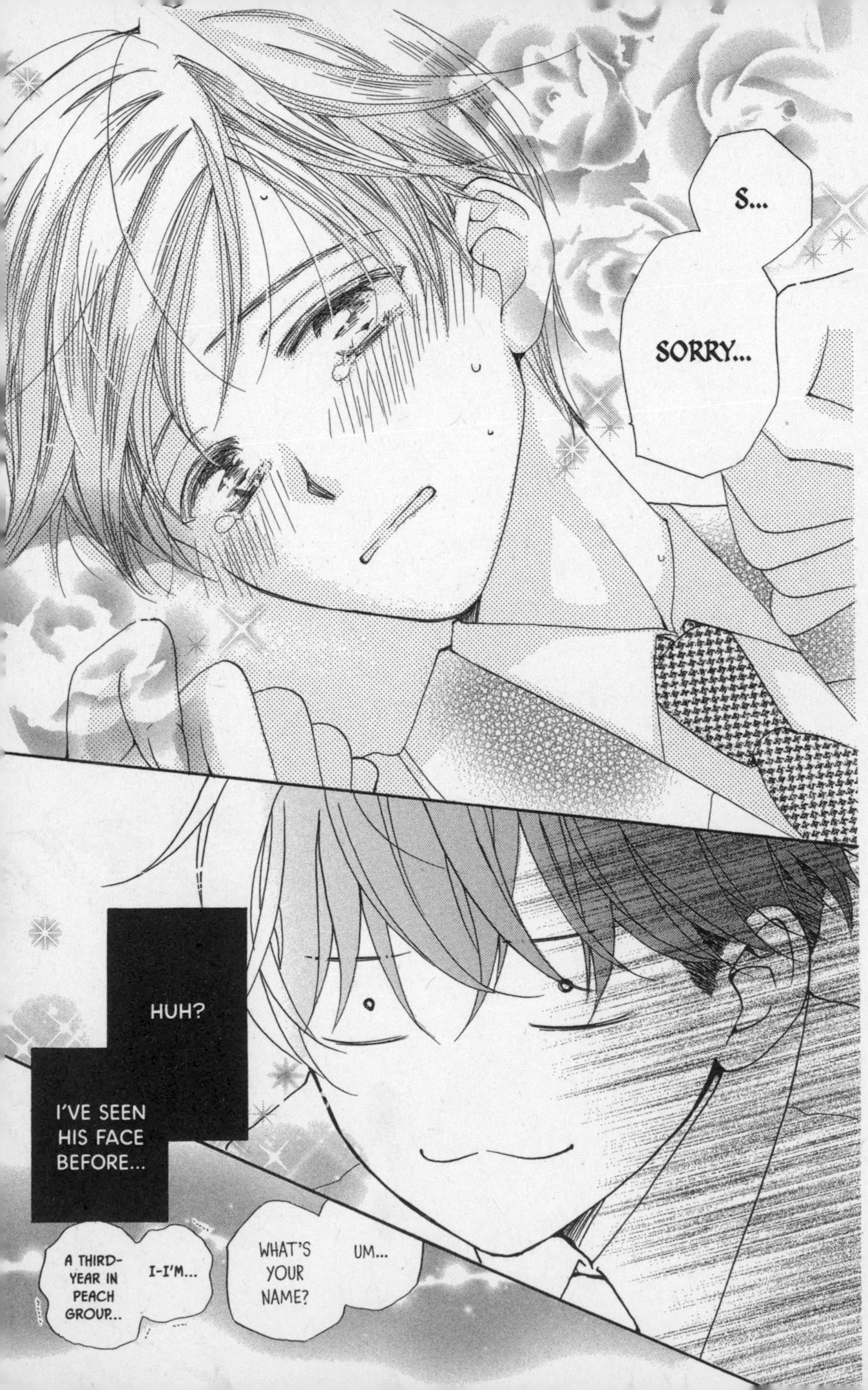
S...
SORRY...
HUH?
I'VE SEEN HIS FACE BEFORE...
UM...
WHAT'S YOUR NAME?
I-I'M...
A THIRD-YEAR IN PEACH GROUP...

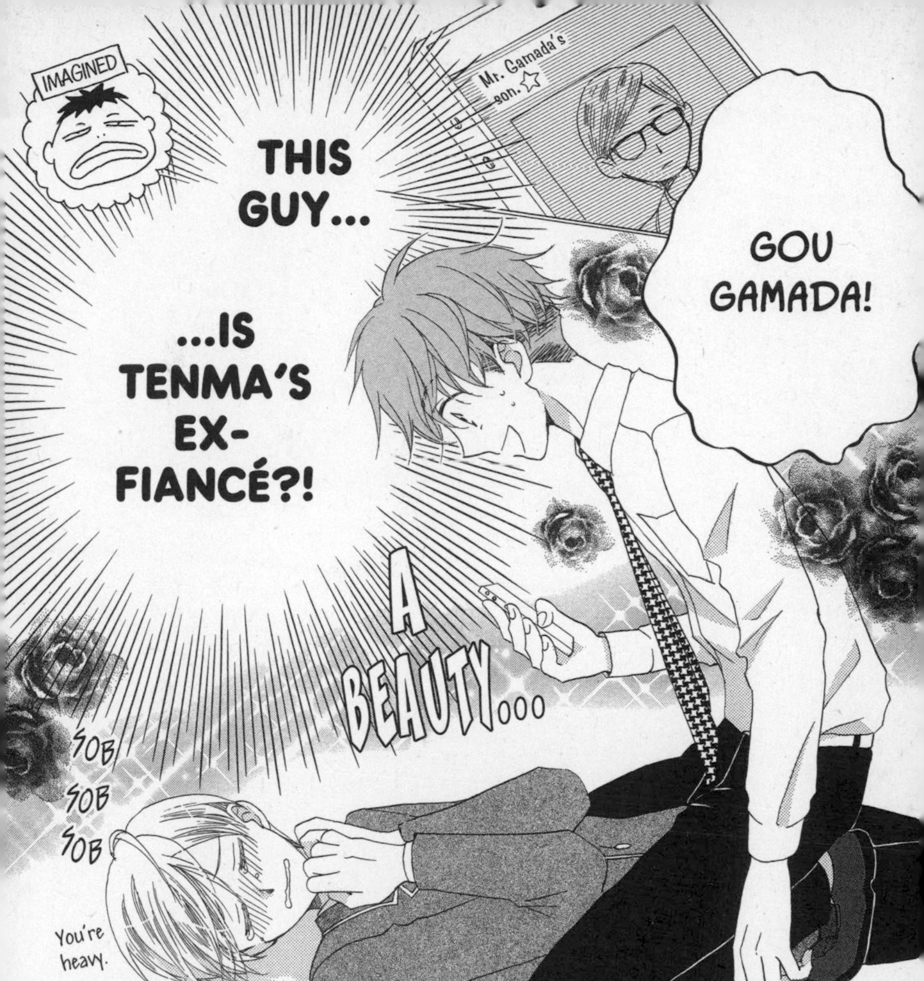
GOU GAMADA!
Mr. Gamada's son.☆
THIS GUY...
IMAGINED
...IS TENMA'S EX-FIANCÉ?!
A BEAUTY...
SOB SOB SOB
You're heavy.

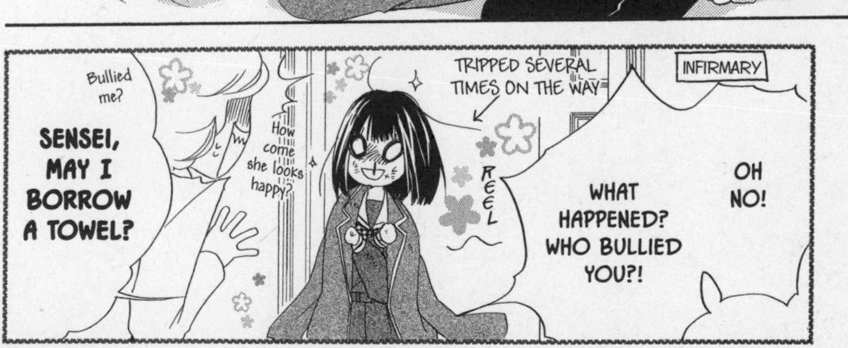
INFIRMARY
OH NO!
WHAT HAPPENED? WHO BULLIED YOU?!
TRIPPED SEVERAL TIMES ON THE WAY
REEL
How come she looks happy?
Bullied me?
SENSEI, MAY I BORROW A TOWEL?

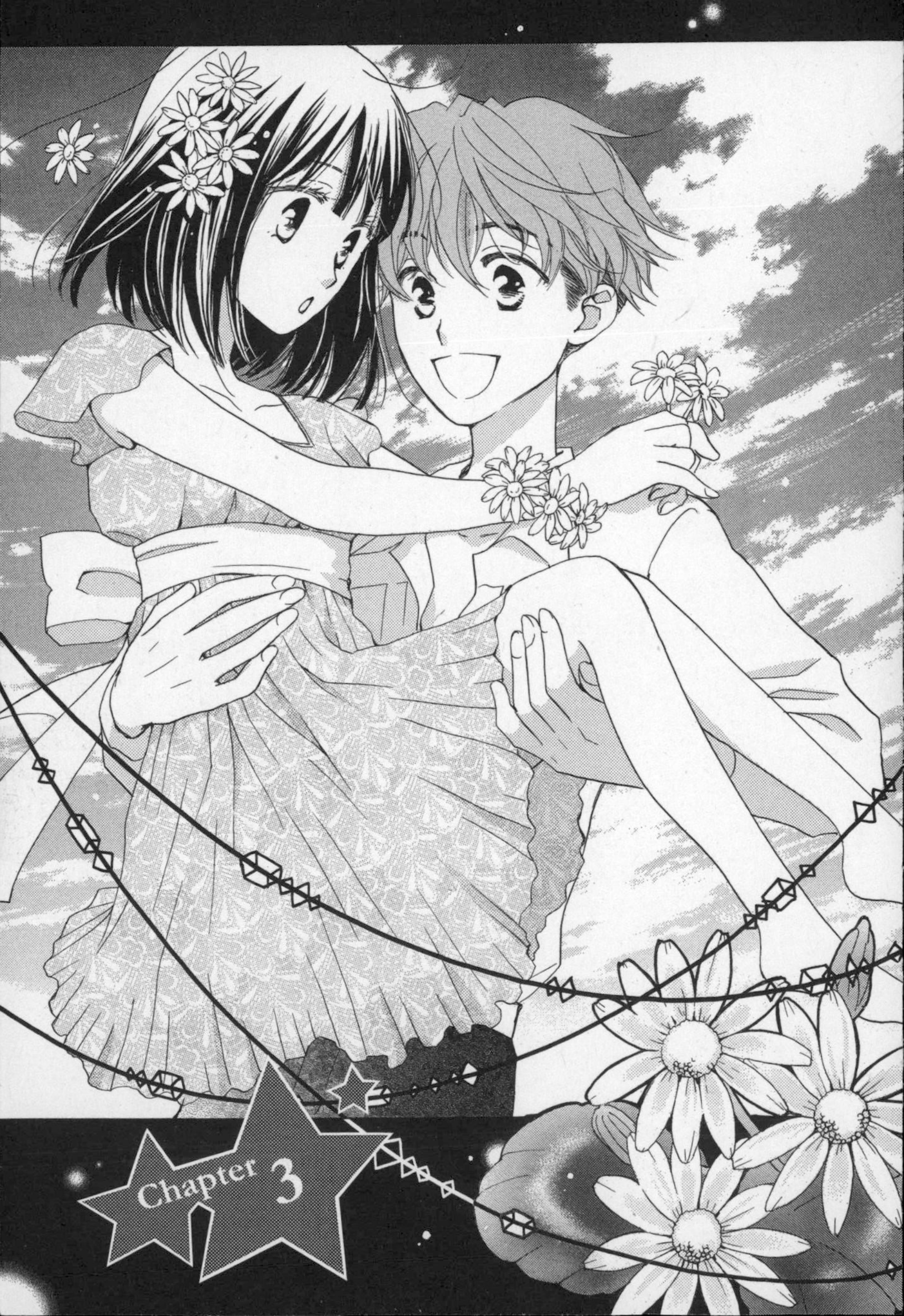
Chapter 3

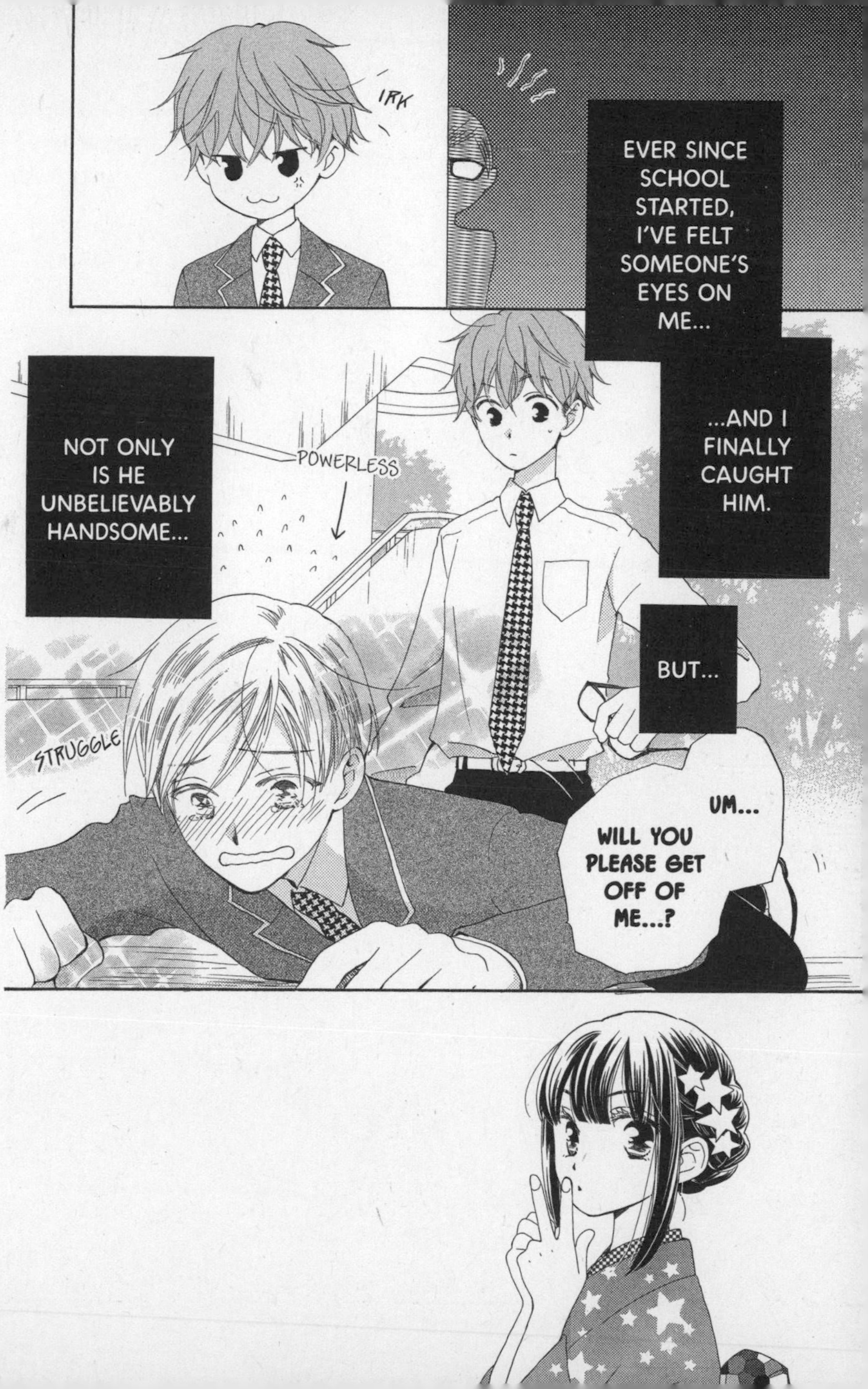
EVER SINCE SCHOOL STARTED, I'VE FELT SOMEONE'S EYES ON ME...
IRK
...AND I FINALLY CAUGHT HIM.
NOT ONLY IS HE UNBELIEVABLY HANDSOME...
POWERLESS
BUT...
UM...
WILL YOU PLEASE GET OFF OF ME...?
STRUGGLE

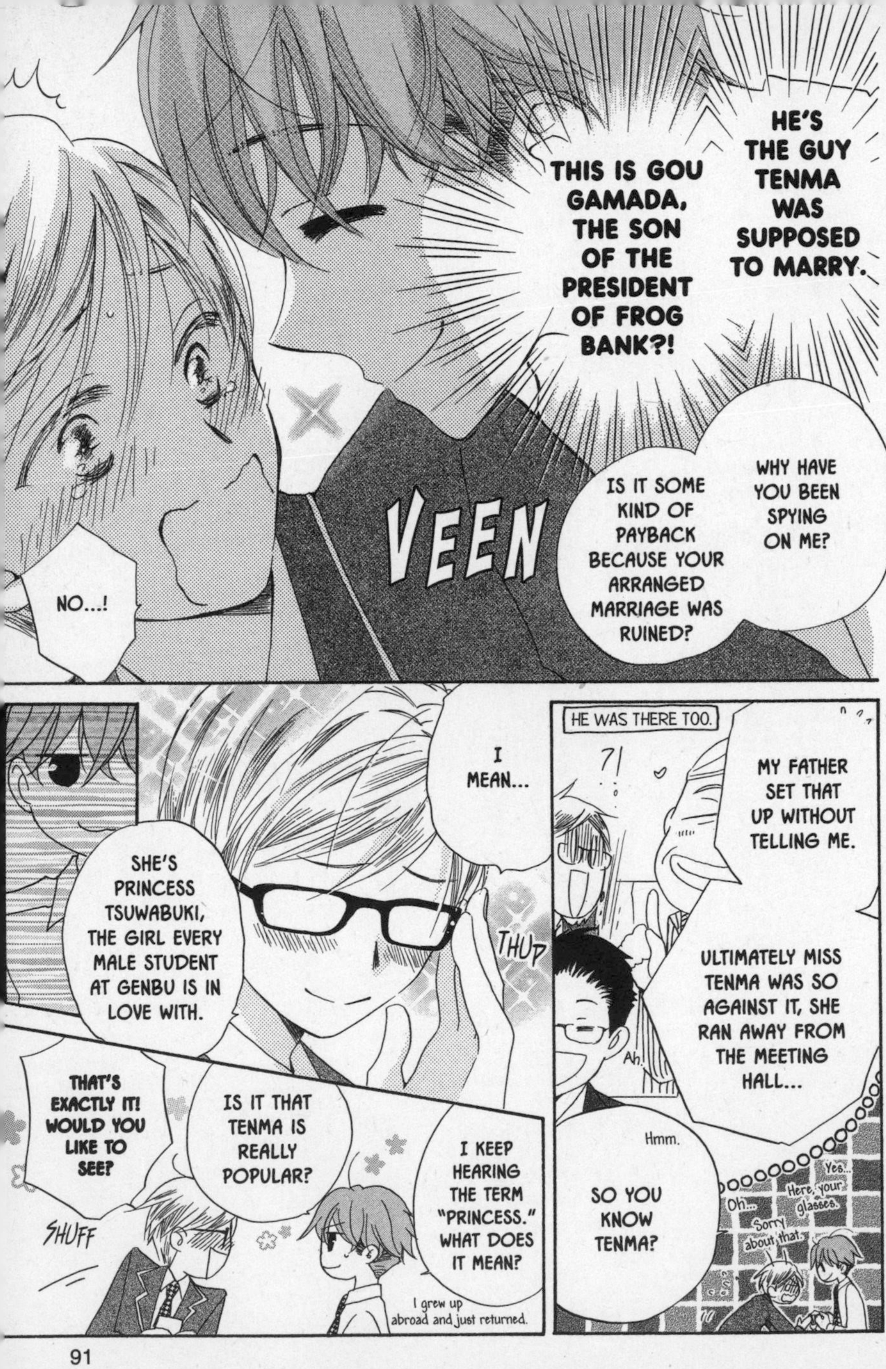
HE'S THE GUY TENMA WAS SUPPOSED TO MARRY.
THIS IS GOU GAMADA, THE SON OF THE PRESIDENT OF FROG BANK?!
WHY HAVE YOU BEEN SPYING ON ME?
IS IT SOME KIND OF PAYBACK BECAUSE YOUR ARRANGED MARRIAGE WAS RUINED?
VEEN
NO...!
HE WAS THERE TOO.
MY FATHER SET THAT UP WITHOUT TELLING ME.
?!
ULTIMATELY MISS TENMA WAS SO AGAINST IT, SHE RAN AWAY FROM THE MEETING HALL...
Ah.
Hmm.
SO YOU KNOW TENMA?
Yes...
Here, your glasses.
Oh...
Sorry about that.
I MEAN...
SHE'S PRINCESS TSUWABUKI, THE GIRL EVERY MALE STUDENT AT GENBU IS IN LOVE WITH.
THUP
I KEEP HEARING THE TERM "PRINCESS." WHAT DOES IT MEAN?
I grew up abroad and just returned.
IS IT THAT TENMA IS REALLY POPULAR?
THAT'S EXACTLY IT! WOULD YOU LIKE TO SEE?
SHUFF

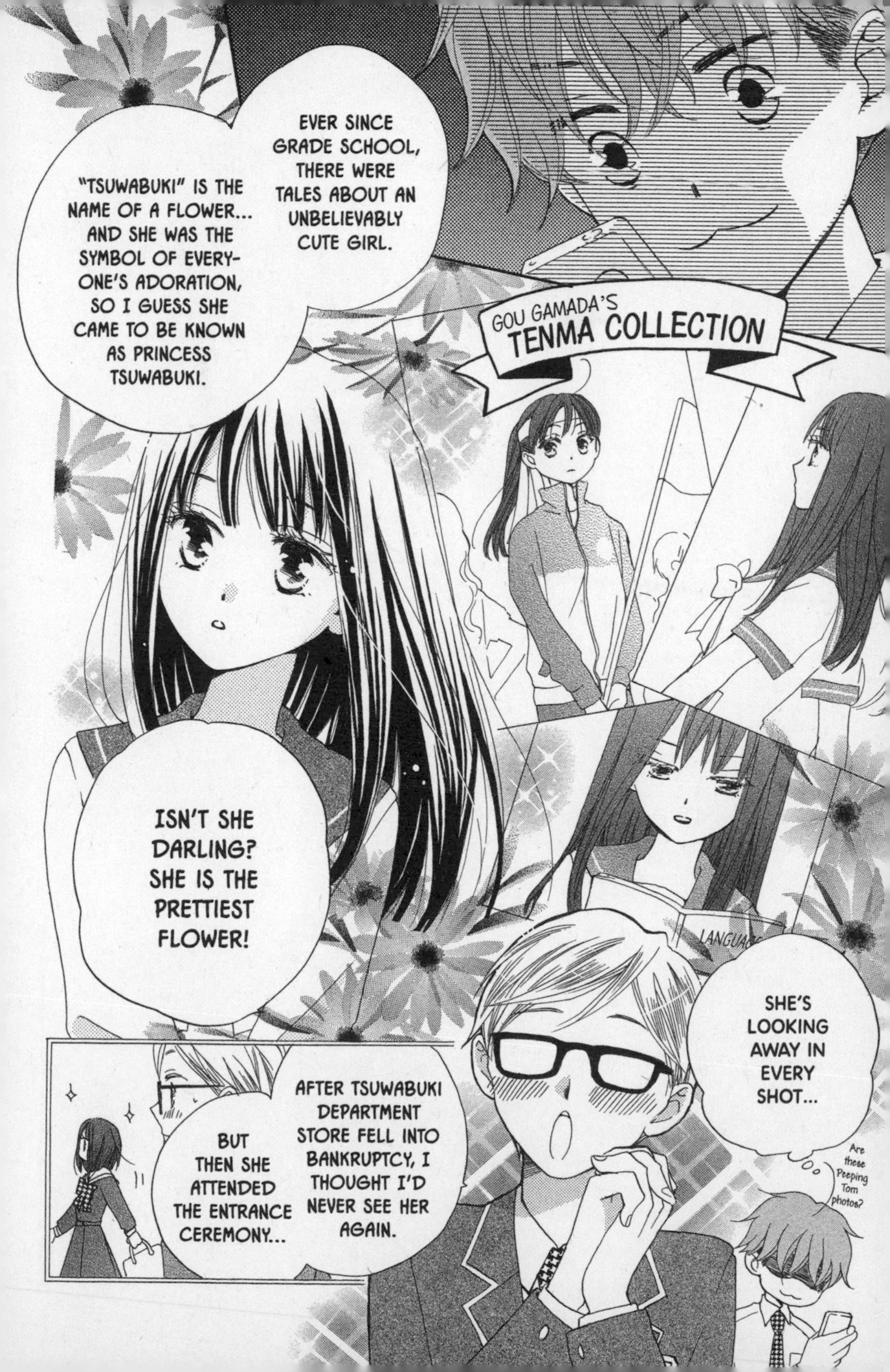
EVER SINCE GRADE SCHOOL, THERE WERE TALES ABOUT AN UNBELIEVABLY CUTE GIRL.
"TSUWABUKI" IS THE NAME OF A FLOWER... AND SHE WAS THE SYMBOL OF EVERY-ONE'S ADORATION, SO I GUESS SHE CAME TO BE KNOWN AS PRINCESS TSUWABUKI.
GOU GAMADA'S TENMA COLLECTION
ISN'T SHE DARLING? SHE IS THE PRETTIEST FLOWER!
SHE'S LOOKING AWAY IN EVERY SHOT...
Are these Peeping Tom photos?
AFTER TSUWABUKI DEPARTMENT STORE FELL INTO BANKRUPTCY, I THOUGHT I'D NEVER SEE HER AGAIN.
BUT THEN SHE ATTENDED THE ENTRANCE CEREMONY...

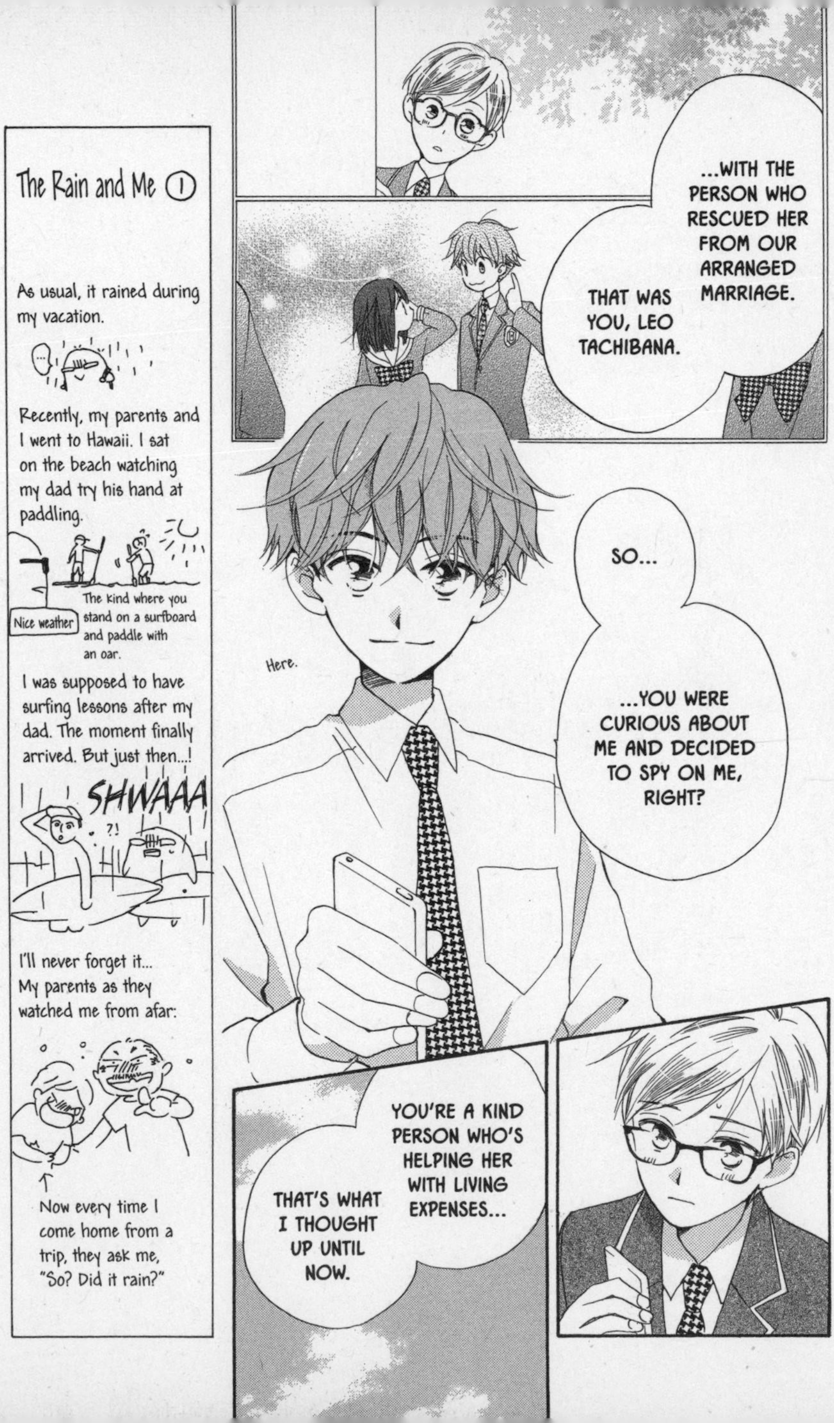
...WITH THE PERSON WHO RESCUED HER FROM OUR ARRANGED MARRIAGE.
THAT WAS YOU, LEO TACHIBANA.
SO...
...YOU WERE CURIOUS ABOUT ME AND DECIDED TO SPY ON ME, RIGHT?
Here.
YOU'RE A KIND PERSON WHO'S HELPING HER WITH LIVING EXPENSES...
THAT'S WHAT I THOUGHT UP UNTIL NOW.

The Rain and Me ①

As usual, it rained during my vacation.

Recently, my parents and I went to Hawaii. I sat on the beach watching my dad try his hand at paddling.

Nice weather

The kind where you stand on a surfboard and paddle with an oar.

I was supposed to have surfing lessons after my dad. The moment finally arrived. But just then...!

SHWAAA

?!

I'll never forget it... My parents as they watched me from afar:

Now every time I come home from a trip, they ask me, "So? Did it rain?"

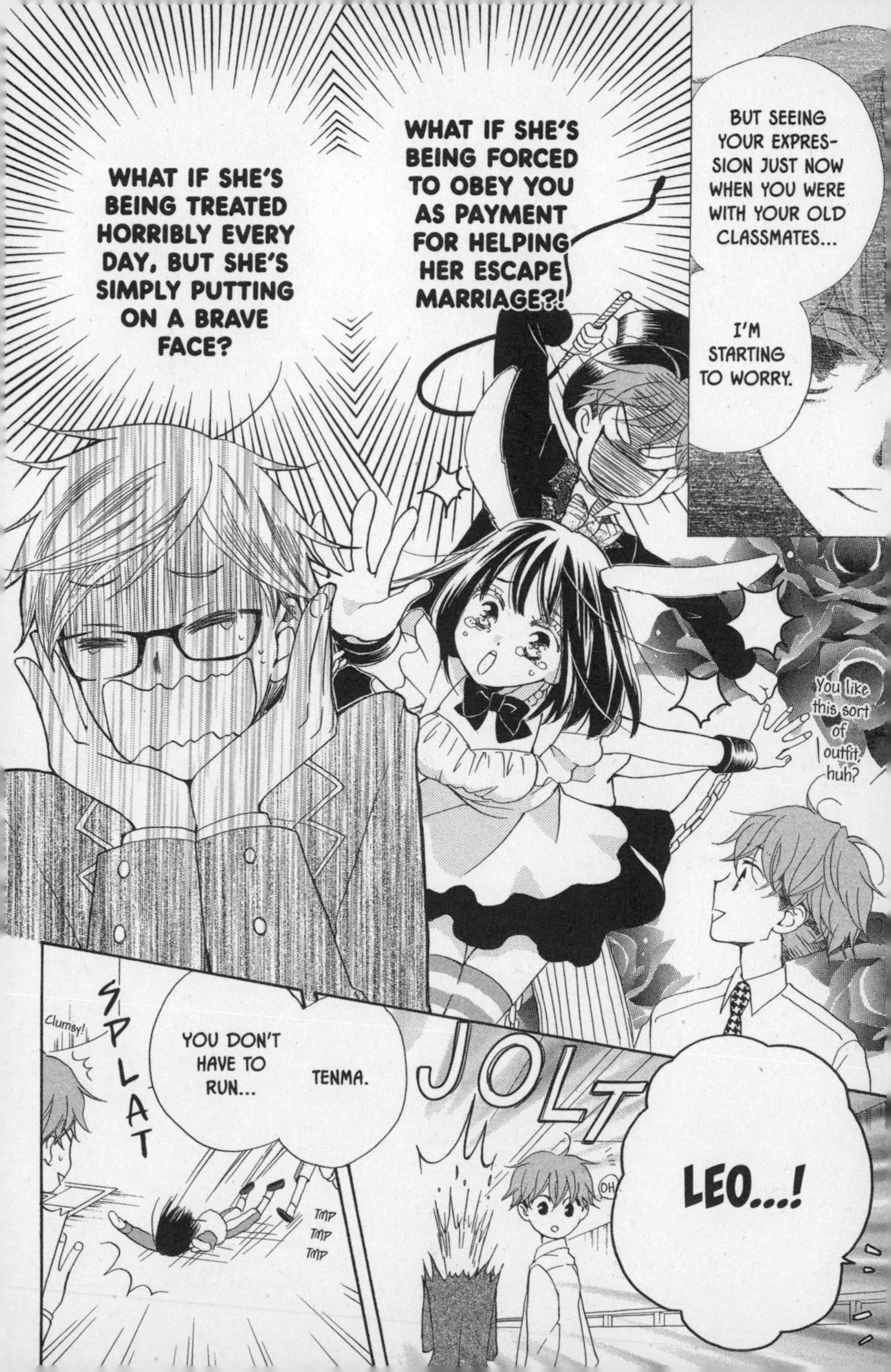
BUT SEEING YOUR EXPRESSION JUST NOW WHEN YOU WERE WITH YOUR OLD CLASSMATES...
I'M STARTING TO WORRY.
WHAT IF SHE'S BEING FORCED TO OBEY YOU AS PAYMENT FOR HELPING HER ESCAPE MARRIAGE?!
WHAT IF SHE'S BEING TREATED HORRIBLY EVERY DAY, BUT SHE'S SIMPLY PUTTING ON A BRAVE FACE?
You like this sort of outfit, huh?
LEO...!
OH
JOLT
TENMA.
YOU DON'T HAVE TO RUN...
SPLAT
Clumsy!
TMP TMP TMP

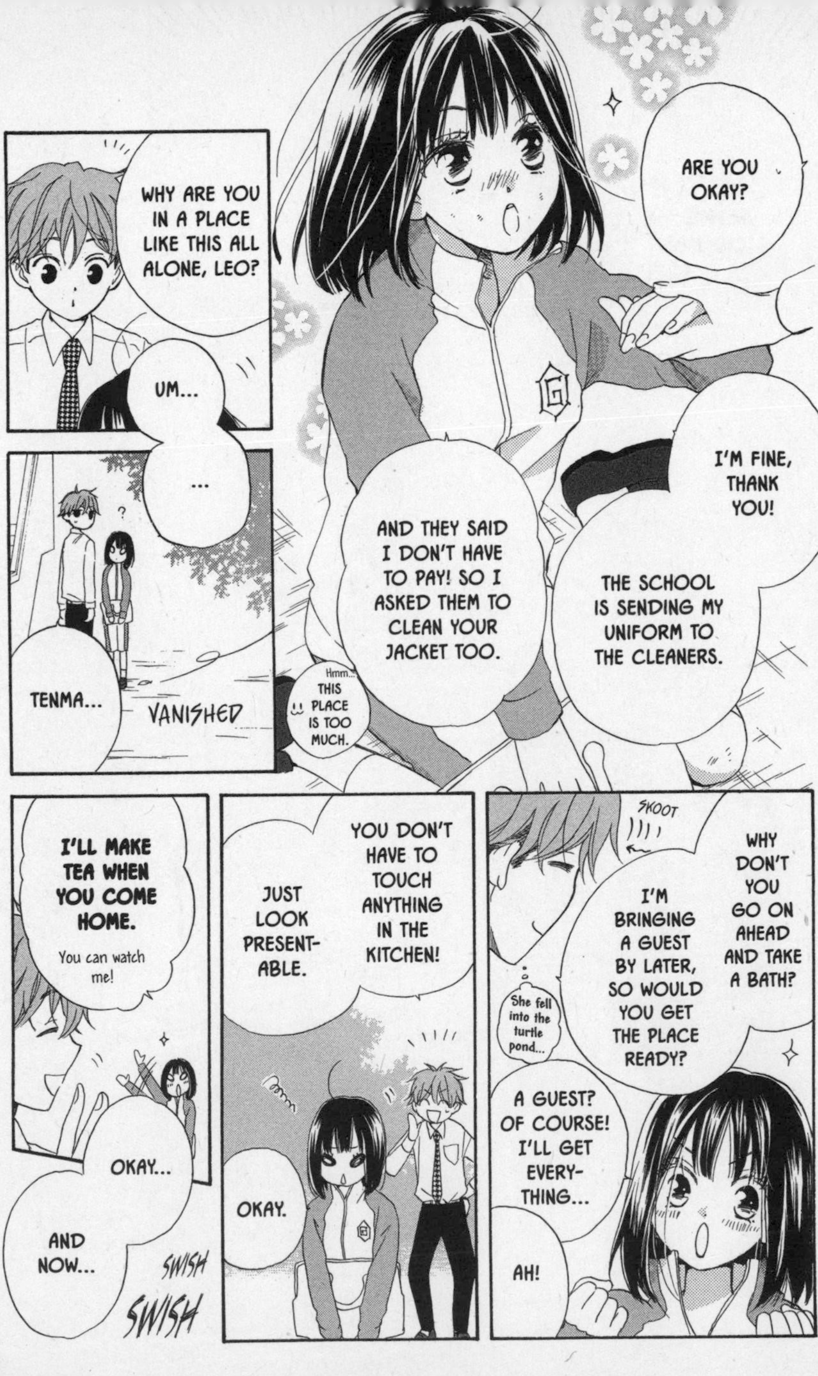
ARE YOU OKAY?
I'M FINE, THANK YOU!
THE SCHOOL IS SENDING MY UNIFORM TO THE CLEANERS.
AND THEY SAID I DON'T HAVE TO PAY! SO I ASKED THEM TO CLEAN YOUR JACKET TOO.
Hmm... THIS PLACE IS TOO MUCH.
WHY ARE YOU IN A PLACE LIKE THIS ALL ALONE, LEO?
UM...
...
TENMA...
VANISHED
SKOOT
WHY DON'T YOU GO ON AHEAD AND TAKE A BATH?
I'M BRINGING A GUEST BY LATER, SO WOULD YOU GET THE PLACE READY?
She fell into the turtle pond...
A GUEST? OF COURSE! I'LL GET EVERY-THING...
AH!
YOU DON'T HAVE TO TOUCH ANYTHING IN THE KITCHEN!
JUST LOOK PRESENT-ABLE.
OKAY.
I'LL MAKE TEA WHEN YOU COME HOME.
You can watch me!
OKAY...
AND NOW...
SWISH
SWISH

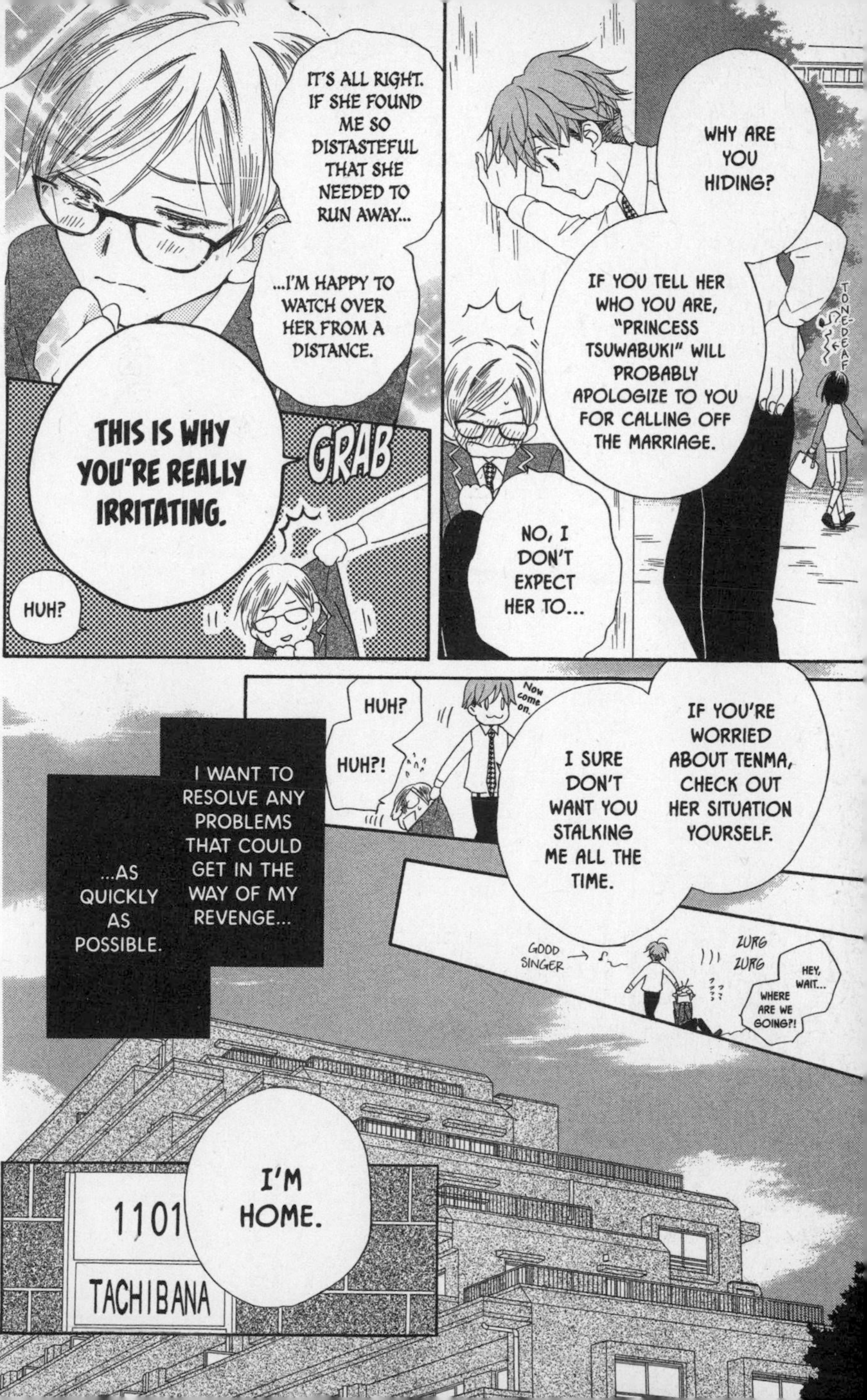
WHY ARE YOU HIDING?
TONE-DEAF
IF YOU TELL HER WHO YOU ARE, "PRINCESS TSUWABUKI" WILL PROBABLY APOLOGIZE TO YOU FOR CALLING OFF THE MARRIAGE.
NO, I DON'T EXPECT HER TO...
IT'S ALL RIGHT. IF SHE FOUND ME SO DISTASTEFUL THAT SHE NEEDED TO RUN AWAY...
...I'M HAPPY TO WATCH OVER HER FROM A DISTANCE.
GRAB
THIS IS WHY YOU'RE REALLY IRRITATING.
HUH?
IF YOU'RE WORRIED ABOUT TENMA, CHECK OUT HER SITUATION YOURSELF.
I SURE DON'T WANT YOU STALKING ME ALL THE TIME.
Now come on.
HUH?
HUH?!
ZURG
ZURG
HEY, WAIT... WHERE ARE WE GOING?!
GOOD SINGER
I WANT TO RESOLVE ANY PROBLEMS THAT COULD GET IN THE WAY OF MY REVENGE...
...AS QUICKLY AS POSSIBLE.
1101
TACHIBANA
I'M HOME.

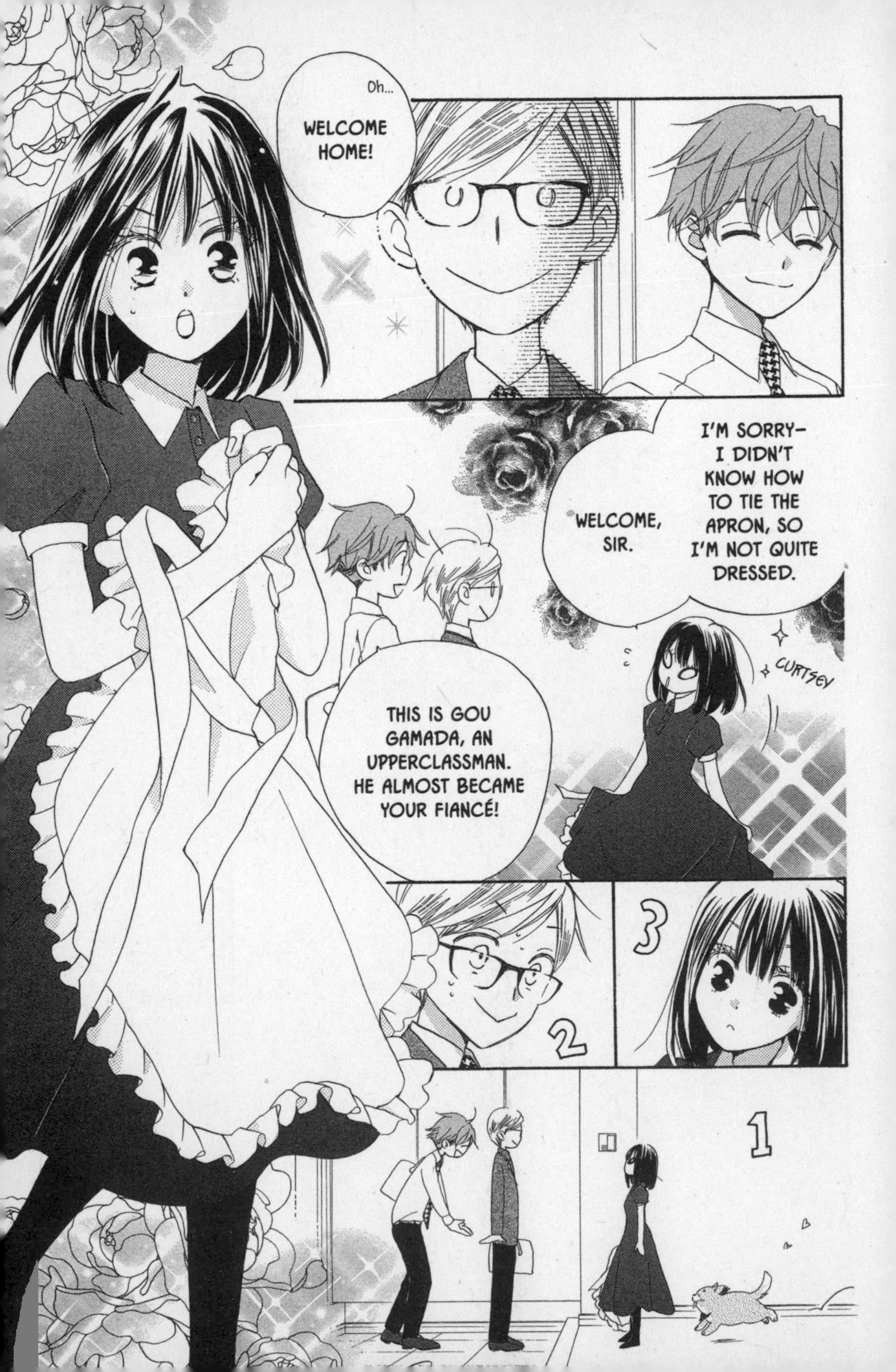
Oh...
WELCOME HOME!
I'M SORRY— I DIDN'T KNOW HOW TO TIE THE APRON, SO I'M NOT QUITE DRESSED.
WELCOME, SIR.
CURTSEY
THIS IS GOU GAMADA, AN UPPERCLASSMAN. HE ALMOST BECAME YOUR FIANCÉ!
3
2
1

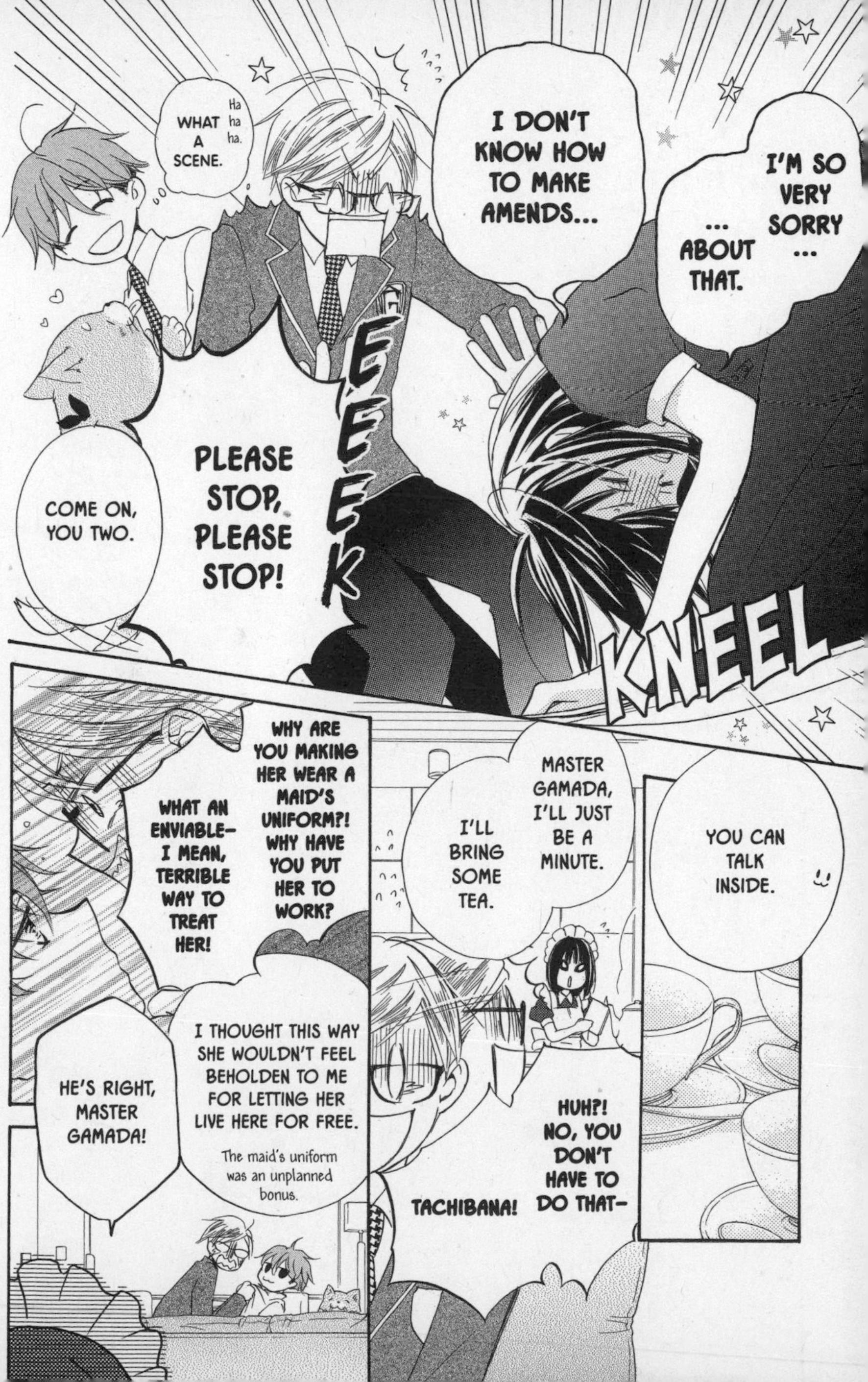
I'M SO VERY SORRY ... ... ABOUT THAT.
I DON'T KNOW HOW TO MAKE AMENDS...
KNEEL
EEEEK
Ha ha ha.
WHAT A SCENE.
PLEASE STOP, PLEASE STOP!
COME ON, YOU TWO.
YOU CAN TALK INSIDE.
MASTER GAMADA, I'LL JUST BE A MINUTE.
I'LL BRING SOME TEA.
HUH?! NO, YOU DON'T HAVE TO DO THAT-
TACHIBANA!
WHY ARE YOU MAKING HER WEAR A MAID'S UNIFORM?! WHY HAVE YOU PUT HER TO WORK?
WHAT AN ENVIABLE- I MEAN, TERRIBLE WAY TO TREAT HER!
I THOUGHT THIS WAY SHE WOULDN'T FEEL BEHOLDEN TO ME FOR LETTING HER LIVE HERE FOR FREE.
The maid's uniform was an unplanned bonus.
HE'S RIGHT, MASTER GAMADA!

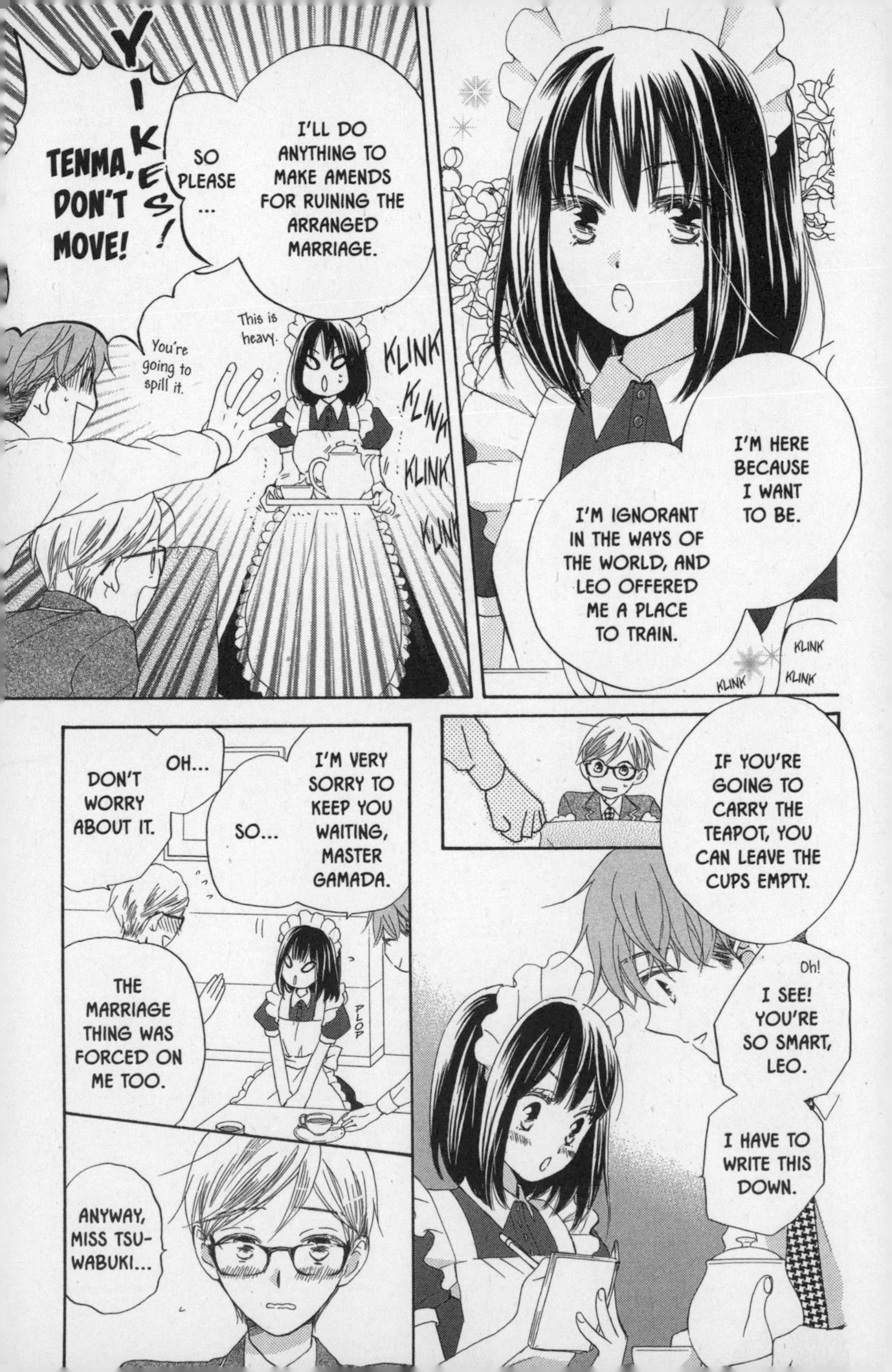

I'M HERE BECAUSE I WANT TO BE.
I'M IGNORANT IN THE WAYS OF THE WORLD, AND LEO OFFERED ME A PLACE TO TRAIN.
KLINK
KLINK
KLINK
I'LL DO ANYTHING TO MAKE AMENDS FOR RUINING THE ARRANGED MARRIAGE.
SO PLEASE ...
YIKES!
TENMA, DON'T MOVE!
KLINK
KLINK
KLINK
KLINK
This is heavy.
You're going to spill it.
IF YOU'RE GOING TO CARRY THE TEAPOT, YOU CAN LEAVE THE CUPS EMPTY.
Oh!
I SEE! YOU'RE SO SMART, LEO.
I HAVE TO WRITE THIS DOWN.
I'M VERY SORRY TO KEEP YOU WAITING, MASTER GAMADA.
SO...
OH...
DON'T WORRY ABOUT IT.
PLOP
THE MARRIAGE THING WAS FORCED ON ME TOO.
ANYWAY, MISS TSU-WABUKI...

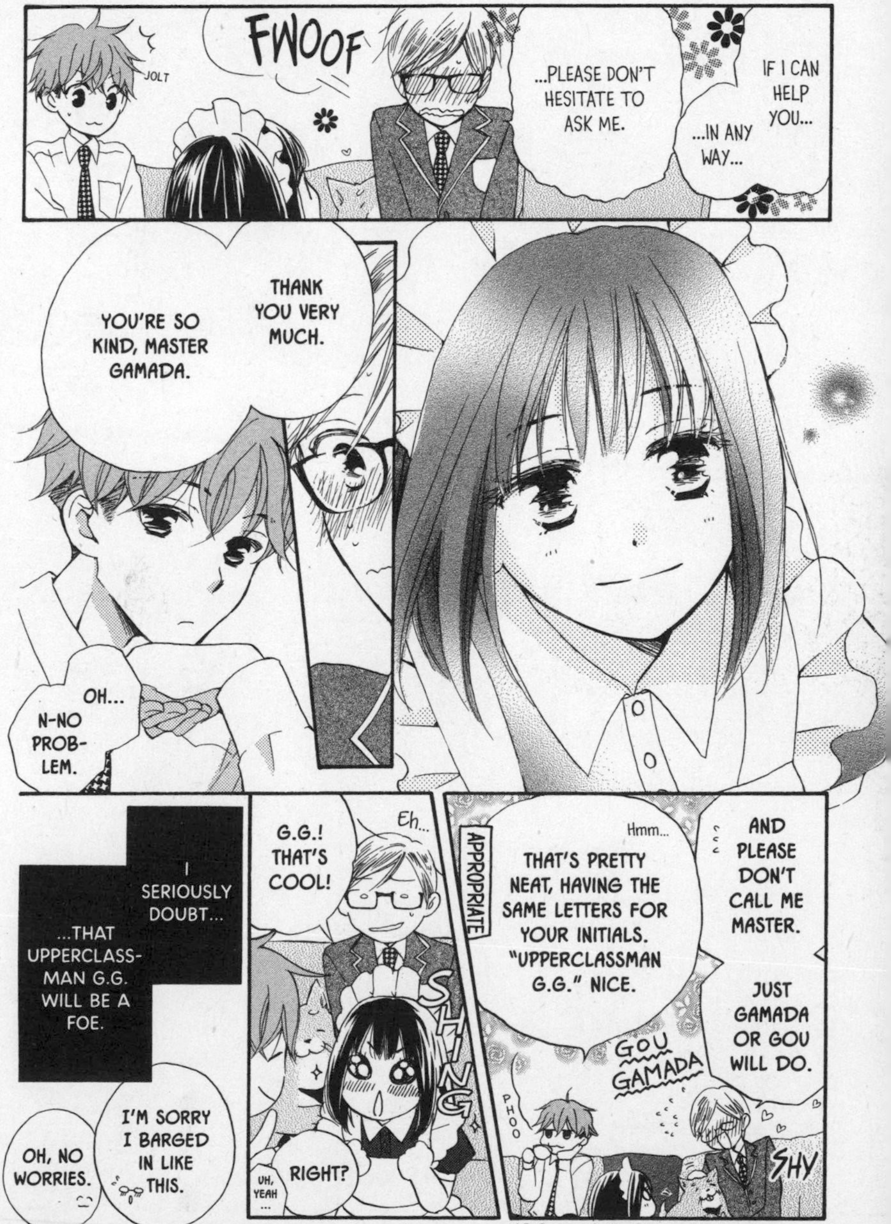
IF I CAN HELP YOU...
...IN ANY WAY...
...PLEASE DON'T HESITATE TO ASK ME.
FWOOF
JOLT
THANK YOU VERY MUCH.
YOU'RE SO KIND, MASTER GAMADA.
OH... N-NO PROB-LEM.
AND PLEASE DON'T CALL ME MASTER.
JUST GAMADA OR GOU WILL DO.
Hmm...
THAT'S PRETTY NEAT, HAVING THE SAME LETTERS FOR YOUR INITIALS. "UPPERCLASSMAN G.G." NICE.
APPROPRIATE
GOU GAMADA
PHOO
SHY
Eh...
G.G.! THAT'S COOL!
SHING
RIGHT?
UH, YEAH...
I SERIOUSLY DOUBT...
...THAT UPPERCLASSMAN G.G. WILL BE A FOE.
I'M SORRY I BARGED IN LIKE THIS.
OH, NO WORRIES.

*G.G. sounds like "old man" in Japanese.

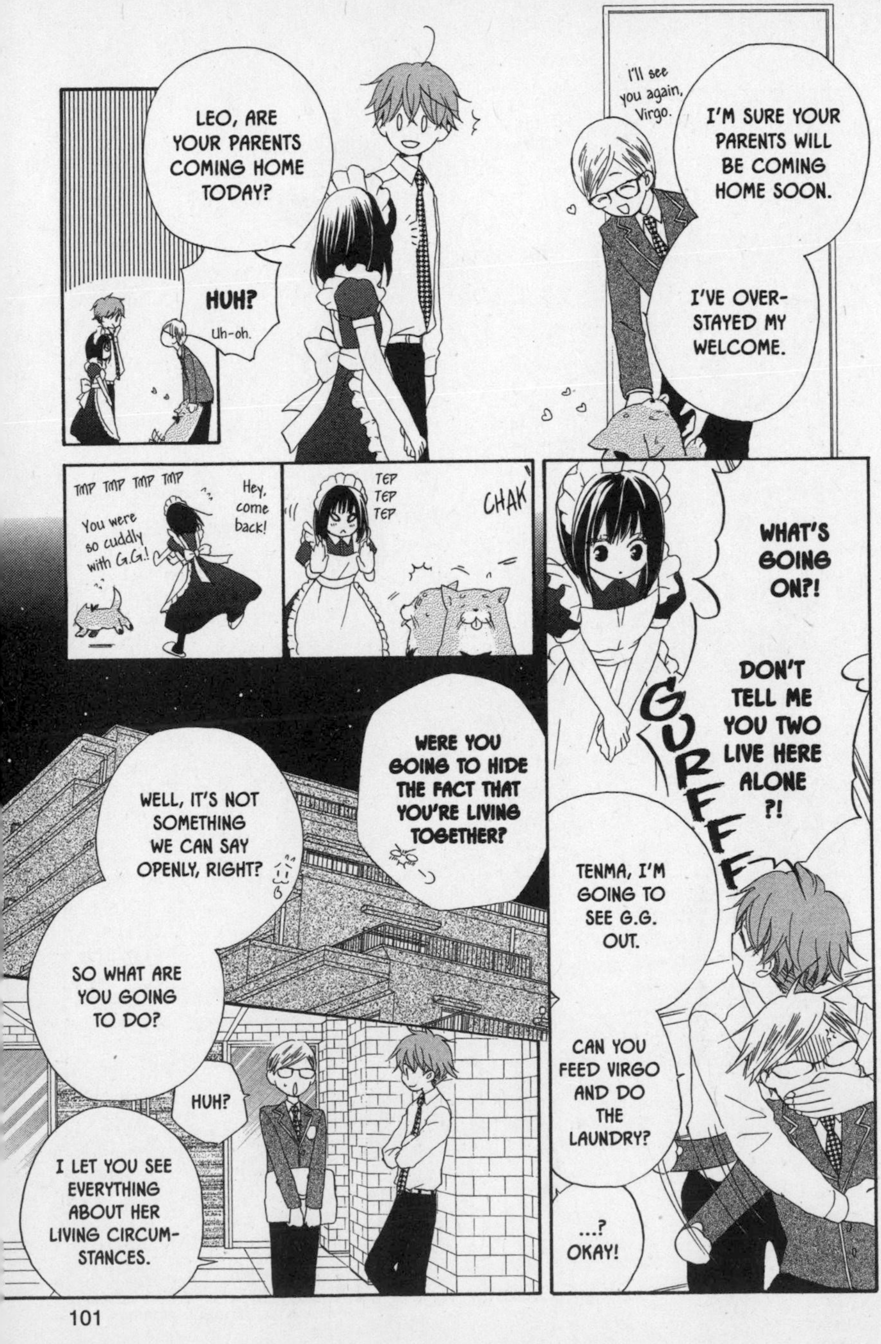
I'll see you again, Virgo.
I'M SURE YOUR PARENTS WILL BE COMING HOME SOON.
I'VE OVER-STAYED MY WELCOME.
LEO, ARE YOUR PARENTS COMING HOME TODAY?
HUH?
Uh-oh.
WHAT'S GOING ON?!
DON'T TELL ME YOU TWO LIVE HERE ALONE ?!
GURFFF
TENMA, I'M GOING TO SEE G.G. OUT.
CAN YOU FEED VIRGO AND DO THE LAUNDRY?
...? OKAY!
TEP TEP TEP
CHAK
TMP TMP TMP TMP
Hey, come back!
You were so cuddly with G.G.!
WERE YOU GOING TO HIDE THE FACT THAT YOU'RE LIVING TOGETHER?
WELL, IT'S NOT SOMETHING WE CAN SAY OPENLY, RIGHT?
SO WHAT ARE YOU GOING TO DO?
HUH?
I LET YOU SEE EVERYTHING ABOUT HER LIVING CIRCUM-STANCES.

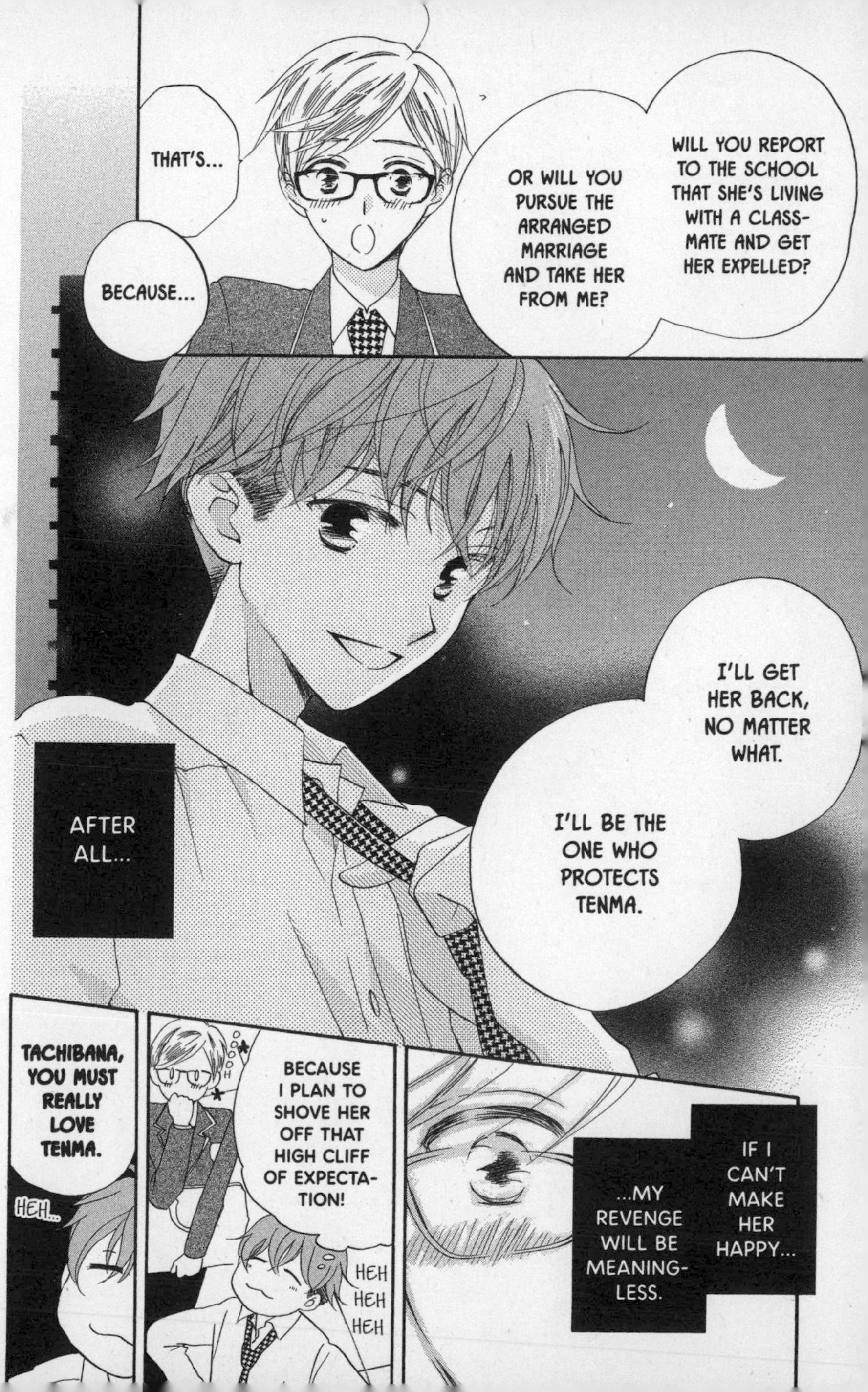
WILL YOU REPORT TO THE SCHOOL THAT SHE'S LIVING WITH A CLASS-MATE AND GET HER EXPELLED?
OR WILL YOU PURSUE THE ARRANGED MARRIAGE AND TAKE HER FROM ME?
THAT'S...
BECAUSE...
I'LL GET HER BACK, NO MATTER WHAT.
I'LL BE THE ONE WHO PROTECTS TENMA.
AFTER ALL...
IF I CAN'T MAKE HER HAPPY...
...MY REVENGE WILL BE MEANING-LESS.
BECAUSE I PLAN TO SHOVE HER OFF THAT HIGH CLIFF OF EXPECTA-TION!
HEH HEH HEH
TACHIBANA, YOU MUST REALLY LOVE TENMA.
HEH...

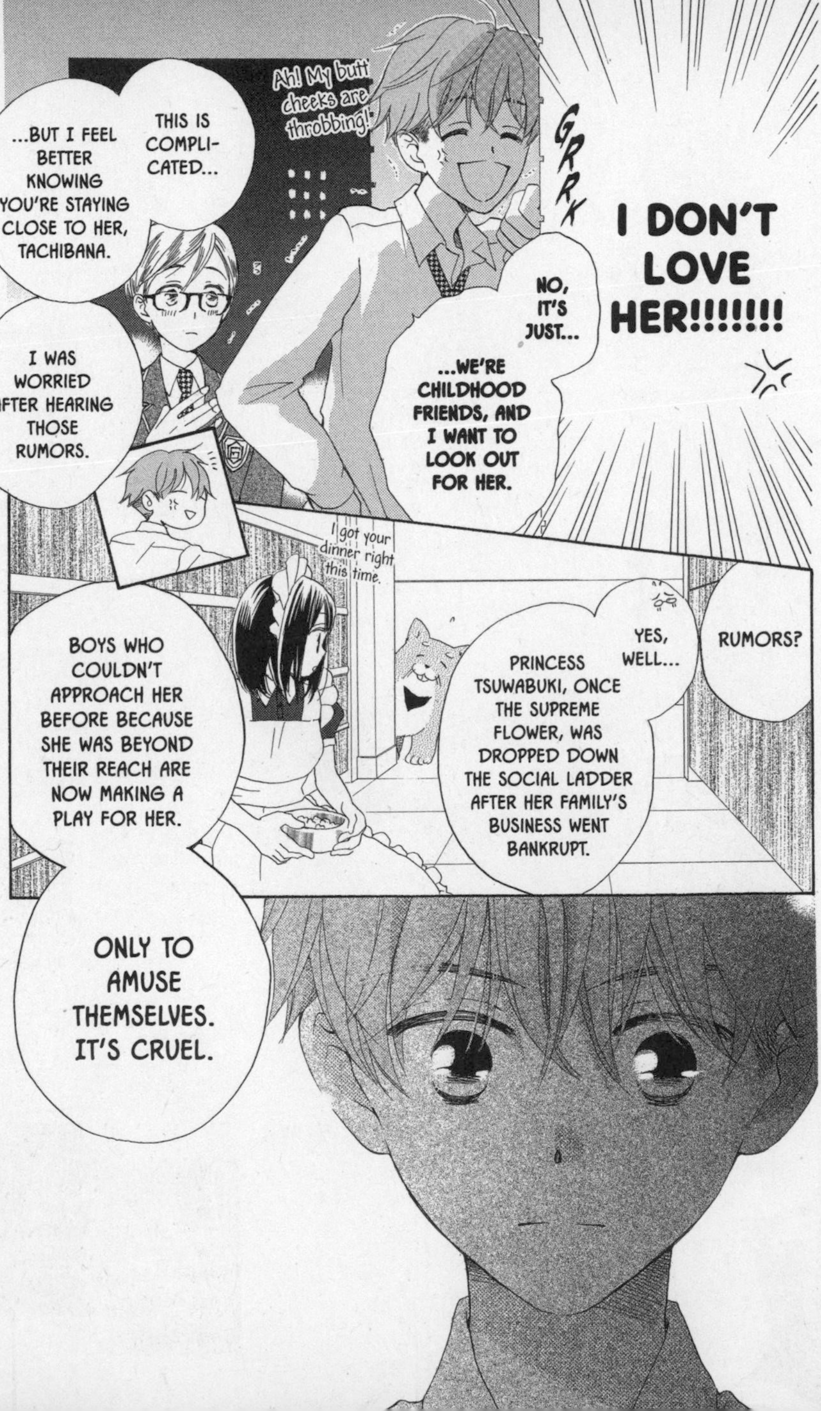
NO, IT'S JUST...
...WE'RE CHILDHOOD FRIENDS, AND I WANT TO LOOK OUT FOR HER.
GRRK
I DON'T LOVE HER!!!!!!!
Ah! My butt cheeks are throbbing!
THIS IS COMPLI-CATED...
...BUT I FEEL BETTER KNOWING YOU'RE STAYING CLOSE TO HER, TACHIBANA.
I WAS WORRIED AFTER HEARING THOSE RUMORS.
RUMORS?
YES, WELL...
PRINCESS TSUWABUKI, ONCE THE SUPREME FLOWER, WAS DROPPED DOWN THE SOCIAL LADDER AFTER HER FAMILY'S BUSINESS WENT BANKRUPT.
I got your dinner right this time.
BOYS WHO COULDN'T APPROACH HER BEFORE BECAUSE SHE WAS BEYOND THEIR REACH ARE NOW MAKING A PLAY FOR HER.
ONLY TO AMUSE THEMSELVES. IT'S CRUEL.

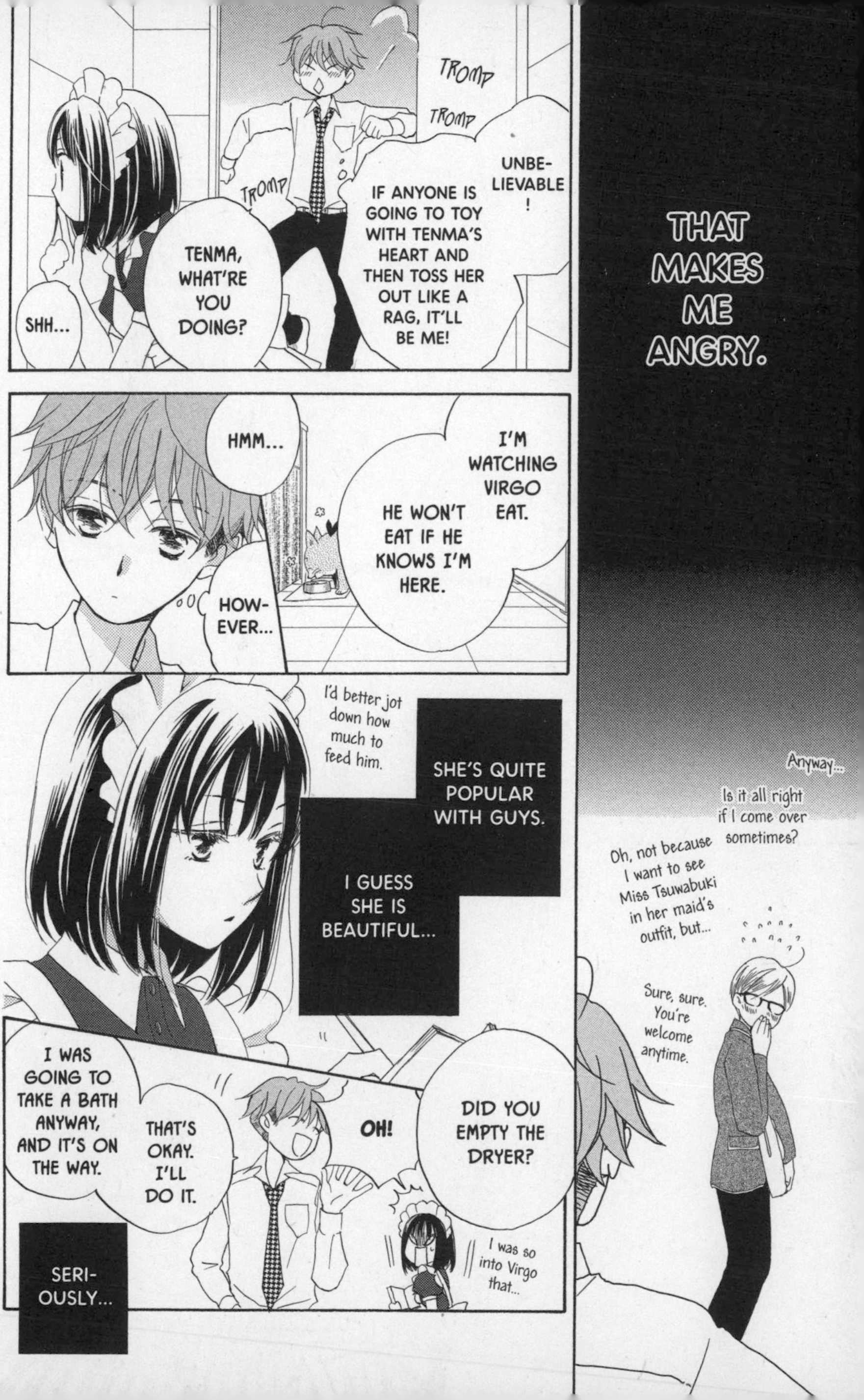
THAT MAKES ME ANGRY.
Anyway...
Is it all right if I come over sometimes?
Oh, not because I want to see Miss Tsuwabuki in her maid's outfit, but...
Sure, sure. You're welcome anytime.
TROMP
TROMP
UNBE-LIEVABLE!
IF ANYONE IS GOING TO TOY WITH TENMA'S HEART AND THEN TOSS HER OUT LIKE A RAG, IT'LL BE ME!
TROMP
TENMA, WHAT'RE YOU DOING?
SHH...
I'M WATCHING VIRGO EAT.
HMM...
HE WON'T EAT IF HE KNOWS I'M HERE.
HOW-EVER...
I'd better jot down how much to feed him.
SHE'S QUITE POPULAR WITH GUYS.
I GUESS SHE IS BEAUTIFUL...
DID YOU EMPTY THE DRYER?
OH!
I was so into Virgo that...
THAT'S OKAY. I'LL DO IT.
I WAS GOING TO TAKE A BATH ANYWAY, AND IT'S ON THE WAY.
SERI-OUSLY...

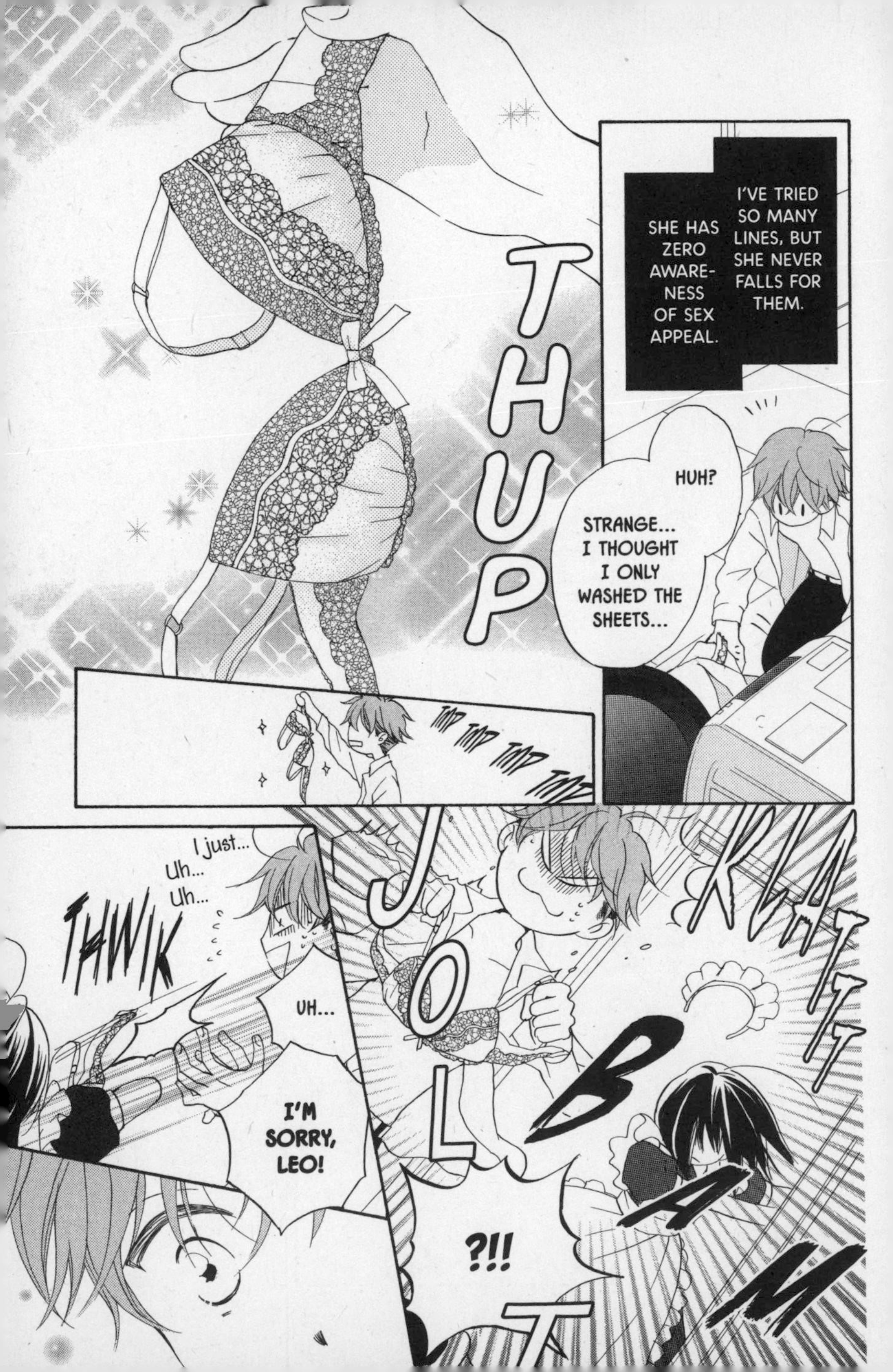
I'VE TRIED SO MANY LINES, BUT SHE NEVER FALLS FOR THEM.
SHE HAS ZERO AWARE-NESS OF SEX APPEAL.
HUH?
STRANGE... I THOUGHT I ONLY WASHED THE SHEETS...
THUP
TMP TMP TMP TMP
KLAT
BAM
JOLT
?!!
I just...
Uh...
Uh...
THWIK
UH...
I'M SORRY, LEO!

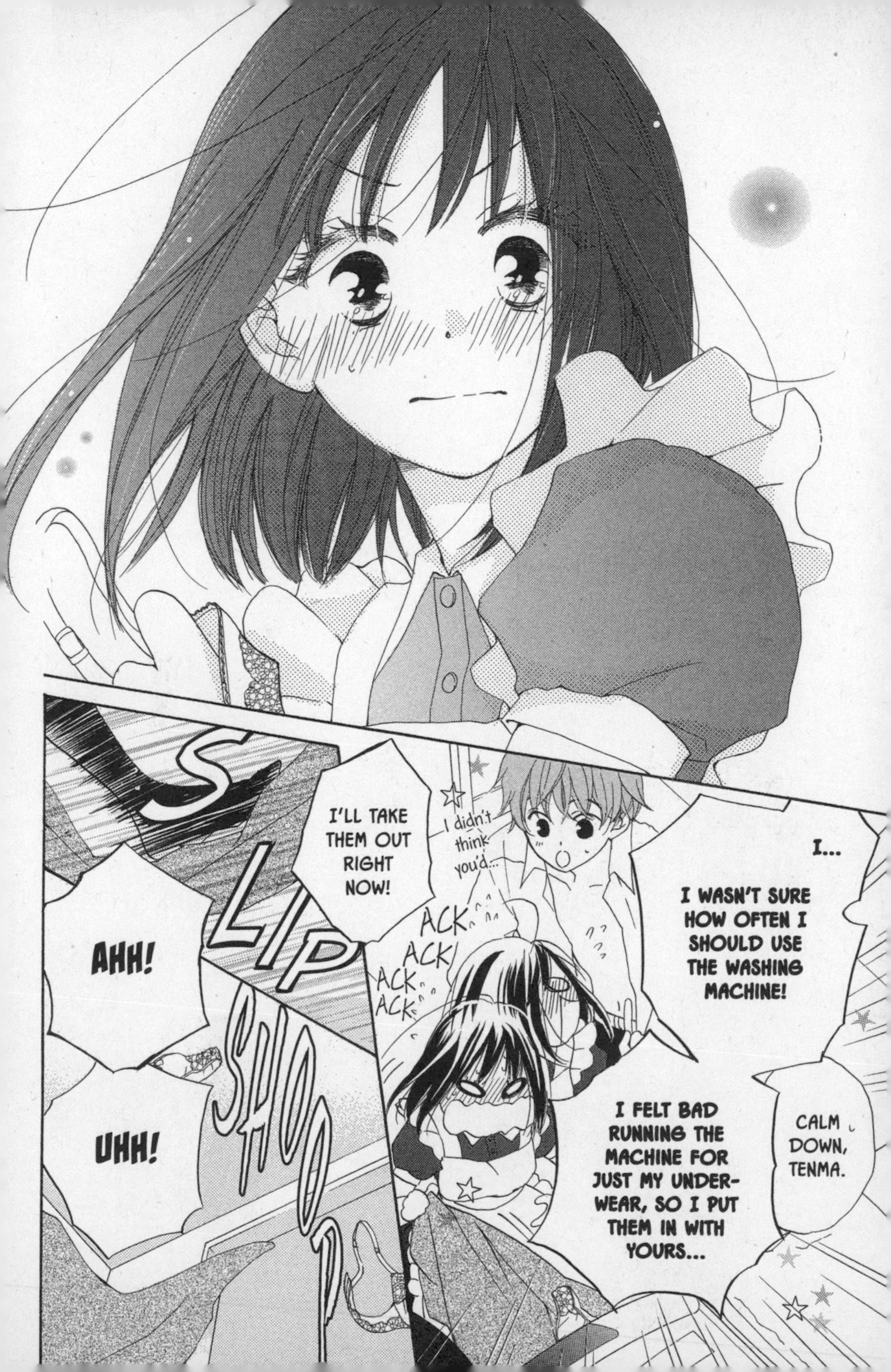
I...
I WASN'T SURE HOW OFTEN I SHOULD USE THE WASHING MACHINE!
CALM DOWN, TENMA.
I FELT BAD RUNNING THE MACHINE FOR JUST MY UNDER-WEAR, SO I PUT THEM IN WITH YOURS...
I didn't think you'd...
ACK ACK ACK ACK
I'LL TAKE THEM OUT RIGHT NOW!
SLIP
AHH!
SHOO
UHH!

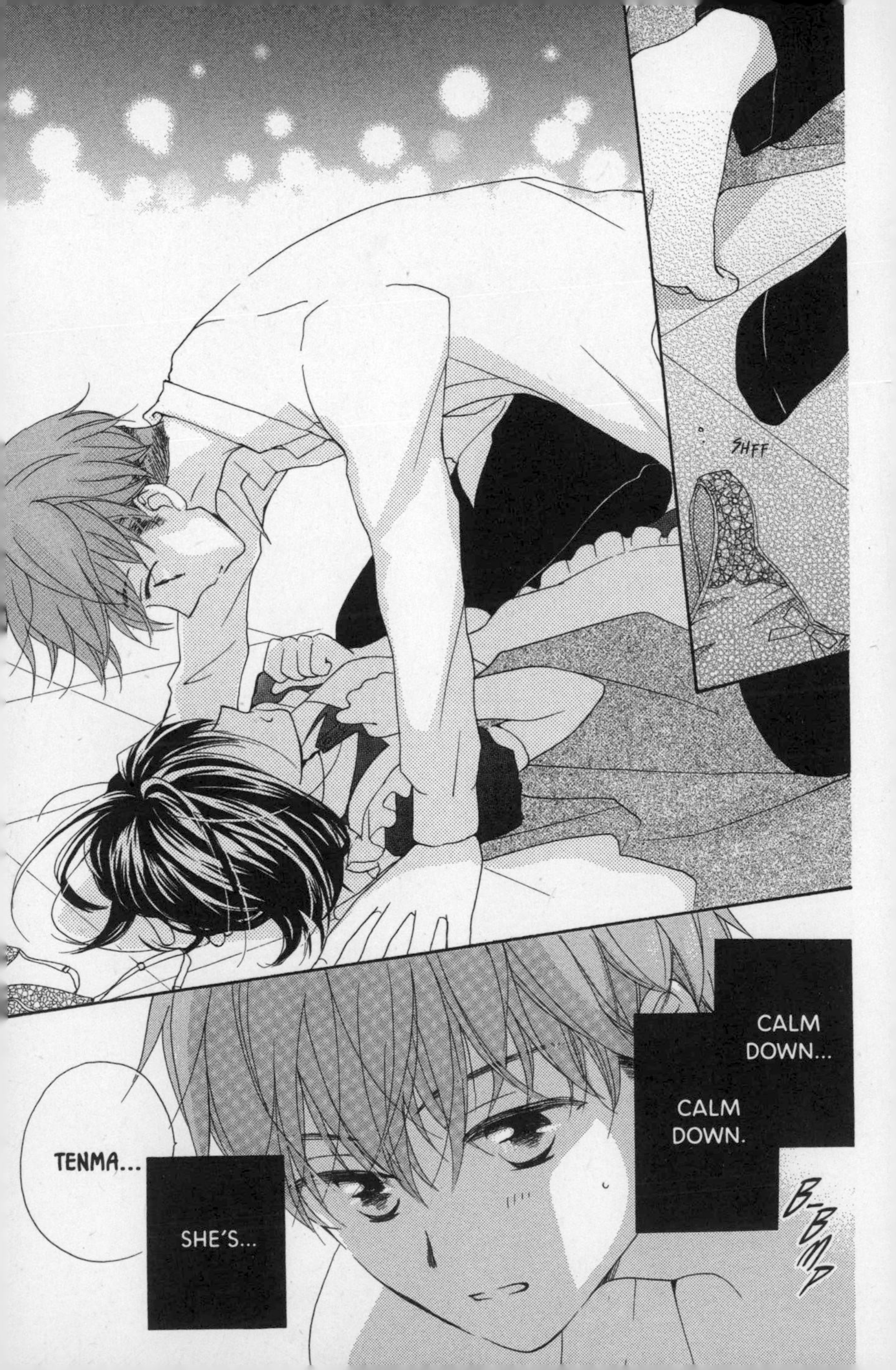
SHFF
CALM DOWN...
CALM DOWN.
B-BMP
TENMA...
SHE'S...

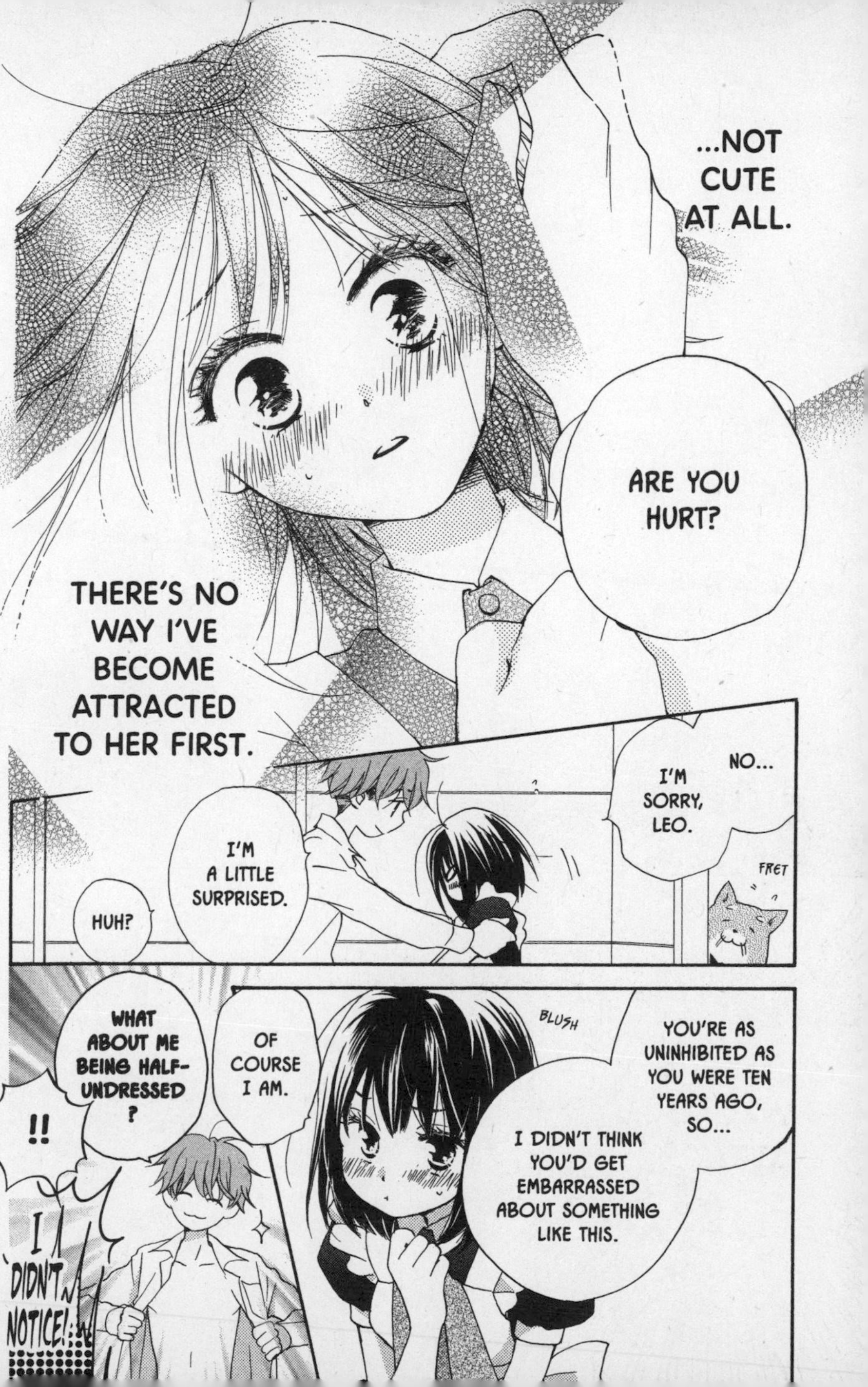
...NOT CUTE AT ALL.
ARE YOU HURT?
THERE'S NO WAY I'VE BECOME ATTRACTED TO HER FIRST.
NO...
I'M SORRY, LEO.
FRET
I'M A LITTLE SURPRISED.
HUH?
BLUSH
YOU'RE AS UNINHIBITED AS YOU WERE TEN YEARS AGO, SO...
I DIDN'T THINK YOU'D GET EMBARRASSED ABOUT SOMETHING LIKE THIS.
OF COURSE I AM.
WHAT ABOUT ME BEING HALF-UNDRESSED?
!!
I DIDN'T NOTICE!

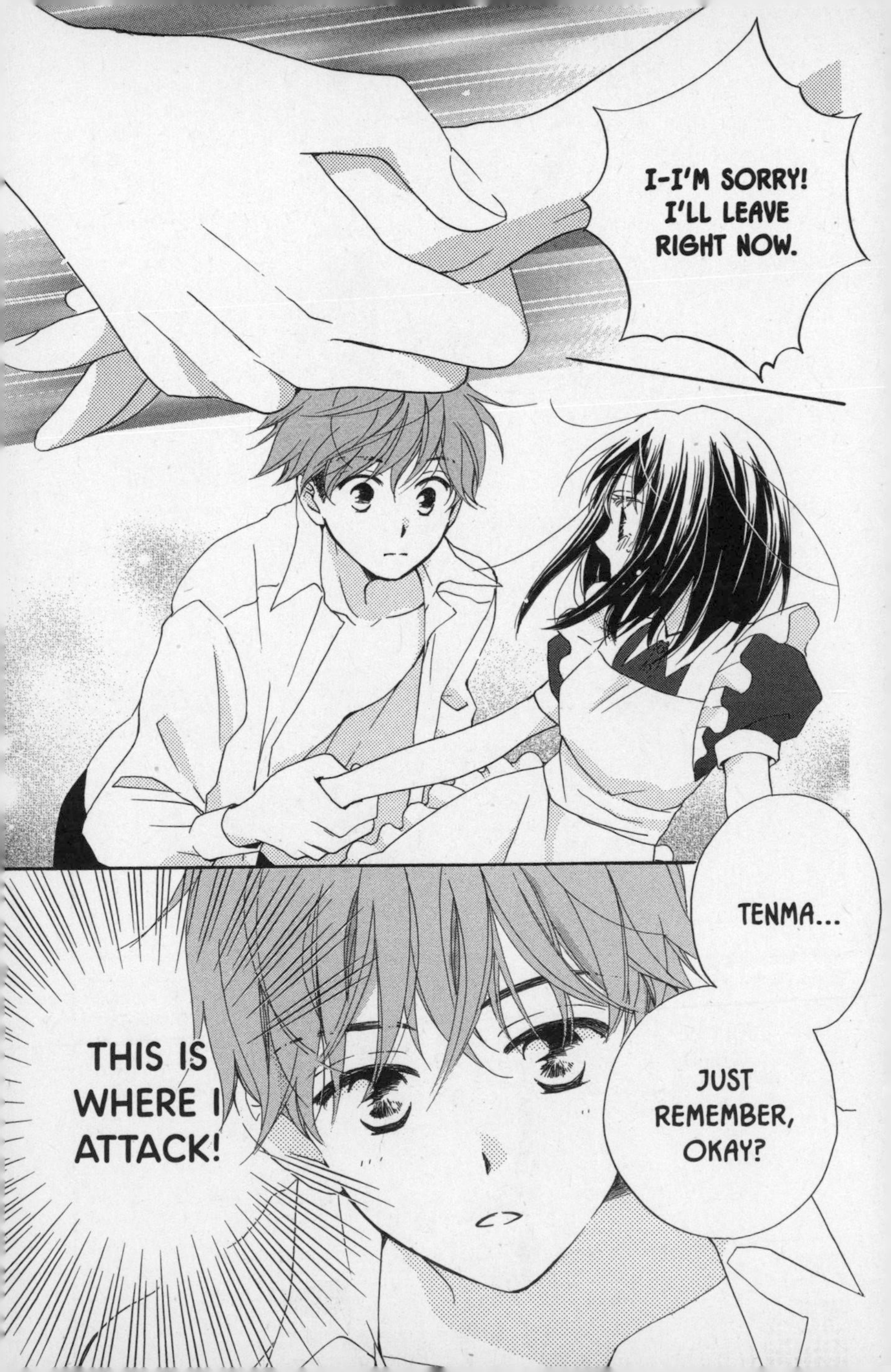
I-I'M SORRY! I'LL LEAVE RIGHT NOW.
TENMA...
JUST REMEMBER, OKAY?
THIS IS WHERE I ATTACK!

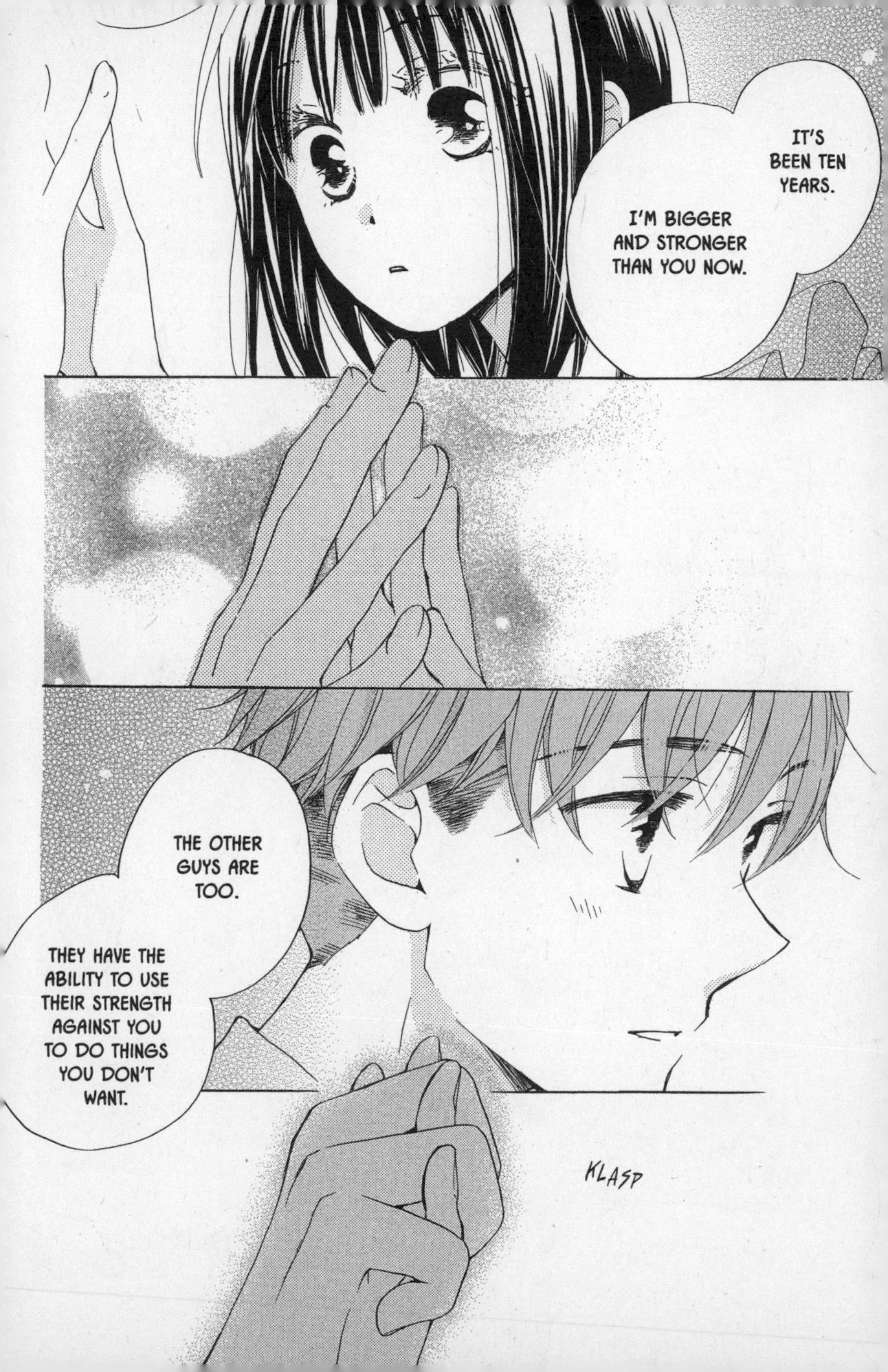
IT'S BEEN TEN YEARS.
I'M BIGGER AND STRONGER THAN YOU NOW.
THE OTHER GUYS ARE TOO.
THEY HAVE THE ABILITY TO USE THEIR STRENGTH AGAINST YOU TO DO THINGS YOU DON'T WANT.
KLASP

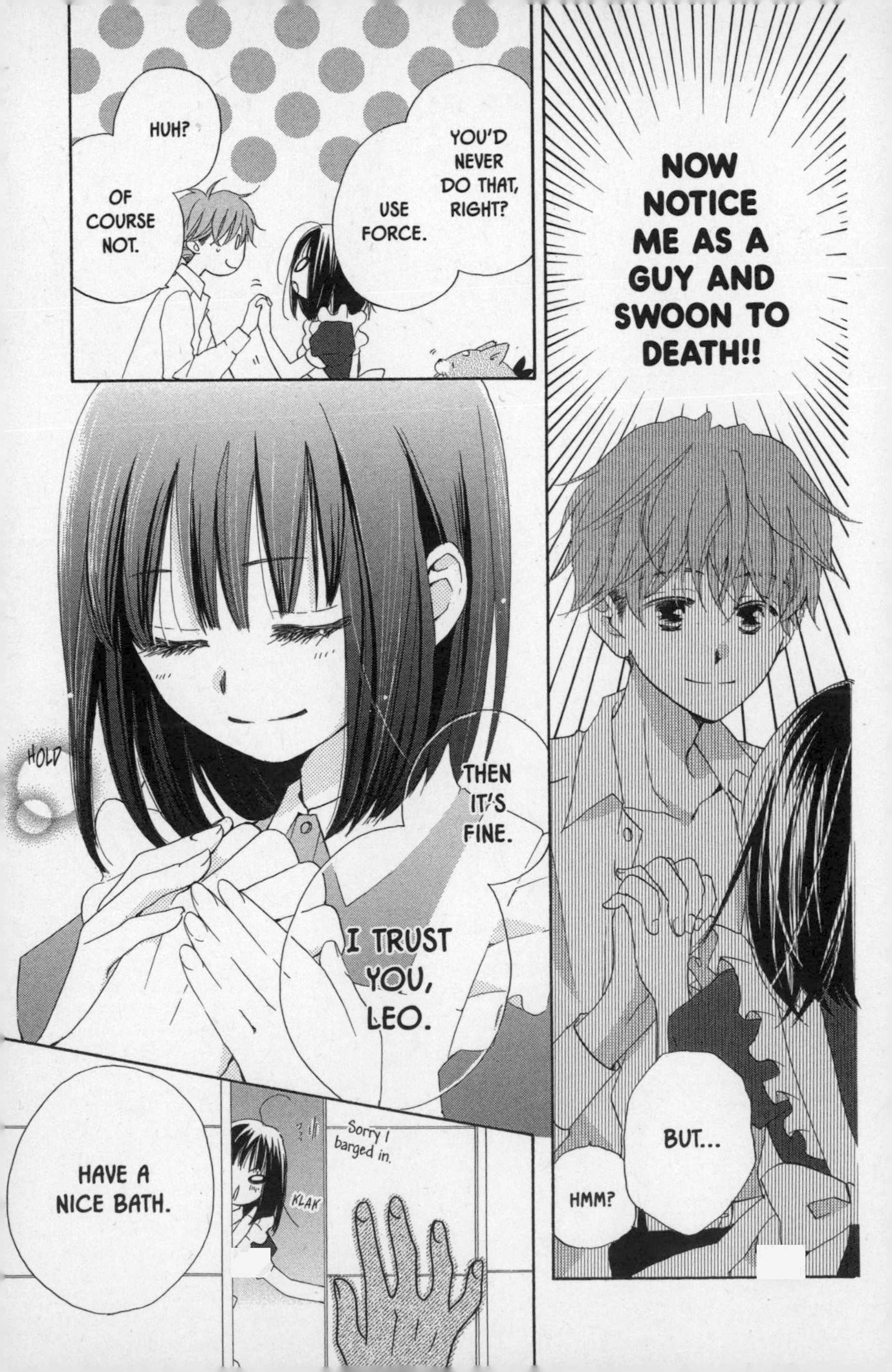
NOW NOTICE ME AS A GUY AND SWOON TO DEATH!!
BUT...
HMM?
YOU'D NEVER DO THAT, RIGHT?
USE FORCE.
HUH?
OF COURSE NOT.
HOLD
THEN IT'S FINE.
I TRUST YOU, LEO.
HAVE A NICE BATH.
Sorry I barged in.
KLAK

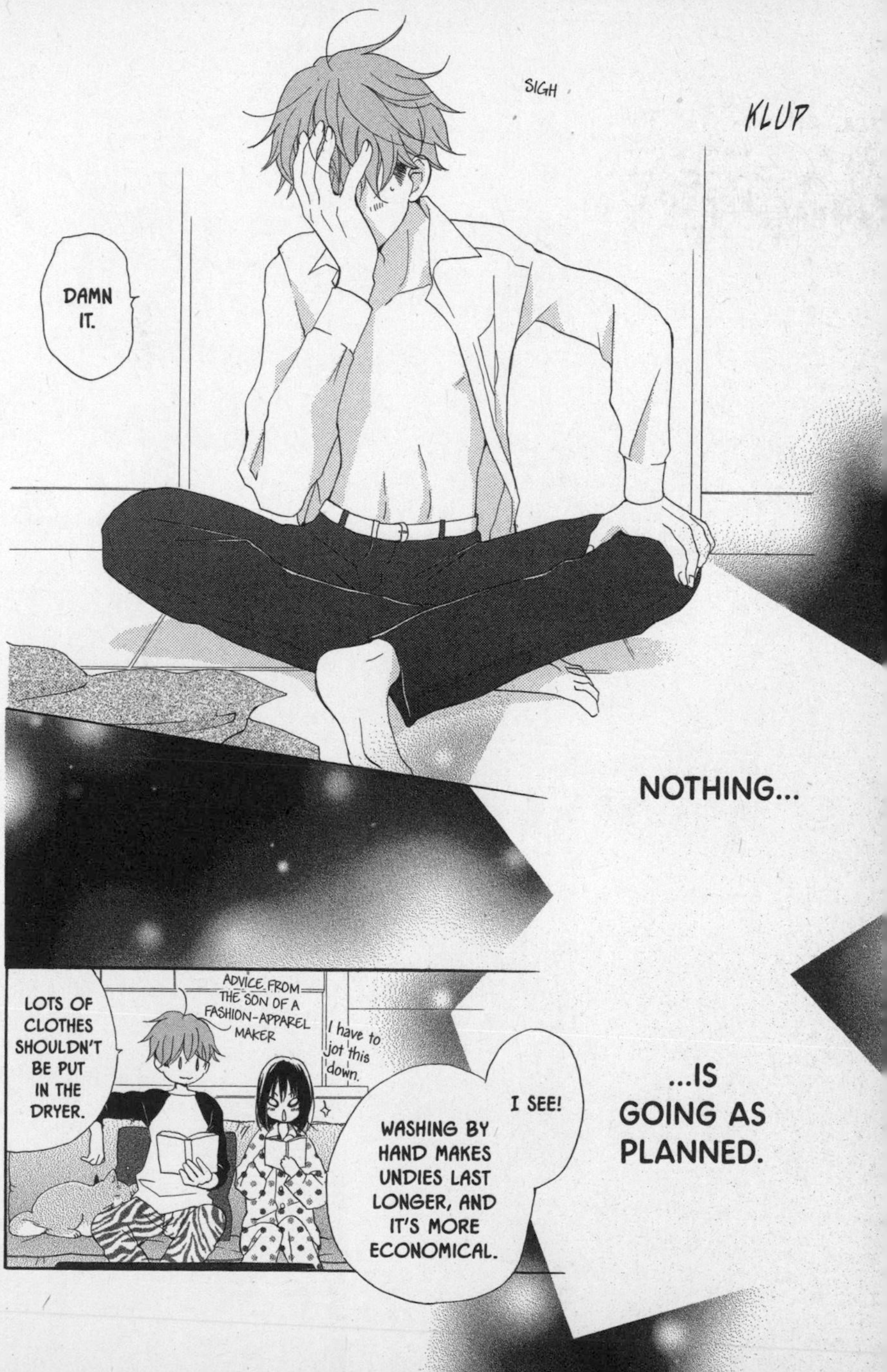
KLUP
SIGH
DAMN IT.
NOTHING...
...IS GOING AS PLANNED.
I SEE!
WASHING BY HAND MAKES UNDIES LAST LONGER, AND IT'S MORE ECONOMICAL.
I have to jot this down.
ADVICE FROM THE SON OF A FASHION-APPAREL MAKER
LOTS OF CLOTHES SHOULDN'T BE PUT IN THE DRYER.

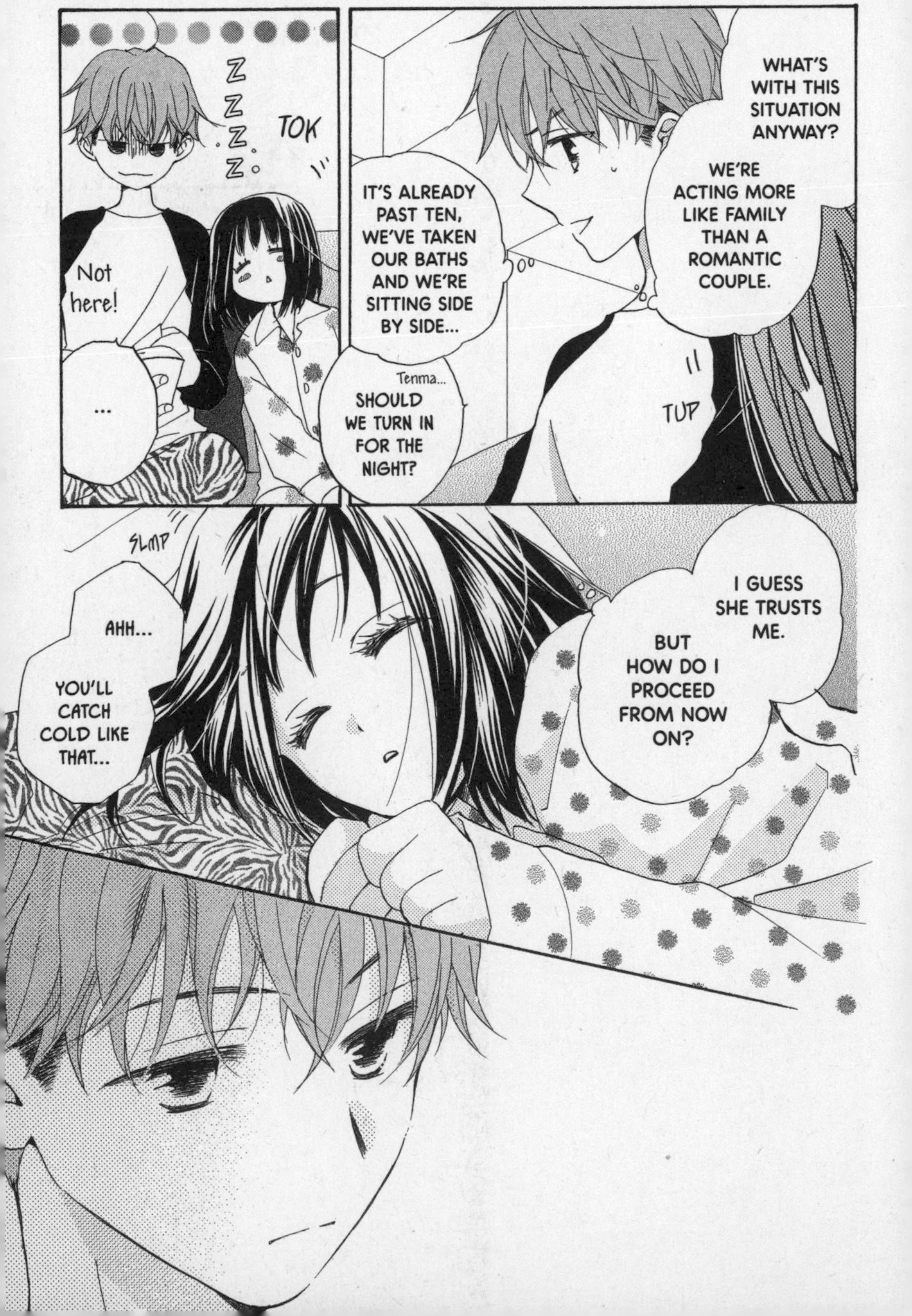
WHAT'S WITH THIS SITUATION ANYWAY?
WE'RE ACTING MORE LIKE FAMILY THAN A ROMANTIC COUPLE.
IT'S ALREADY PAST TEN, WE'VE TAKEN OUR BATHS AND WE'RE SITTING SIDE BY SIDE...
TUP
Tenma...
SHOULD WE TURN IN FOR THE NIGHT?
ZZZZ
TOK
Not here!
...
I GUESS SHE TRUSTS ME.
BUT HOW DO I PROCEED FROM NOW ON?
SLMP
AHH...
YOU'LL CATCH COLD LIKE THAT...

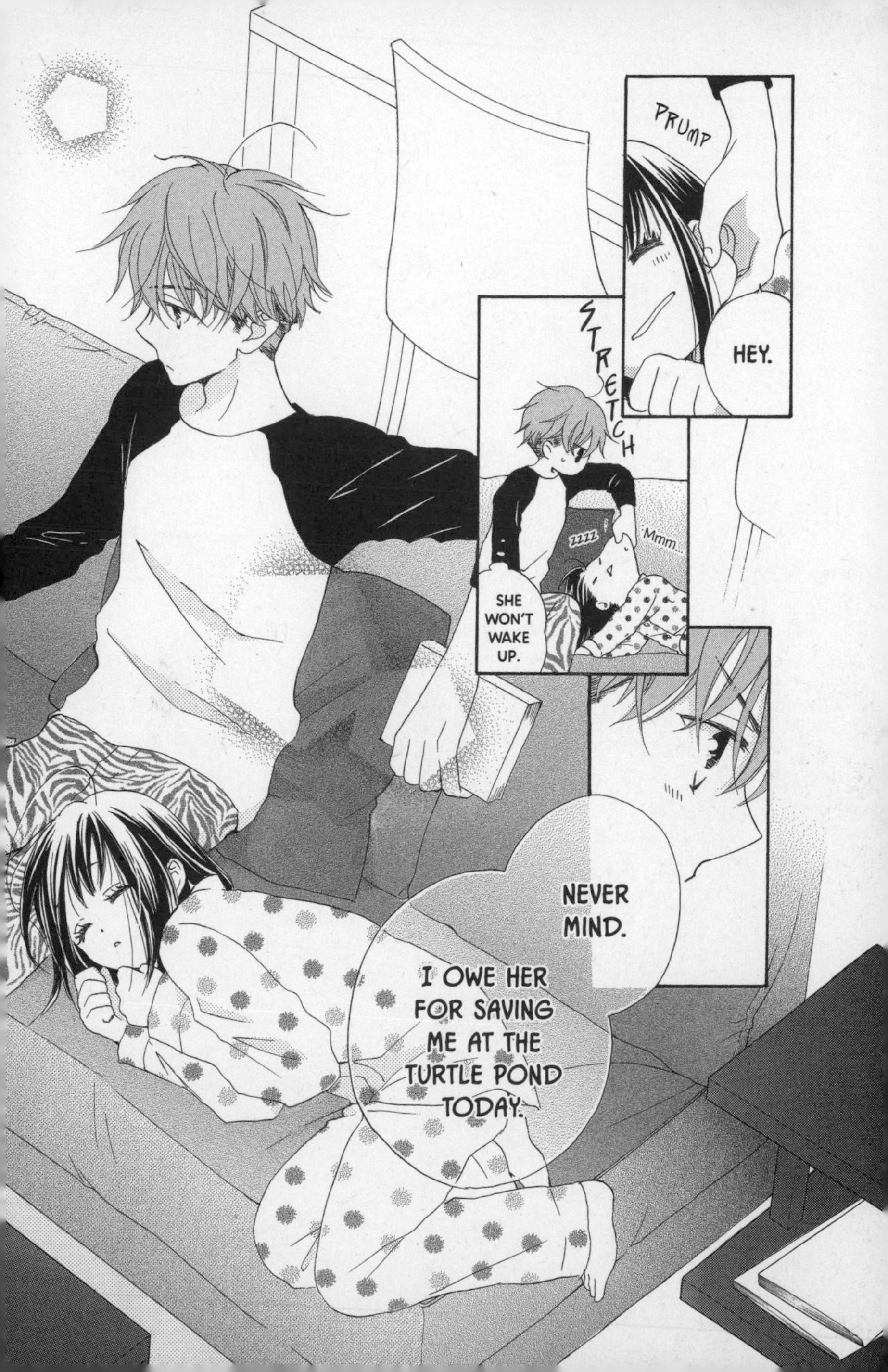
PRUMP
HEY.
STRETCH
Mmm...
ZZZZ
SHE WON'T WAKE UP.
NEVER MIND.
I OWE HER FOR SAVING ME AT THE TURTLE POND TODAY.

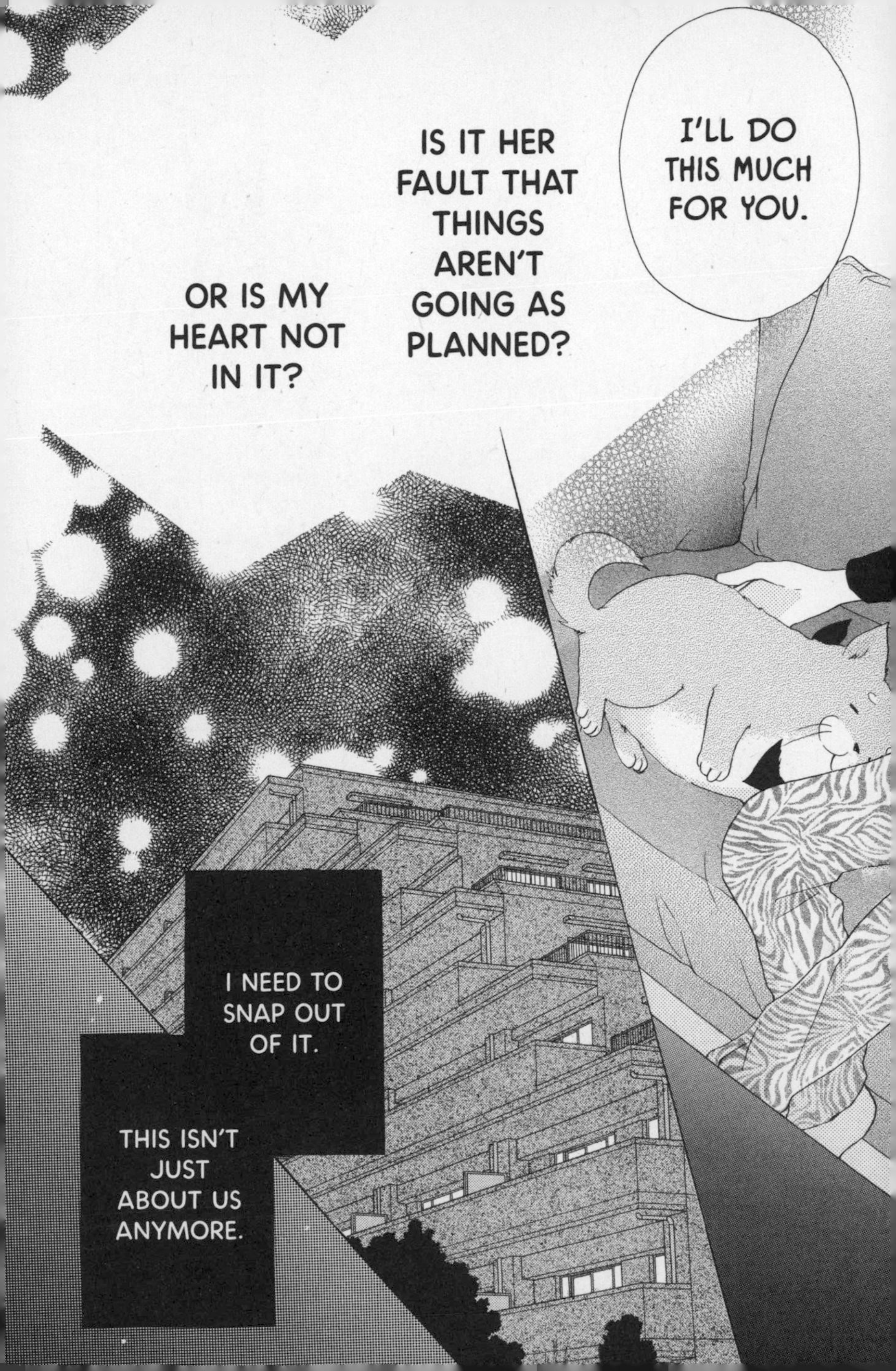
I'LL DO THIS MUCH FOR YOU.
IS IT HER FAULT THAT THINGS AREN'T GOING AS PLANNED?
OR IS MY HEART NOT IN IT?
I NEED TO SNAP OUT OF IT.
THIS ISN'T JUST ABOUT US ANYMORE.

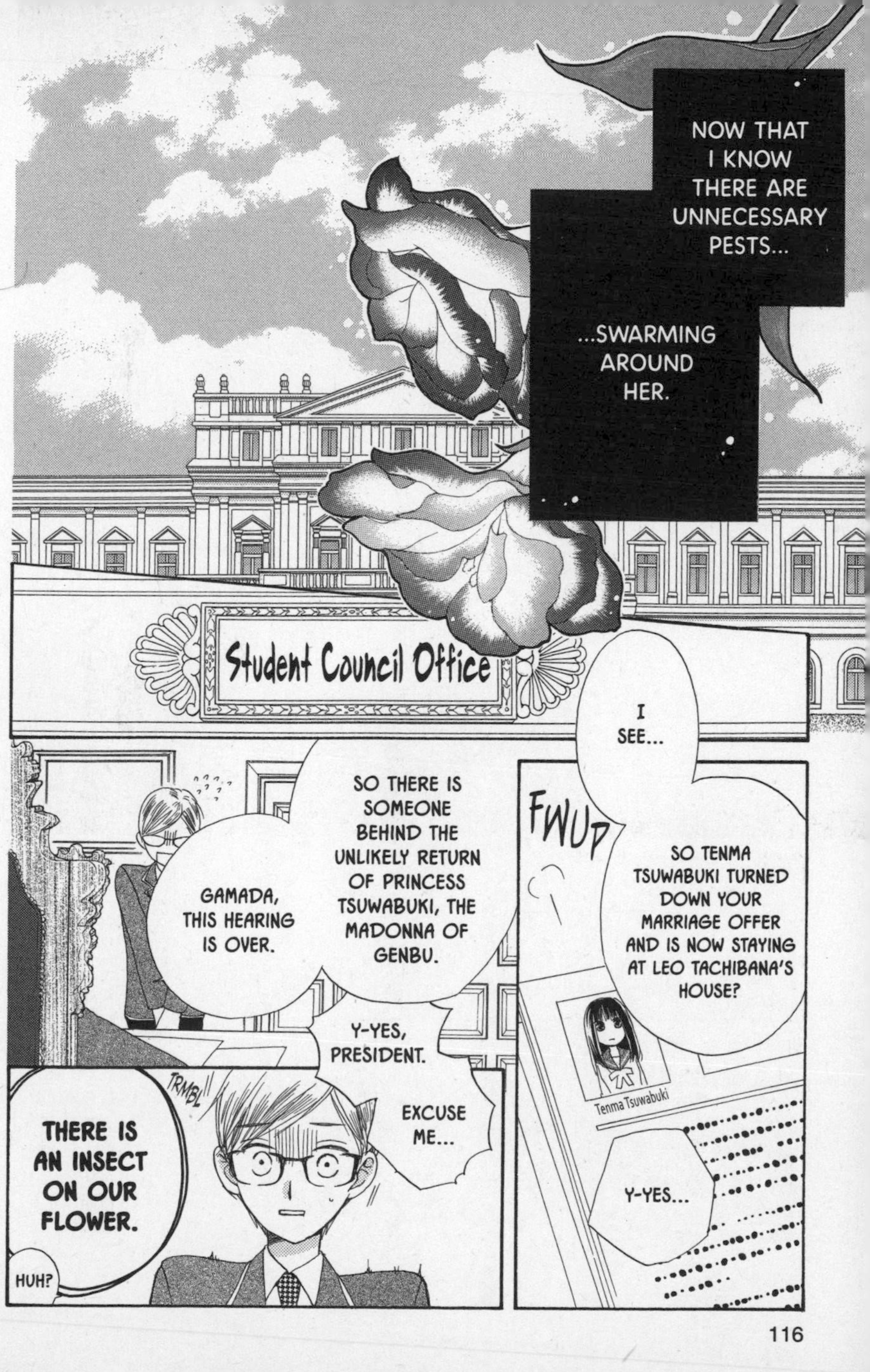
NOW THAT I KNOW THERE ARE UNNECESSARY PESTS...
...SWARMING AROUND HER.
Student Council Office
I SEE...
FWUP
SO TENMA TSUWABUKI TURNED DOWN YOUR MARRIAGE OFFER AND IS NOW STAYING AT LEO TACHIBANA'S HOUSE?
Tenma Tsuwabuki
Y-YES...
SO THERE IS SOMEONE BEHIND THE UNLIKELY RETURN OF PRINCESS TSUWABUKI, THE MADONNA OF GENBU.
GAMADA, THIS HEARING IS OVER.
Y-YES, PRESIDENT.
EXCUSE ME...
TRMBL
THERE IS AN INSECT ON OUR FLOWER.
HUH?

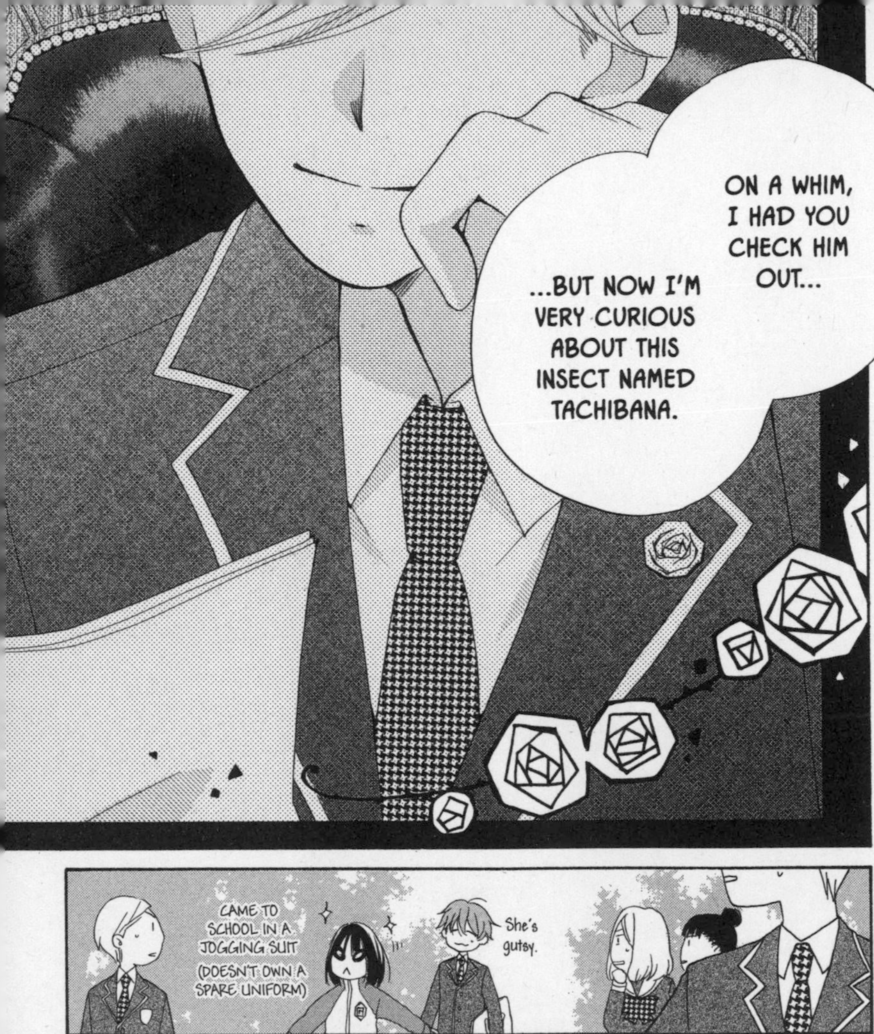
ON A WHIM, I HAD YOU CHECK HIM OUT...
...BUT NOW I'M VERY CURIOUS ABOUT THIS INSECT NAMED TACHIBANA.

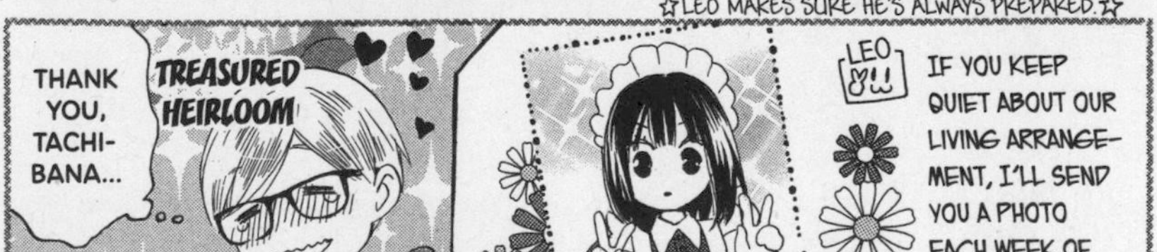
She's gutsy.
CAME TO SCHOOL IN A JOGGING SUIT (DOESN'T OWN A SPARE UNIFORM)

☆LEO MAKES SURE HE'S ALWAYS PREPARED.☆

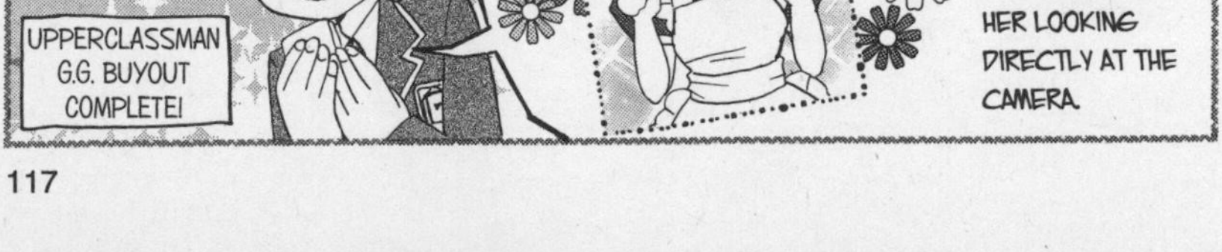
LEO
IF YOU KEEP QUIET ABOUT OUR LIVING ARRANGEMENT, I'LL SEND YOU A PHOTO EACH WEEK OF HER LOOKING DIRECTLY AT THE CAMERA.
THANK YOU, TACHIBANA...
TREASURED HEIRLOOM
UPPERCLASSMAN G.G. BUYOUT COMPLETE!

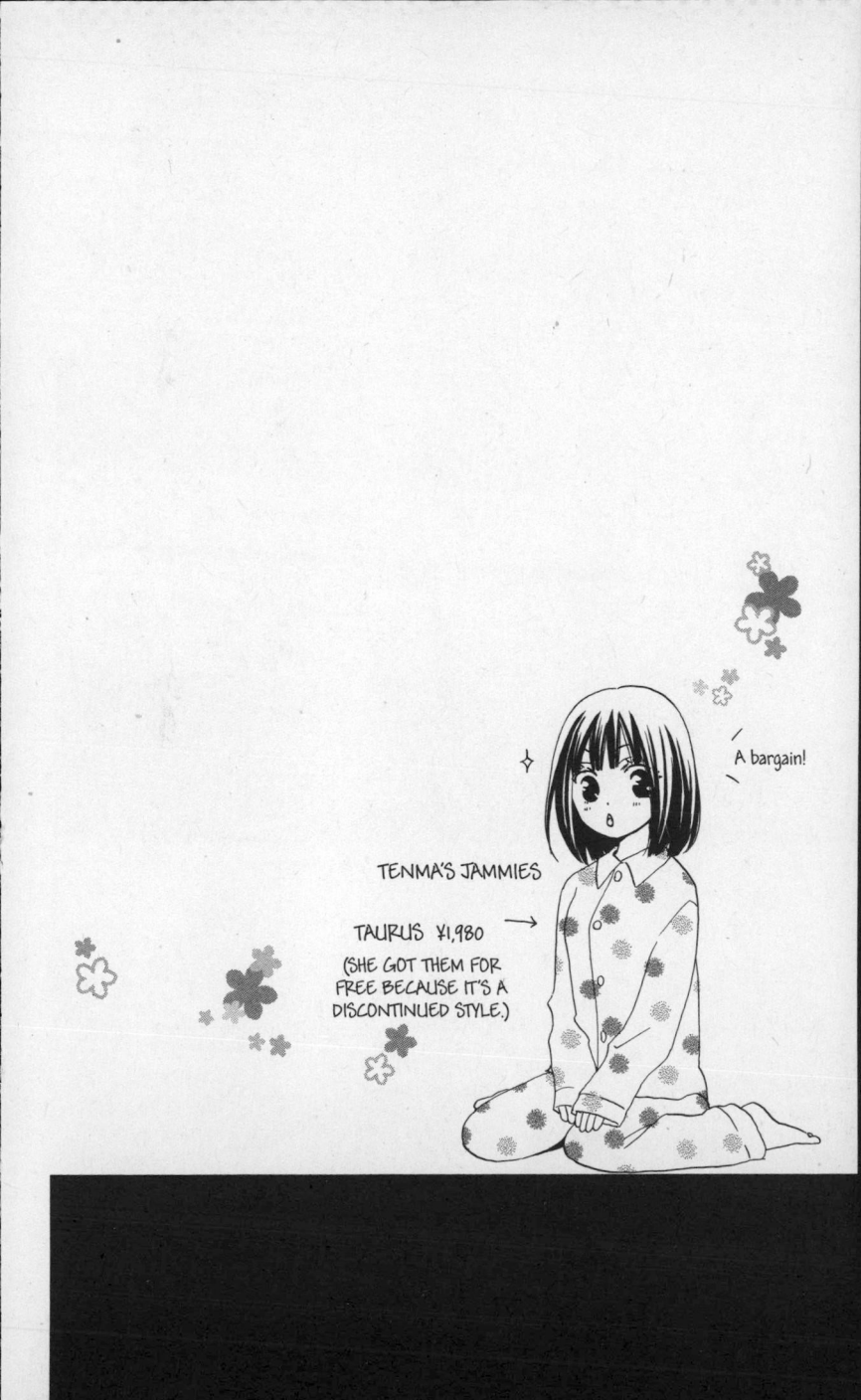

A bargain!

TENMA'S JAMMIES

TAURUS ¥1,980 →
(SHE GOT THEM FOR FREE BECAUSE IT'S A DISCONTINUED STYLE.)

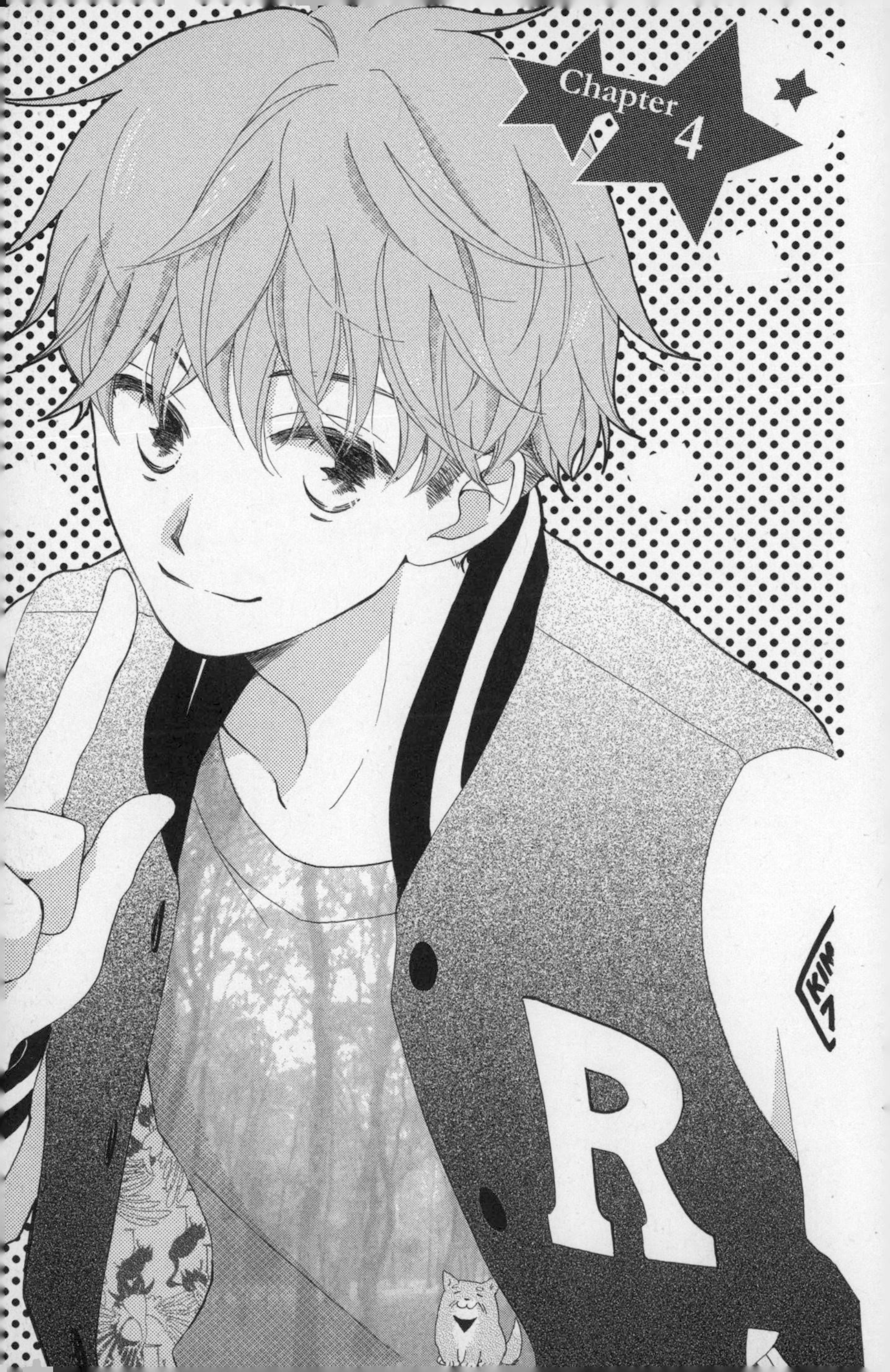
Chapter 4
R
KIM 1

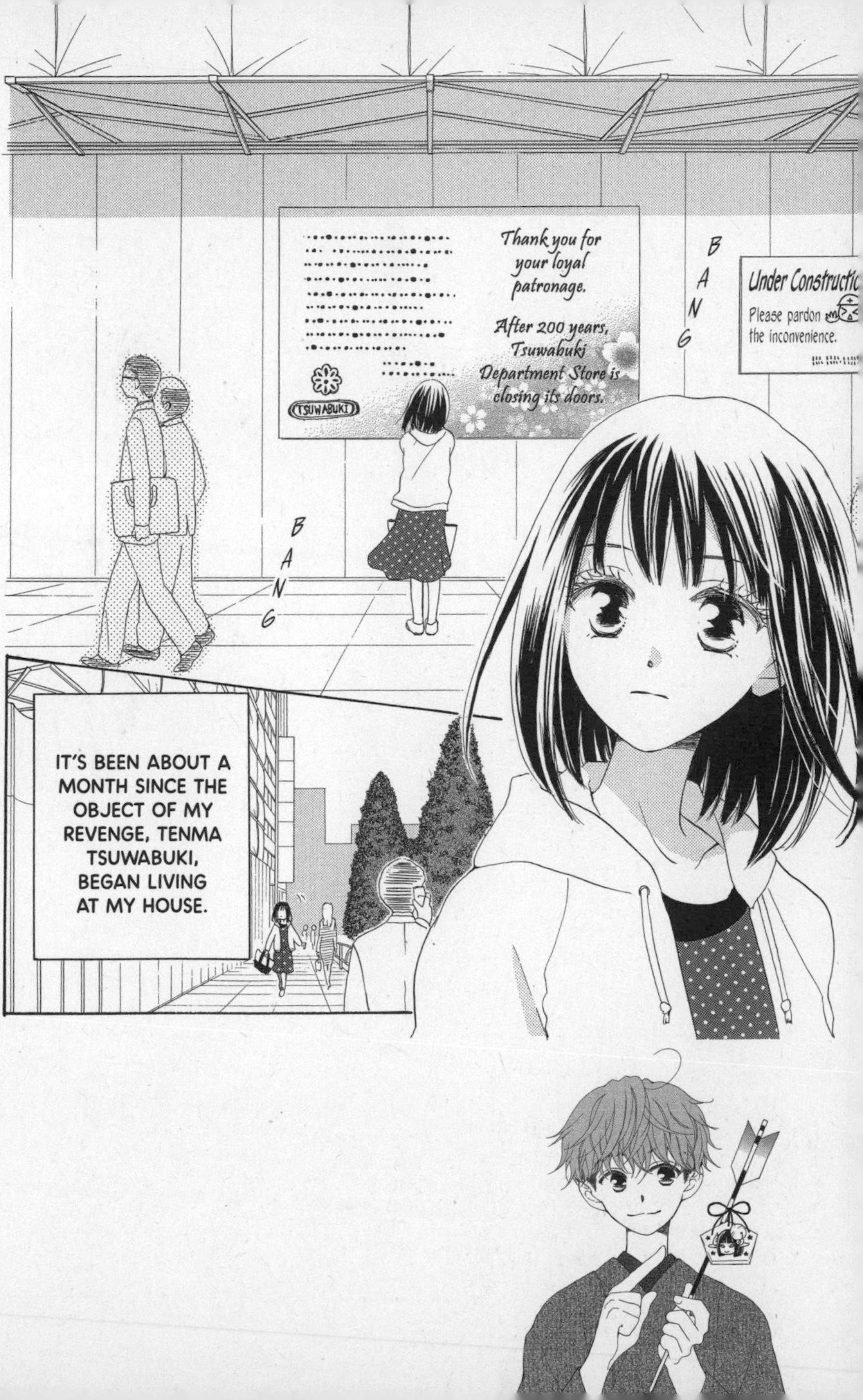
Under Constructio
Please pardon the inconvenience.
BANG
Thank you for your loyal patronage.
After 200 years, Tsuwabuki Department Store is closing its doors.
TSUWABUKI
BANG
IT'S BEEN ABOUT A MONTH SINCE THE OBJECT OF MY REVENGE, TENMA TSUWABUKI, BEGAN LIVING AT MY HOUSE.

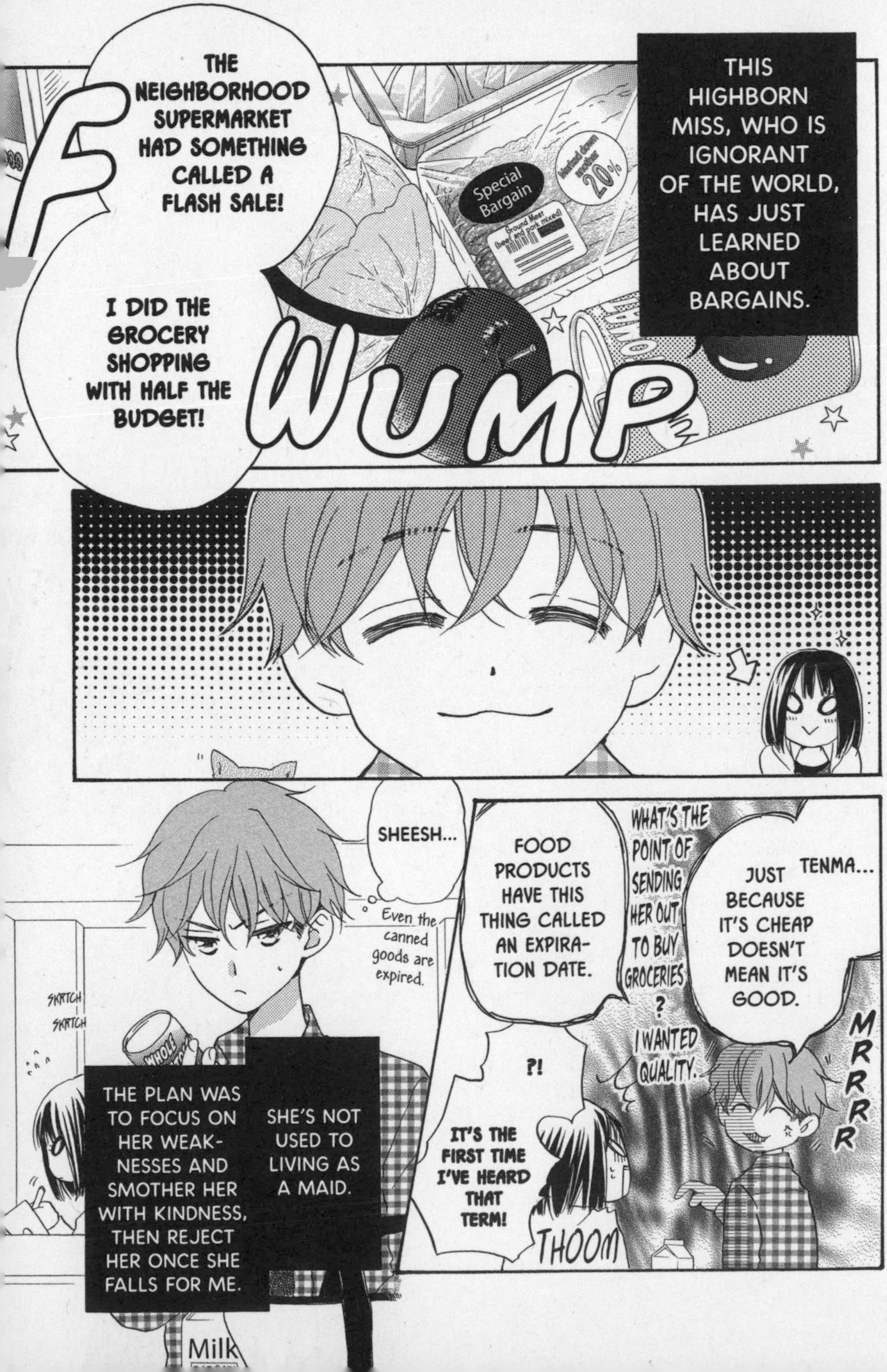
THIS HIGHBORN MISS, WHO IS IGNORANT OF THE WORLD, HAS JUST LEARNED ABOUT BARGAINS.
THE NEIGHBORHOOD SUPERMARKET HAD SOMETHING CALLED A FLASH SALE!
I DID THE GROCERY SHOPPING WITH HALF THE BUDGET!
Special Bargain
Ground Meat (beef and pork mixed)
WUMP
TENMA...
JUST BECAUSE IT'S CHEAP DOESN'T MEAN IT'S GOOD.
MRRRR
WHAT'S THE POINT OF SENDING HER OUT TO BUY GROCERIES?
I WANTED QUALITY.
FOOD PRODUCTS HAVE THIS THING CALLED AN EXPIRATION DATE.
?!
IT'S THE FIRST TIME I'VE HEARD THAT TERM!
THOOM
SHEESH...
Even the canned goods are expired.
SKRTCH SKRTCH
SHE'S NOT USED TO LIVING AS A MAID.
THE PLAN WAS TO FOCUS ON HER WEAKNESSES AND SMOTHER HER WITH KINDNESS, THEN REJECT HER ONCE SHE FALLS FOR ME.
Milk

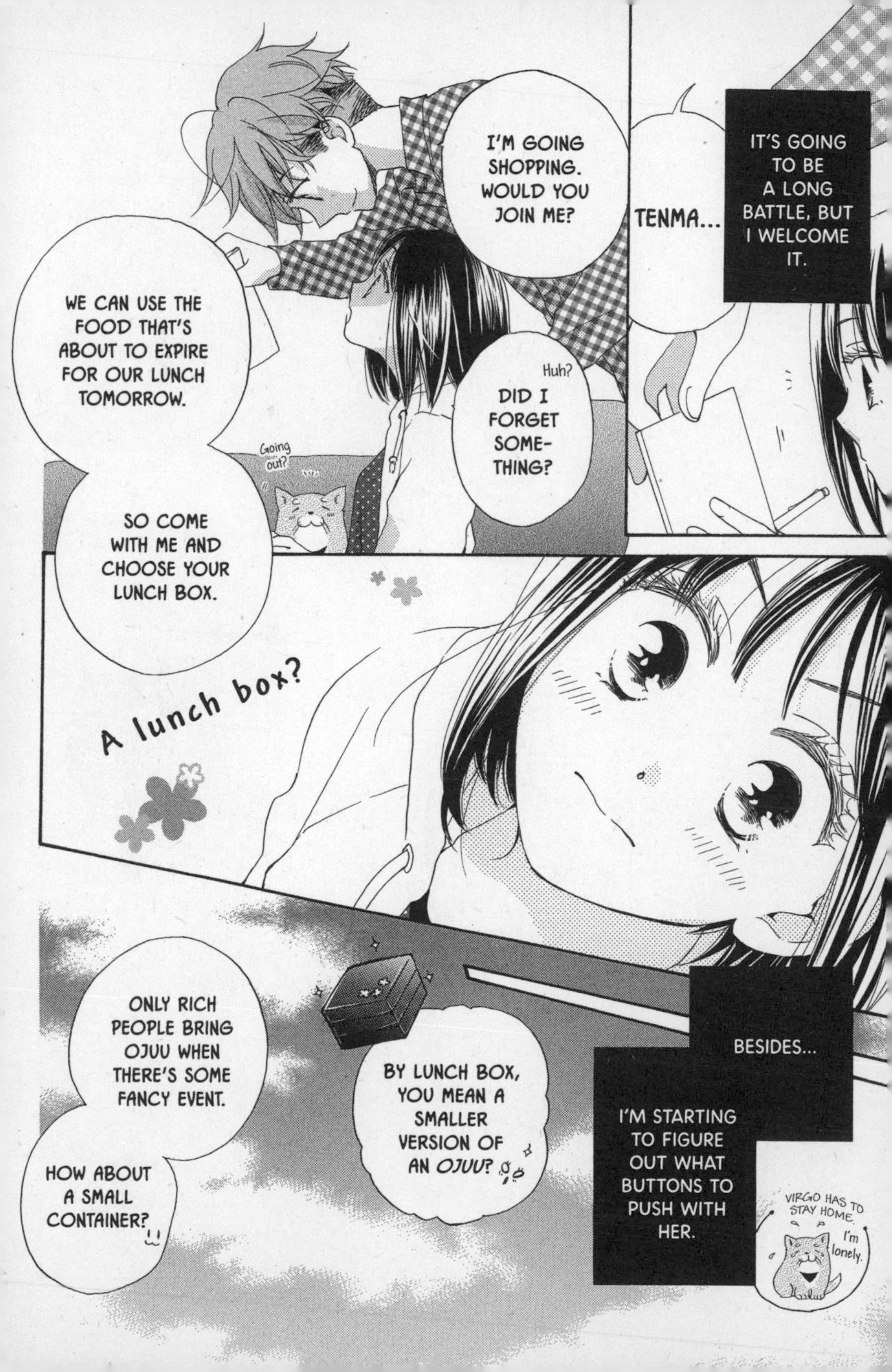
IT'S GOING TO BE A LONG BATTLE, BUT I WELCOME IT.
TENMA...
I'M GOING SHOPPING. WOULD YOU JOIN ME?
Huh?
DID I FORGET SOME-THING?
WE CAN USE THE FOOD THAT'S ABOUT TO EXPIRE FOR OUR LUNCH TOMORROW.
Going out?
SO COME WITH ME AND CHOOSE YOUR LUNCH BOX.
A lunch box?
BESIDES...
I'M STARTING TO FIGURE OUT WHAT BUTTONS TO PUSH WITH HER.
VIRGO HAS TO STAY HOME.
I'm lonely.
BY LUNCH BOX, YOU MEAN A SMALLER VERSION OF AN *OJUU*?
ONLY RICH PEOPLE BRING OJUU WHEN THERE'S SOME FANCY EVENT.
HOW ABOUT A SMALL CONTAINER?

The Rain and Me ②

And in July, I went to the West Coast of America where it's guaranteed to be dry. (Arid region)

I arrived at the Grand Canyon...

The rainy season began today.

Guide

A towel

When I went to Las Vegas... (Practically a desert)

It rained last night.

First time in three months.

So unusual.

Inside the bus

"I'm sorry. Maybe it's because I'm here..." said my super-assistant who was also on the trip.

You know, Meca, maybe you should travel to the world's driest regions.

You know, to bring them rain.

I've found my calling!

I'm not joking. The amount of rain isn't funny...

So, people of the world who are waiting for rain, send me your letters.

In 2014...

America (rain) Hawaii (rain locally)

Taiwan (rain) Hakone (snow-storm)

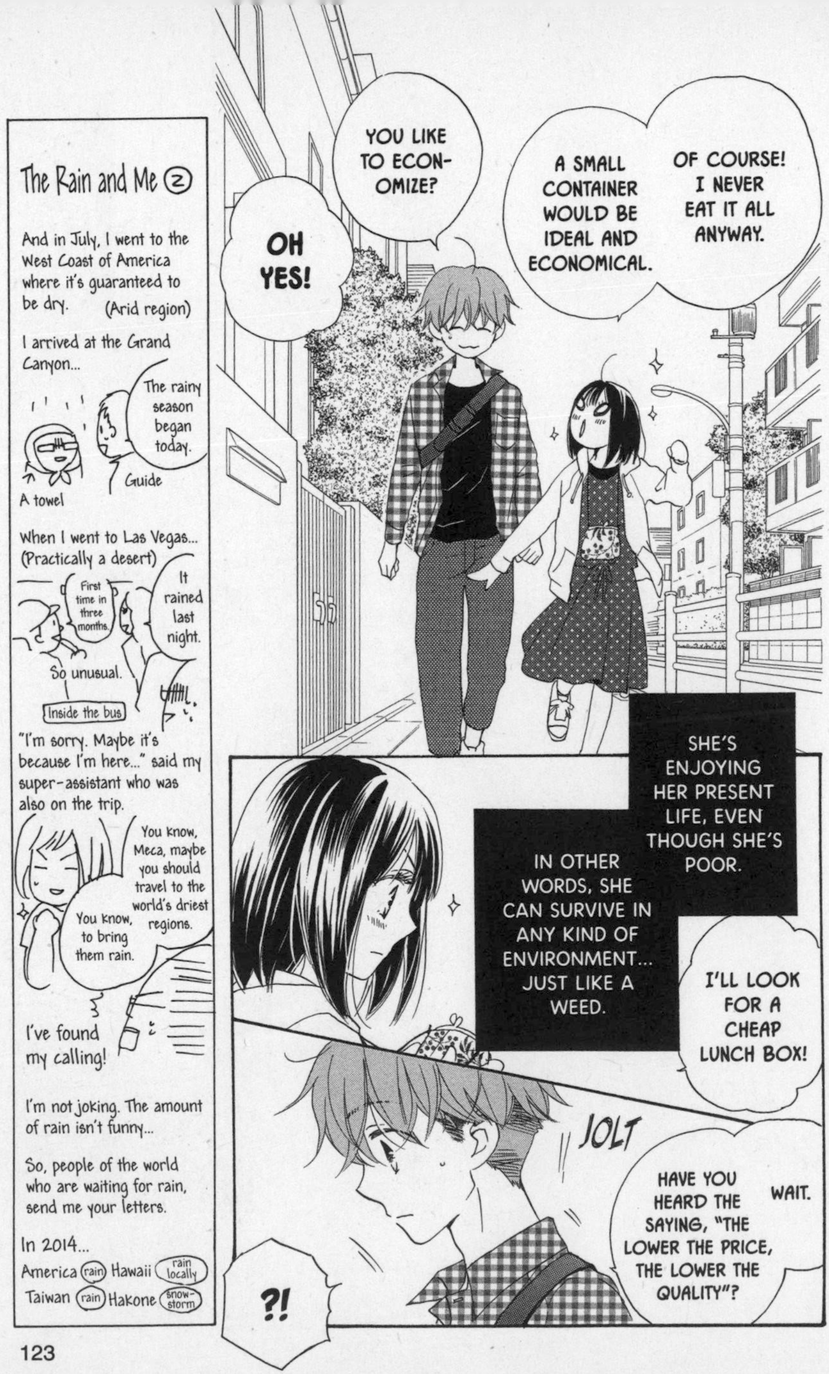
OF COURSE! I NEVER EAT IT ALL ANYWAY.
A SMALL CONTAINER WOULD BE IDEAL AND ECONOMICAL.
YOU LIKE TO ECON-OMIZE?
OH YES!
SHE'S ENJOYING HER PRESENT LIFE, EVEN THOUGH SHE'S POOR.
IN OTHER WORDS, SHE CAN SURVIVE IN ANY KIND OF ENVIRONMENT... JUST LIKE A WEED.
I'LL LOOK FOR A CHEAP LUNCH BOX!
WAIT.
HAVE YOU HEARD THE SAYING, "THE LOWER THE PRICE, THE LOWER THE QUALITY"?
JOLT
?!

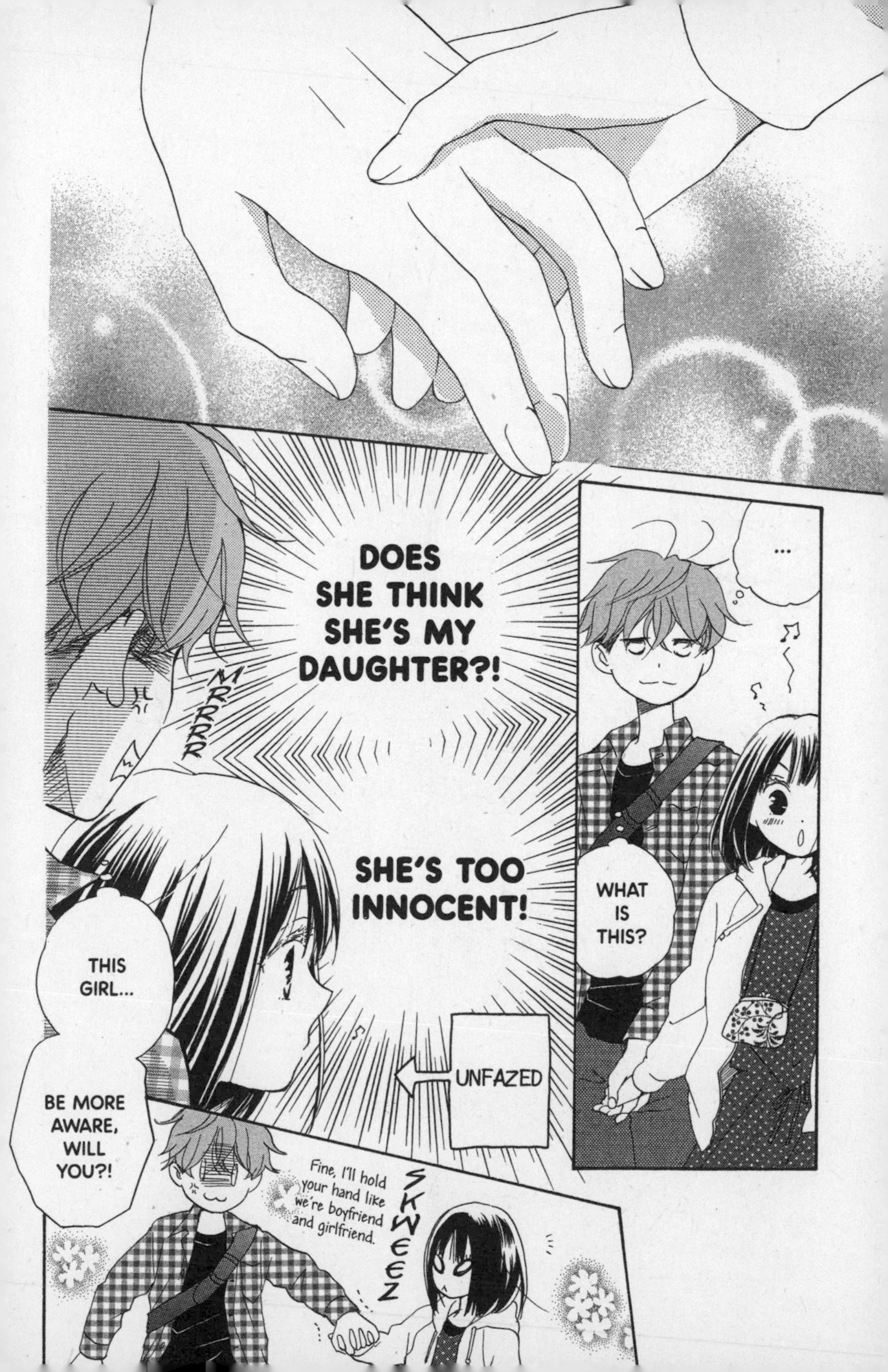
...
WHAT IS THIS?
DOES SHE THINK SHE'S MY DAUGHTER?!
SHE'S TOO INNOCENT!
MRRRRR
UNFAZED
THIS GIRL...
BE MORE AWARE, WILL YOU?!
SKWEEZ
Fine, I'll hold your hand like we're boyfriend and girlfriend.

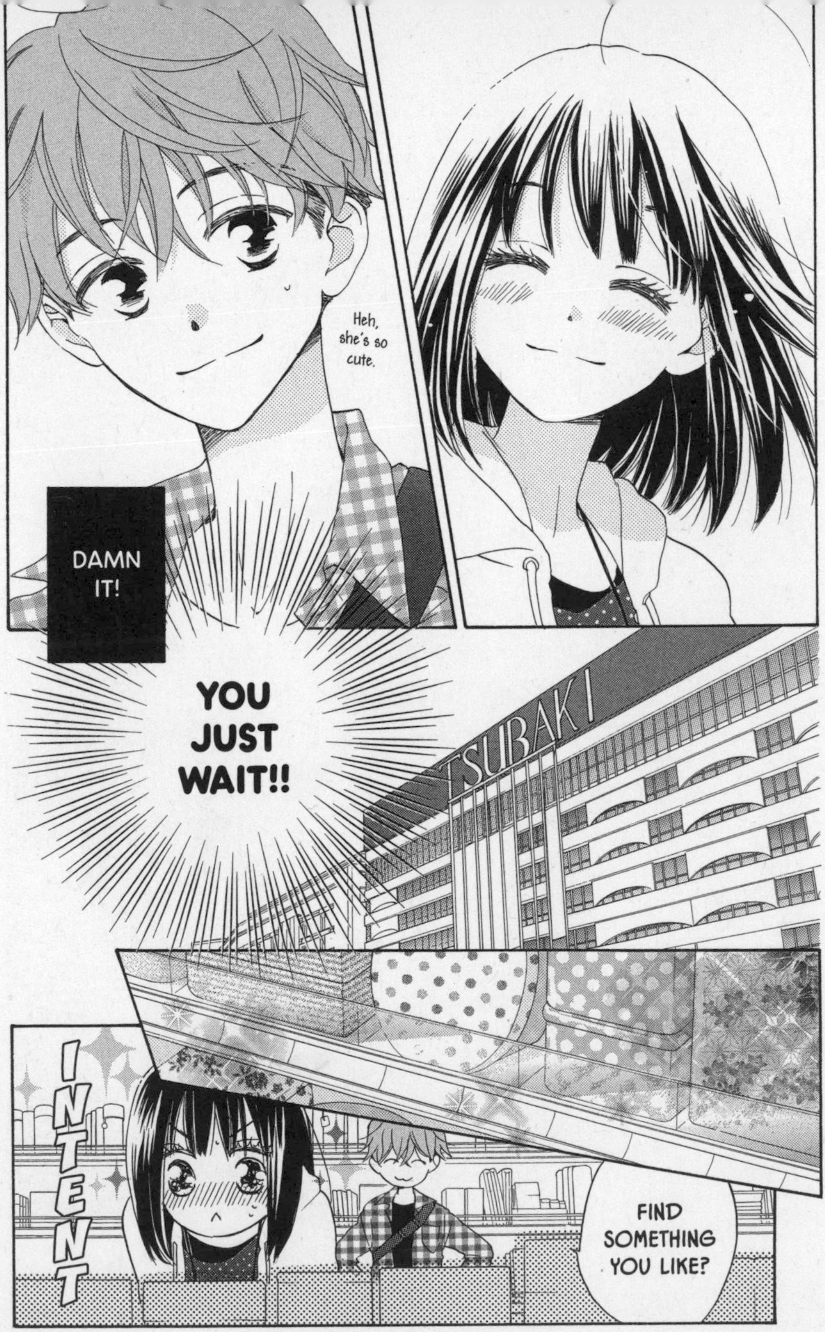
Heh, she's so cute.
DAMN IT!
YOU JUST WAIT!!
TSUBAKI
FIND SOMETHING YOU LIKE?
INTENT

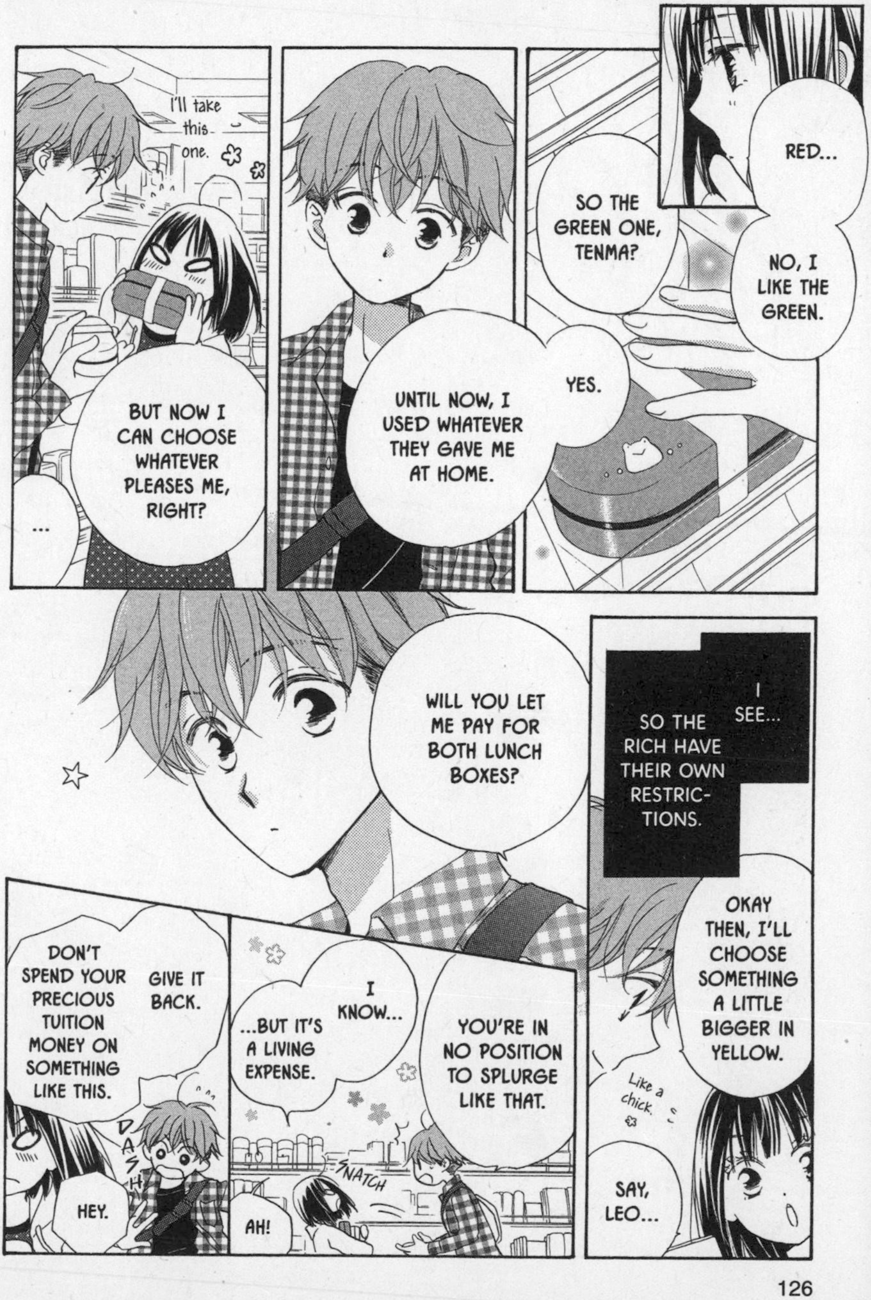
RED...
NO, I LIKE THE GREEN.
SO THE GREEN ONE, TENMA?
YES.
UNTIL NOW, I USED WHATEVER THEY GAVE ME AT HOME.
I'll take this one.
BUT NOW I CAN CHOOSE WHATEVER PLEASES ME, RIGHT?
...
I SEE...
SO THE RICH HAVE THEIR OWN RESTRICTIONS.
WILL YOU LET ME PAY FOR BOTH LUNCH BOXES?
OKAY THEN, I'LL CHOOSE SOMETHING A LITTLE BIGGER IN YELLOW.
Like a chick.
SAY, LEO...
YOU'RE IN NO POSITION TO SPLURGE LIKE THAT.
I KNOW...
...BUT IT'S A LIVING EXPENSE.
SNATCH
AH!
GIVE IT BACK.
DON'T SPEND YOUR PRECIOUS TUITION MONEY ON SOMETHING LIKE THIS.
DASH
HEY.

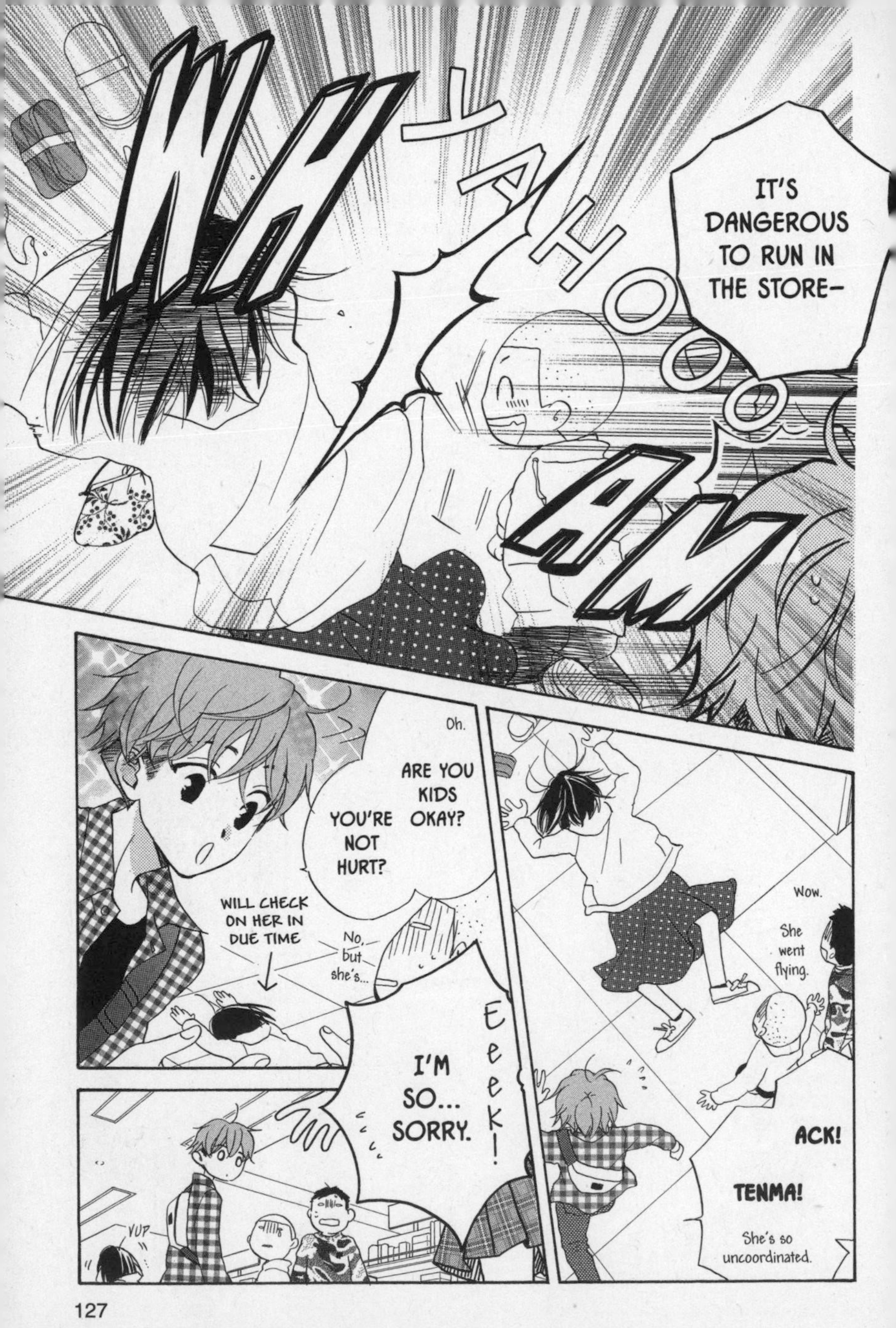
IT'S DANGEROUS TO RUN IN THE STORE–
YAHOOOO
WHAM
Wow.
She went flying.
ACK!
TENMA!
She's so uncoordinated.
Oh.
ARE YOU KIDS OKAY?
YOU'RE NOT HURT?
WILL CHECK ON HER IN DUE TIME
No, but she's...
Eeek!
I'M SO... SORRY.
YUP

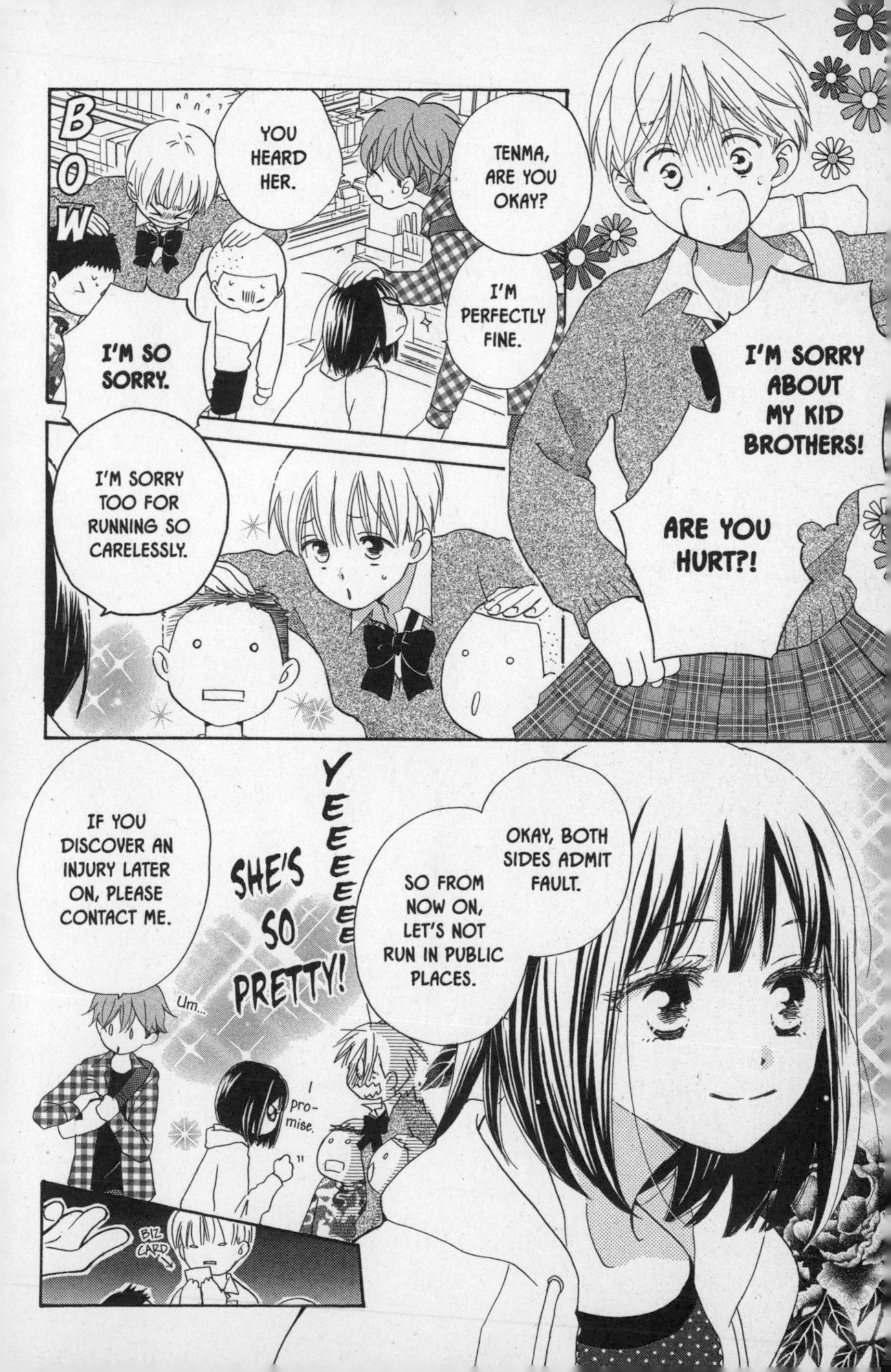
I'M SORRY ABOUT MY KID BROTHERS!
ARE YOU HURT?!
TENMA, ARE YOU OKAY?
I'M PERFECTLY FINE.
YOU HEARD HER.
BOW
I'M SO SORRY.
I'M SORRY TOO FOR RUNNING SO CARELESSLY.
OKAY, BOTH SIDES ADMIT FAULT.
SO FROM NOW ON, LET'S NOT RUN IN PUBLIC PLACES.
YEEEEEEE
SHE'S SO PRETTY!
IF YOU DISCOVER AN INJURY LATER ON, PLEASE CONTACT ME.
Um...
I pro-mise.
BIZ CARD

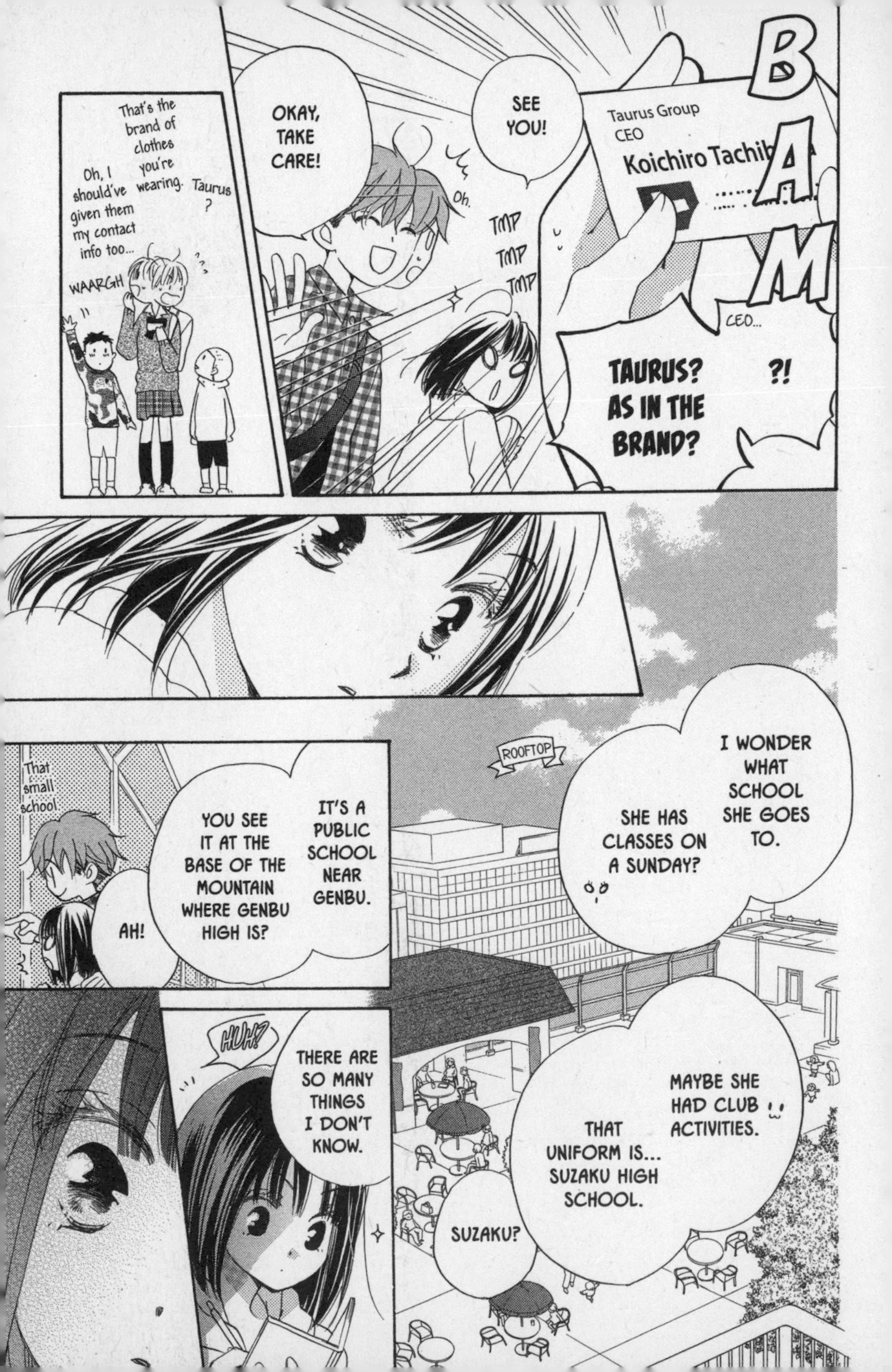
BAM
Taurus Group
CEO
Koichiro Tachib
CEO...
TAURUS? AS IN THE BRAND?
?!
SEE YOU!
Oh.
TMP
TMP
TMP
OKAY, TAKE CARE!
That's the brand of clothes you're wearing.
Taurus?
Oh, I should've given them my contact info too...
WAARGH
ROOFTOP
I WONDER WHAT SCHOOL SHE GOES TO.
SHE HAS CLASSES ON A SUNDAY?
IT'S A PUBLIC SCHOOL NEAR GENBU.
YOU SEE IT AT THE BASE OF THE MOUNTAIN WHERE GENBU HIGH IS?
AH!
That small school
MAYBE SHE HAD CLUB ACTIVITIES.
THAT UNIFORM IS... SUZAKU HIGH SCHOOL.
SUZAKU?
HUH?
THERE ARE SO MANY THINGS I DON'T KNOW.

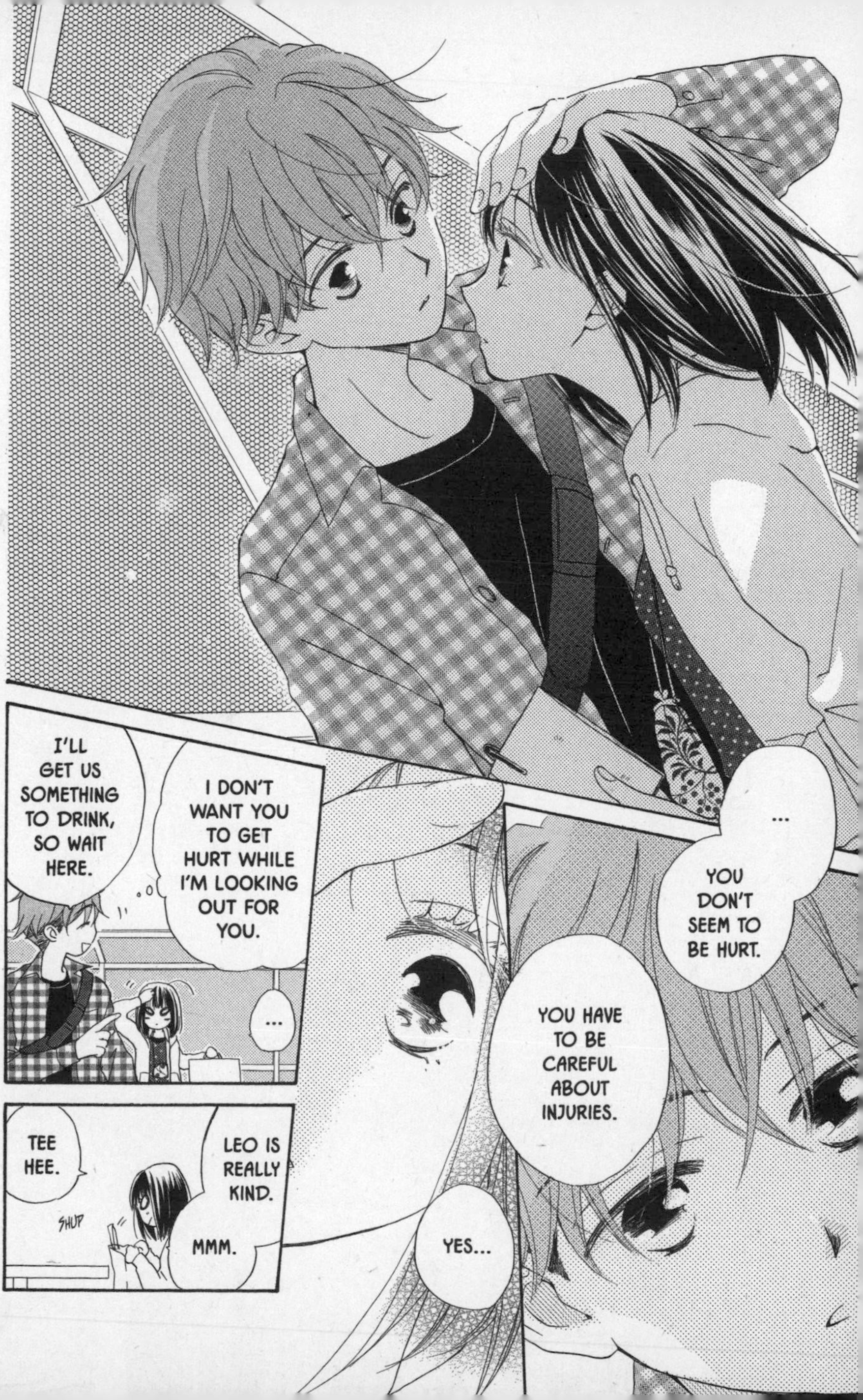
...
YOU DON'T SEEM TO BE HURT.
YOU HAVE TO BE CAREFUL ABOUT INJURIES.
YES...
I'LL GET US SOMETHING TO DRINK, SO WAIT HERE.
I DON'T WANT YOU TO GET HURT WHILE I'M LOOKING OUT FOR YOU.
...
TEE HEE.
LEO IS REALLY KIND.
MMM.
SHUP

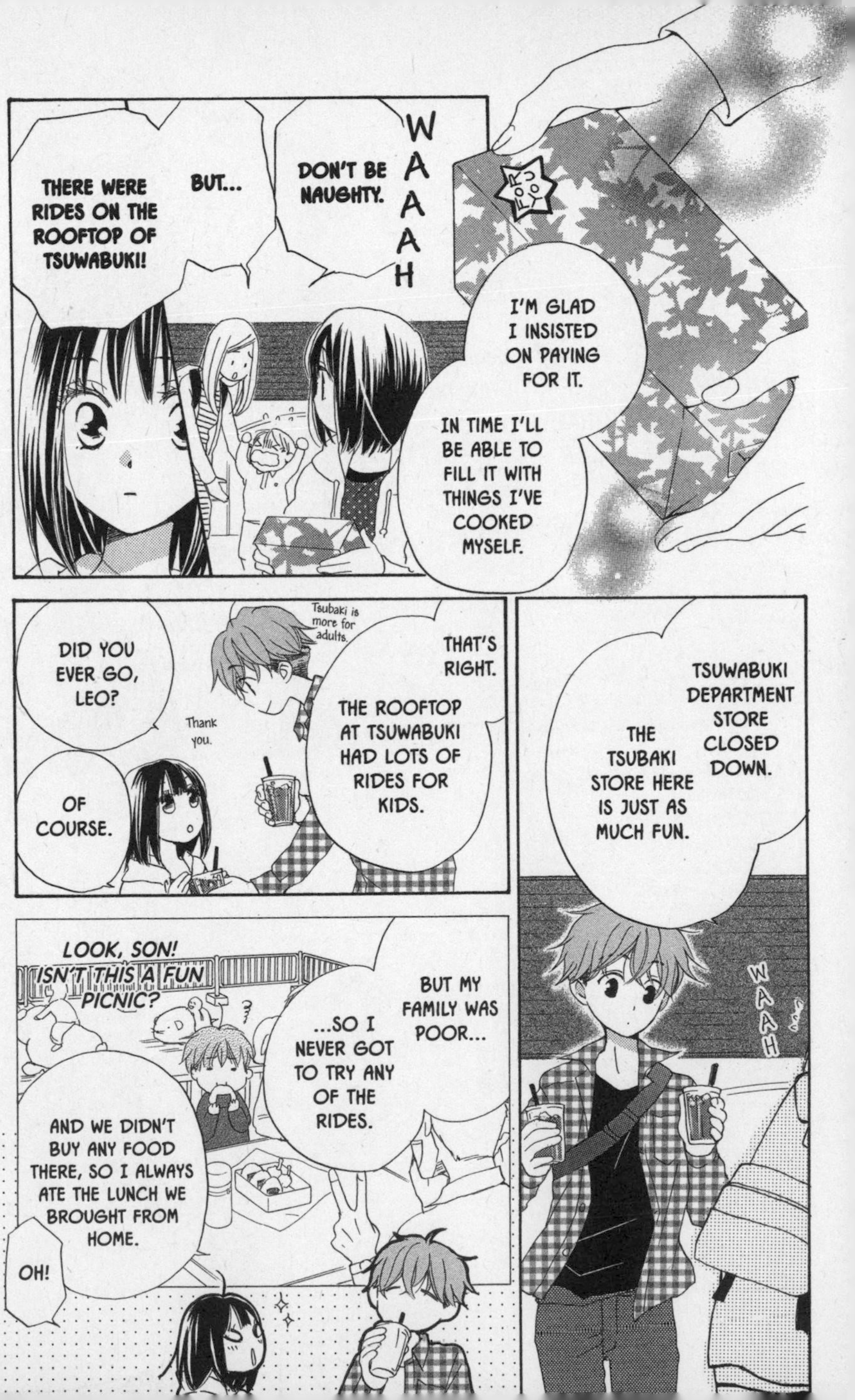
FOR YOU
I'M GLAD I INSISTED ON PAYING FOR IT.
IN TIME I'LL BE ABLE TO FILL IT WITH THINGS I'VE COOKED MYSELF.
WAAAH
DON'T BE NAUGHTY.
BUT...
THERE WERE RIDES ON THE ROOFTOP OF TSUWABUKI!
TSUWABUKI DEPARTMENT STORE CLOSED DOWN.
THE TSUBAKI STORE HERE IS JUST AS MUCH FUN.
WAAAH
Tsubaki is more for adults.
THAT'S RIGHT.
THE ROOFTOP AT TSUWABUKI HAD LOTS OF RIDES FOR KIDS.
DID YOU EVER GO, LEO?
Thank you.
OF COURSE.
BUT MY FAMILY WAS POOR...
...SO I NEVER GOT TO TRY ANY OF THE RIDES.
LOOK, SON! ISN'T THIS A FUN PICNIC?
AND WE DIDN'T BUY ANY FOOD THERE, SO I ALWAYS ATE THE LUNCH WE BROUGHT FROM HOME.
OH!

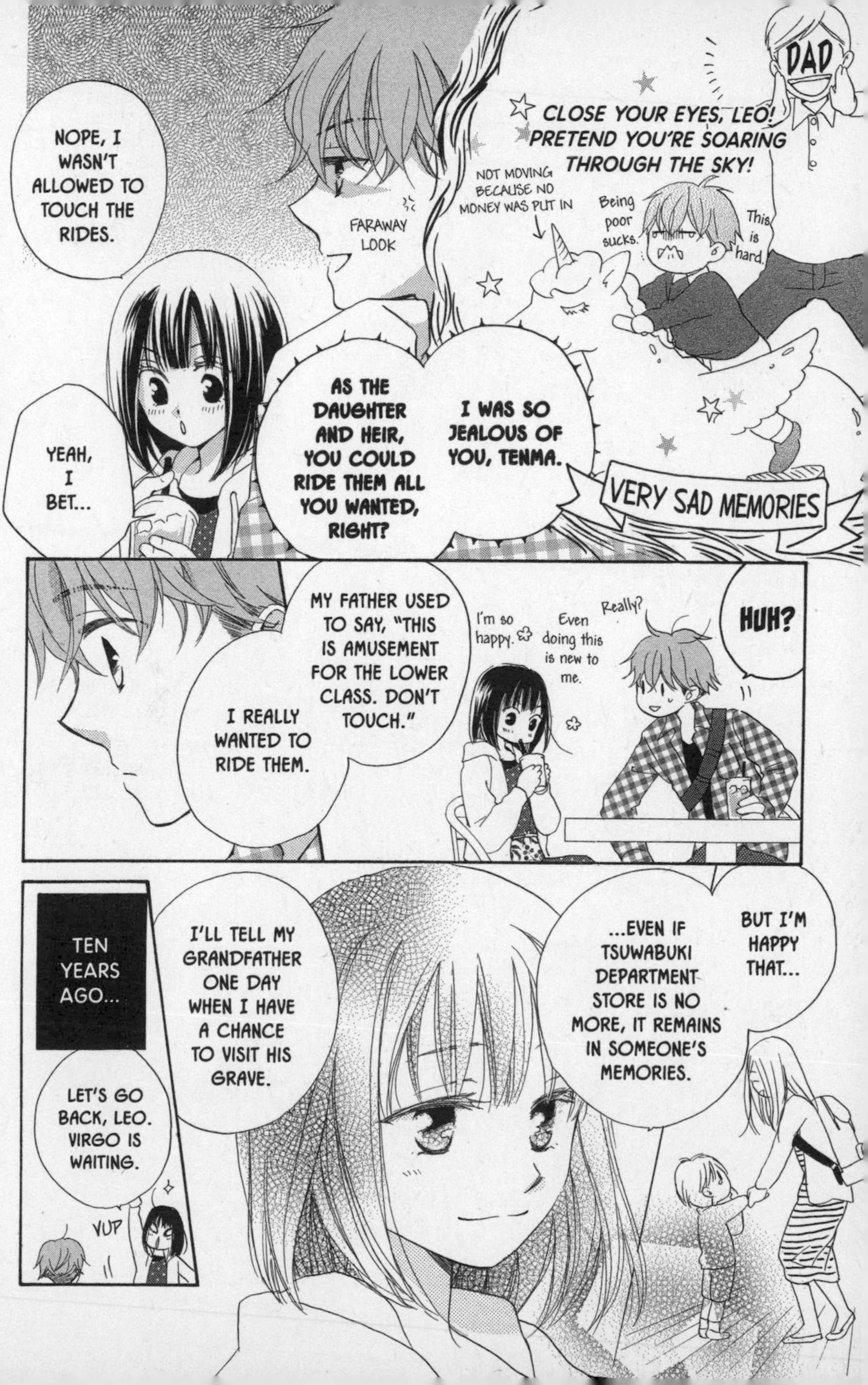
DAD
CLOSE YOUR EYES, LEO! PRETEND YOU'RE SOARING THROUGH THE SKY!
NOT MOVING BECAUSE NO MONEY WAS PUT IN
Being poor sucks.
This is hard.
FARAWAY LOOK
NOPE, I WASN'T ALLOWED TO TOUCH THE RIDES.
I WAS SO JEALOUS OF YOU, TENMA.
AS THE DAUGHTER AND HEIR, YOU COULD RIDE THEM ALL YOU WANTED, RIGHT?
VERY SAD MEMORIES
YEAH, I BET...
HUH?
Really?
Even doing this is new to me.
I'm so happy.
MY FATHER USED TO SAY, "THIS IS AMUSEMENT FOR THE LOWER CLASS. DON'T TOUCH."
I REALLY WANTED TO RIDE THEM.
BUT I'M HAPPY THAT...
...EVEN IF TSUWABUKI DEPARTMENT STORE IS NO MORE, IT REMAINS IN SOMEONE'S MEMORIES.
I'LL TELL MY GRANDFATHER ONE DAY WHEN I HAVE A CHANCE TO VISIT HIS GRAVE.
TEN YEARS AGO...
LET'S GO BACK, LEO. VIRGO IS WAITING.
YUP

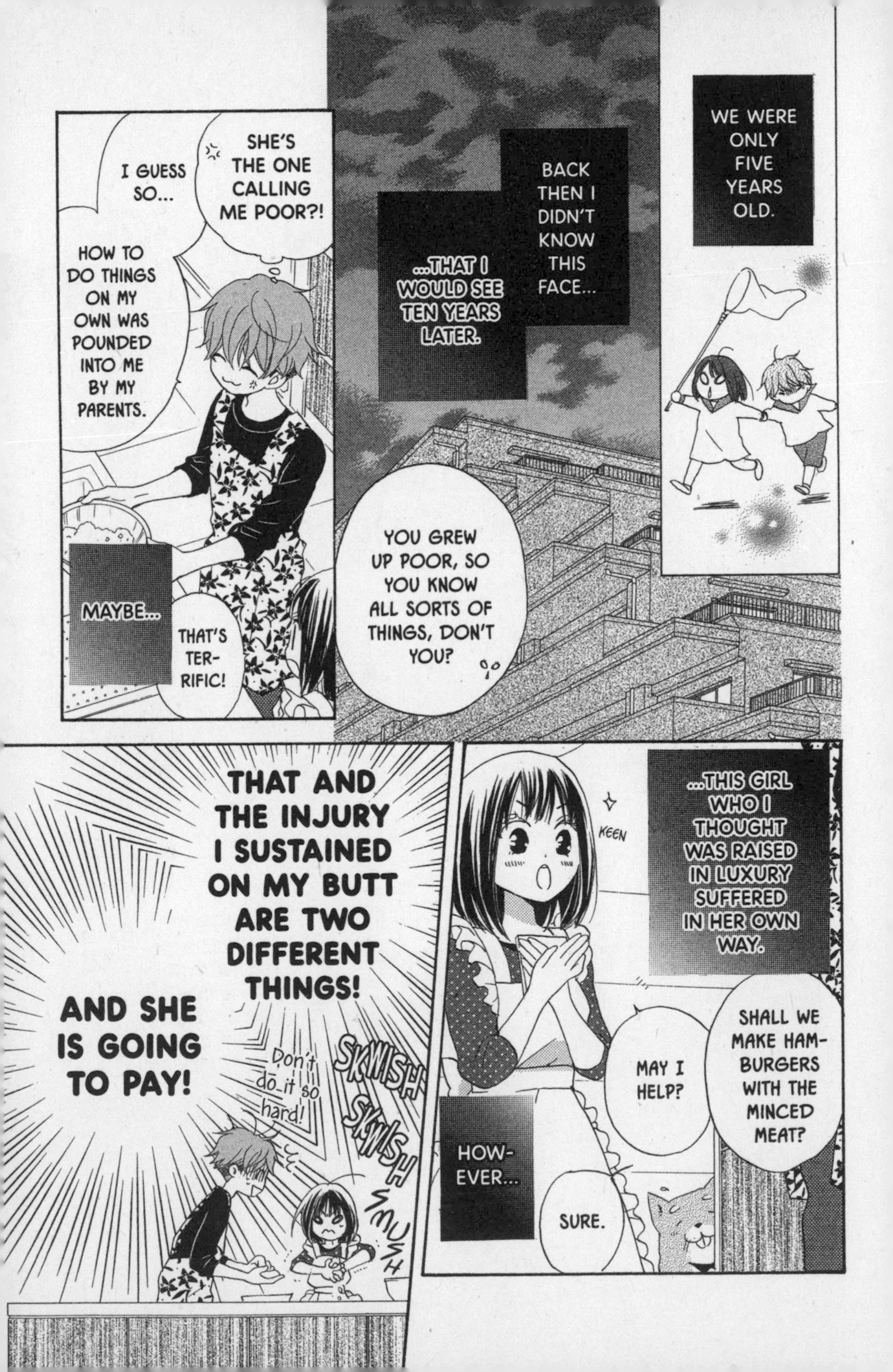
WE WERE ONLY FIVE YEARS OLD.
BACK THEN I DIDN'T KNOW THIS FACE...
...THAT I WOULD SEE TEN YEARS LATER.
YOU GREW UP POOR, SO YOU KNOW ALL SORTS OF THINGS, DON'T YOU?
SHE'S THE ONE CALLING ME POOR?!
I GUESS SO...
HOW TO DO THINGS ON MY OWN WAS POUNDED INTO ME BY MY PARENTS.
MAYBE...
THAT'S TER-RIFIC!
...THIS GIRL WHO I THOUGHT WAS RAISED IN LUXURY SUFFERED IN HER OWN WAY.
KEEN
SHALL WE MAKE HAM-BURGERS WITH THE MINCED MEAT?
MAY I HELP?
HOW-EVER...
SURE.
THAT AND THE INJURY I SUSTAINED ON MY BUTT ARE TWO DIFFERENT THINGS!
AND SHE IS GOING TO PAY!
Don't do it so hard!
SKWISH
SKWISH
SMUSH

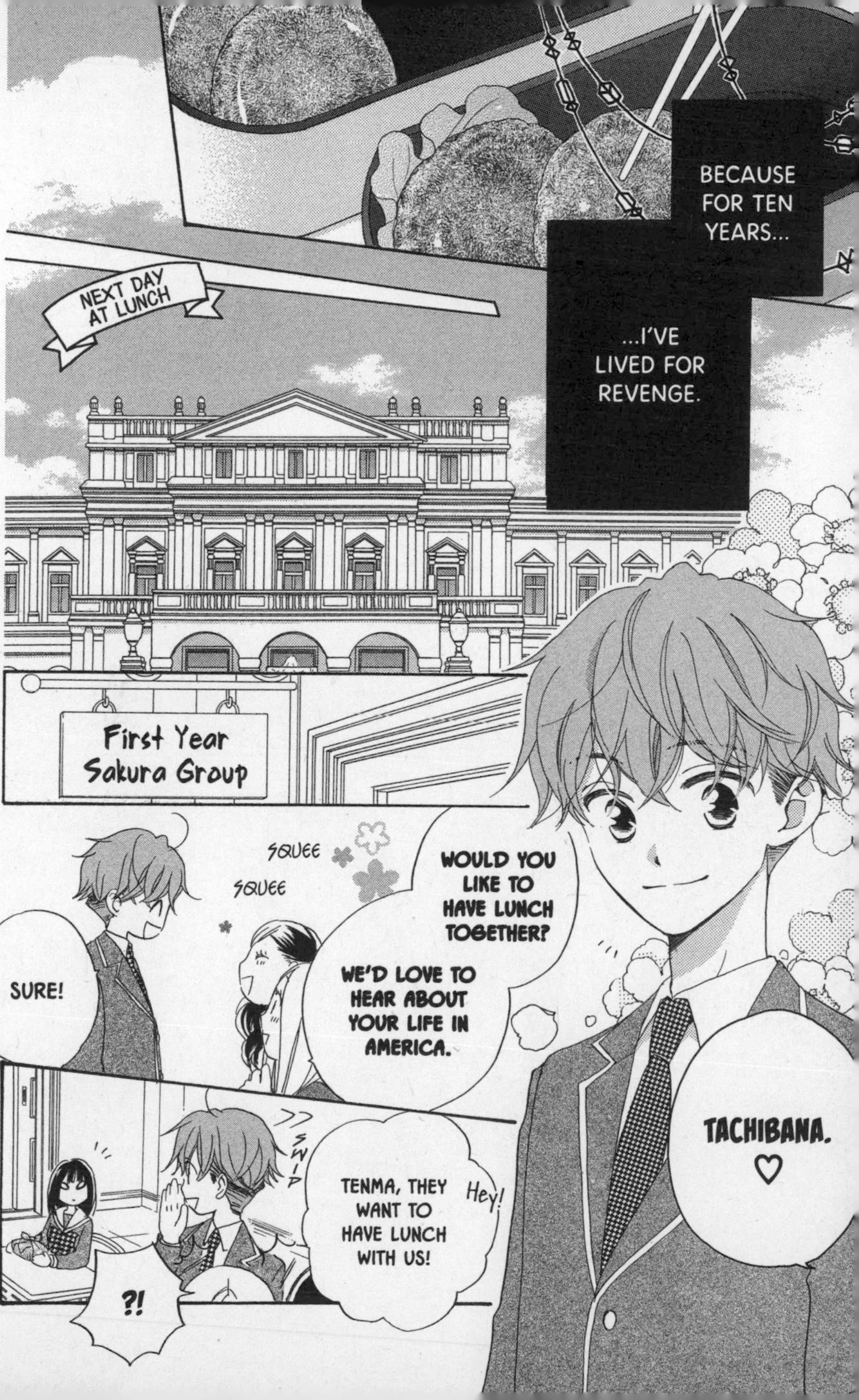
BECAUSE FOR TEN YEARS...
...I'VE LIVED FOR REVENGE.
NEXT DAY AT LUNCH
First Year Sakura Group
TACHIBANA. ♡
WOULD YOU LIKE TO HAVE LUNCH TOGETHER?
WE'D LOVE TO HEAR ABOUT YOUR LIFE IN AMERICA.
SQUEE
SQUEE
SURE!
Hey!
SWIP
TENMA, THEY WANT TO HAVE LUNCH WITH US!
?!

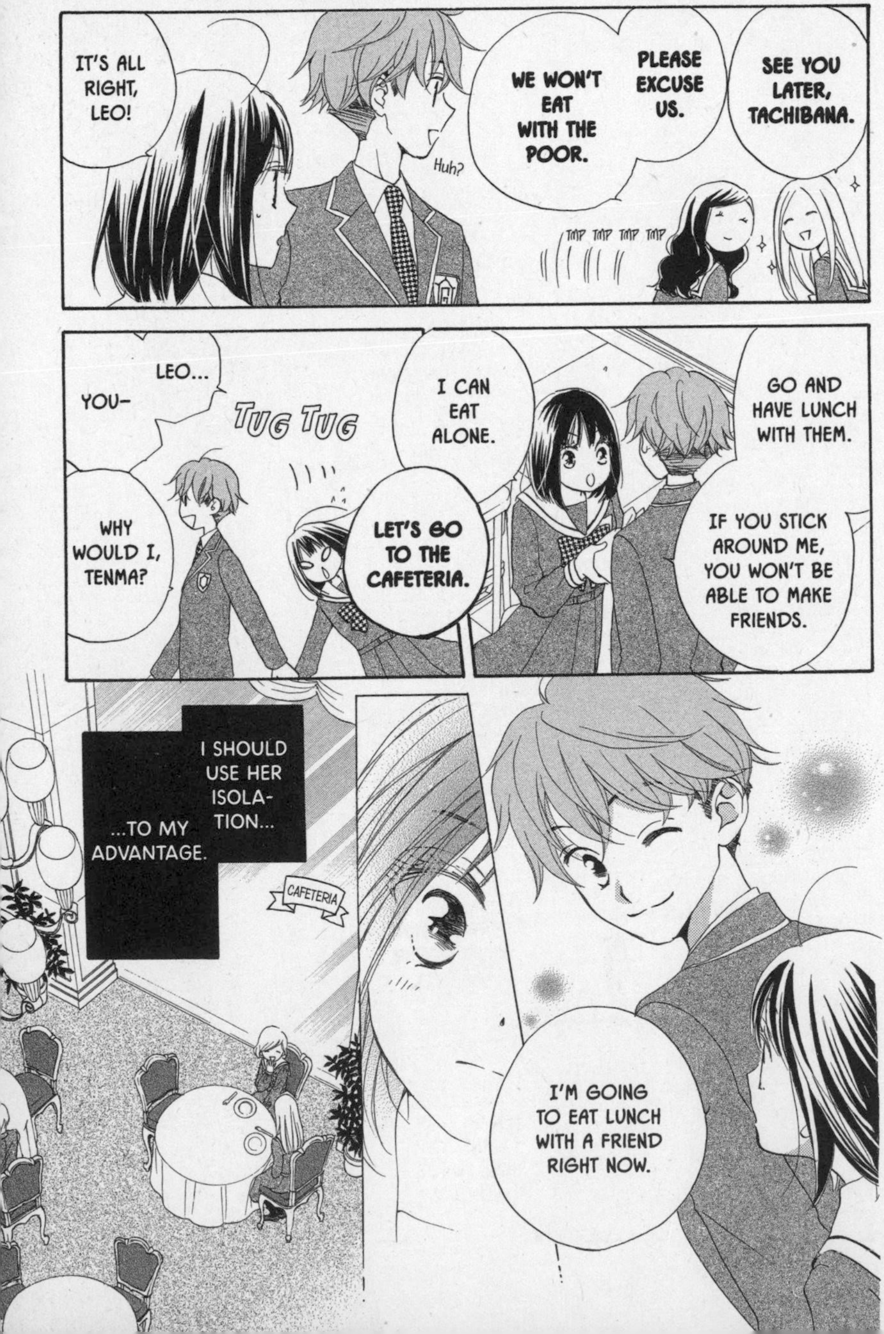
SEE YOU LATER, TACHIBANA.
PLEASE EXCUSE US.
WE WON'T EAT WITH THE POOR.
Huh?
TMP TMP TMP TMP
IT'S ALL RIGHT, LEO!
GO AND HAVE LUNCH WITH THEM.
IF YOU STICK AROUND ME, YOU WON'T BE ABLE TO MAKE FRIENDS.
I CAN EAT ALONE.
LET'S GO TO THE CAFETERIA.
TUG TUG
LEO... YOU-
WHY WOULD I, TENMA?
I'M GOING TO EAT LUNCH WITH A FRIEND RIGHT NOW.
I SHOULD USE HER ISOLATION...
...TO MY ADVANTAGE.
CAFETERIA

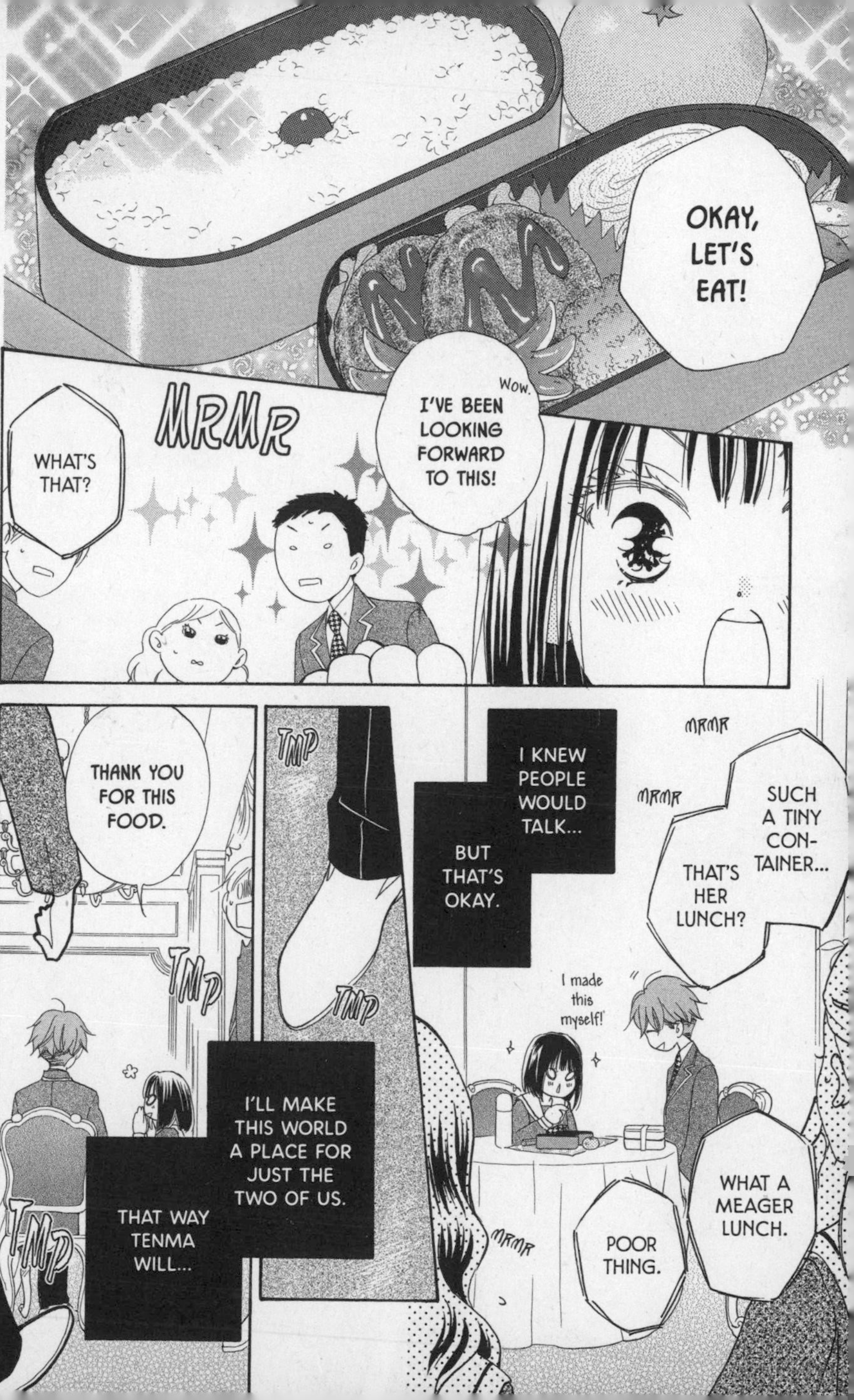
OKAY, LET'S EAT!
Wow.
I'VE BEEN LOOKING FORWARD TO THIS!
MRMR
WHAT'S THAT?
MRMR
SUCH A TINY CON-TAINER...
MRMR
THAT'S HER LUNCH?
I KNEW PEOPLE WOULD TALK...
BUT THAT'S OKAY.
I made this myself!
WHAT A MEAGER LUNCH.
MRMR
POOR THING.
TMP
TMP
THANK YOU FOR THIS FOOD.
TMP
I'LL MAKE THIS WORLD A PLACE FOR JUST THE TWO OF US.
THAT WAY TENMA WILL...
TMP

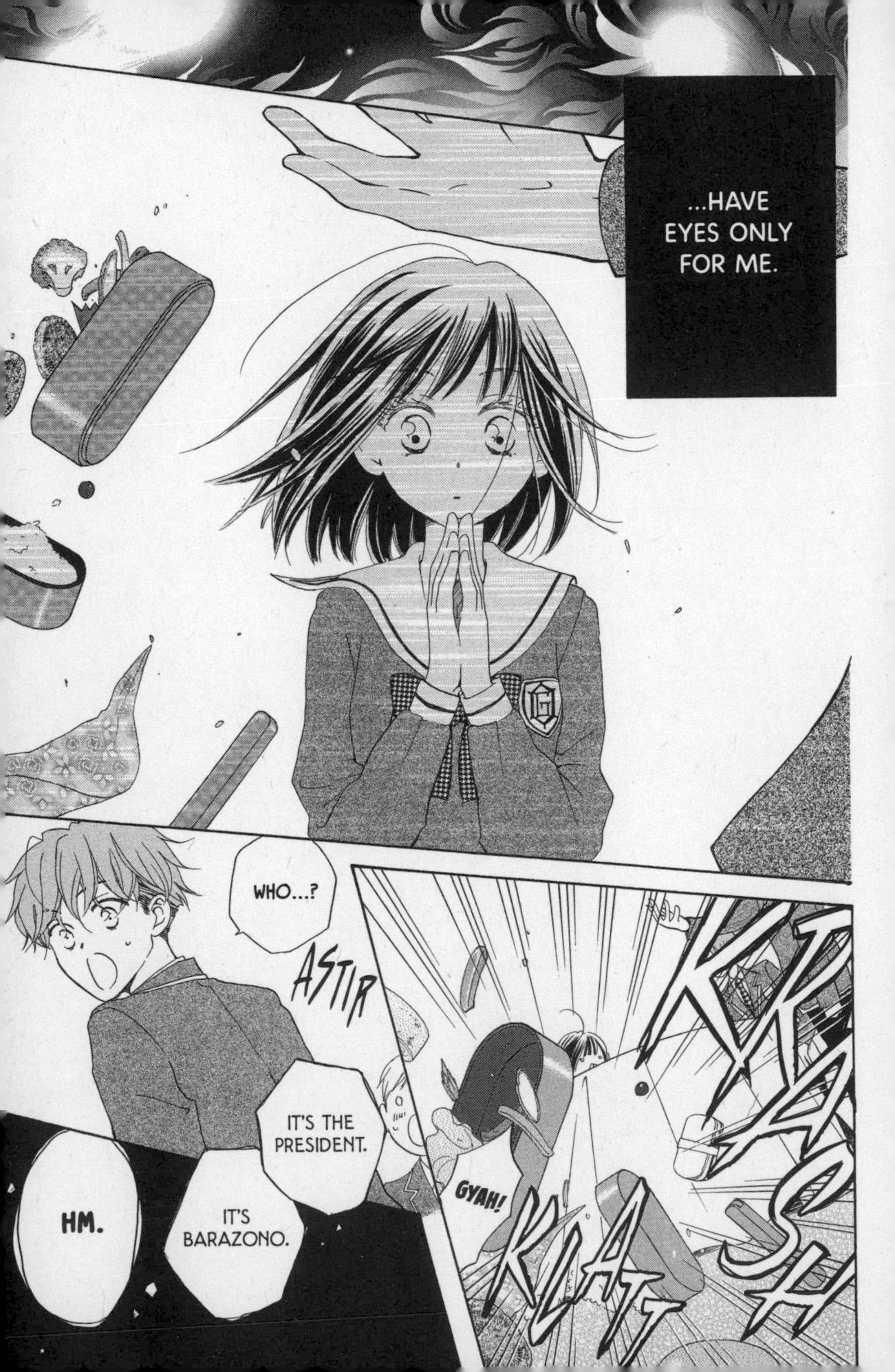
...HAVE EYES ONLY FOR ME.
KRASH
KLATT
GYAH!
WHO...?
ASTIR
IT'S THE PRESIDENT.
IT'S BARAZONO.
HM.

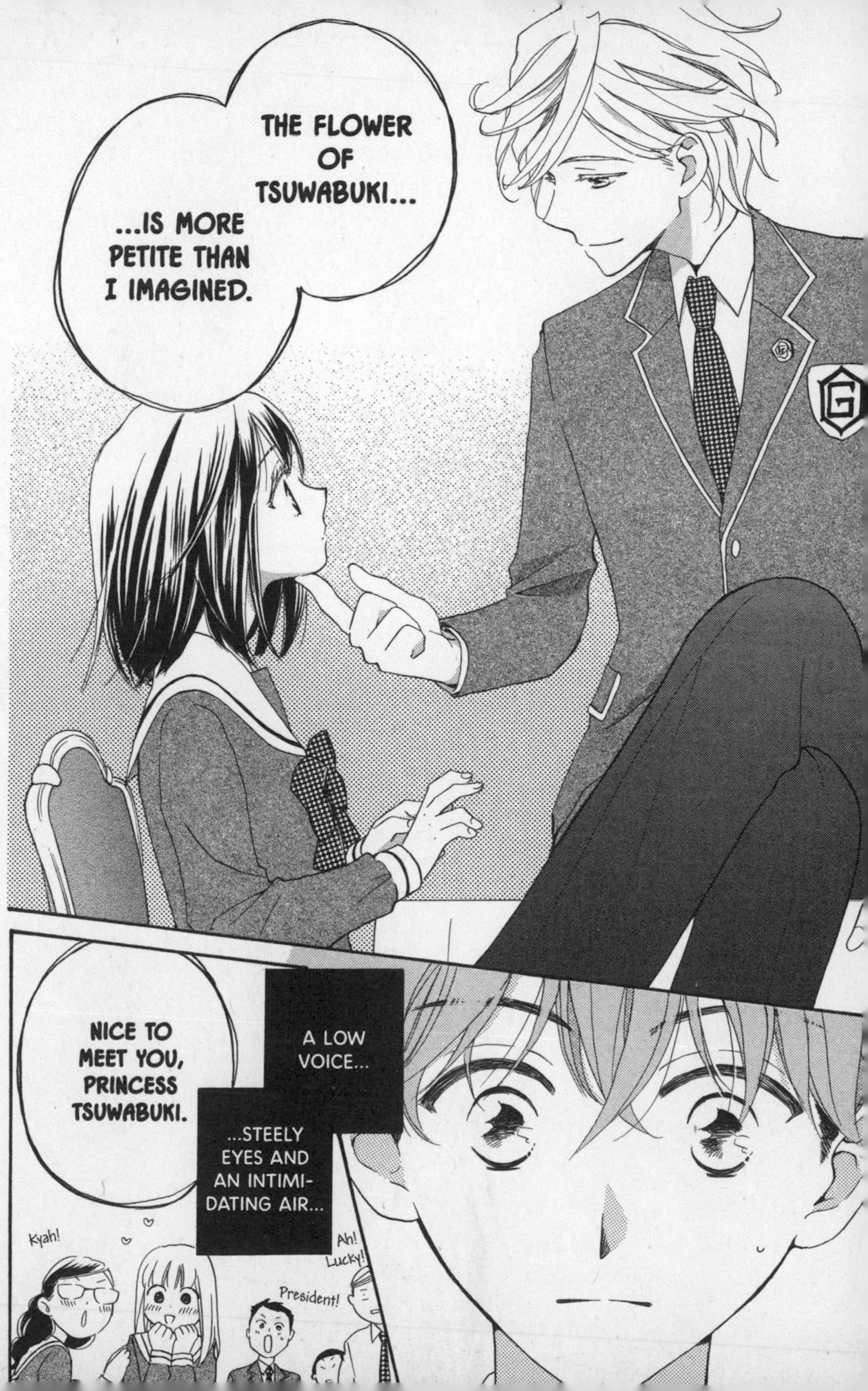
THE FLOWER OF TSUWABUKI...
...IS MORE PETITE THAN I IMAGINED.
A LOW VOICE...
...STEELY EYES AND AN INTIMI-DATING AIR...
NICE TO MEET YOU, PRINCESS TSUWABUKI.
Ah! Lucky!
President!
Kyah!

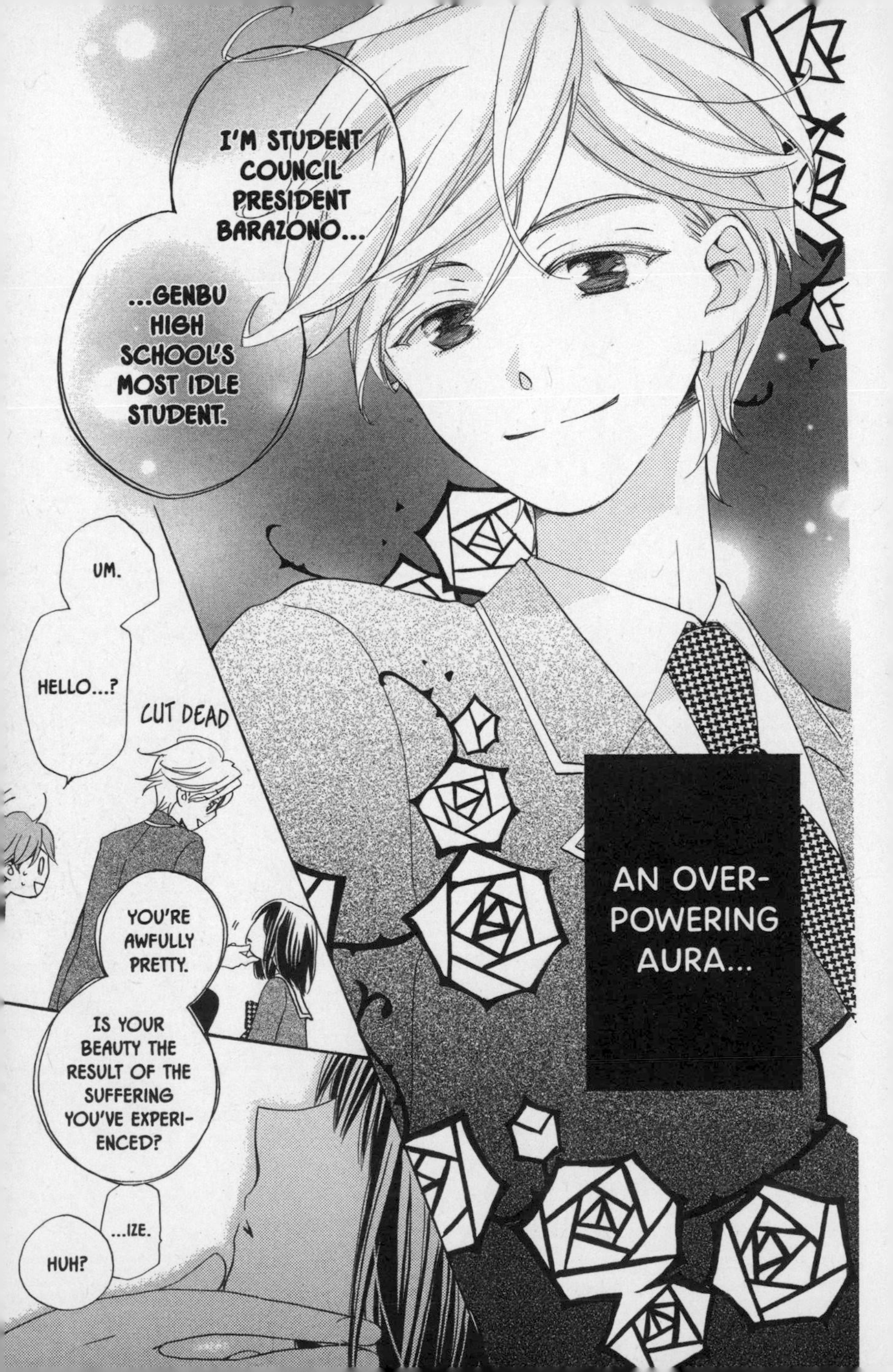
I'M STUDENT COUNCIL PRESIDENT BARAZONO...
...GENBU HIGH SCHOOL'S MOST IDLE STUDENT.
AN OVER-POWERING AURA...
UM.
HELLO...?
CUT DEAD
YOU'RE AWFULLY PRETTY.
IS YOUR BEAUTY THE RESULT OF THE SUFFERING YOU'VE EXPERI-ENCED?
...IZE.
HUH?

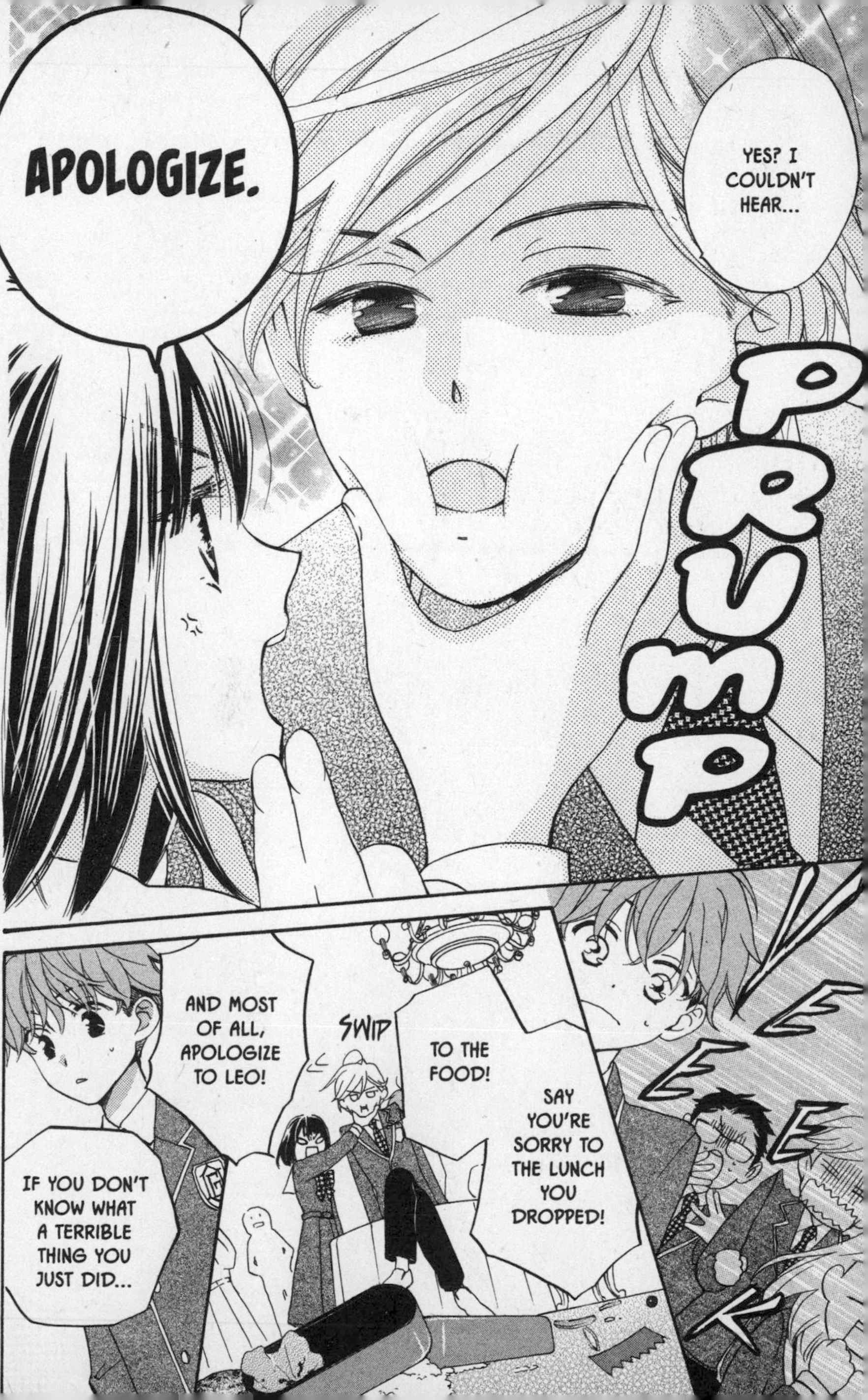
YES? I COULDN'T HEAR...
PRUMP
APOLOGIZE.
EEEEK
SAY YOU'RE SORRY TO THE LUNCH YOU DROPPED!
TO THE FOOD!
SWIP
AND MOST OF ALL, APOLOGIZE TO LEO!
IF YOU DON'T KNOW WHAT A TERRIBLE THING YOU JUST DID...

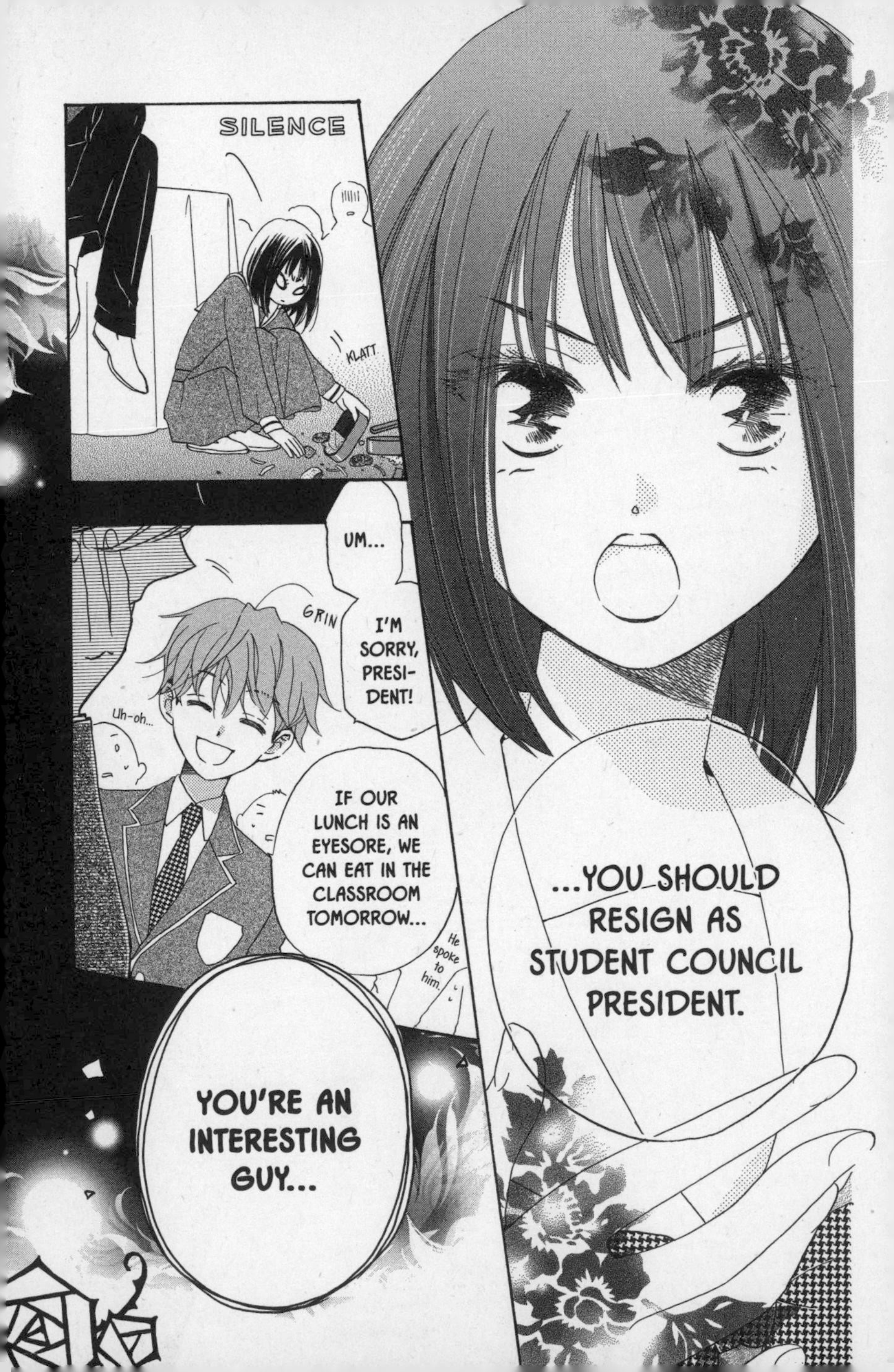

...YOU SHOULD RESIGN AS STUDENT COUNCIL PRESIDENT.
SILENCE
KLATT
UM...
GRIN
I'M SORRY, PRESI-DENT!
Uh-oh...
IF OUR LUNCH IS AN EYESORE, WE CAN EAT IN THE CLASSROOM TOMORROW...
He spoke to him.
YOU'RE AN INTERESTING GUY...

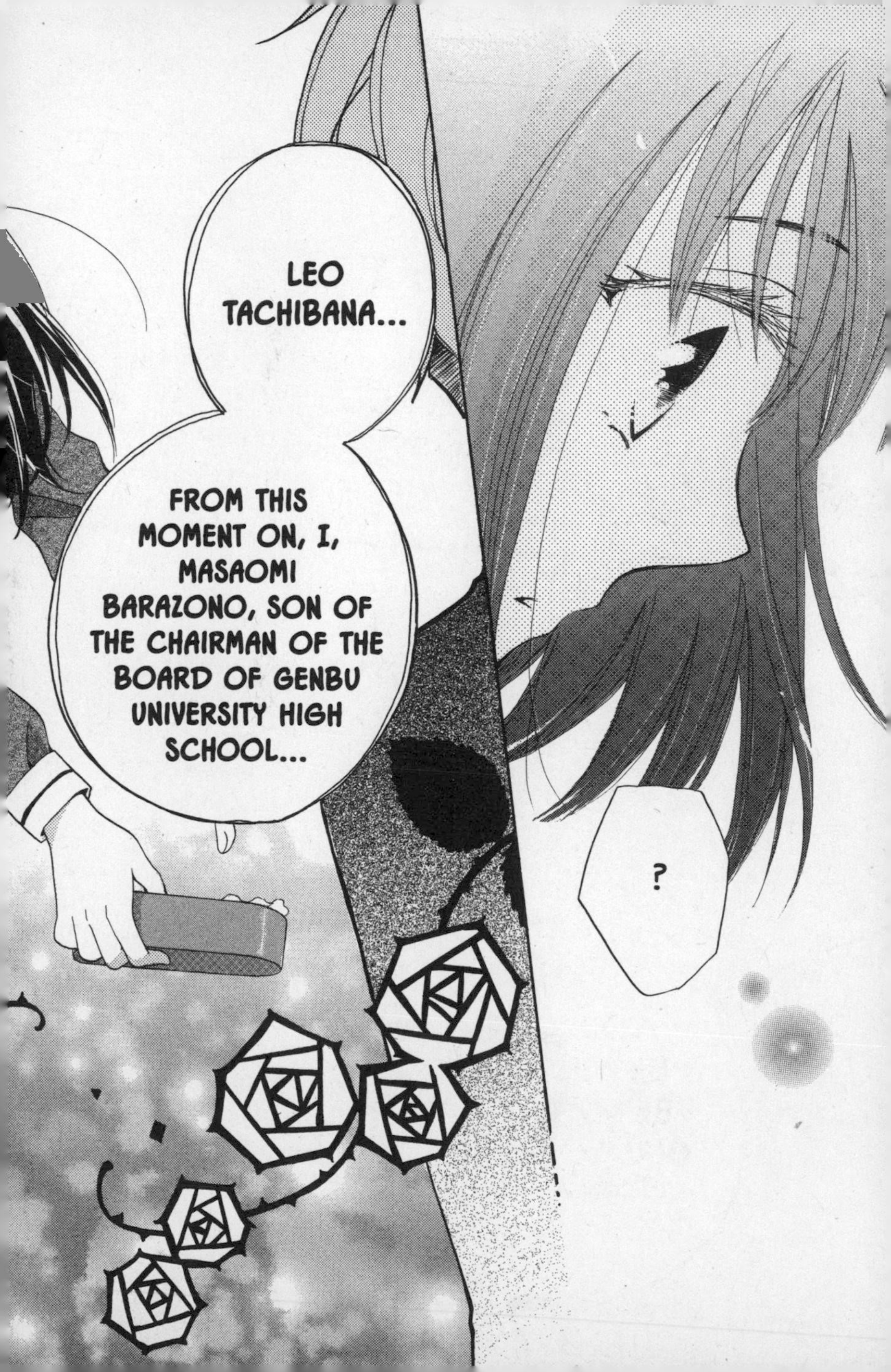
?
LEO TACHIBANA...
FROM THIS MOMENT ON, I, MASAOMI BARAZONO, SON OF THE CHAIRMAN OF THE BOARD OF GENBU UNIVERSITY HIGH SCHOOL...

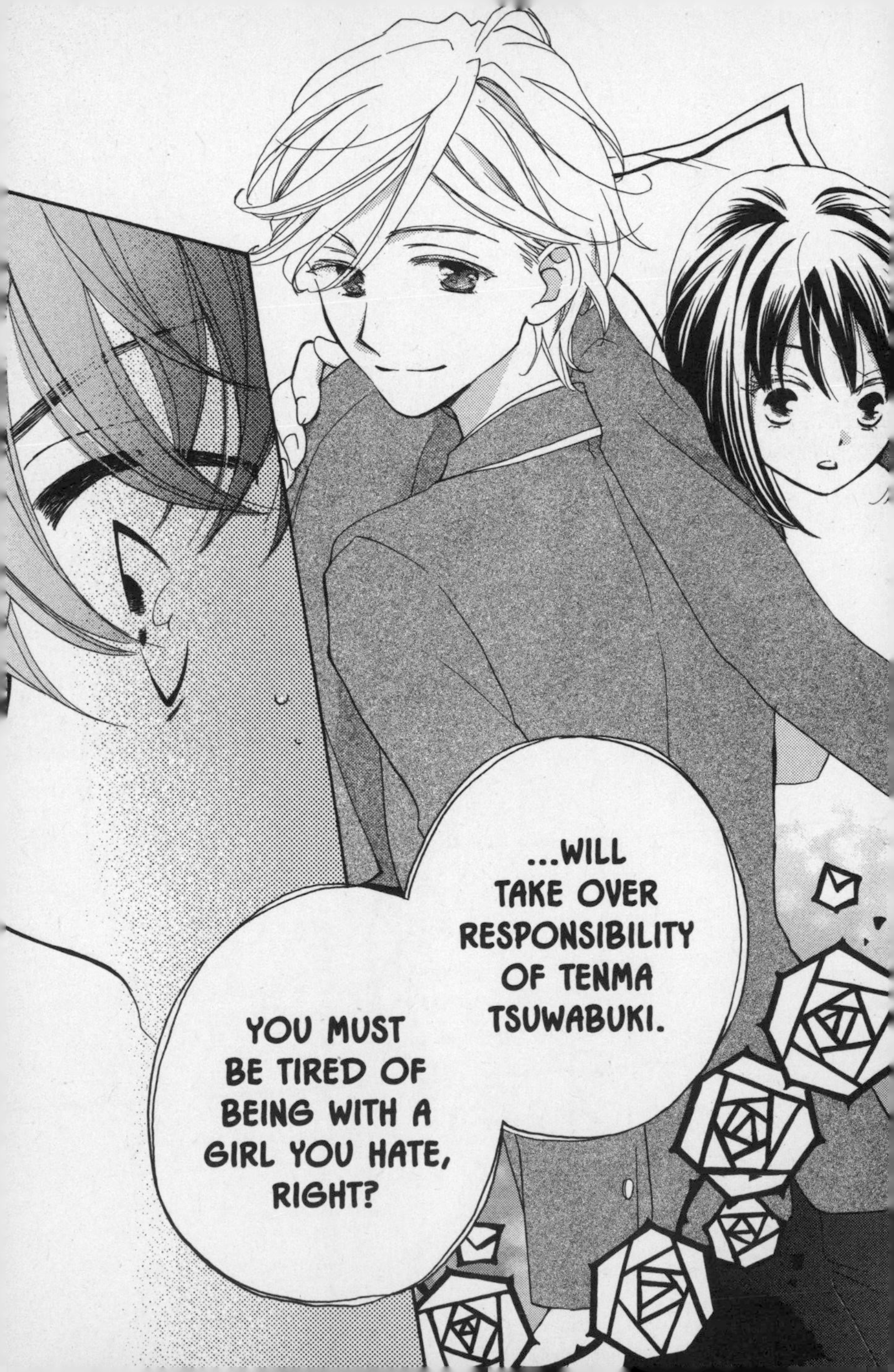
...WILL TAKE OVER RESPONSIBILITY OF TENMA TSUWABUKI.
YOU MUST BE TIRED OF BEING WITH A GIRL YOU HATE, RIGHT?

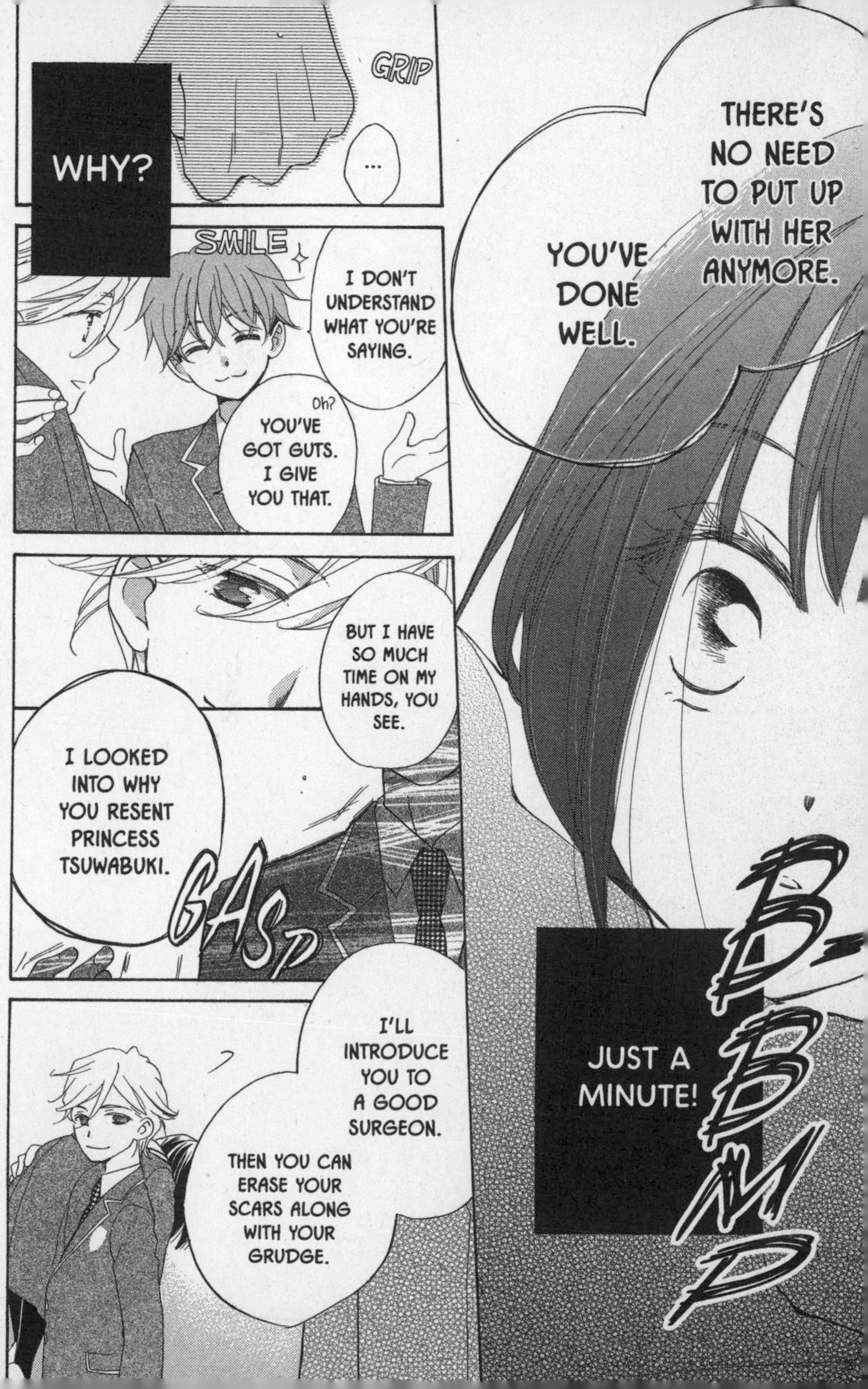

THERE'S NO NEED TO PUT UP WITH HER ANYMORE.
YOU'VE DONE WELL.
B-BUMP
JUST A MINUTE!
GRIP
...
WHY?
SMILE
I DON'T UNDERSTAND WHAT YOU'RE SAYING.
Oh?
YOU'VE GOT GUTS. I GIVE YOU THAT.
BUT I HAVE SO MUCH TIME ON MY HANDS, YOU SEE.
I LOOKED INTO WHY YOU RESENT PRINCESS TSUWABUKI.
GASP
I'LL INTRODUCE YOU TO A GOOD SURGEON.
THEN YOU CAN ERASE YOUR SCARS ALONG WITH YOUR GRUDGE.

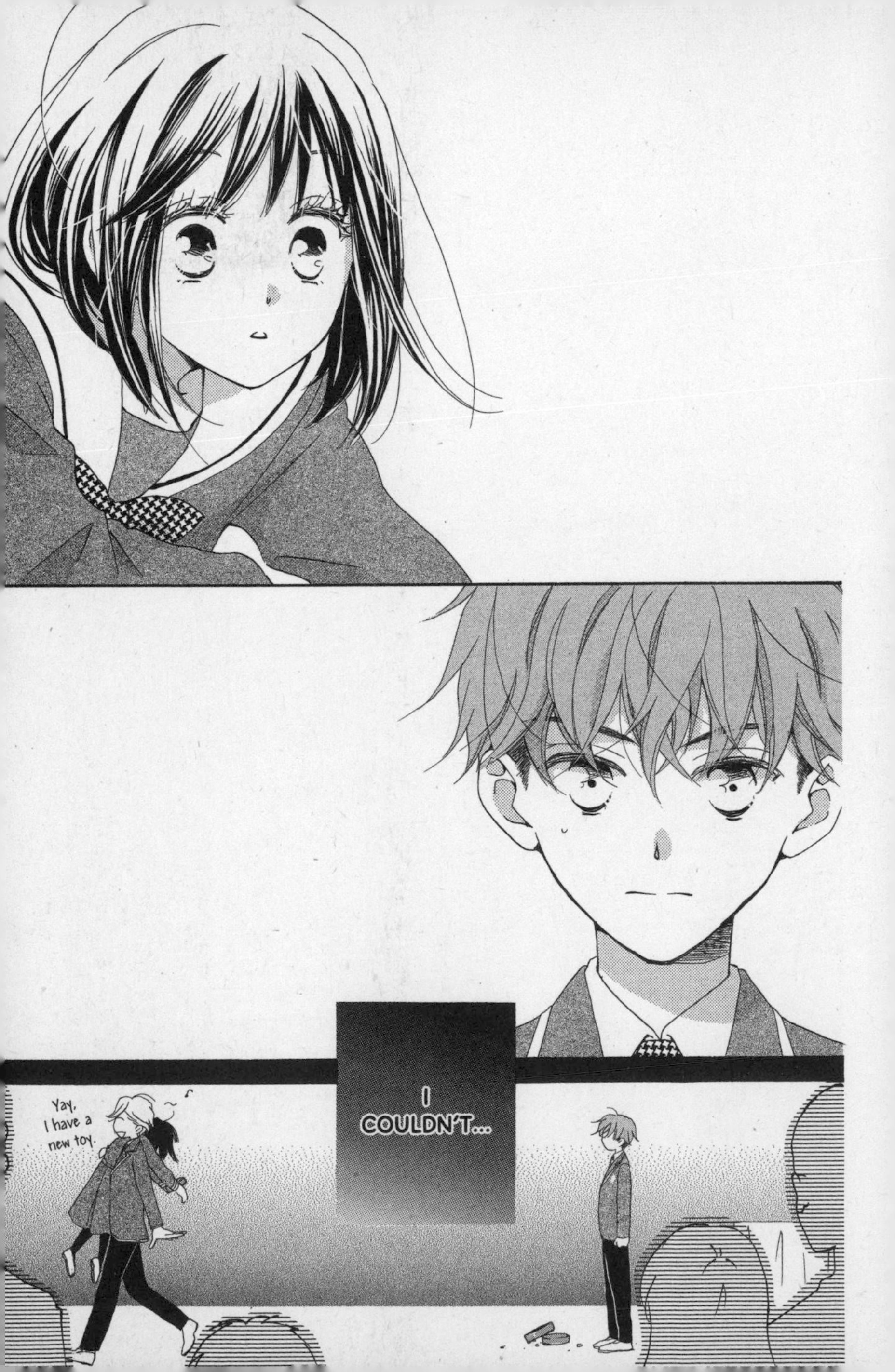
I COULDN'T...
Yay, I have a new toy.

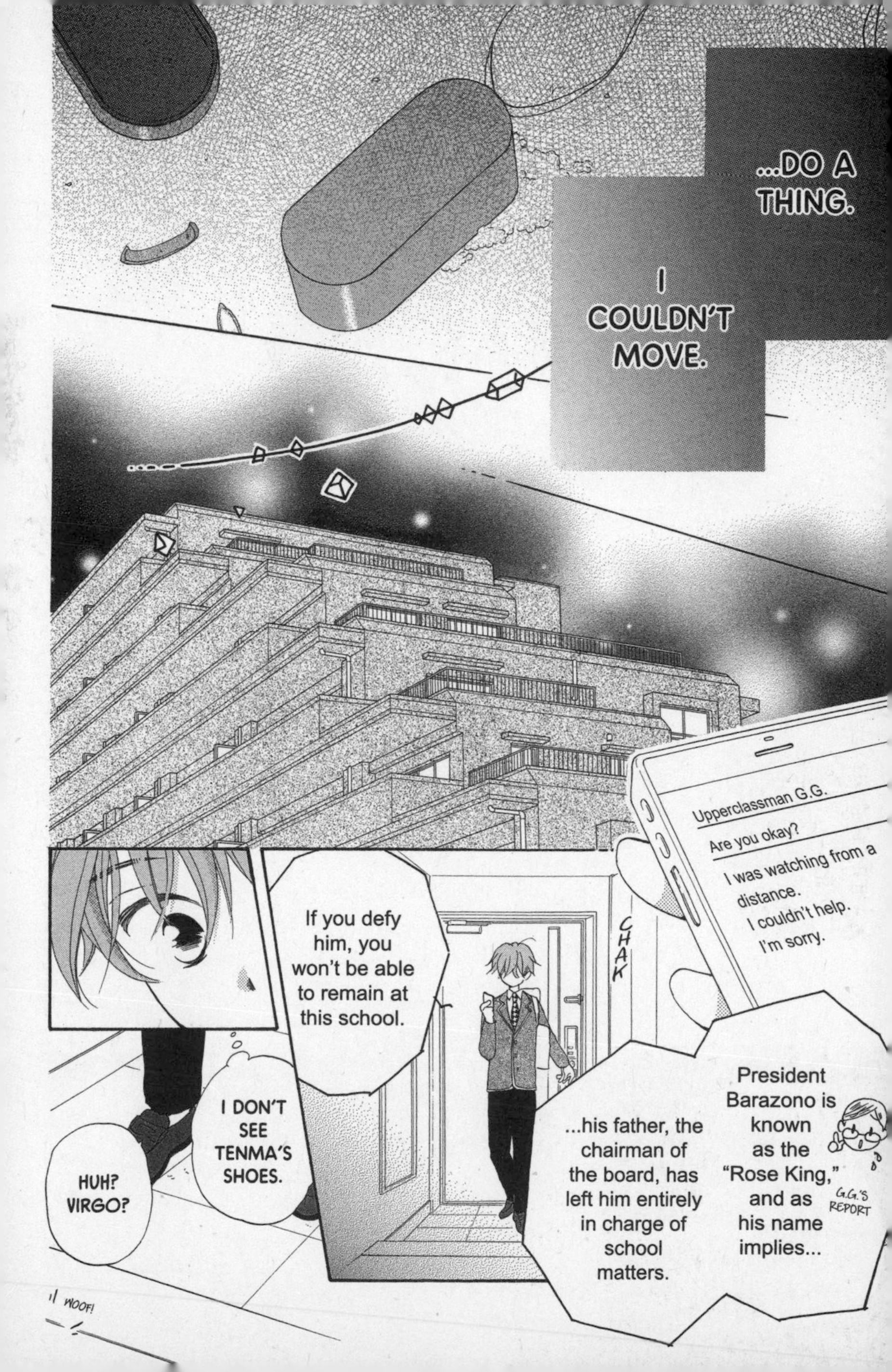
...DO A THING.
I COULDN'T MOVE.
Upperclassman G.G.
Are you okay?
I was watching from a distance.
I couldn't help.
I'm sorry.
President Barazono is known as the "Rose King," and as his name implies...
G.G.'S REPORT
...his father, the chairman of the board, has left him entirely in charge of school matters.
CHAK
If you defy him, you won't be able to remain at this school.
I DON'T SEE TENMA'S SHOES.
HUH? VIRGO?
WOOF!

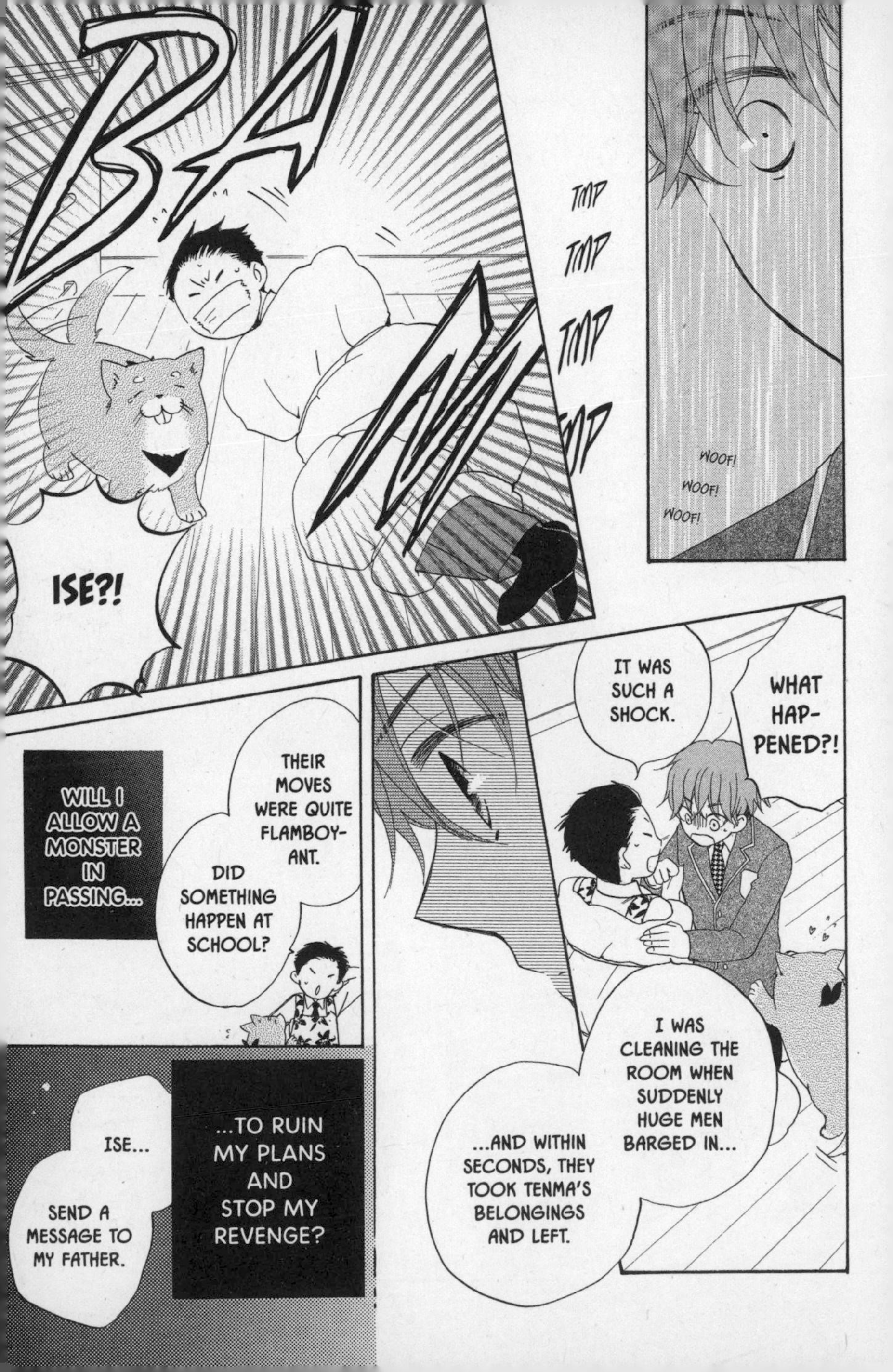
WOOF!
WOOF!
WOOF!
TMP
TMP
TMP
TMP
BAM
ISE?!
WHAT HAP-PENED?!
IT WAS SUCH A SHOCK.
I WAS CLEANING THE ROOM WHEN SUDDENLY HUGE MEN BARGED IN...
...AND WITHIN SECONDS, THEY TOOK TENMA'S BELONGINGS AND LEFT.
THEIR MOVES WERE QUITE FLAMBOY-ANT.
DID SOMETHING HAPPEN AT SCHOOL?
WILL I ALLOW A MONSTER IN PASSING...
...TO RUIN MY PLANS AND STOP MY REVENGE?
ISE...
SEND A MESSAGE TO MY FATHER.

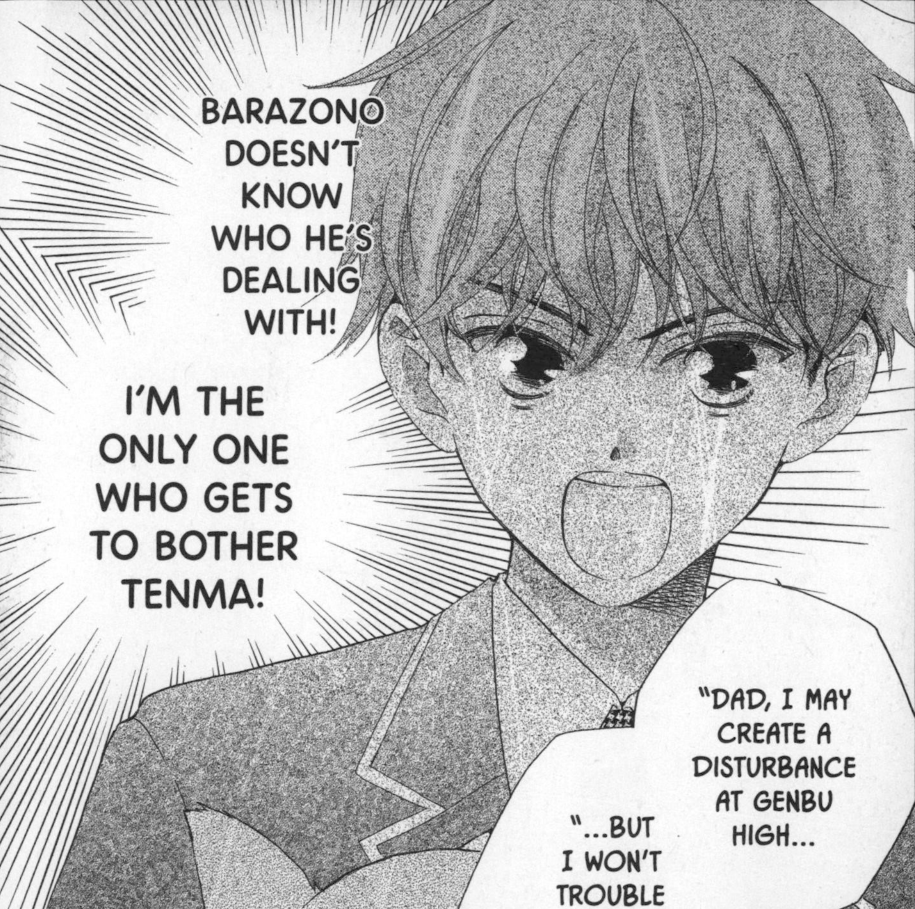
"DAD, I MAY CREATE A DISTURBANCE AT GENBU HIGH...
"...BUT I WON'T TROUBLE YOU."
BARAZONO DOESN'T KNOW WHO HE'S DEALING WITH!
I'M THE ONLY ONE WHO GETS TO BOTHER TENMA!
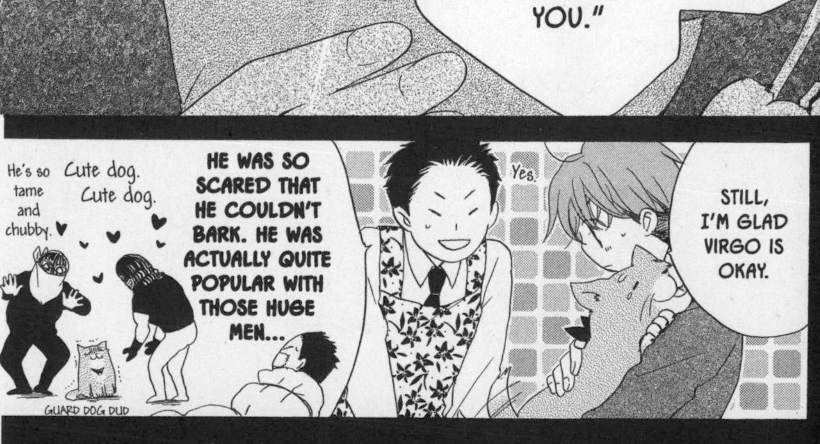
STILL, I'M GLAD VIRGO IS OKAY.
Yes.
HE WAS SO SCARED THAT HE COULDN'T BARK. HE WAS ACTUALLY QUITE POPULAR WITH THOSE HUGE MEN...
Cute dog. Cute dog.
He's so tame and chubby.
GUARD DOG DUD

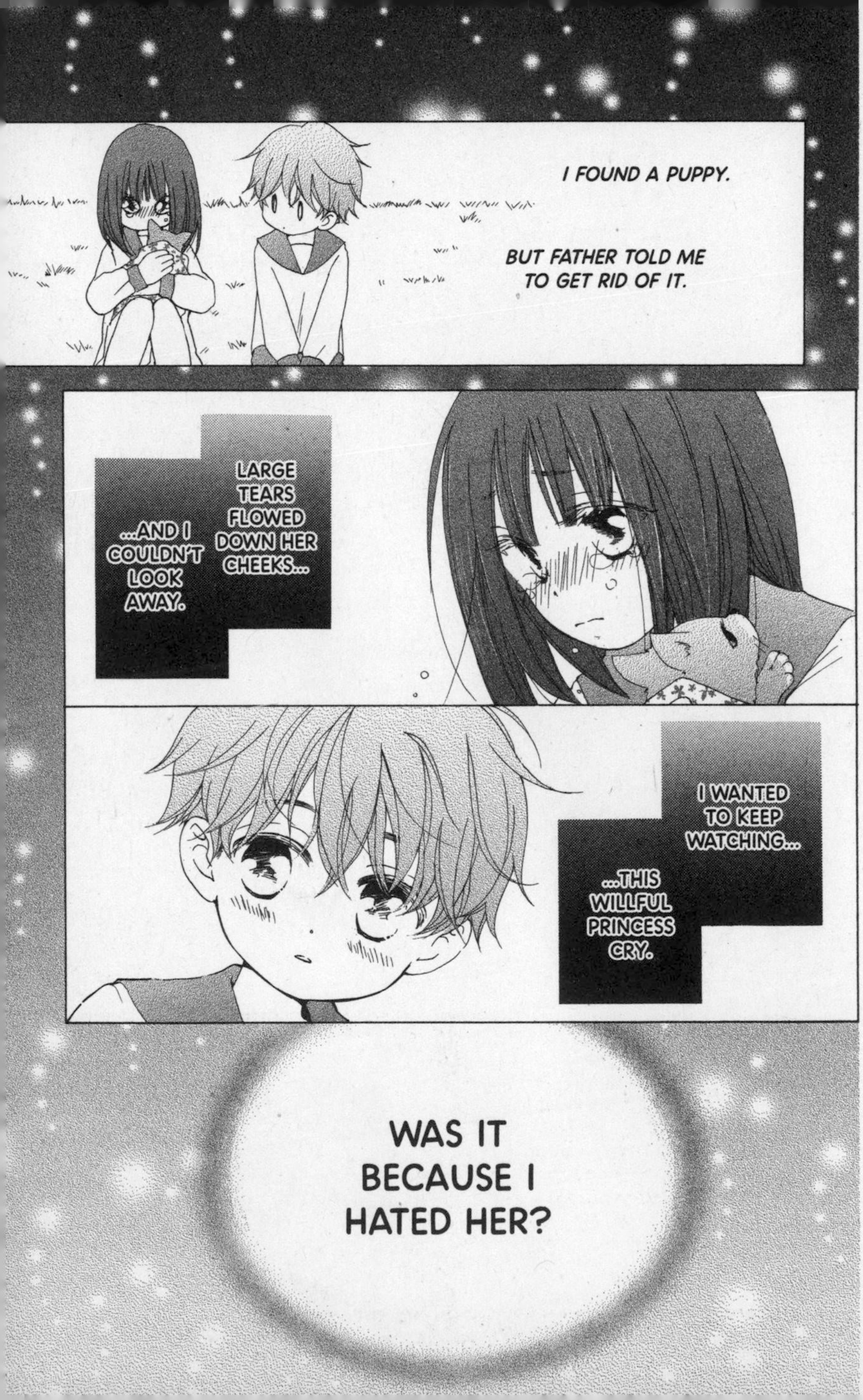
I FOUND A PUPPY.
BUT FATHER TOLD ME TO GET RID OF IT.
LARGE TEARS FLOWED DOWN HER CHEEKS...
...AND I COULDN'T LOOK AWAY.
I WANTED TO KEEP WATCHING...
...THIS WILLFUL PRINCESS CRY.
WAS IT BECAUSE I HATED HER?

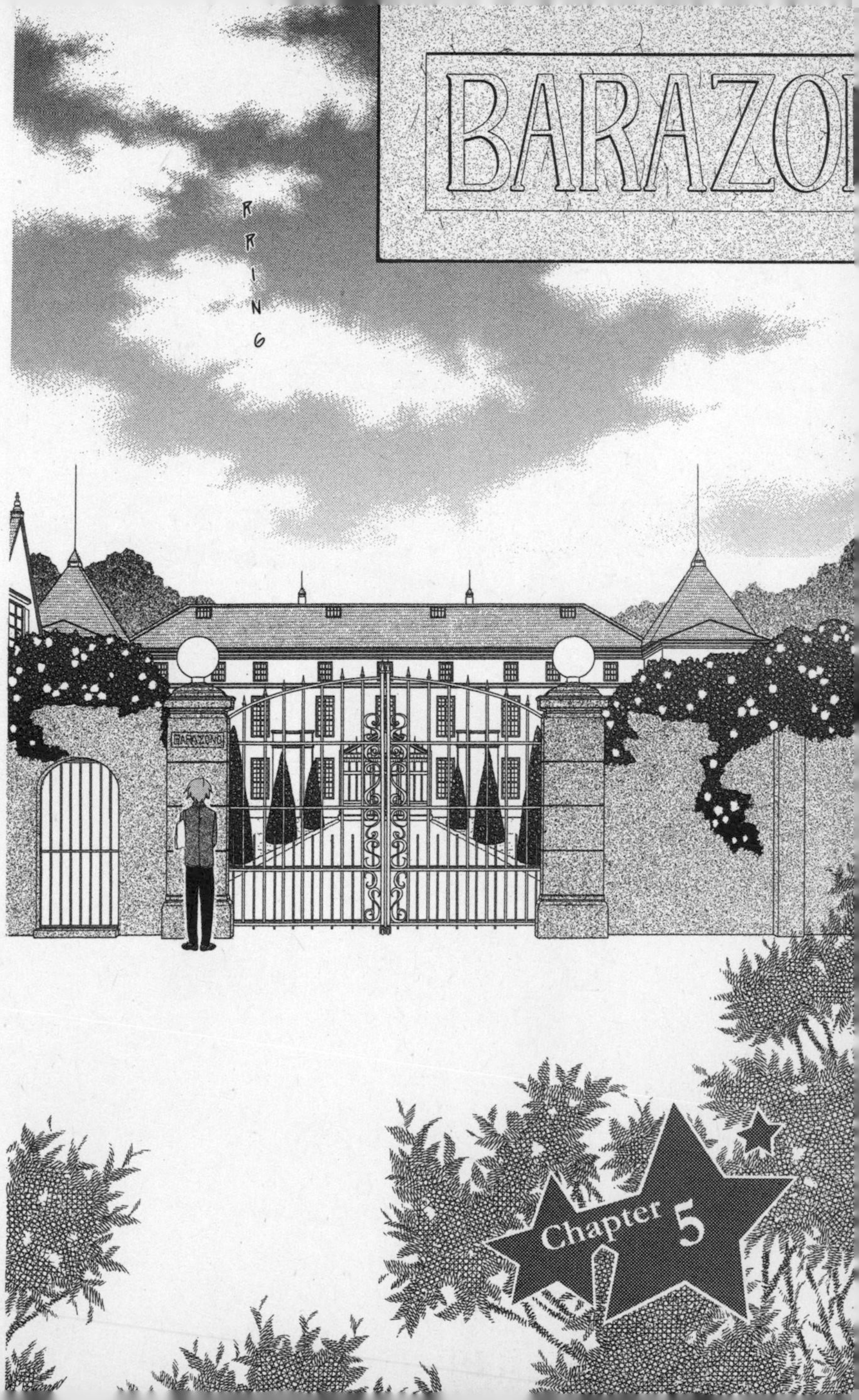
BARAZO
RRING
BARAZONO
Chapter 5

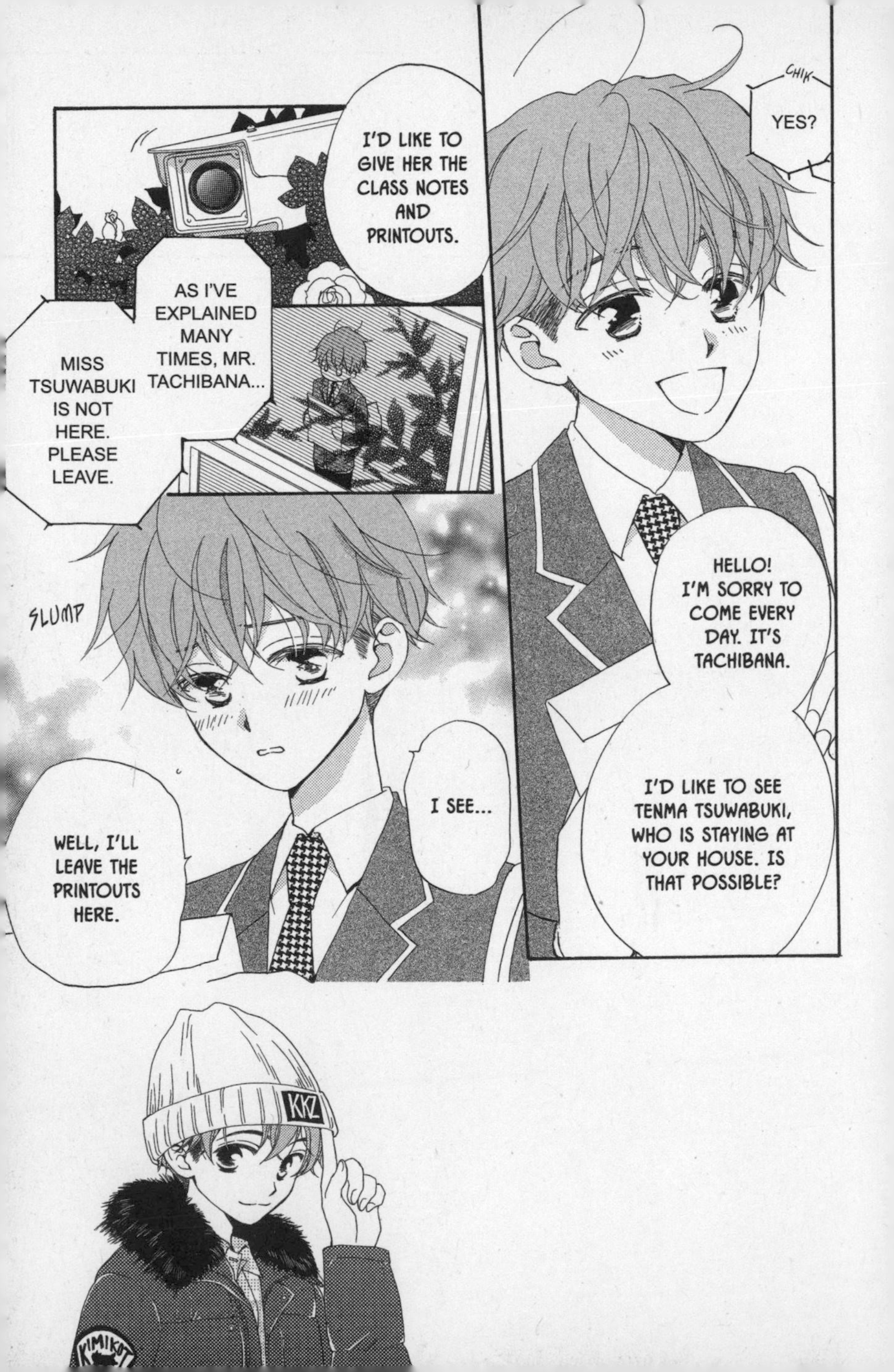
CHIK
YES?
HELLO! I'M SORRY TO COME EVERY DAY. IT'S TACHIBANA.
I'D LIKE TO SEE TENMA TSUWABUKI, WHO IS STAYING AT YOUR HOUSE. IS THAT POSSIBLE?
I'D LIKE TO GIVE HER THE CLASS NOTES AND PRINTOUTS.
AS I'VE EXPLAINED MANY TIMES, MR. TACHIBANA...
MISS TSUWABUKI IS NOT HERE. PLEASE LEAVE.
SLUMP
I SEE...
WELL, I'LL LEAVE THE PRINTOUTS HERE.
KKZ
KIMIKOI

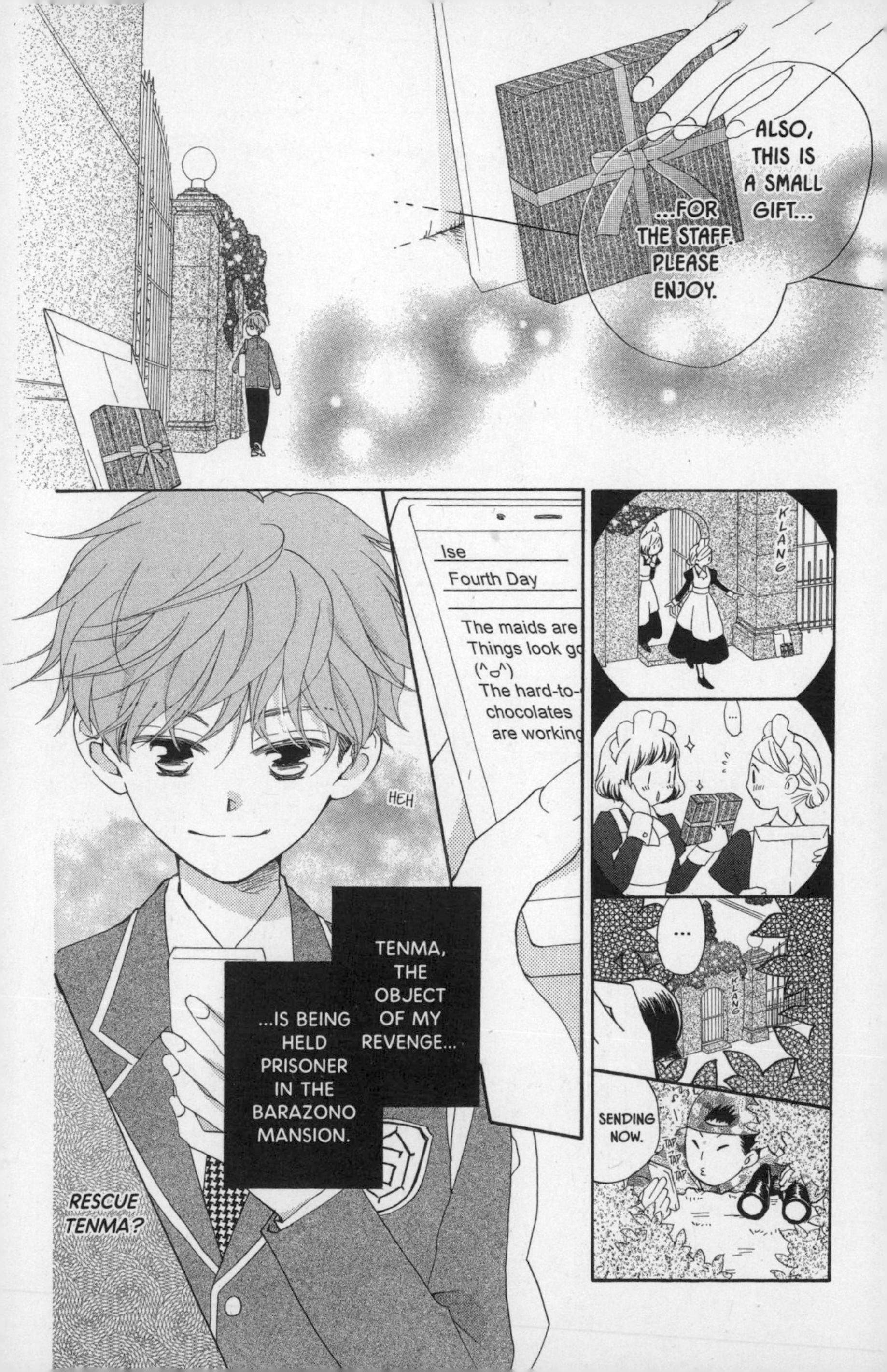
ALSO, THIS IS A SMALL GIFT...
...FOR THE STAFF. PLEASE ENJOY.
KLANG
...
...
KLANG
SENDING NOW.
TAP TAP TAP
Ise
Fourth Day
The maids are
Things look go
(^o^)
The hard-to-
chocolates
are working
HEH
TENMA, THE OBJECT OF MY REVENGE...
...IS BEING HELD PRISONER IN THE BARAZONO MANSION.
RESCUE TENMA?

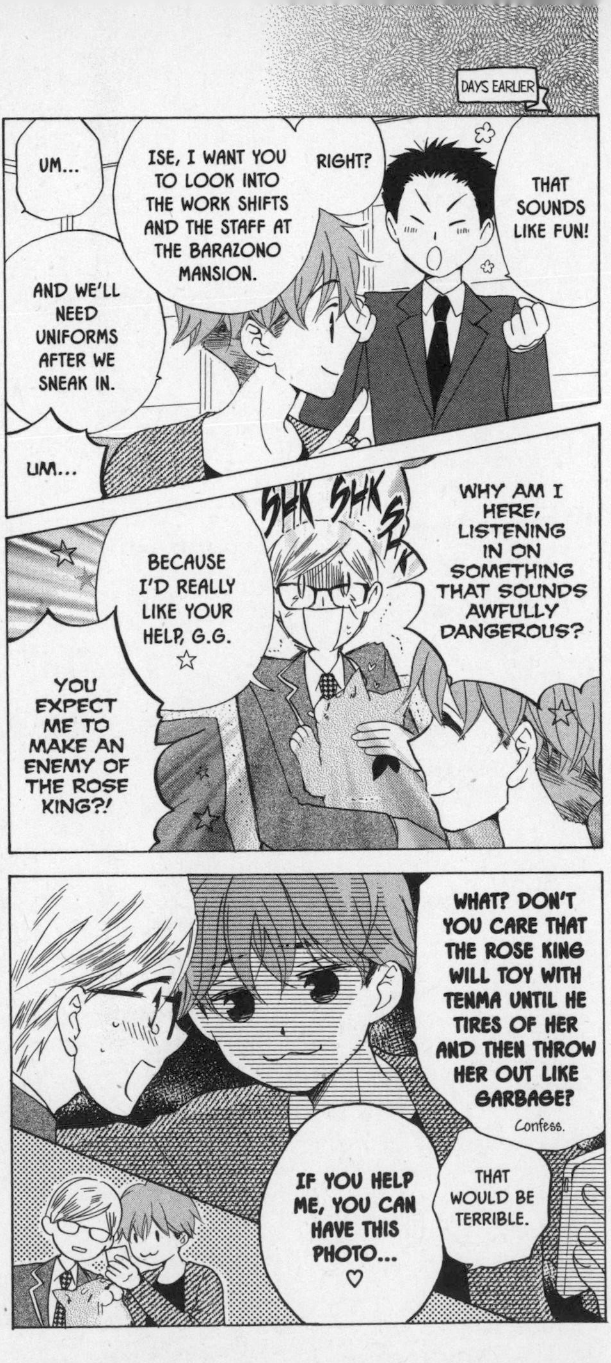
DAYS EARLIER
THAT SOUNDS LIKE FUN!
RIGHT?
ISE, I WANT YOU TO LOOK INTO THE WORK SHIFTS AND THE STAFF AT THE BARAZONO MANSION.
AND WE'LL NEED UNIFORMS AFTER WE SNEAK IN.
UM...
UM...
WHY AM I HERE, LISTENING IN ON SOMETHING THAT SOUNDS AWFULLY DANGEROUS?
SHK SHK SHK
BECAUSE I'D REALLY LIKE YOUR HELP, G.G. ☆
YOU EXPECT ME TO MAKE AN ENEMY OF THE ROSE KING?!
WHAT? DON'T YOU CARE THAT THE ROSE KING WILL TOY WITH TENMA UNTIL HE TIRES OF HER AND THEN THROW HER OUT LIKE GARBAGE?
Confess.
THAT WOULD BE TERRIBLE.
IF YOU HELP ME, YOU CAN HAVE THIS PHOTO... ♡

Many Thanks

I'm able to work because I have the support of an editor who overflows with refreshing energy.

Thank you so much!
I love you!

And I have assistants who help me with the drawings and help relieve my tension.

A big thank-you for all you do!

And to the readers who take time to send me letters, even when there's a simple tool like Twitter.

Thank you so much!
I love you!

On to the end of the volume!

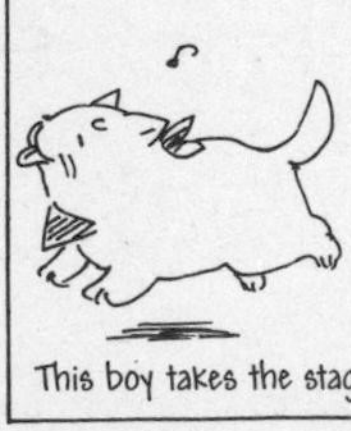

This boy takes the stage!

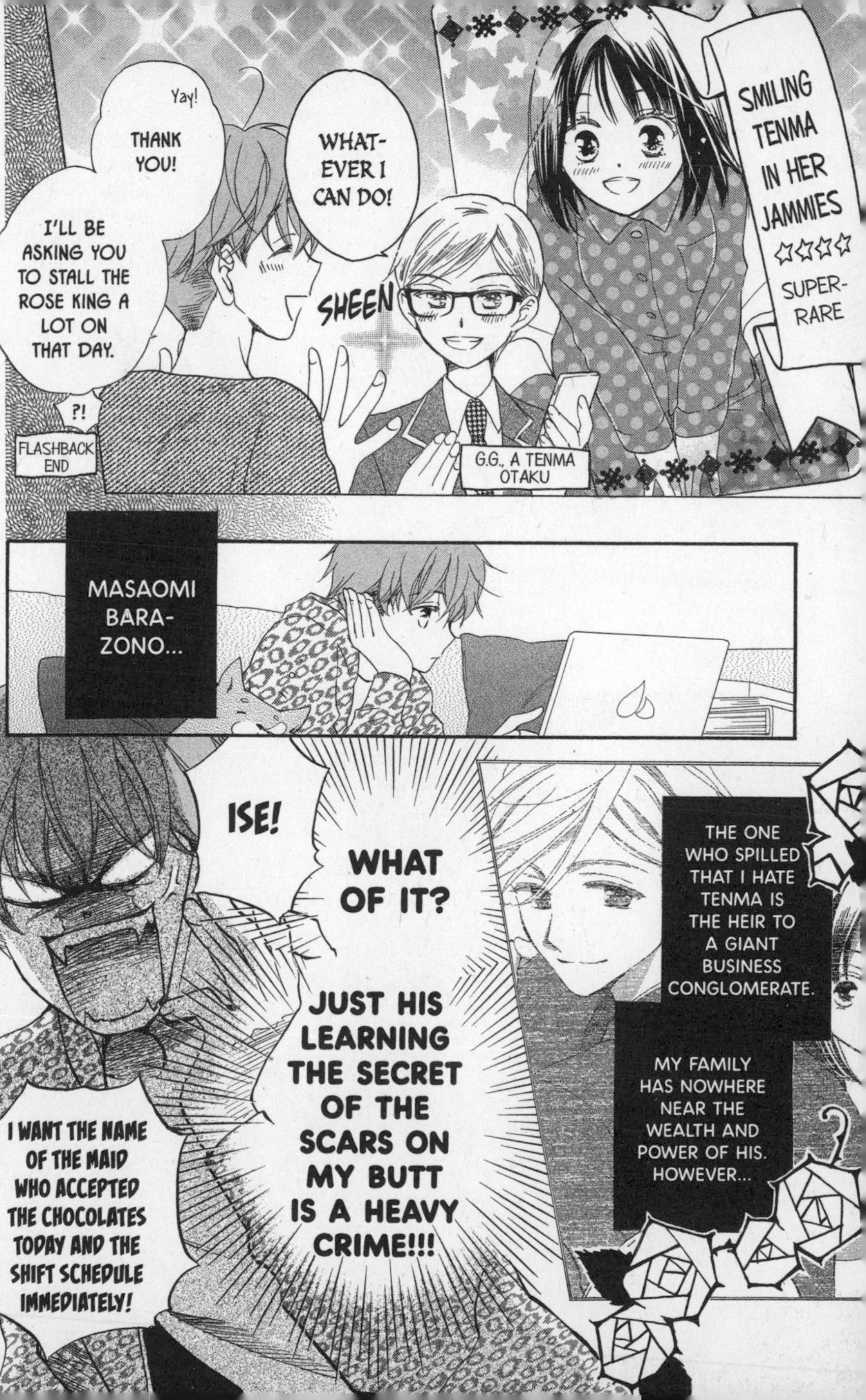
SMILING TENMA IN HER JAMMIES ☆☆☆☆ SUPER-RARE
G.G., A TENMA OTAKU
WHAT-EVER I CAN DO!
SHEEN
Yay!
THANK YOU!
I'LL BE ASKING YOU TO STALL THE ROSE KING A LOT ON THAT DAY.
?!
FLASHBACK END
MASAOMI BARA-ZONO...
THE ONE WHO SPILLED THAT I HATE TENMA IS THE HEIR TO A GIANT BUSINESS CONGLOMERATE.
MY FAMILY HAS NOWHERE NEAR THE WEALTH AND POWER OF HIS. HOWEVER...
WHAT OF IT?
JUST HIS LEARNING THE SECRET OF THE SCARS ON MY BUTT IS A HEAVY CRIME!!!
ISE!
I WANT THE NAME OF THE MAID WHO ACCEPTED THE CHOCOLATES TODAY AND THE SHIFT SCHEDULE IMMEDIATELY!

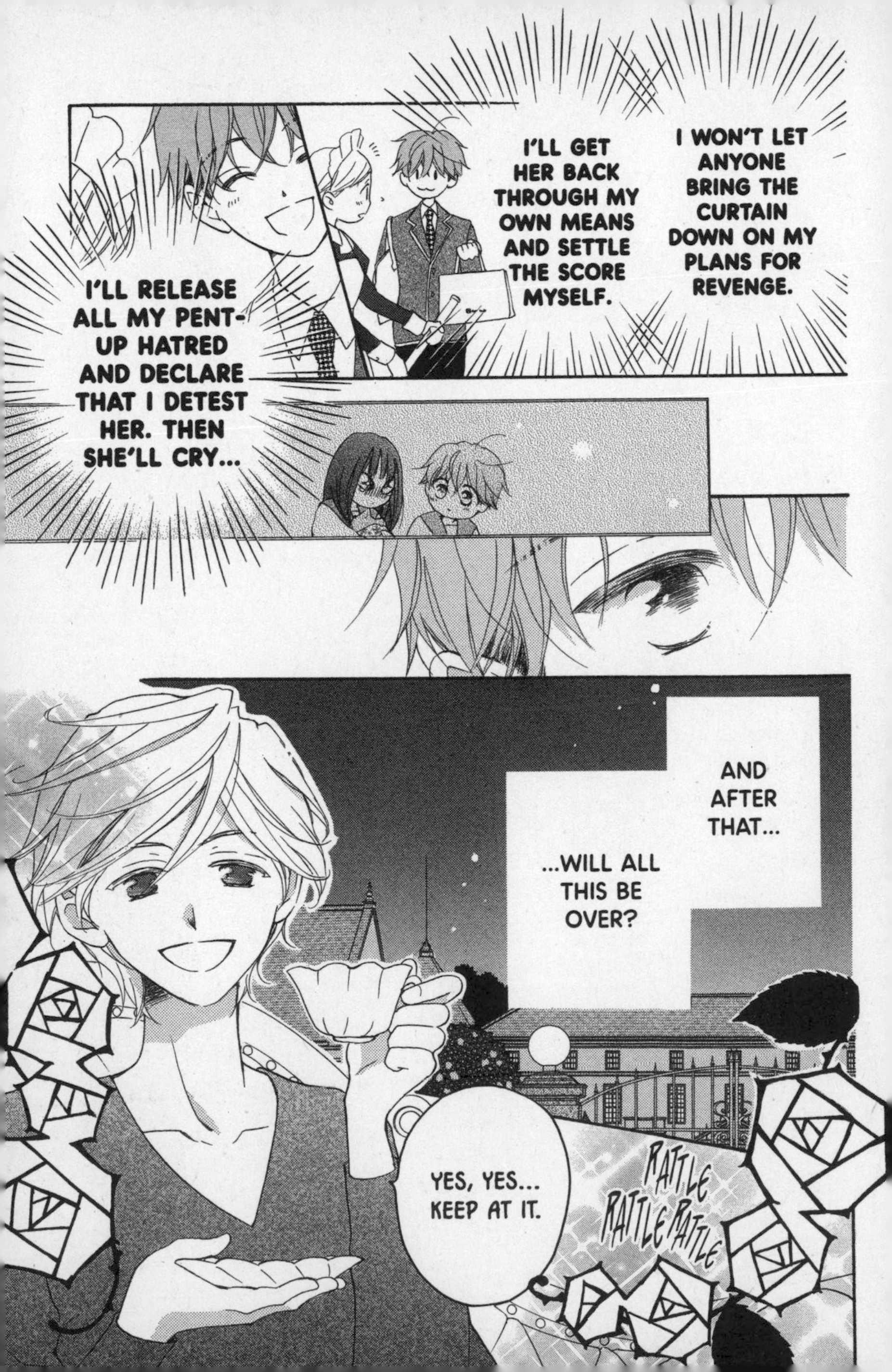
I WON'T LET ANYONE BRING THE CURTAIN DOWN ON MY PLANS FOR REVENGE.
I'LL GET HER BACK THROUGH MY OWN MEANS AND SETTLE THE SCORE MYSELF.
I'LL RELEASE ALL MY PENT-UP HATRED AND DECLARE THAT I DETEST HER. THEN SHE'LL CRY...
AND AFTER THAT...
...WILL ALL THIS BE OVER?
RATTLE RATTLE RATTLE
YES, YES... KEEP AT IT.

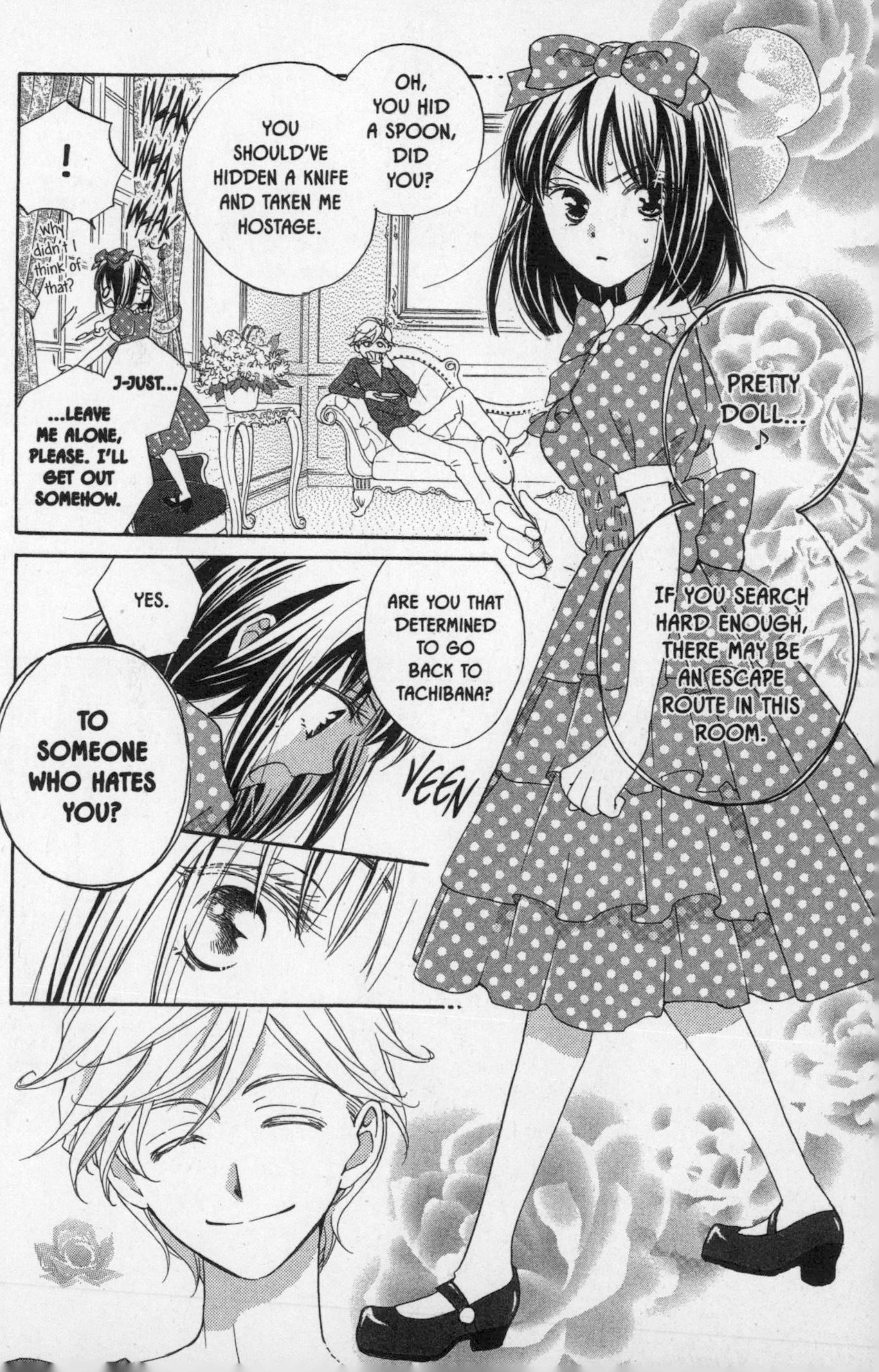
PRETTY DOLL... ♪
IF YOU SEARCH HARD ENOUGH, THERE MAY BE AN ESCAPE ROUTE IN THIS ROOM.
OH, YOU HID A SPOON, DID YOU?
YOU SHOULD'VE HIDDEN A KNIFE AND TAKEN ME HOSTAGE.
!
WHAK WHAK WHAK
Why didn't I think of that?
J-JUST...
...LEAVE ME ALONE, PLEASE. I'LL GET OUT SOMEHOW.
ARE YOU THAT DETERMINED TO GO BACK TO TACHIBANA?
YES.
VEEN
TO SOMEONE WHO HATES YOU?

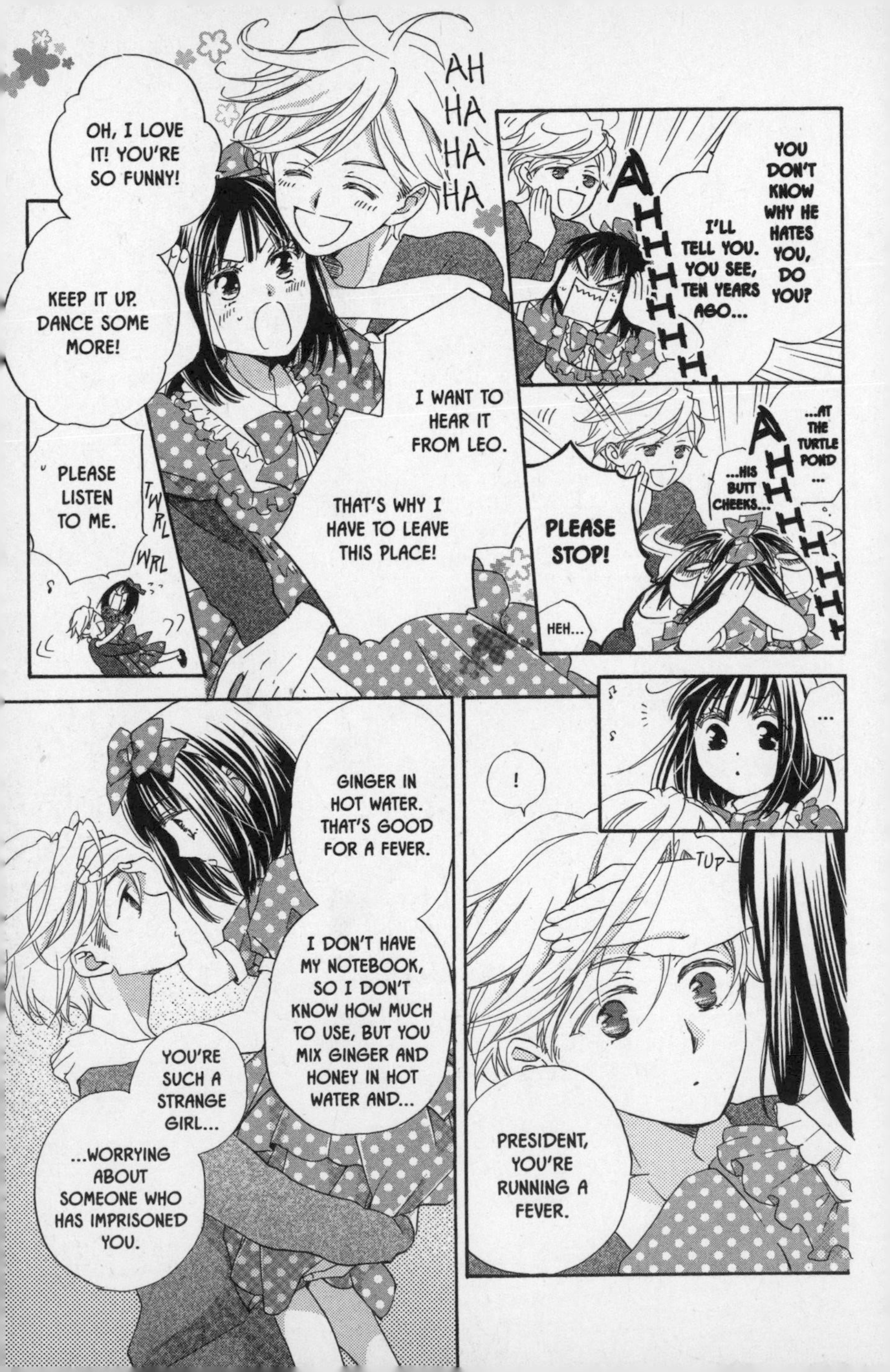
YOU DON'T KNOW WHY HE HATES YOU, DO YOU?
I'LL TELL YOU. YOU SEE, TEN YEARS AGO...
AHHHHH
...AT THE TURTLE POND...
...HIS BUTT CHEEKS...
AHHHHHHH
PLEASE STOP!
HEH...
AH HA HA HA
OH, I LOVE IT! YOU'RE SO FUNNY!
KEEP IT UP. DANCE SOME MORE!
PLEASE LISTEN TO ME.
TWRL WRL
I WANT TO HEAR IT FROM LEO.
THAT'S WHY I HAVE TO LEAVE THIS PLACE!
...
!
TUP
PRESIDENT, YOU'RE RUNNING A FEVER.
GINGER IN HOT WATER. THAT'S GOOD FOR A FEVER.
I DON'T HAVE MY NOTEBOOK, SO I DON'T KNOW HOW MUCH TO USE, BUT YOU MIX GINGER AND HONEY IN HOT WATER AND...
YOU'RE SUCH A STRANGE GIRL...
...WORRYING ABOUT SOMEONE WHO HAS IMPRISONED YOU.

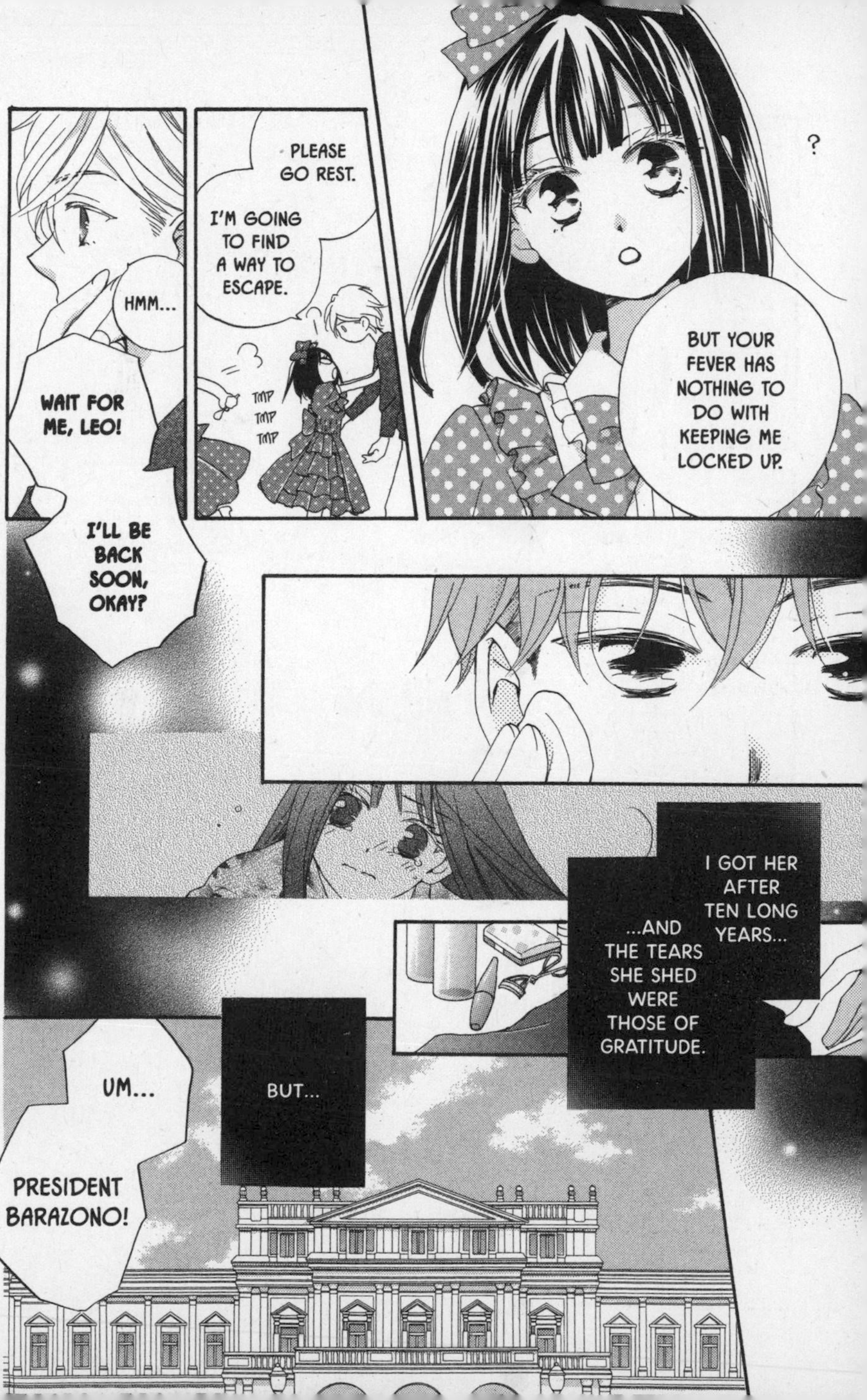
?
BUT YOUR FEVER HAS NOTHING TO DO WITH KEEPING ME LOCKED UP.
PLEASE GO REST.
I'M GOING TO FIND A WAY TO ESCAPE.
TMP TMP TMP
HMM...
WAIT FOR ME, LEO!
I'LL BE BACK SOON, OKAY?
I GOT HER AFTER TEN LONG YEARS...
...AND THE TEARS SHE SHED WERE THOSE OF GRATITUDE.
BUT...
UM...
PRESIDENT BARAZONO!

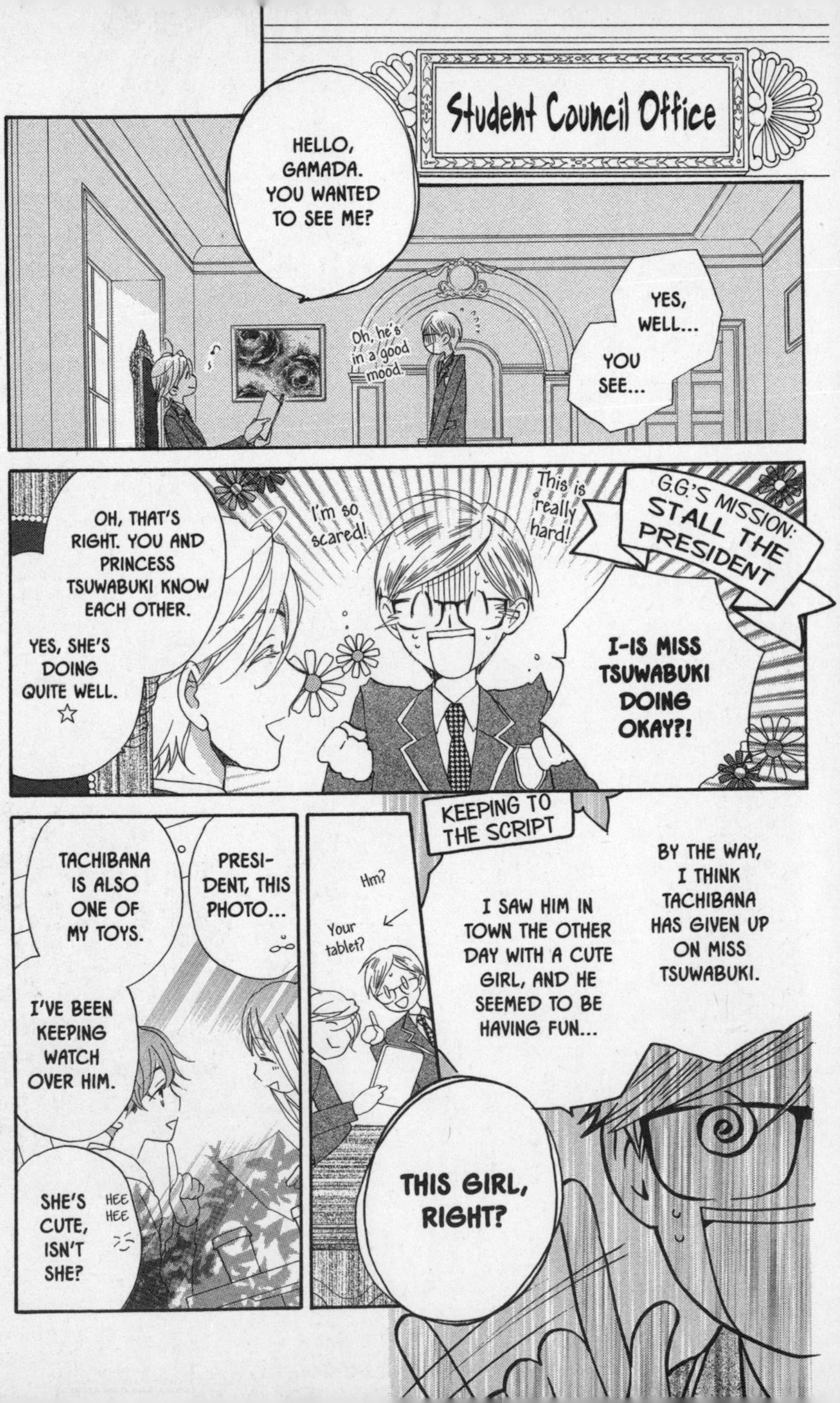
Student Council Office
HELLO, GAMADA. YOU WANTED TO SEE ME?
YES, WELL... YOU SEE...
Oh, he's in a good mood.
G.G.'S MISSION: STALL THE PRESIDENT
This is really hard!
I-IS MISS TSUWABUKI DOING OKAY?!
I'm so scared!
OH, THAT'S RIGHT. YOU AND PRINCESS TSUWABUKI KNOW EACH OTHER.
YES, SHE'S DOING QUITE WELL. ☆
KEEPING TO THE SCRIPT
BY THE WAY, I THINK TACHIBANA HAS GIVEN UP ON MISS TSUWABUKI.
I SAW HIM IN TOWN THE OTHER DAY WITH A CUTE GIRL, AND HE SEEMED TO BE HAVING FUN...
Hm?
Your tablet?
THIS GIRL, RIGHT?
PRESI-DENT, THIS PHOTO...
TACHIBANA IS ALSO ONE OF MY TOYS.
I'VE BEEN KEEPING WATCH OVER HIM.
SHE'S CUTE, ISN'T SHE?
HEE HEE

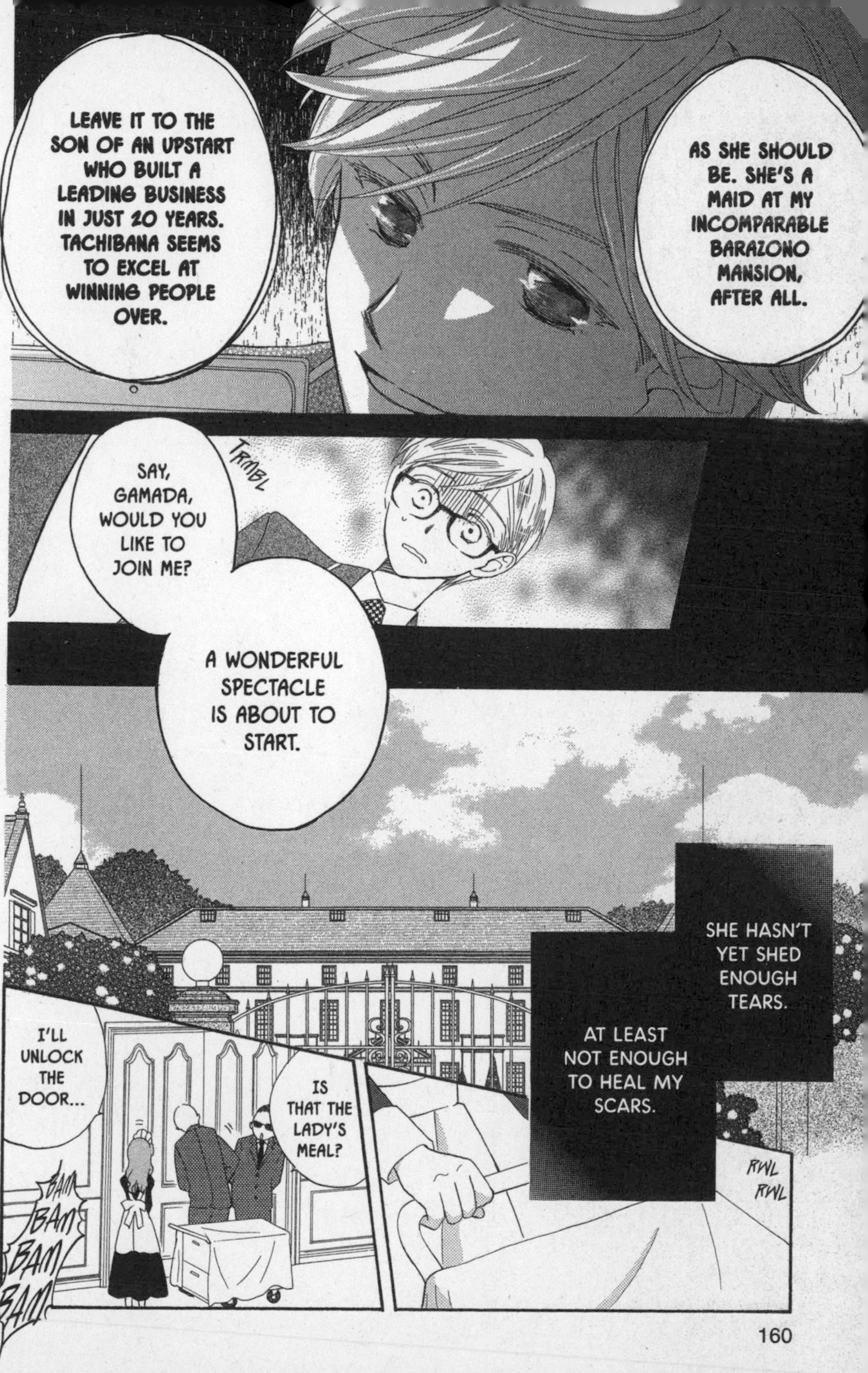
AS SHE SHOULD BE. SHE'S A MAID AT MY INCOMPARABLE BARAZONO MANSION, AFTER ALL.
LEAVE IT TO THE SON OF AN UPSTART WHO BUILT A LEADING BUSINESS IN JUST 20 YEARS. TACHIBANA SEEMS TO EXCEL AT WINNING PEOPLE OVER.
TRMBL
SAY, GAMADA, WOULD YOU LIKE TO JOIN ME?
A WONDERFUL SPECTACLE IS ABOUT TO START.
SHE HASN'T YET SHED ENOUGH TEARS.
AT LEAST NOT ENOUGH TO HEAL MY SCARS.
RWL RWL
IS THAT THE LADY'S MEAL?
I'LL UNLOCK THE DOOR...
BAM BAM BAM BAM

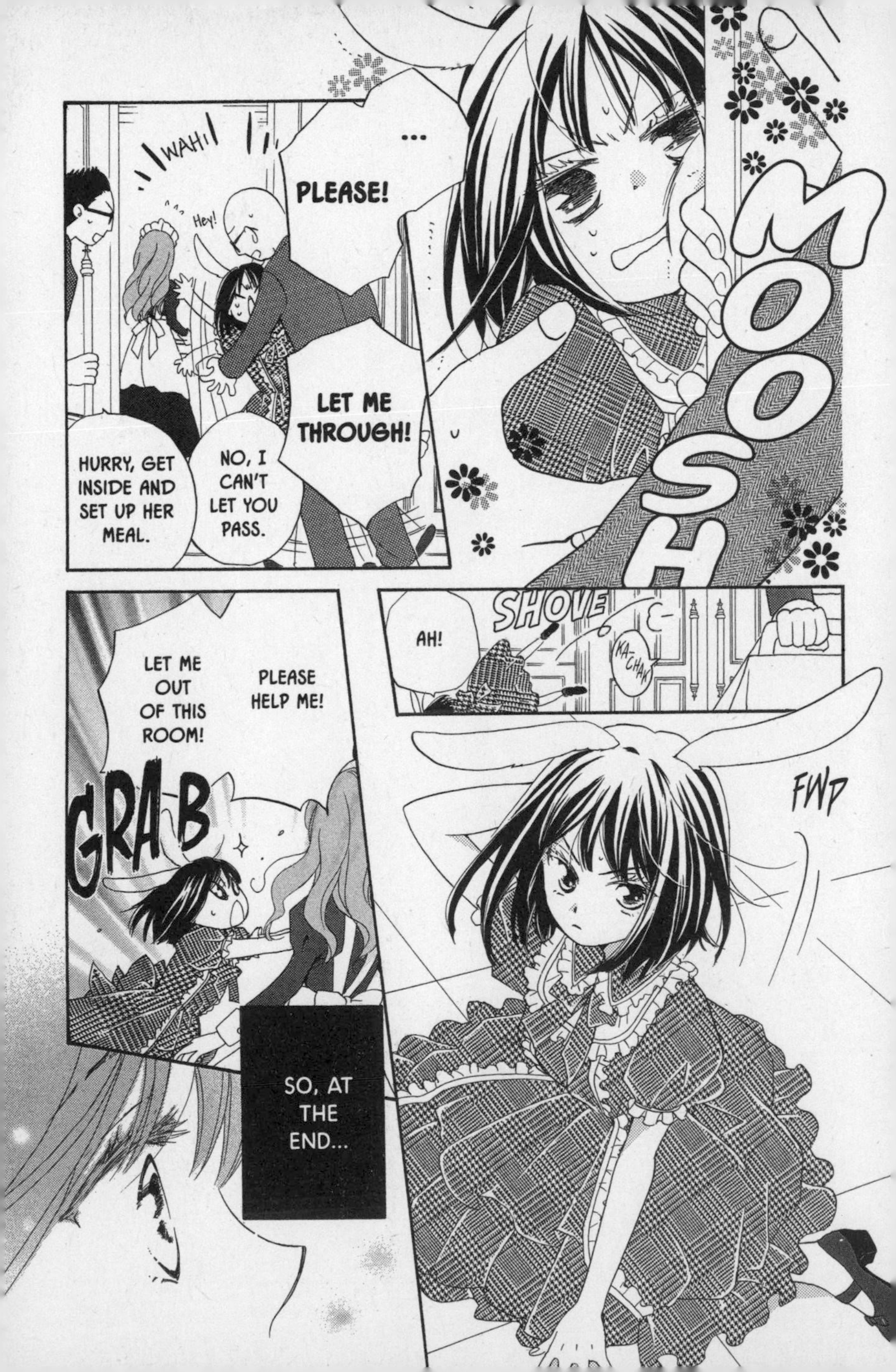
MOOSH
...
PLEASE!
LET ME THROUGH!
NO, I CAN'T LET YOU PASS.
WAH!
Hey!
HURRY, GET INSIDE AND SET UP HER MEAL.
SHOVE
KA-CHAK
AH!
FWP
PLEASE HELP ME!
LET ME OUT OF THIS ROOM!
GRAB
SO, AT THE END...

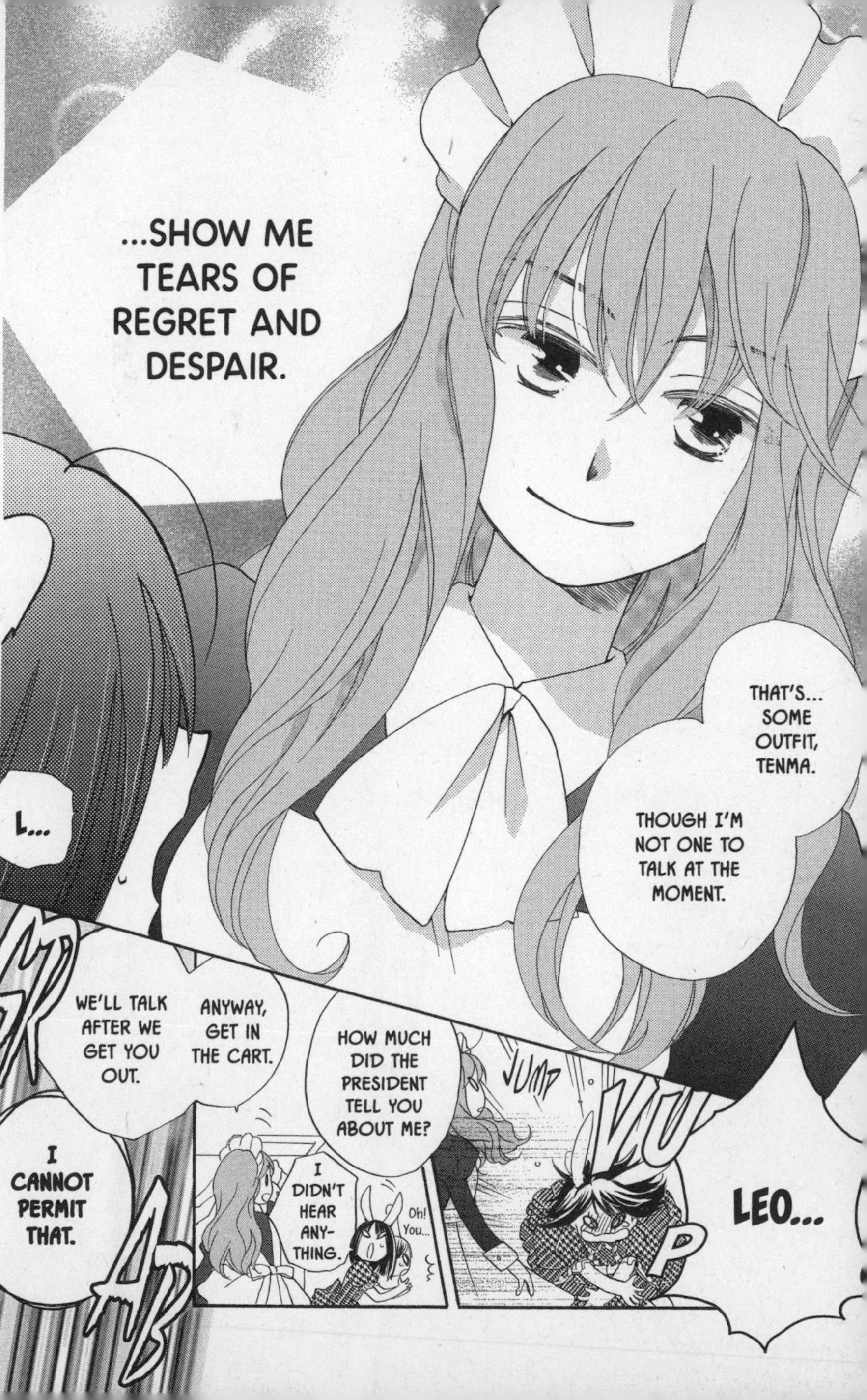
...SHOW ME TEARS OF REGRET AND DESPAIR.
THAT'S... SOME OUTFIT, TENMA.
THOUGH I'M NOT ONE TO TALK AT THE MOMENT.
L...
VUP
JUMP
P
LEO...
HOW MUCH DID THE PRESIDENT TELL YOU ABOUT ME?
Oh! You...
I DIDN'T HEAR ANY-THING.
ANYWAY, GET IN THE CART.
WE'LL TALK AFTER WE GET YOU OUT.
GRAB
I CANNOT PERMIT THAT.

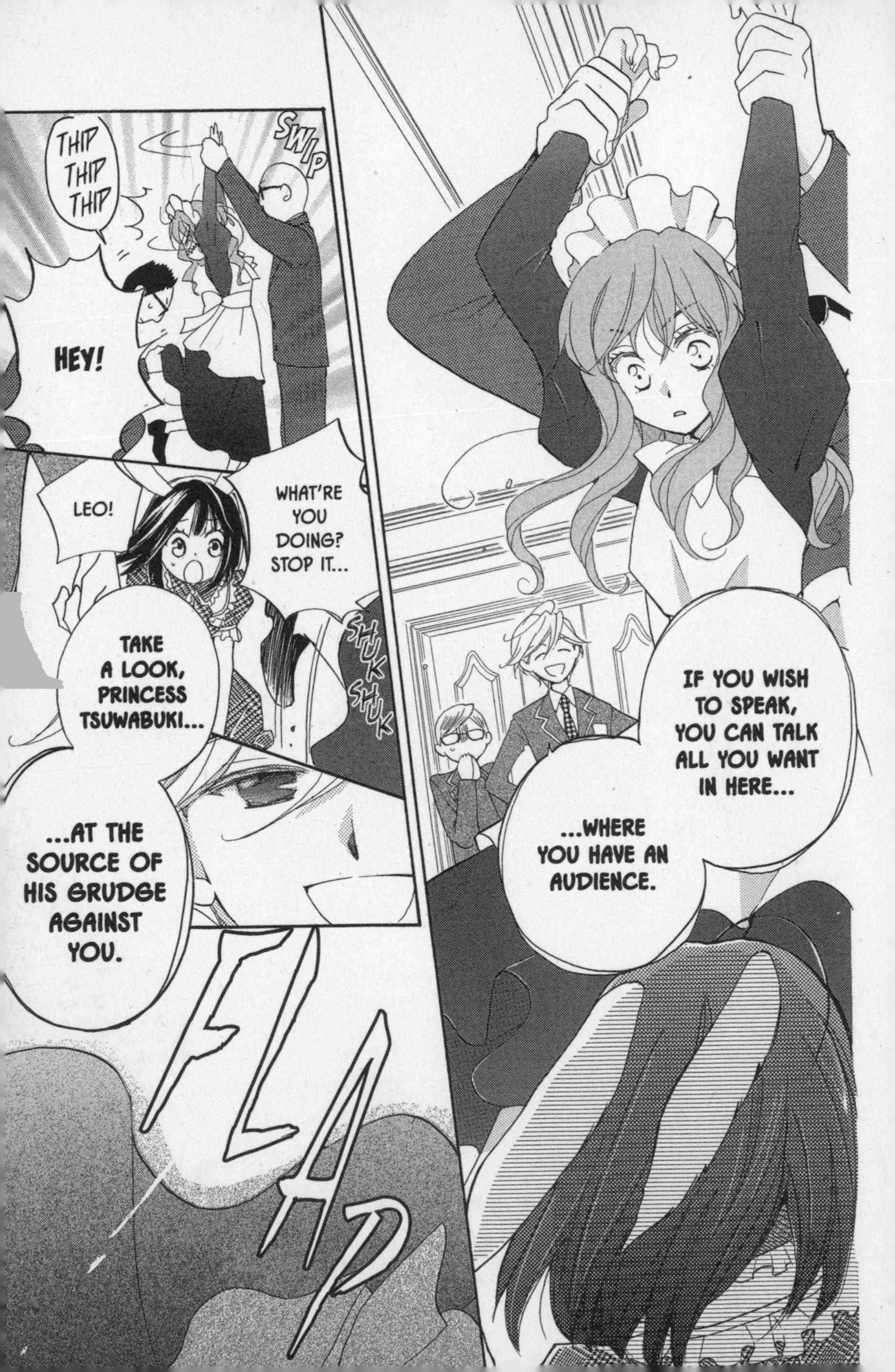
IF YOU WISH TO SPEAK, YOU CAN TALK ALL YOU WANT IN HERE...
...WHERE YOU HAVE AN AUDIENCE.
SWIP
THIP THIP THIP
HEY!
WHAT'RE YOU DOING? STOP IT...
LEO!
SHUK SHUK
TAKE A LOOK, PRINCESS TSUWABUKI...
...AT THE SOURCE OF HIS GRUDGE AGAINST YOU.
FLAP

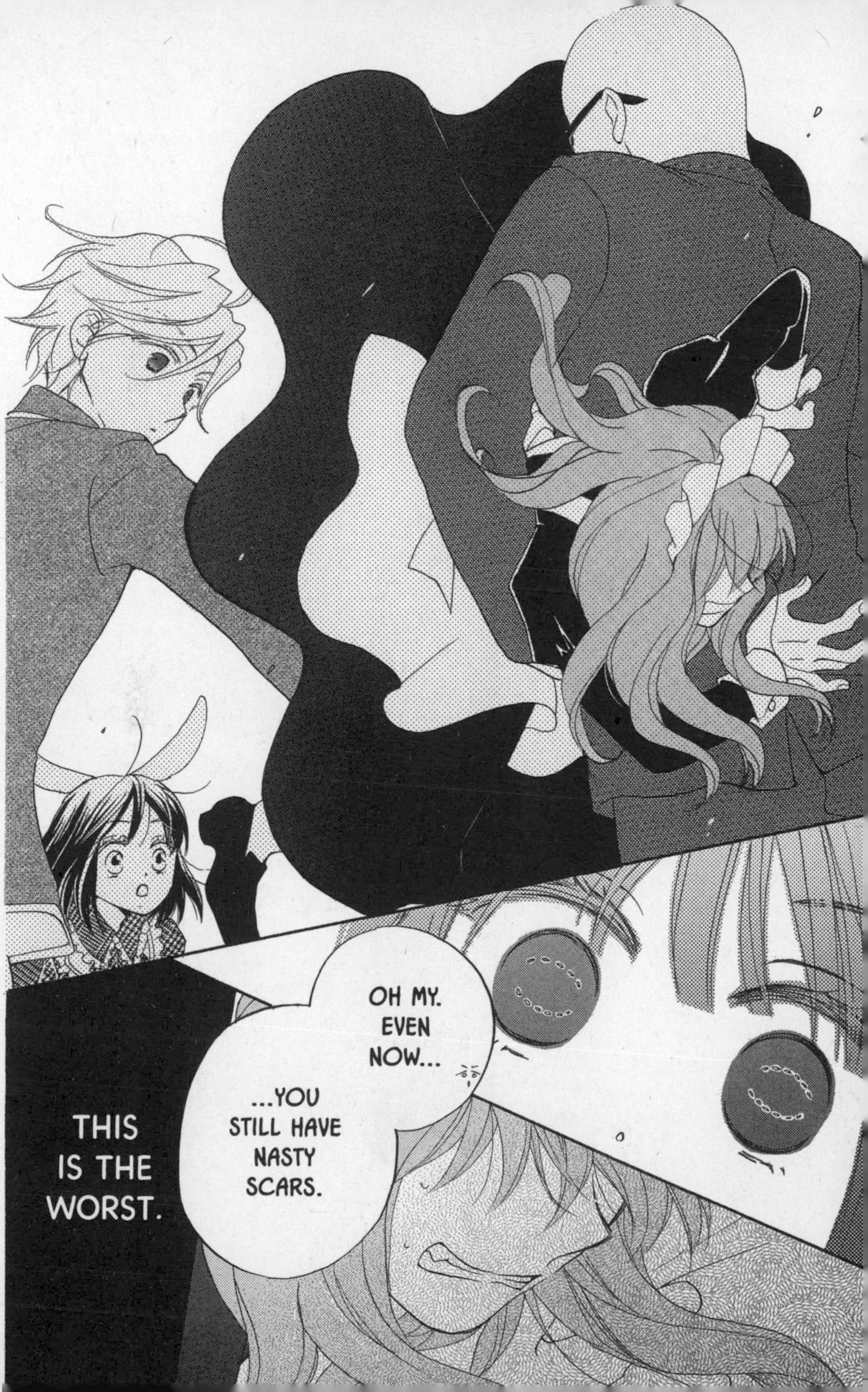
OH MY. EVEN NOW...
...YOU STILL HAVE NASTY SCARS.
THIS IS THE WORST.

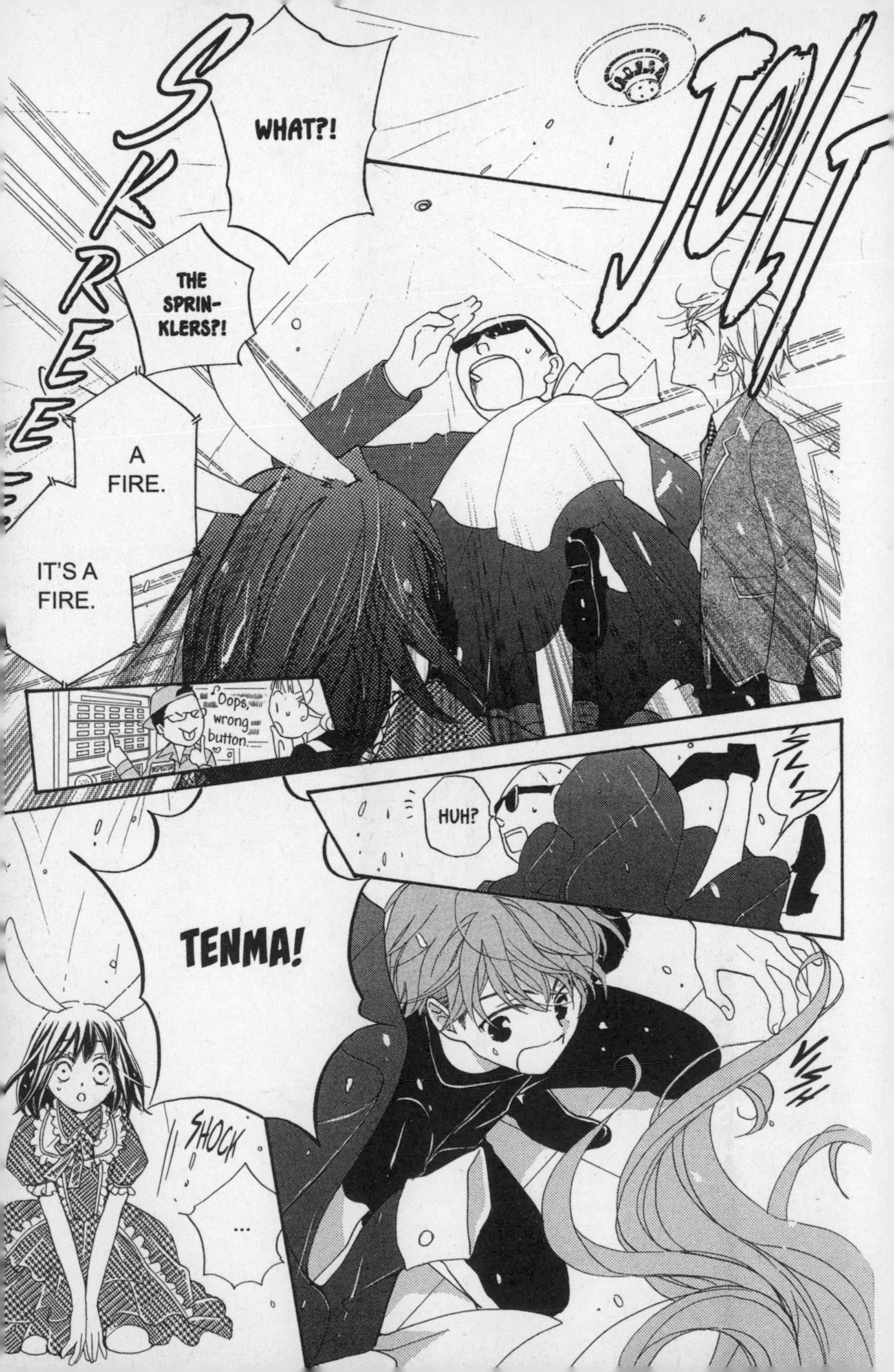
JOLT
WHAT?!
THE SPRIN-KLERS?!
SKREEE
A FIRE.
IT'S A FIRE.
Oops, wrong button.
INSPECTOR
SLIP
HUH?
TENMA!
VISH
SHOCK
...

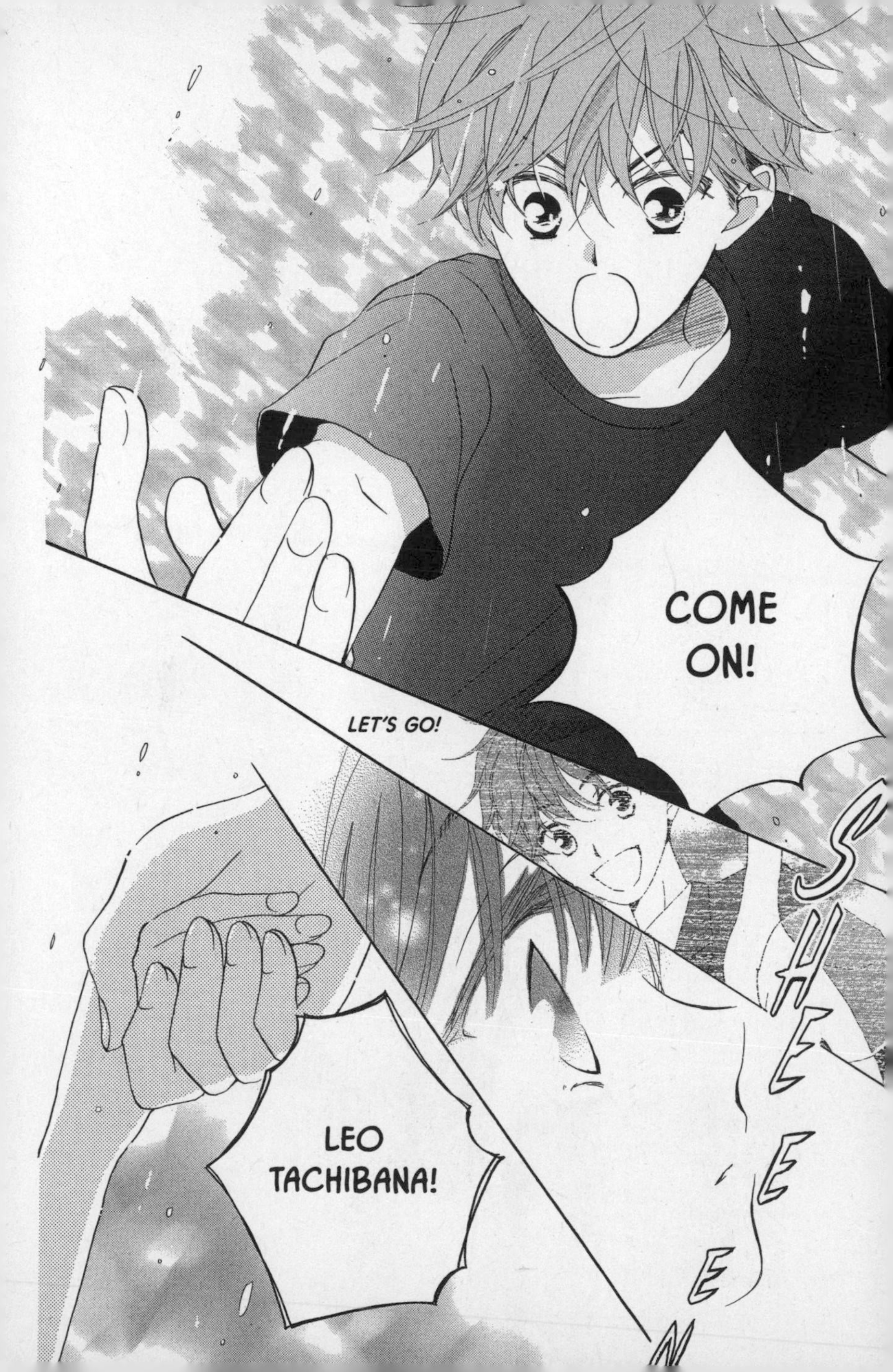
COME ON!
LET'S GO!
SHEEEEN
LEO TACHIBANA!

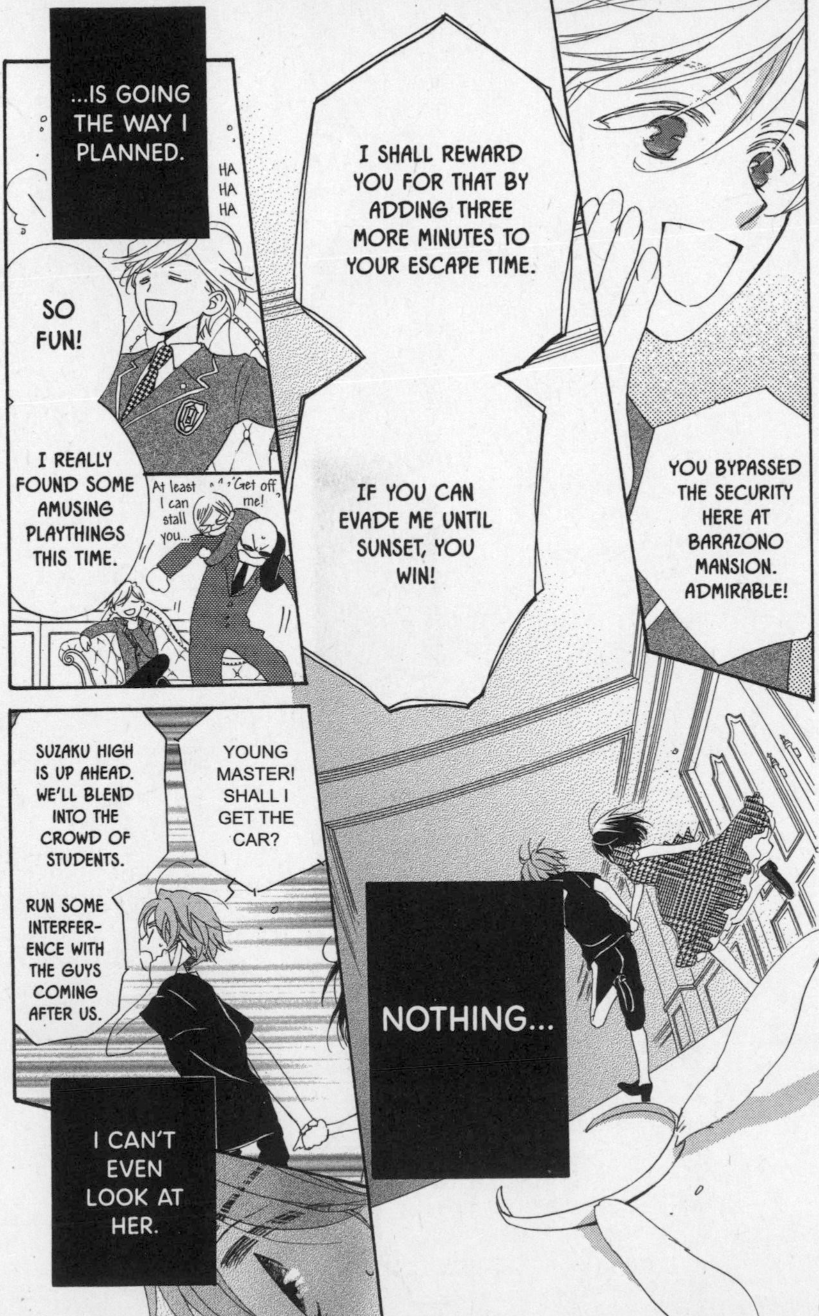
YOU BYPASSED THE SECURITY HERE AT BARAZONO MANSION. ADMIRABLE!
I SHALL REWARD YOU FOR THAT BY ADDING THREE MORE MINUTES TO YOUR ESCAPE TIME.
IF YOU CAN EVADE ME UNTIL SUNSET, YOU WIN!
...IS GOING THE WAY I PLANNED.
HA HA HA
SO FUN!
I REALLY FOUND SOME AMUSING PLAYTHINGS THIS TIME.
"Get off me!"
At least I can stall you...
NOTHING...
YOUNG MASTER! SHALL I GET THE CAR?
SUZAKU HIGH IS UP AHEAD. WE'LL BLEND INTO THE CROWD OF STUDENTS.
RUN SOME INTERFER-ENCE WITH THE GUYS COMING AFTER US.
I CAN'T EVEN LOOK AT HER.

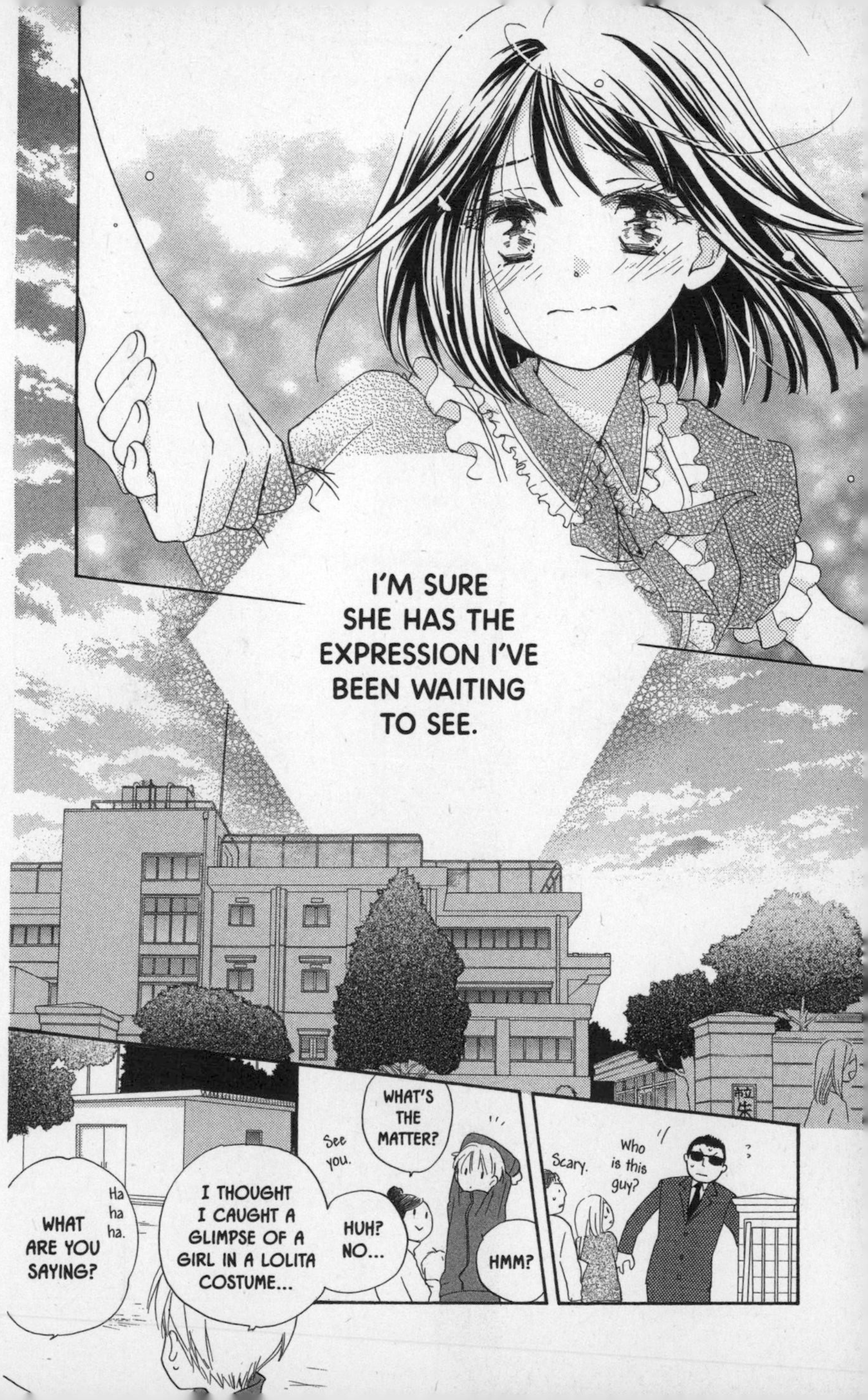
I'M SURE SHE HAS THE EXPRESSION I'VE BEEN WAITING TO SEE.
Who is this guy?
Scary.
HMM?
WHAT'S THE MATTER?
See you.
HUH? NO...
I THOUGHT I CAUGHT A GLIMPSE OF A GIRL IN A LOLITA COSTUME...
Ha ha ha.
WHAT ARE YOU SAYING?

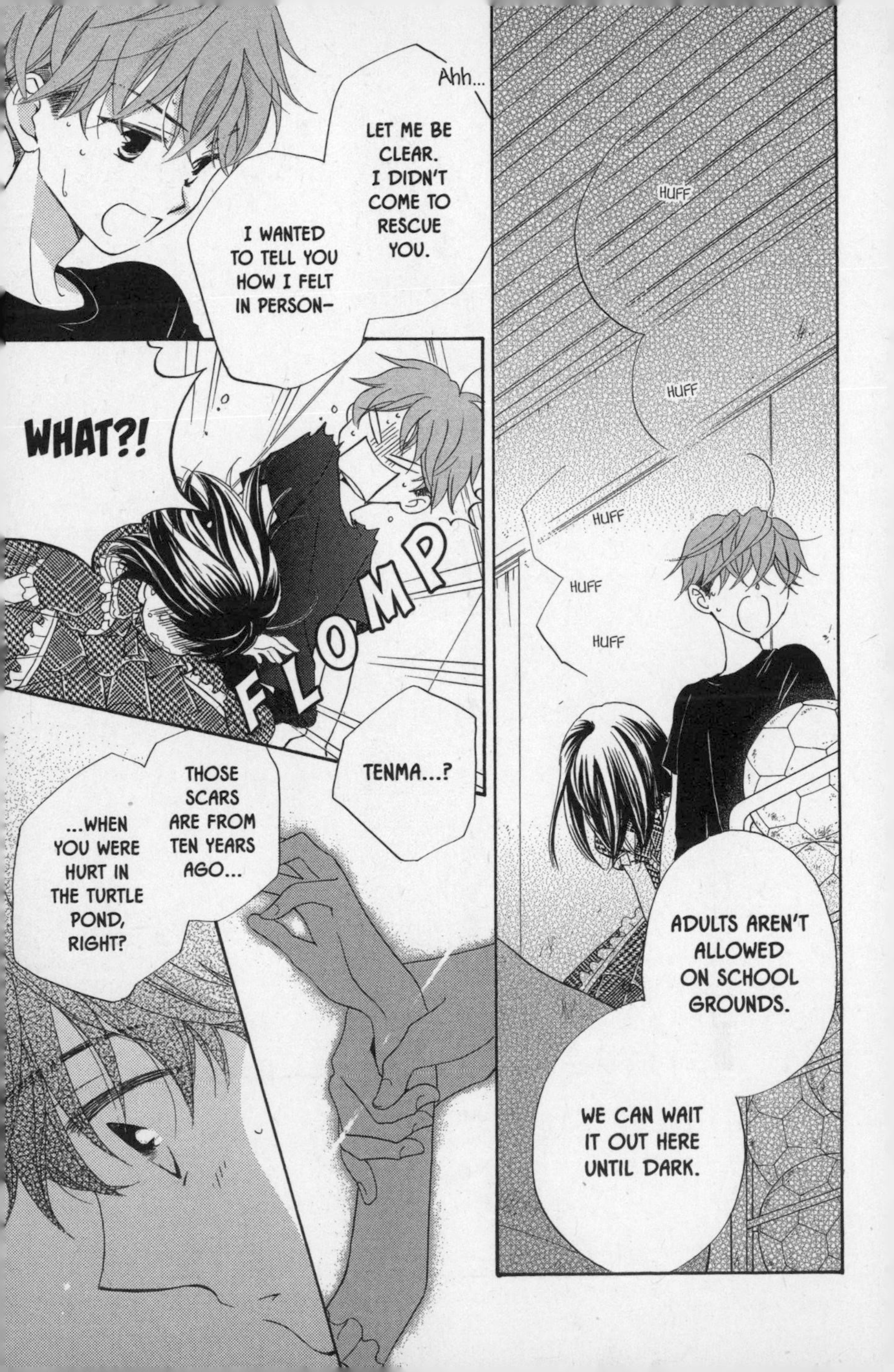
HUFF
HUFF
HUFF
HUFF
HUFF
ADULTS AREN'T ALLOWED ON SCHOOL GROUNDS.
WE CAN WAIT IT OUT HERE UNTIL DARK.
Ahh...
LET ME BE CLEAR. I DIDN'T COME TO RESCUE YOU.
I WANTED TO TELL YOU HOW I FELT IN PERSON—
WHAT?!
FLOMP
TENMA...?
THOSE SCARS ARE FROM TEN YEARS AGO...
...WHEN YOU WERE HURT IN THE TURTLE POND, RIGHT?

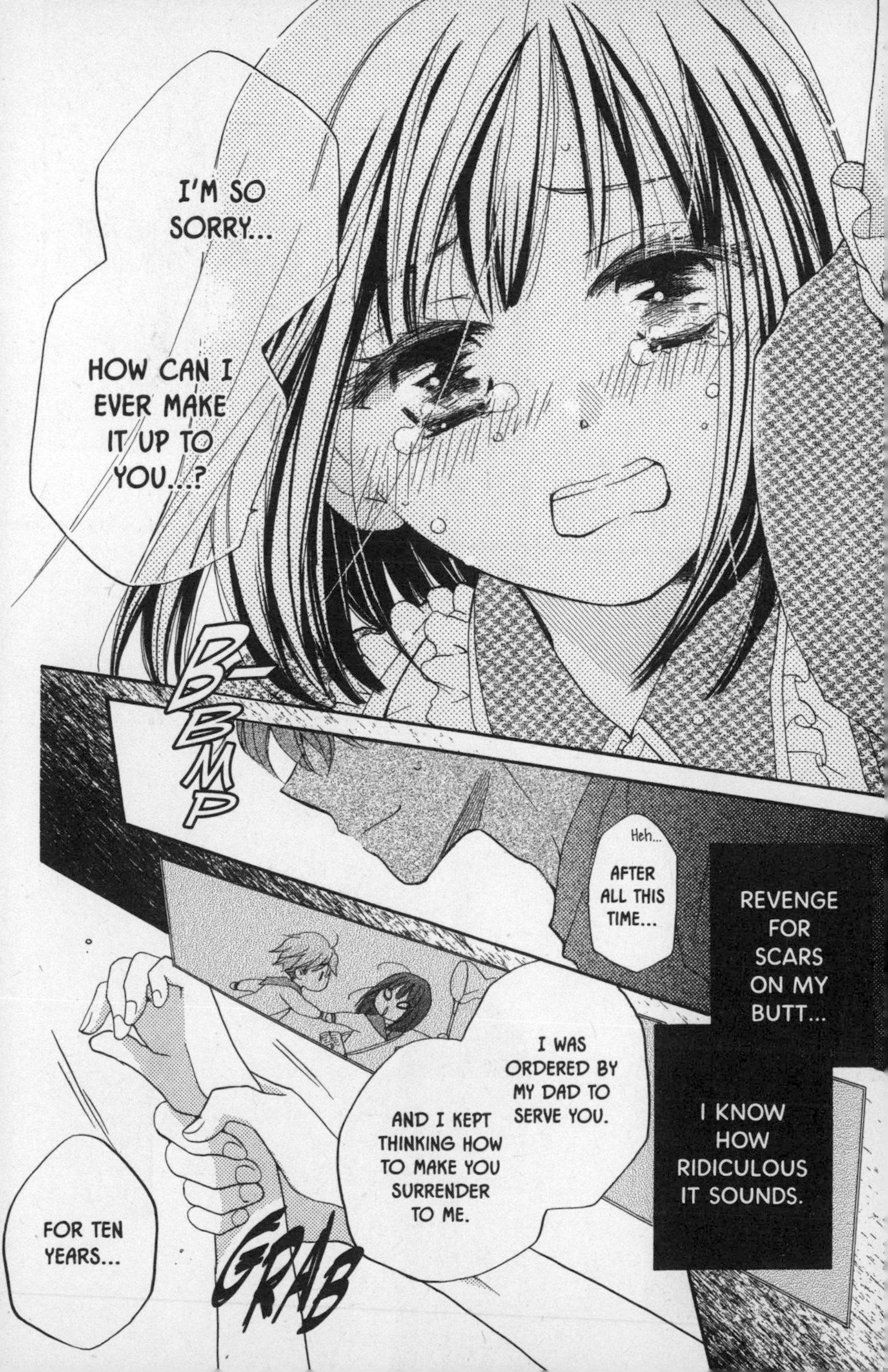
I'M SO SORRY...
HOW CAN I EVER MAKE IT UP TO YOU...?
B-BUMP
REVENGE FOR SCARS ON MY BUTT...
Heh... AFTER ALL THIS TIME...
I KNOW HOW RIDICULOUS IT SOUNDS.
I WAS ORDERED BY MY DAD TO SERVE YOU.
AND I KEPT THINKING HOW TO MAKE YOU SURRENDER TO ME.
FOR TEN YEARS...
GRAB

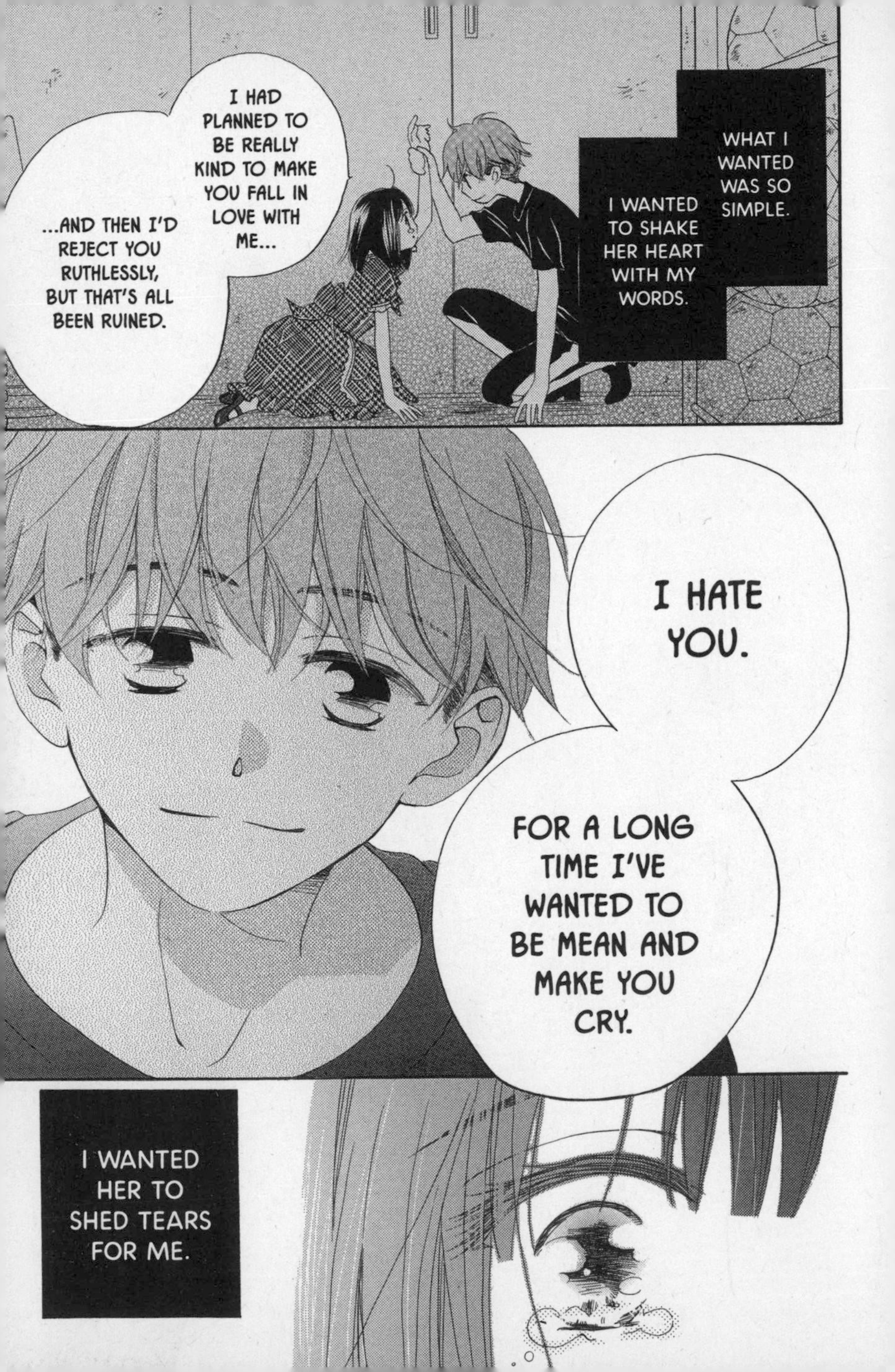
WHAT I WANTED WAS SO SIMPLE.
I WANTED TO SHAKE HER HEART WITH MY WORDS.
I HAD PLANNED TO BE REALLY KIND TO MAKE YOU FALL IN LOVE WITH ME...
...AND THEN I'D REJECT YOU RUTHLESSLY, BUT THAT'S ALL BEEN RUINED.
I HATE YOU.
FOR A LONG TIME I'VE WANTED TO BE MEAN AND MAKE YOU CRY.
I WANTED HER TO SHED TEARS FOR ME.

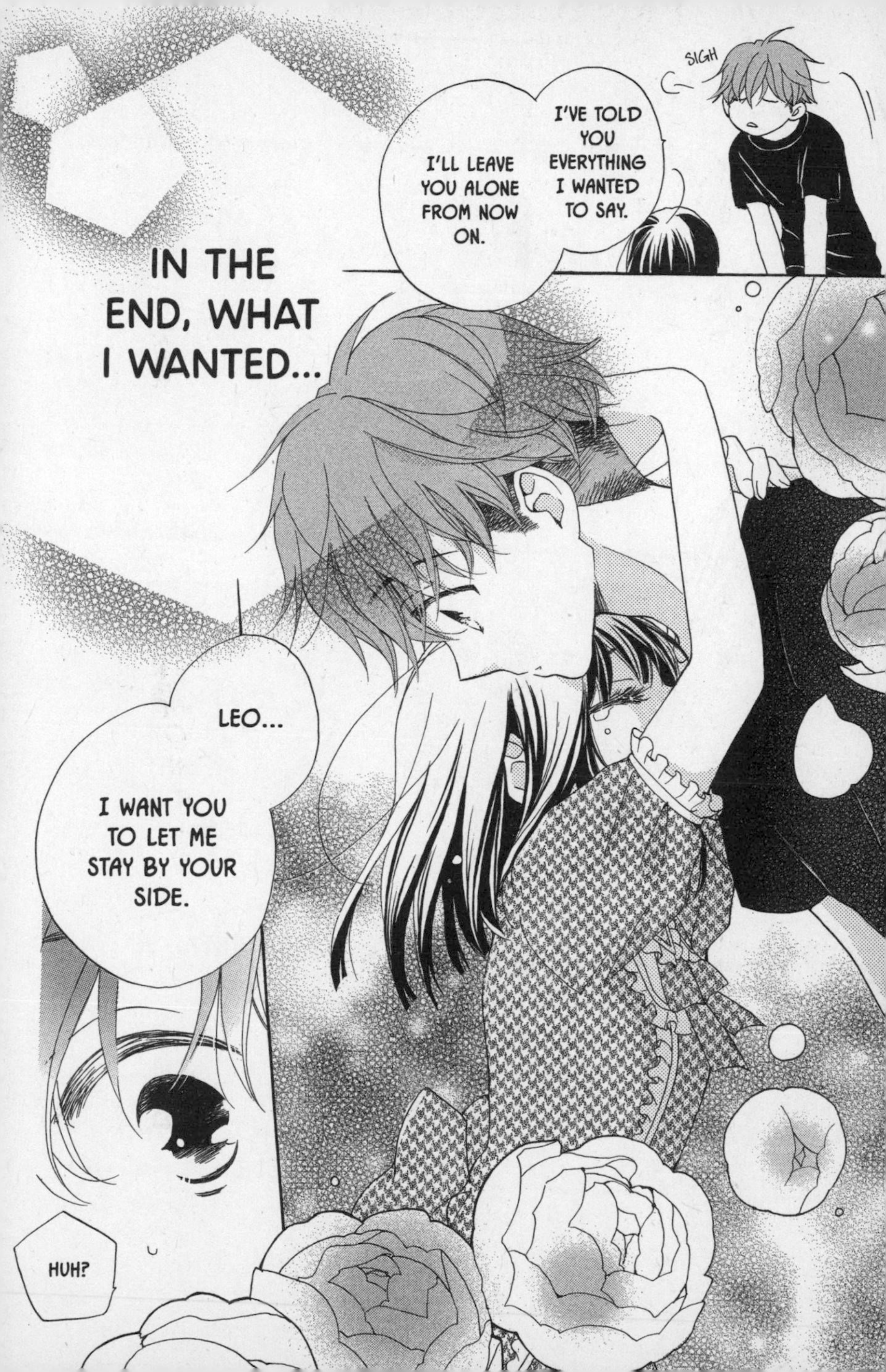
SIGH
I'VE TOLD YOU EVERYTHING I WANTED TO SAY.
I'LL LEAVE YOU ALONE FROM NOW ON.
IN THE END, WHAT I WANTED...
LEO...
I WANT YOU TO LET ME STAY BY YOUR SIDE.
HUH?

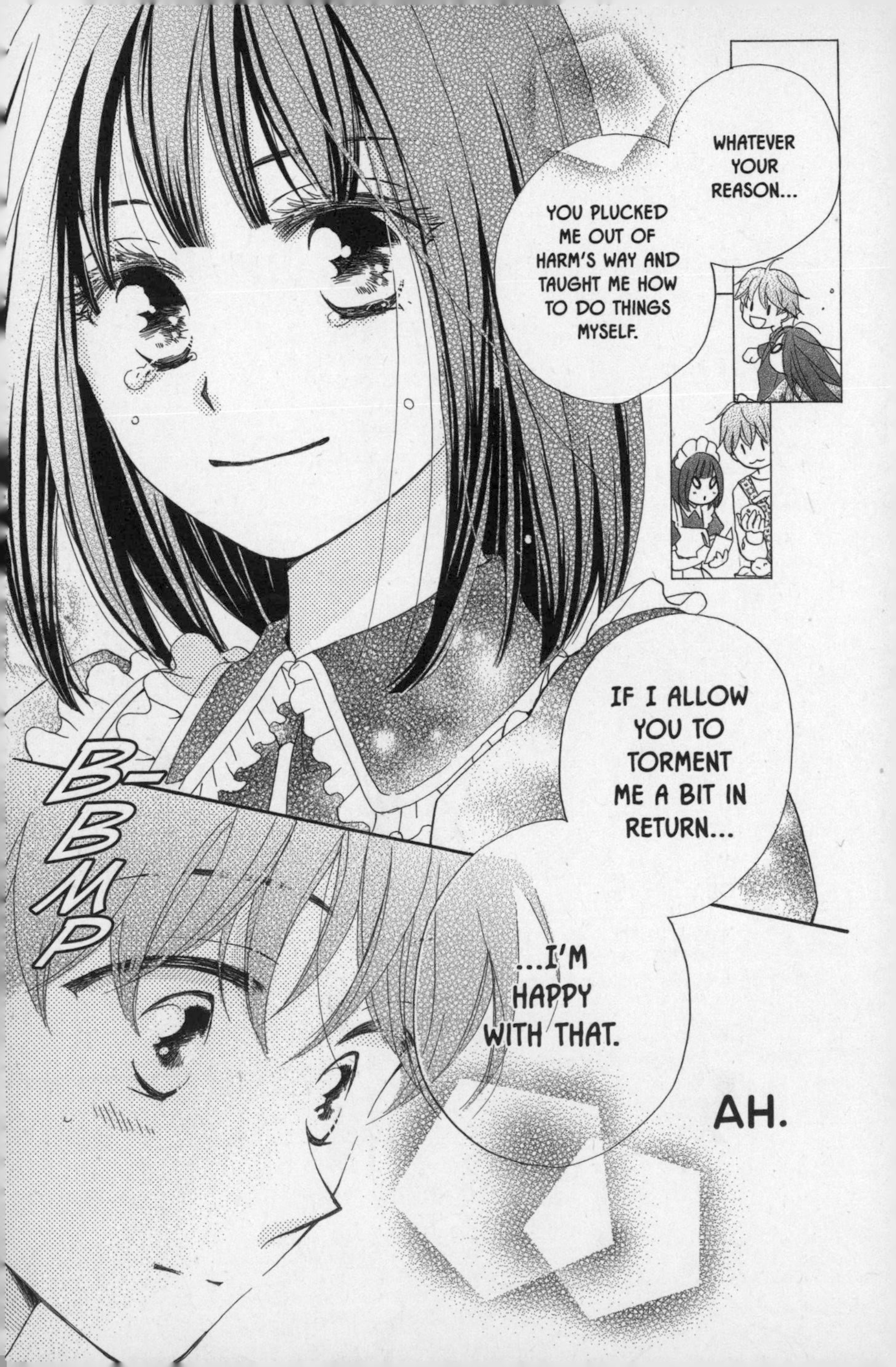
WHATEVER YOUR REASON...
YOU PLUCKED ME OUT OF HARM'S WAY AND TAUGHT ME HOW TO DO THINGS MYSELF.
IF I ALLOW YOU TO TORMENT ME A BIT IN RETURN...
B-BMP
...I'M HAPPY WITH THAT.
AH.

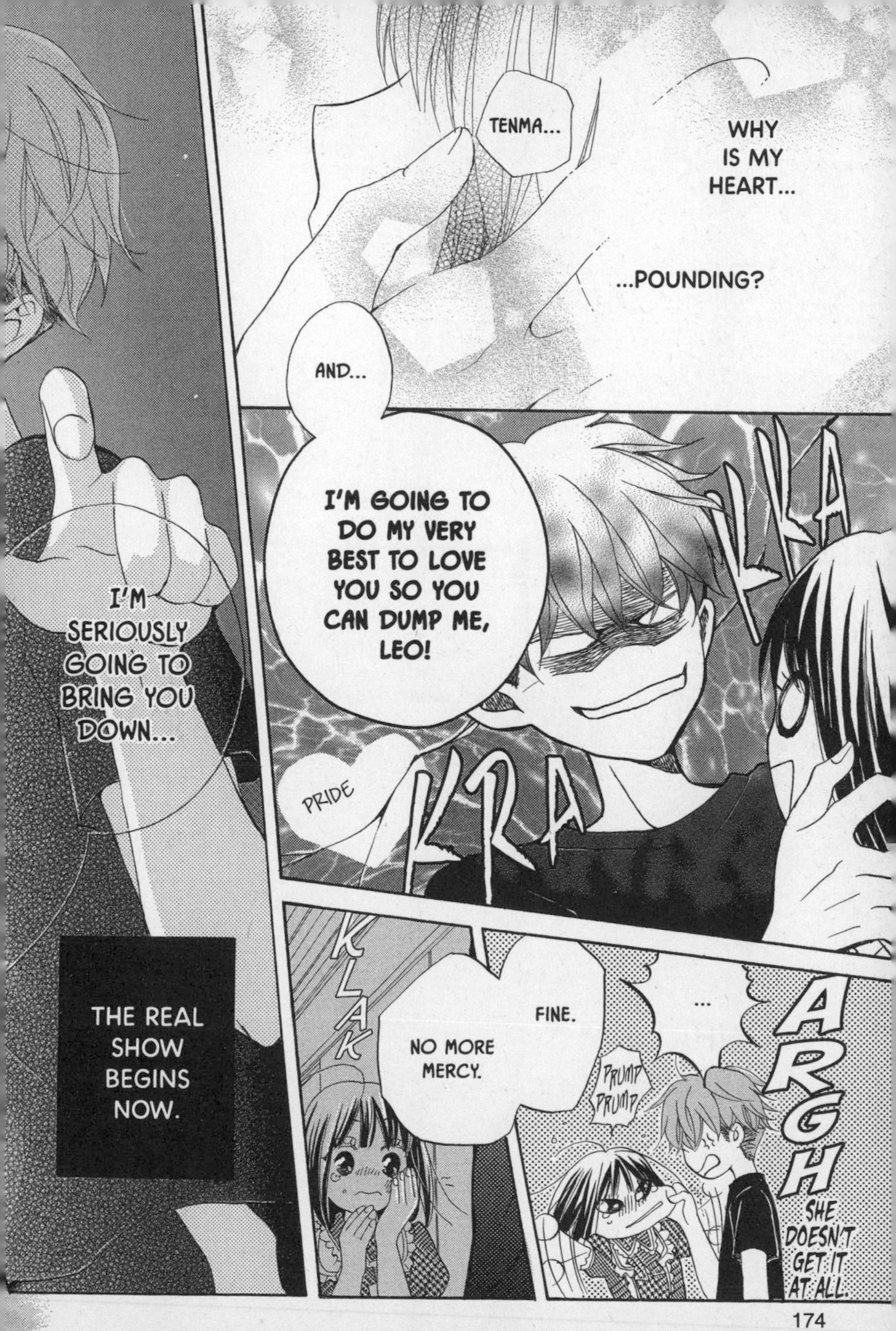
WHY IS MY HEART...
...POUNDING?
TENMA...
AND...
I'M GOING TO DO MY VERY BEST TO LOVE YOU SO YOU CAN DUMP ME, LEO!
KKA
KRA
PRIDE
I'M SERIOUSLY GOING TO BRING YOU DOWN...
ARGH
SHE DOESN'T GET IT AT ALL.
...
PRUMP PRUMP
FINE.
NO MORE MERCY.
KLAK
THE REAL SHOW BEGINS NOW.

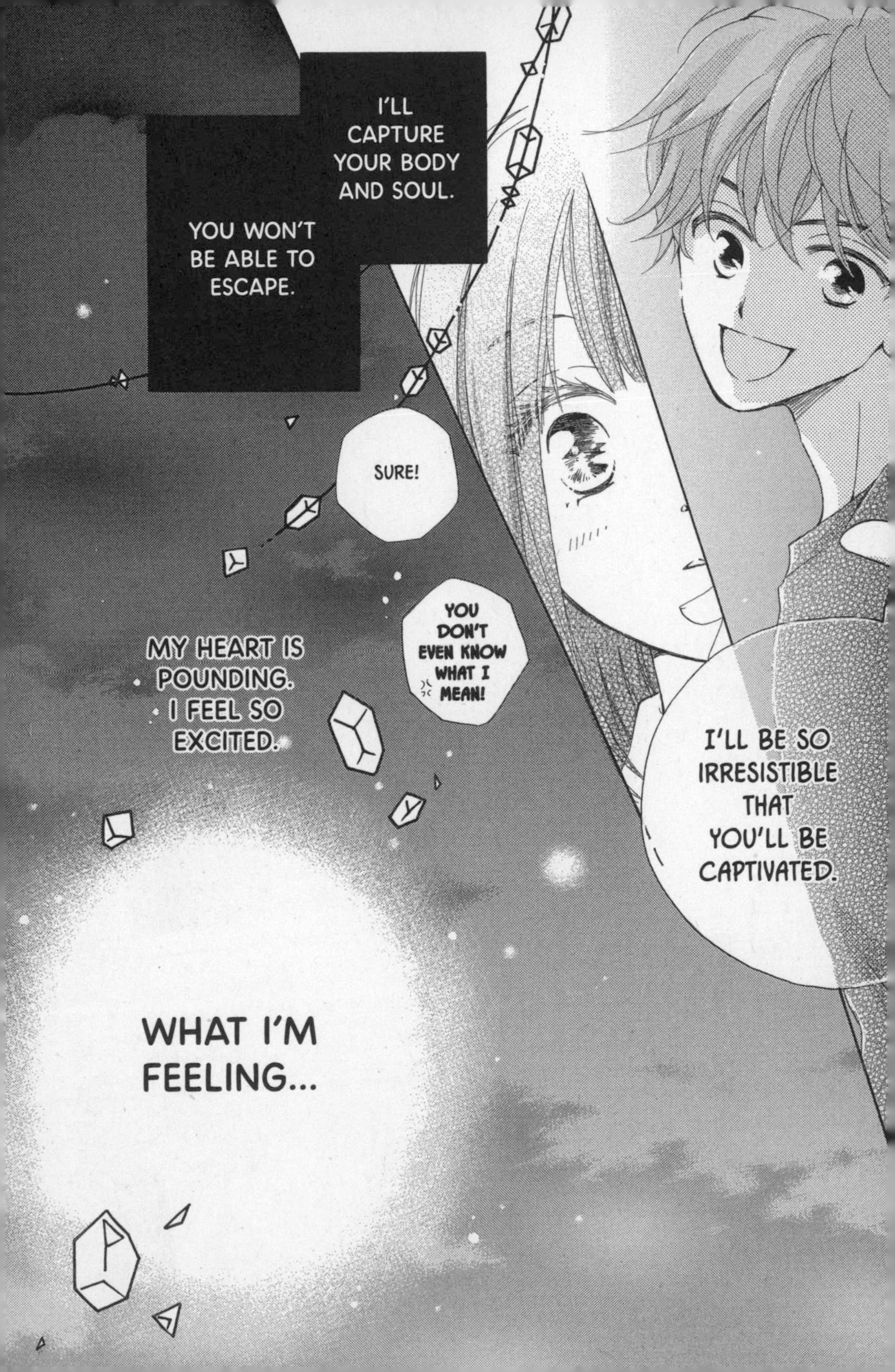
I'LL CAPTURE YOUR BODY AND SOUL.
YOU WON'T BE ABLE TO ESCAPE.
SURE!
I'LL BE SO IRRESISTIBLE THAT YOU'LL BE CAPTIVATED.
YOU DON'T EVEN KNOW WHAT I MEAN!
MY HEART IS POUNDING. I FEEL SO EXCITED.
WHAT I'M FEELING...

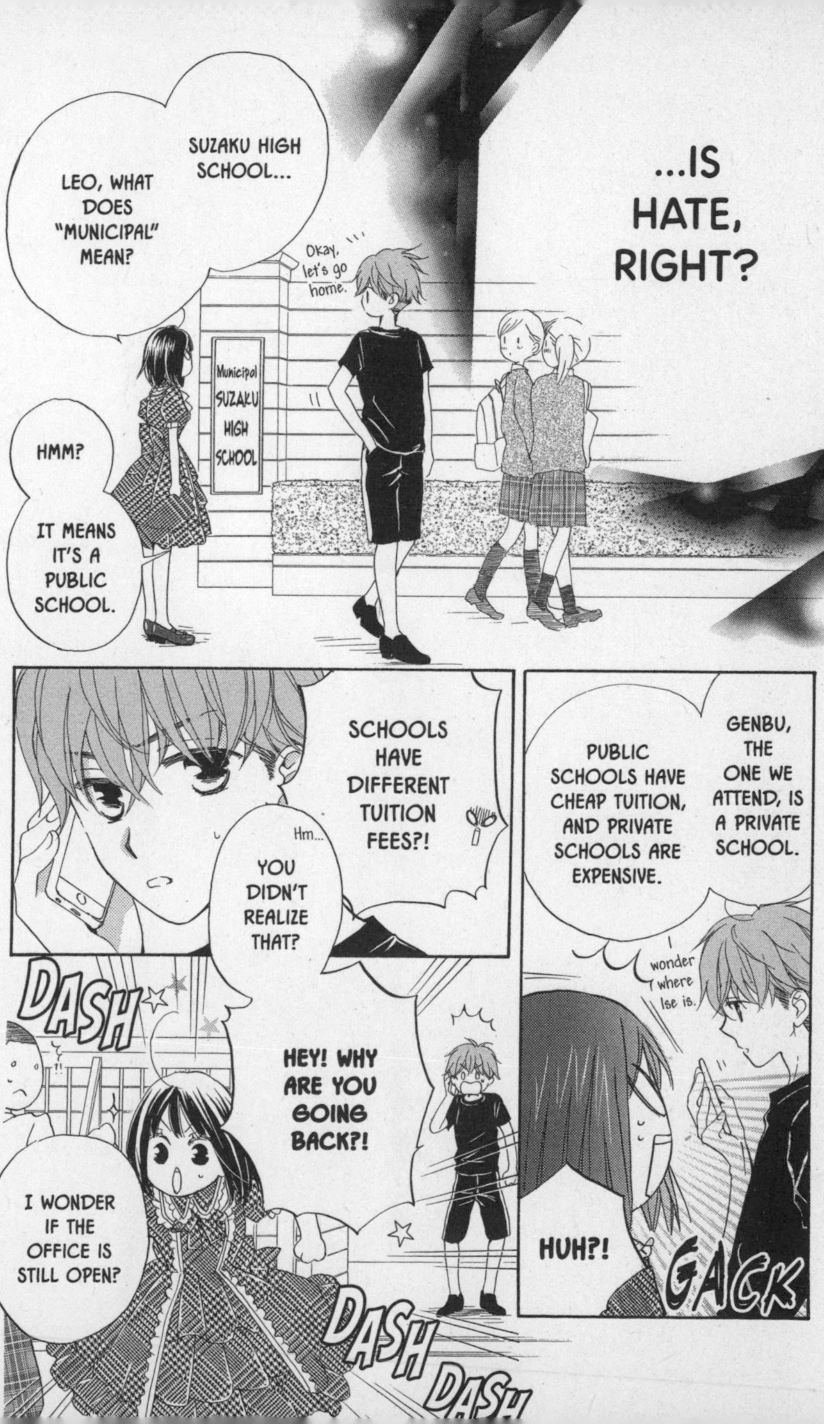
...IS HATE, RIGHT?
Okay, let's go home.
SUZAKU HIGH SCHOOL...
LEO, WHAT DOES "MUNICIPAL" MEAN?
Municipal SUZAKU HIGH SCHOOL
HMM?
IT MEANS IT'S A PUBLIC SCHOOL.
GENBU, THE ONE WE ATTEND, IS A PRIVATE SCHOOL.
PUBLIC SCHOOLS HAVE CHEAP TUITION, AND PRIVATE SCHOOLS ARE EXPENSIVE.
SCHOOLS HAVE DIFFERENT TUITION FEES?!
Hm...
YOU DIDN'T REALIZE THAT?
I wonder where Ise is.
HUH?!
GACK
HEY! WHY ARE YOU GOING BACK?!
DASH
I WONDER IF THE OFFICE IS STILL OPEN?
DASH DASH

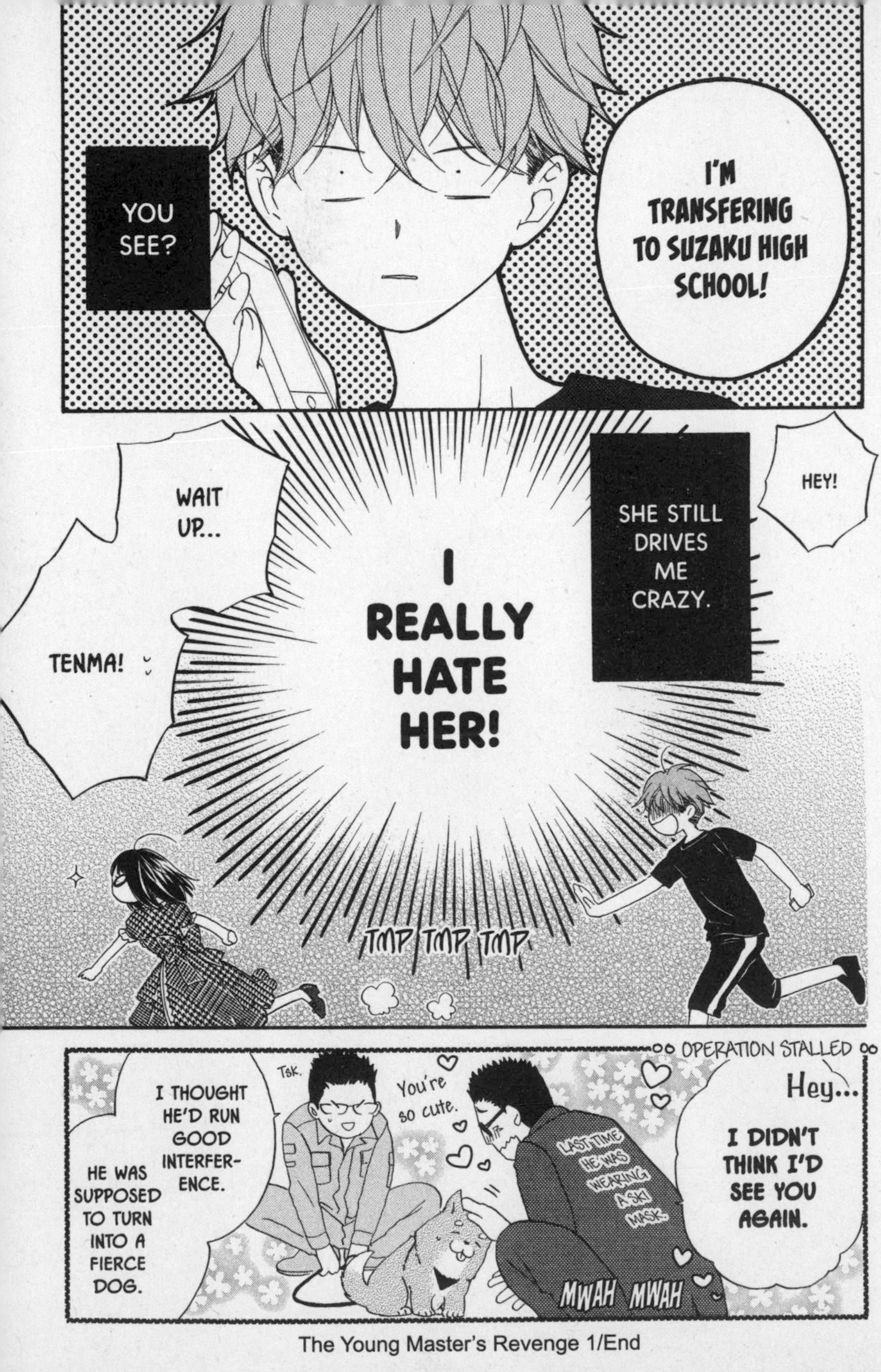
I'M TRANSFERING TO SUZAKU HIGH SCHOOL!
YOU SEE?
HEY!
SHE STILL DRIVES ME CRAZY.
I REALLY HATE HER!
WAIT UP...
TENMA!
TMP TMP TMP
OPERATION STALLED
Hey...
I DIDN'T THINK I'D SEE YOU AGAIN.
LAST TIME HE WAS WEARING A SKI MASK.
MWAH MWAH
You're so cute.
Tsk.
I THOUGHT HE'D RUN GOOD INTERFERENCE.
HE WAS SUPPOSED TO TURN INTO A FIERCE DOG.

The Young Master's Revenge 1/End

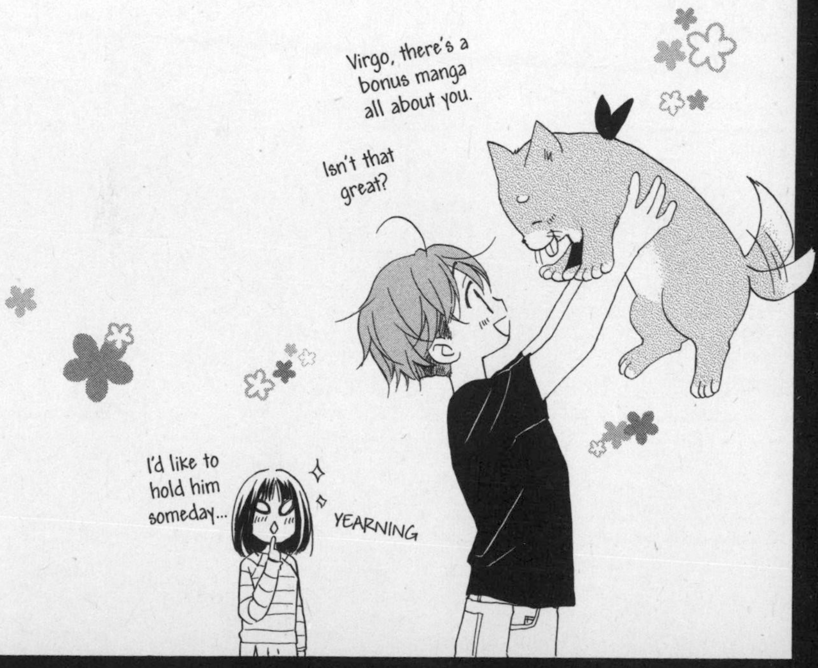
Virgo, there's a bonus manga all about you.
Isn't that great?
I'd like to hold him someday...
YEARNING

Bonus Manga

If It's About Me, Keep It Brief

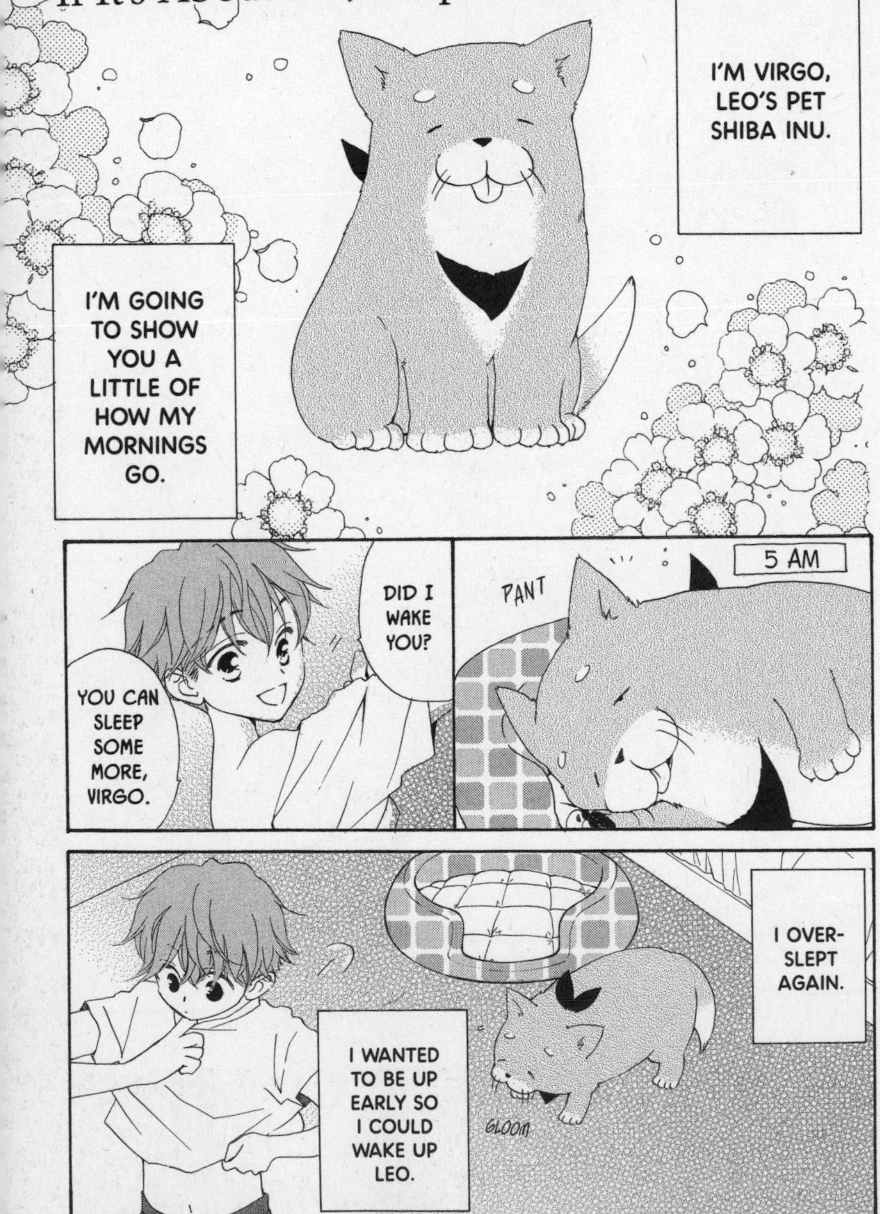
I'M VIRGO, LEO'S PET SHIBA INU.
I'M GOING TO SHOW YOU A LITTLE OF HOW MY MORNINGS GO.
5 AM
PANT
DID I WAKE YOU?
YOU CAN SLEEP SOME MORE, VIRGO.
I OVER-SLEPT AGAIN.
GLOOM
I WANTED TO BE UP EARLY SO I COULD WAKE UP LEO.

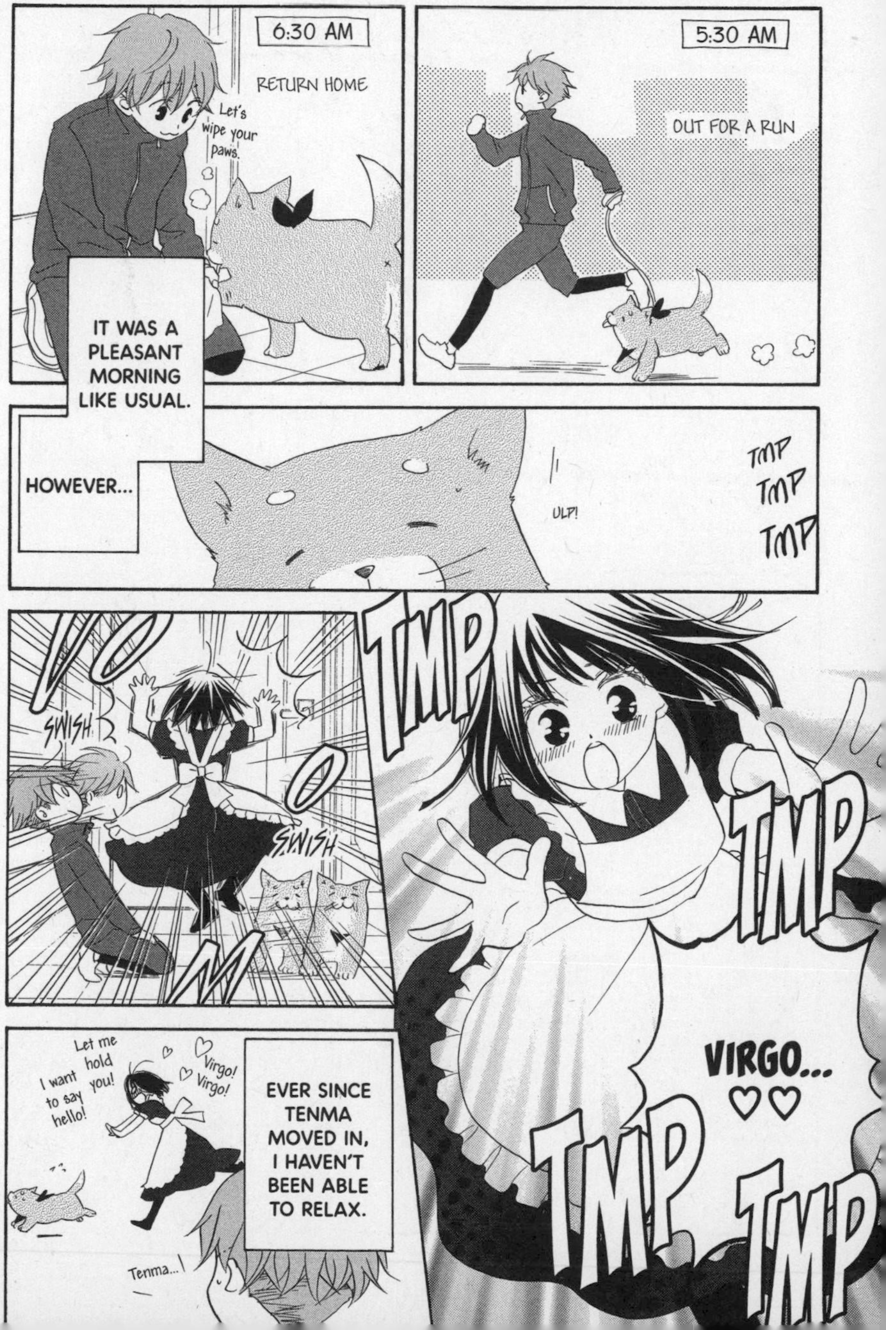
5:30 AM
OUT FOR A RUN
6:30 AM
RETURN HOME
Let's wipe your paws.
IT WAS A PLEASANT MORNING LIKE USUAL.
TMP
TMP
TMP
ULP!
HOWEVER...
TMP
TMP
VIRGO... ♡♡
TMP
TMP
VOOM
SWISH
SWISH
EVER SINCE TENMA MOVED IN, I HAVEN'T BEEN ABLE TO RELAX.
Virgo! Virgo!
Let me hold you!
I want to say hello!
Tenma...!

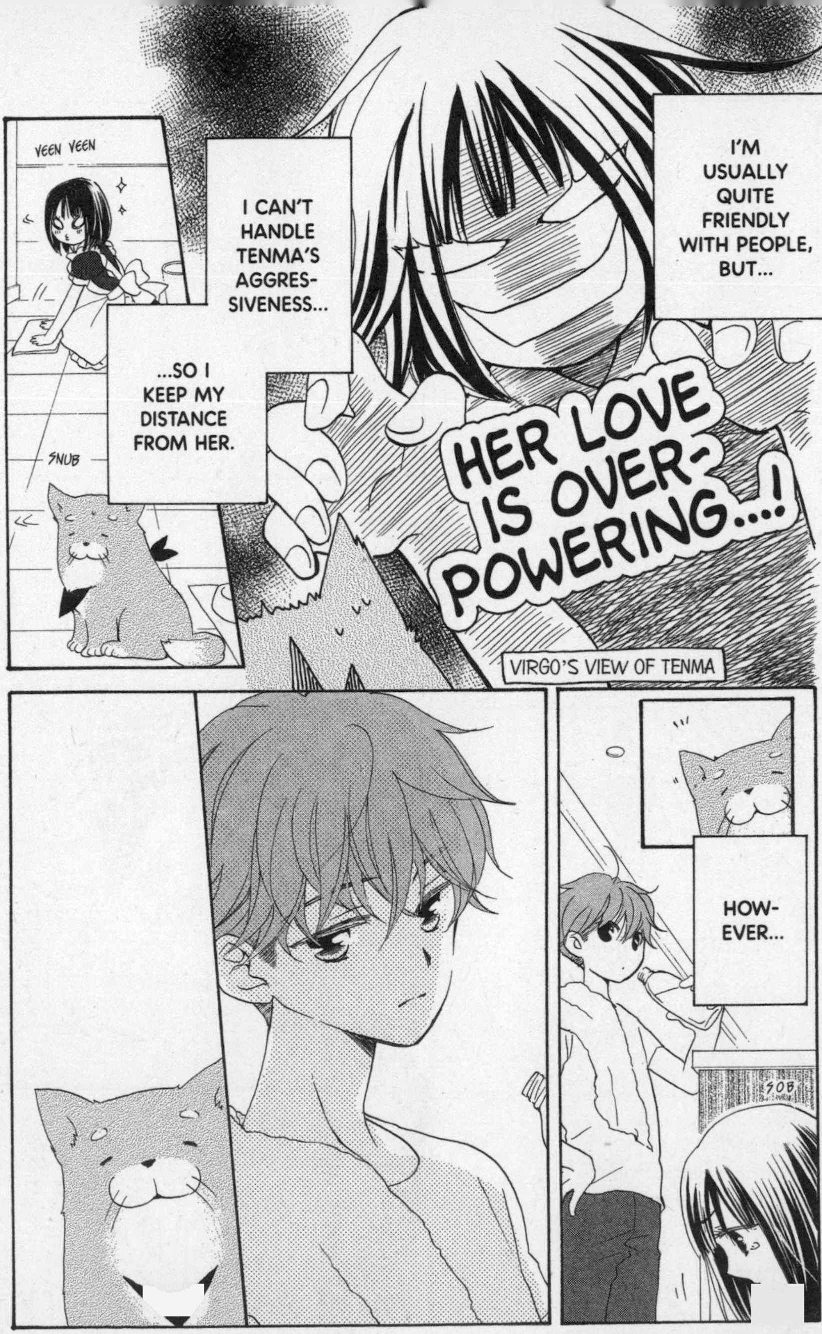
I'M USUALLY QUITE FRIENDLY WITH PEOPLE, BUT...
HER LOVE IS OVER-POWERING...!
VIRGO'S VIEW OF TENMA
I CAN'T HANDLE TENMA'S AGGRES-SIVENESS...
...SO I KEEP MY DISTANCE FROM HER.
VEEN VEEN
SNUB
HOW-EVER...
SOB

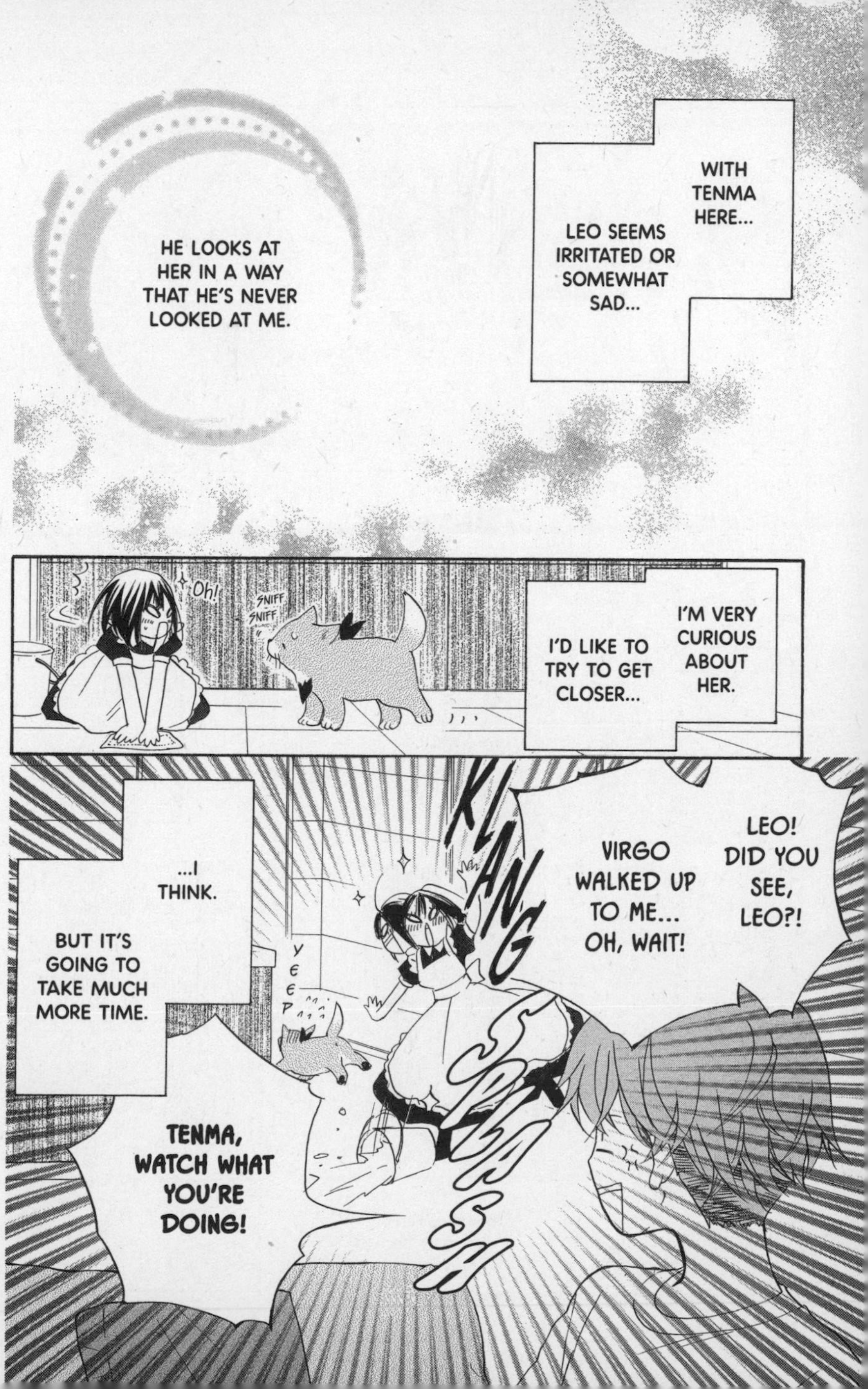
WITH TENMA HERE...
LEO SEEMS IRRITATED OR SOMEWHAT SAD...
HE LOOKS AT HER IN A WAY THAT HE'S NEVER LOOKED AT ME.
I'M VERY CURIOUS ABOUT HER.
I'D LIKE TO TRY TO GET CLOSER...
SNIFF SNIFF
Oh!
LEO! DID YOU SEE, LEO?!
VIRGO WALKED UP TO ME... OH, WAIT!
KLANG
SCHWASH
YEEP
...I THINK.
BUT IT'S GOING TO TAKE MUCH MORE TIME.
TENMA, WATCH WHAT YOU'RE DOING!

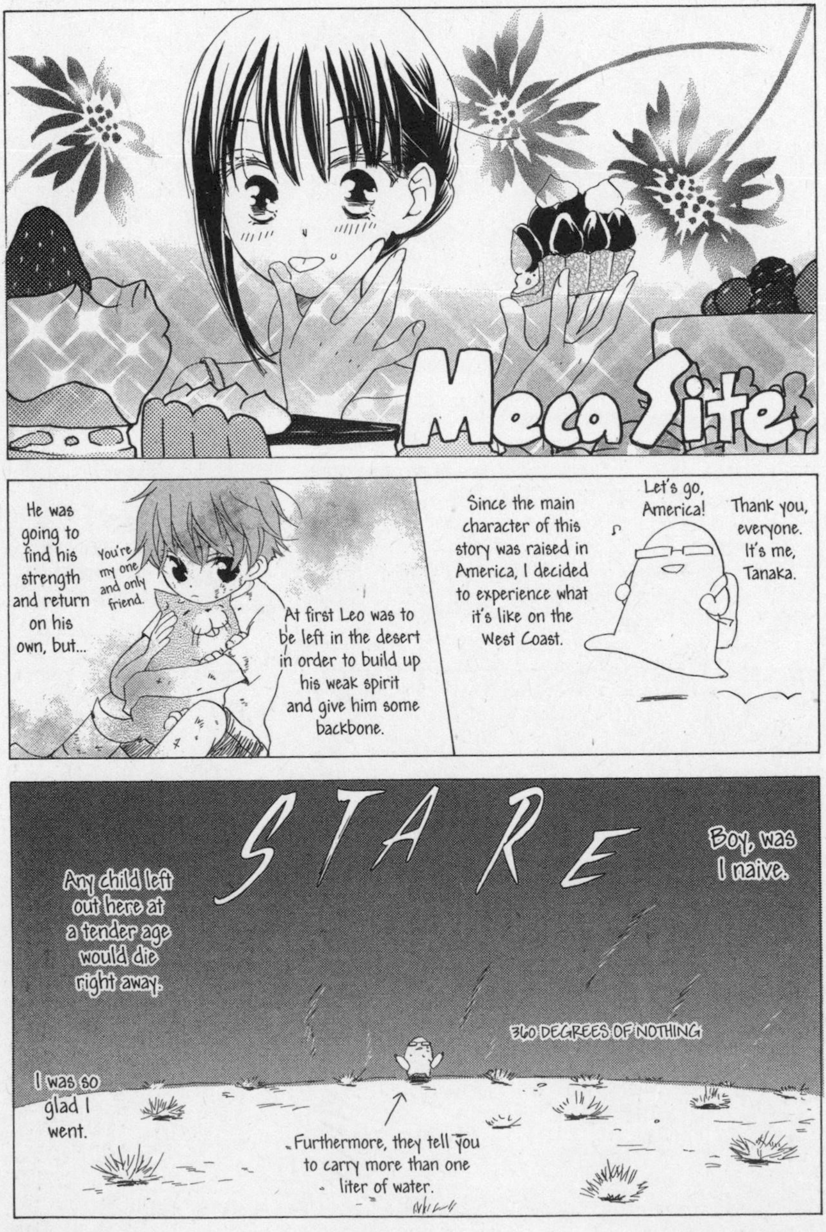
Meca Site
Thank you, everyone. It's me, Tanaka.
Let's go, America!
Since the main character of this story was raised in America, I decided to experience what it's like on the West Coast.
At first Leo was to be left in the desert in order to build up his weak spirit and give him some backbone.
You're my one and only friend.
He was going to find his strength and return on his own, but...
Boy, was I naive.
STARE
Any child left out here at a tender age would die right away.
360 DEGREES OF NOTHING
Furthermore, they tell you to carry more than one liter of water.
I was so glad I went.

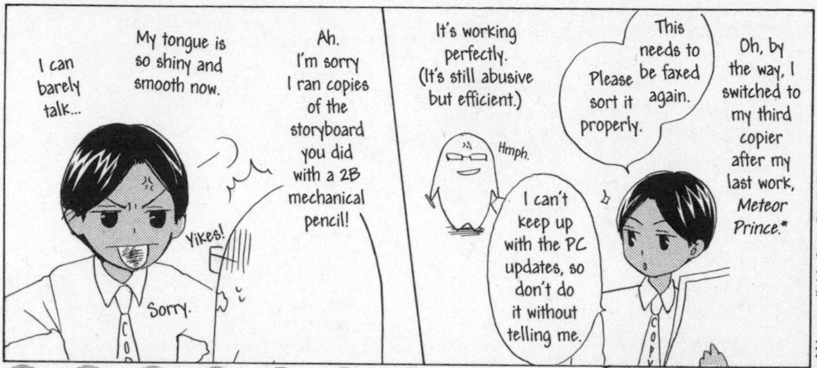

Oh, by the way, I switched to my third copier after my last work, Meteor Prince.*
This needs to be faxed again.
Please sort it properly.
It's working perfectly. (It's still abusive but efficient.)
Hmph.
I can't keep up with the PC updates, so don't do it without telling me.
Ah. I'm sorry I ran copies of the storyboard you did with a 2B mechanical pencil!
Yikes!
Sorry.
My tongue is so shiny and smooth now.
I can barely talk...

*Also available from Shojo Beat!

When I draw Leo, I have to keep in mind that he's a 16-year-old in his first year of high school. I'm always tempted to make him muscular...
This year my nephew (firstborn) began high school!
Eek, how time flies!
My nephew is very macho.
When he returns home, we always pester him to show us his abs.

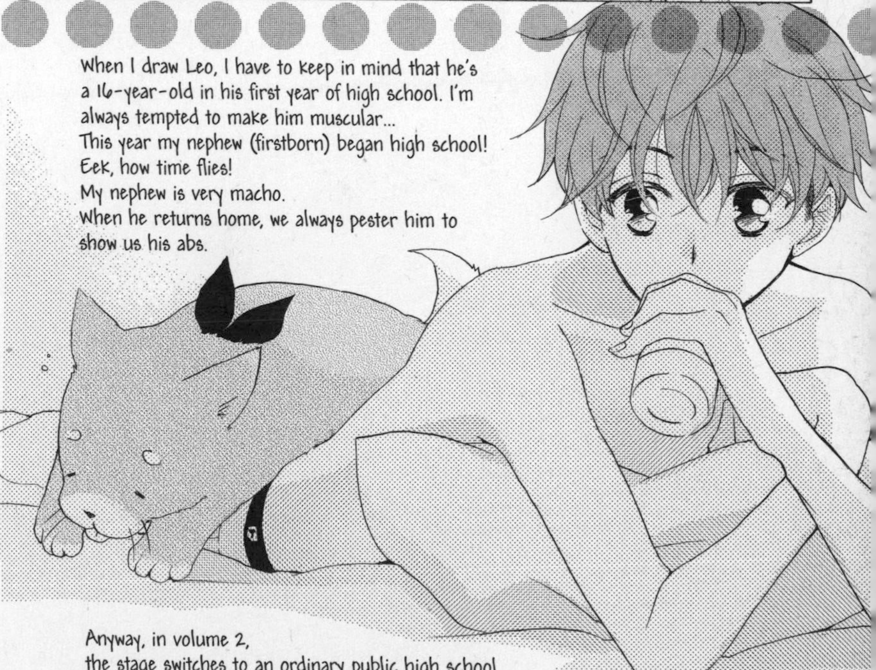

Anyway, in volume 2,
the stage switches to an ordinary public high school.
Will Leo's twisted emotions get straightened out?
Will it be true love that Tenma feels for Leo?
I'd be grateful if you'd follow their story.

THANKS!

Yamamoto-sama
My editor
My mother

Uchida-sama
Sano-sama
Hayashi-sama
Shiino-sama
Haremoto-sama
Karasawa-sama
Nakano-sama
Mikawa-sama
Shiojima-sama

To everyone who has supported me and my manga.

Thank you so, so much!

It's time to say goodbye for now!

Meca Tanaka

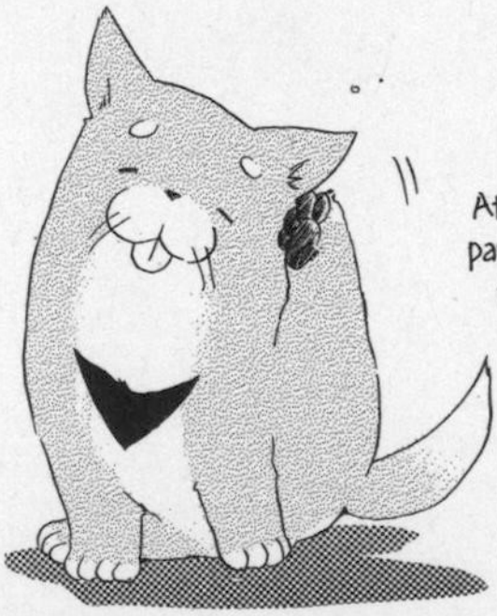
At least my paw reaches my ear.

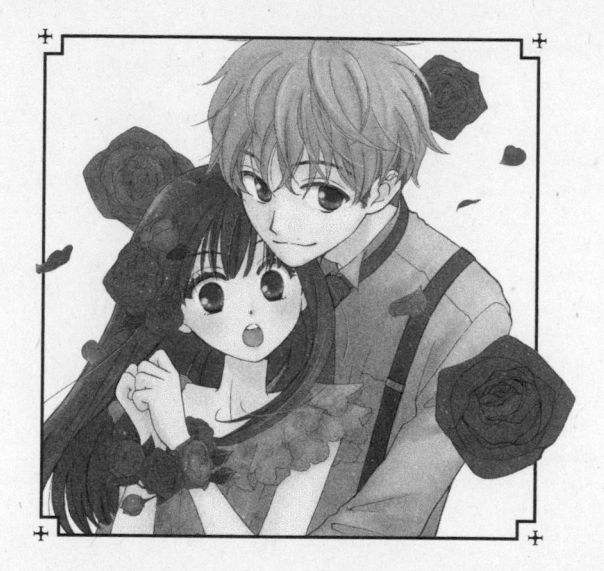

I love dogs.
Big dogs, little dogs, Western breeds
and Japanese breeds.
I haven't been able to have a dog, so all my
desires for one are crammed into this manga.
Ah, dogs! Dogs are so cute!
Do you know or own a dog like Virgo?
I'll be waiting to hear from you!
—**Meca Tanaka**

Meca Tanaka made her manga debut in 1998.
Her previous works include *Omukae Desu*,
Tennen Pearl Pink (Pearl Pink) and *Kiss Yori mo
Hayaku* (Faster than a Kiss). Her series *Meteor
Prince* is also published by VIZ Media.

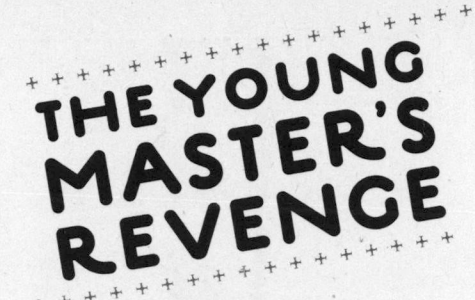

THE YOUNG MASTER'S REVENGE

Shojo Beat Edition
Volume 1

STORY AND ART BY
Meca Tanaka

Translation—**JN Productions**
Touch-Up Art & Lettering—**Inori Fukuda Trant**
Graphic Design—**Alice Lewis**
Editor—**Nancy Thistlethwaite**

Kimi no Kotonado Zettaini by Meca Tanaka
© Meca Tanaka 2015
All rights reserved.
First published in Japan in 2015 by HAKUSENSHA, Inc., Tokyo.
English language translation rights arranged with HAKUSENSHA, Inc., Tokyo.

Printed in the U.S.A.

Published by VIZ Media, LLC
P.O. Box 77010
San Francisco, CA 94107

10 9 8 7 6 5 4 3 2 1
First printing, March 2018

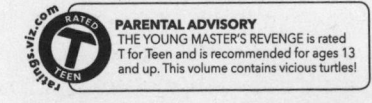

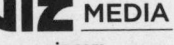

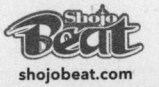

viz.com   shojobeat.com

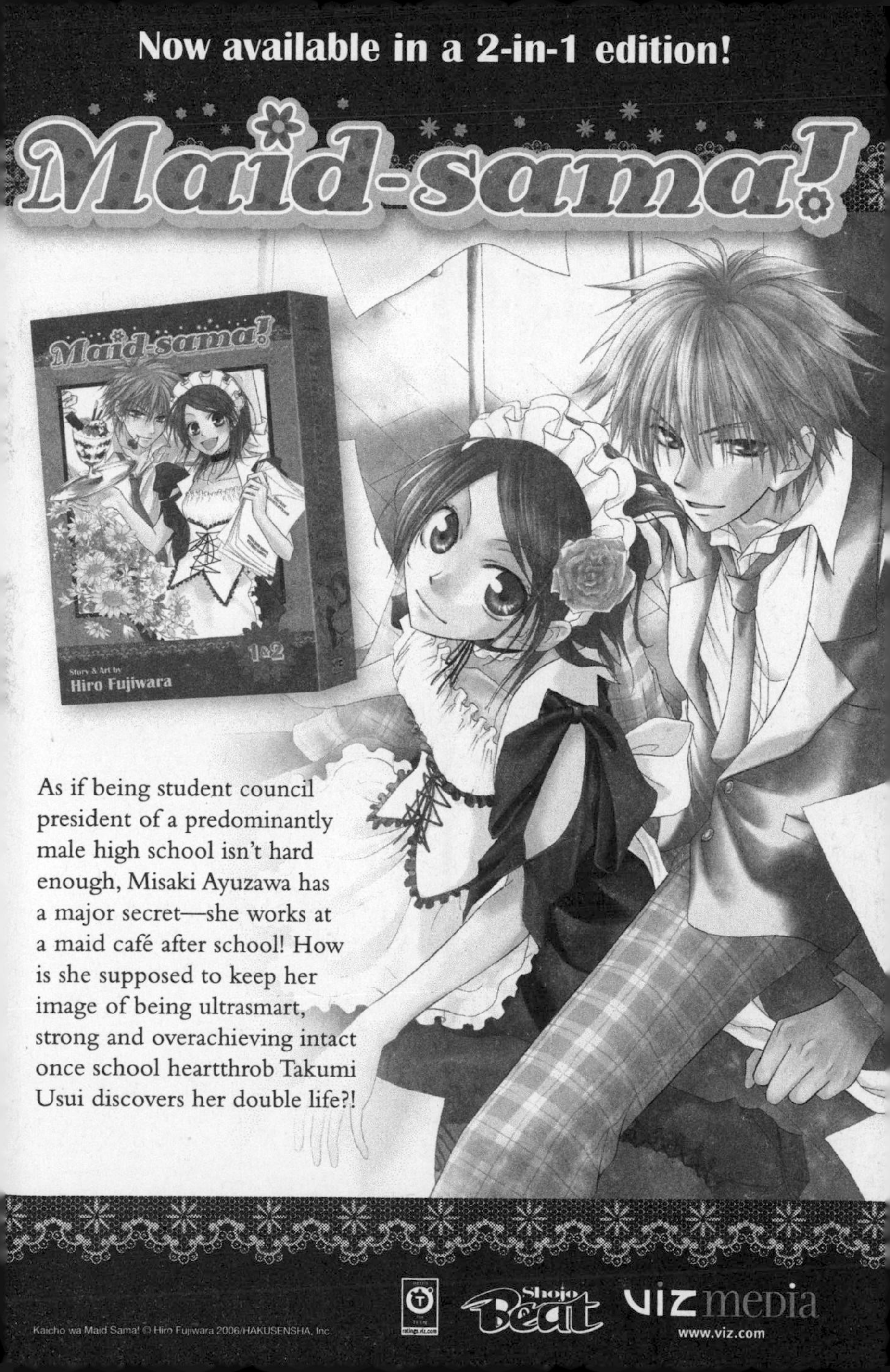

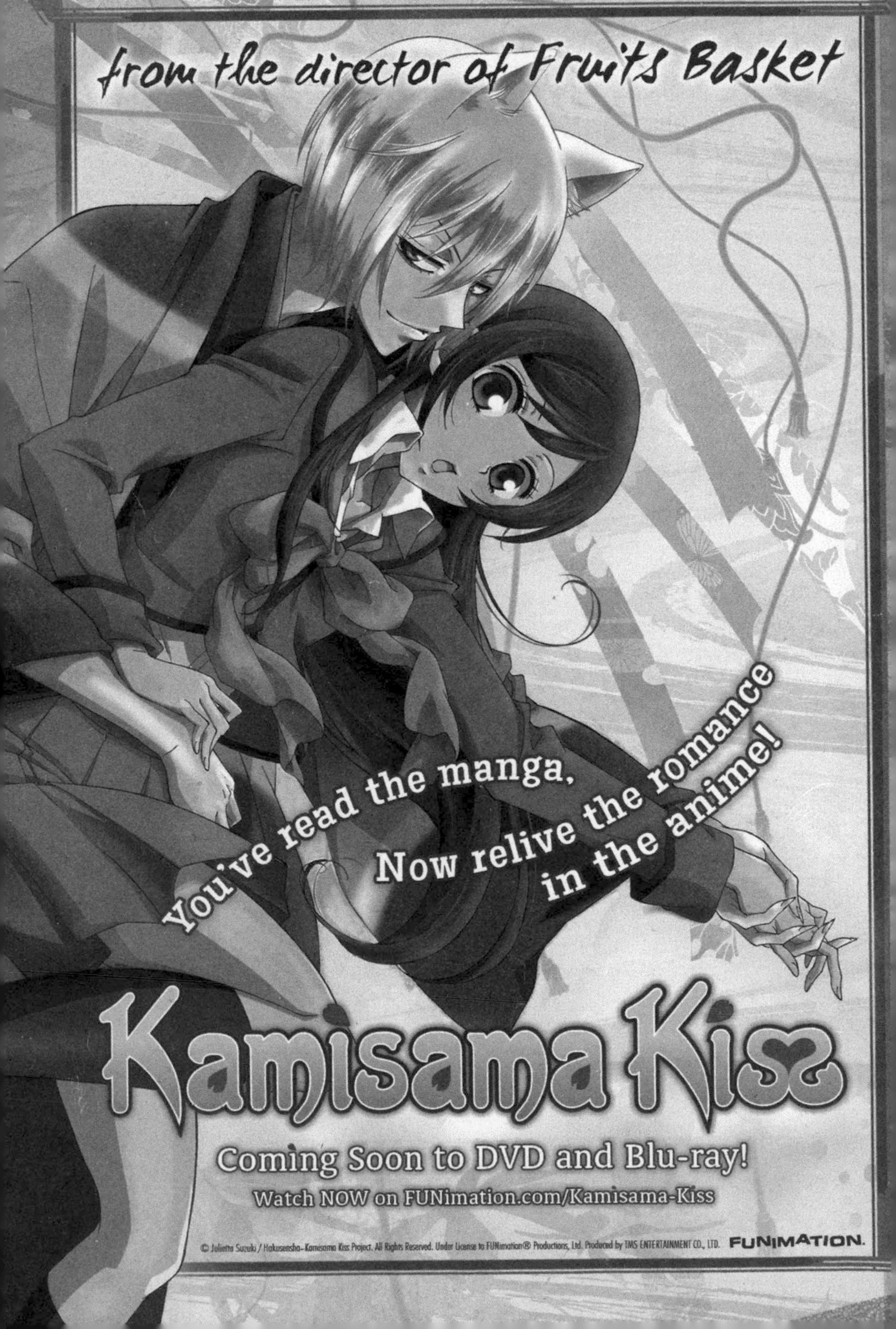
from the director of Fruits Basket
You've read the manga,
Now relive the romance
in the anime!
Kamisama Kiss
Coming Soon to DVD and Blu-ray!
Watch NOW on FUNimation.com/Kamisama-Kiss
© Julietta Suzuki / Hakusensha–Kamisama Kiss Project. All Rights Reserved. Under License to FUNimation® Productions, Ltd. Produced by TMS ENTERTAINMENT CO., LTD.
FUNIMATION.

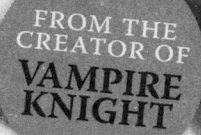

Shuriken
and Pleats

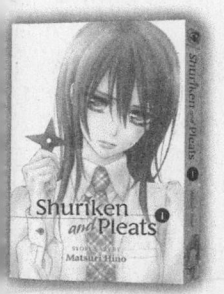

When the master she has sworn to protect is killed, Mikage Kirio,
a skilled ninja, travels to Japan to start a new, peaceful life for
herself. But as soon as she arrives, she finds herself fighting to
protect the life of Mahito Wakashimatsu, a man who is under
attack by a band of ninja. From that time on, Mikage is drawn
deeper into the machinations of his powerful family.

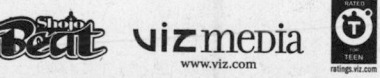

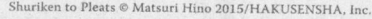

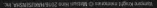
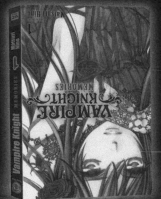

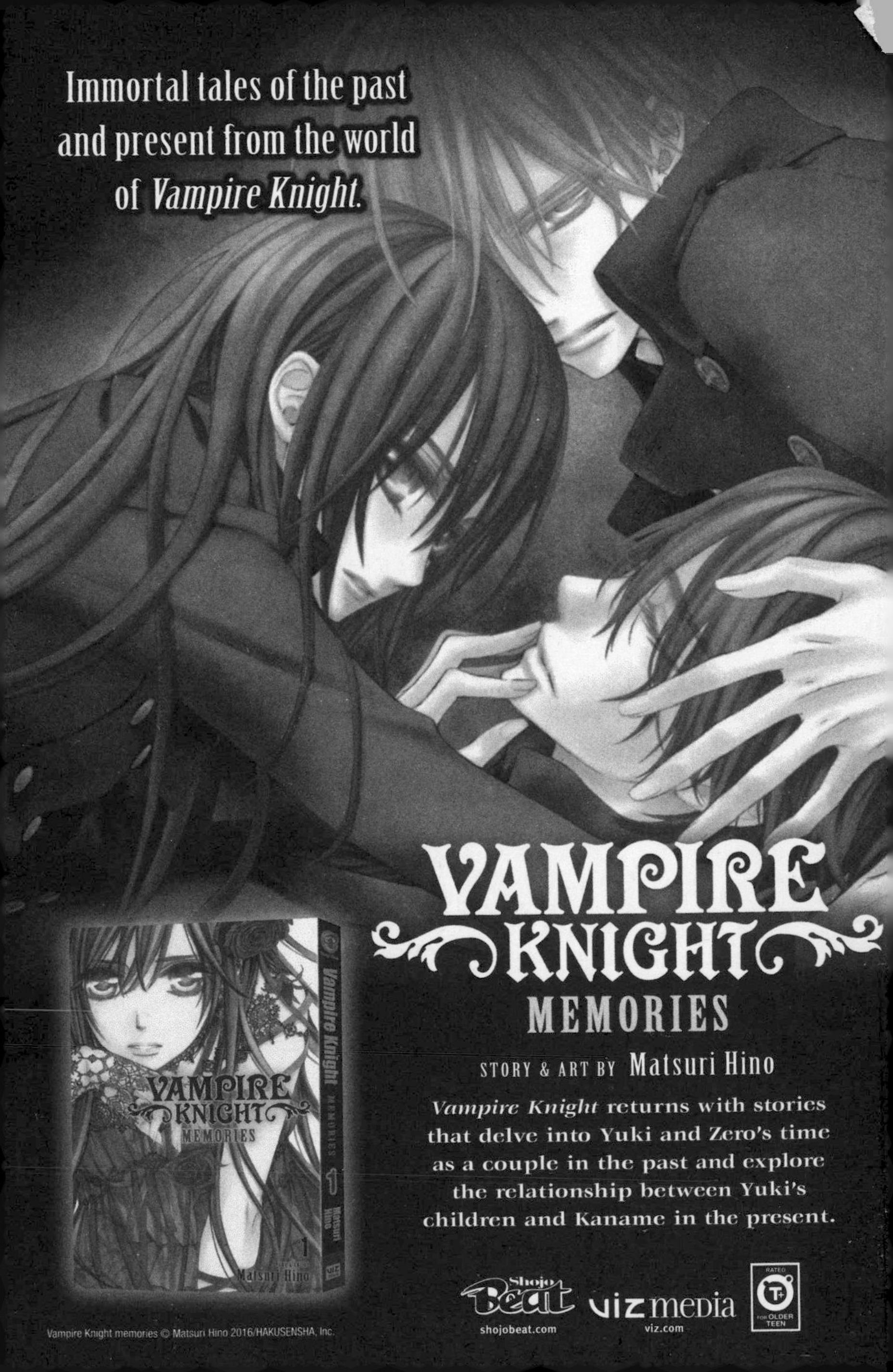

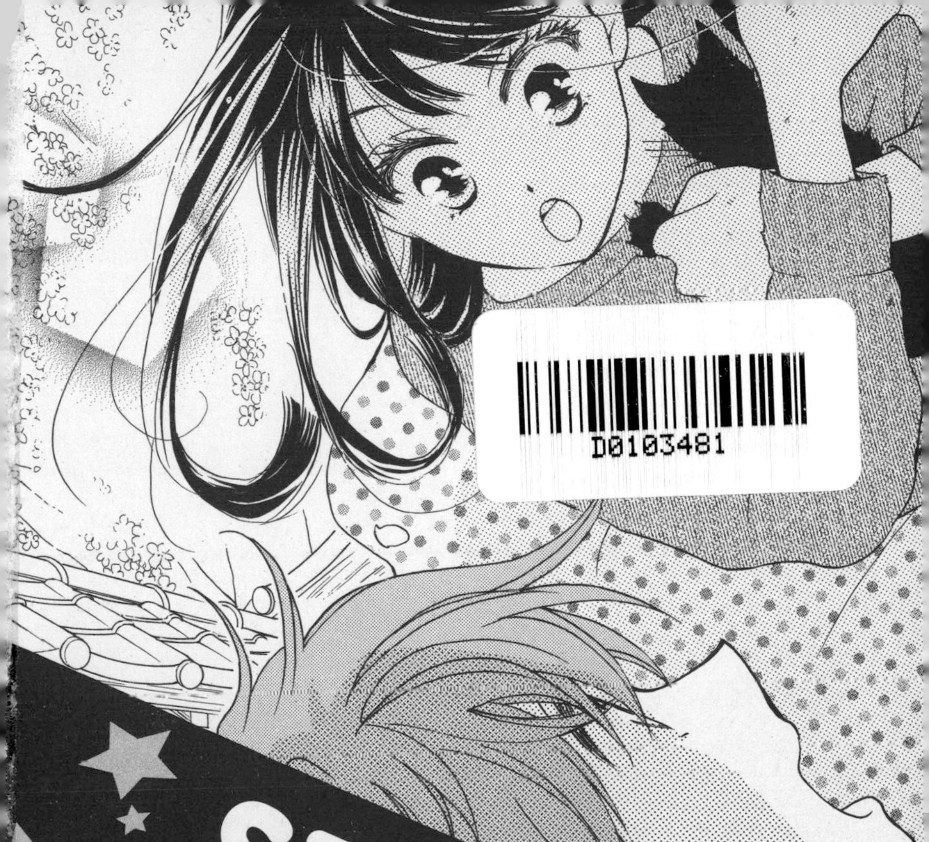

STOP!

You may be reading the wrong way!

In keeping with the original Japanese comic format, this book reads from right to left—so action, sound effects and word balloons are completely reversed to preserve the orientation of the original artwork.

Check out the diagram shown here to get the hang of things, and then turn to the other side of the book to get started!

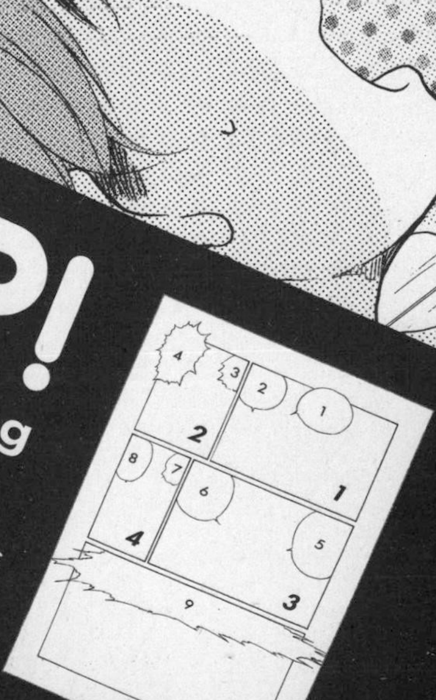
1
2
3
4
5
1
2
3
4
5
6
7
8
9